Understanding Cavell, Understanding Modernism

Understanding Philosophy, Understanding Modernism

The aim of each volume in **Understanding Philosophy, Understanding Modernism** is to understand a philosophical thinker more fully through literary and cultural modernism and consequently to understand literary modernism better through a key philosophical figure. In this way, the series also rethinks the limits of modernism, calling attention to lacunae in modernist studies and sometimes in the philosophical work under examination.

Series Editors:
Paul Ardoin, S. E. Gontarski, and Laci Mattison

Volumes in the Series:
Understanding Bergson, Understanding Modernism
Edited by Paul Ardoin, S. E. Gontarski, and Laci Mattison
Understanding Deleuze, Understanding Modernism
Edited by S. E. Gontarski, Paul Ardoin, and Laci Mattison
Understanding Wittgenstein, Understanding Modernism
Edited by Anat Matar
Understanding Foucault, Understanding Modernism
Edited by David Scott
Understanding James, Understanding Modernism
Edited by David H. Evans
Understanding Rancière, Understanding Modernism
Edited by Patrick M. Bray
Understanding Blanchot, Understanding Modernism
Edited by Christopher Langlois
Understanding Merleau-Ponty, Understanding Modernism
Edited by Ariane Mildenberg
Understanding Nietzsche, Understanding Modernism
Edited by Douglas Burnham and Brian Pines
Understanding Derrida, Understanding Modernism
Edited by Jean-Michel Rabaté
Understanding Adorno, Understanding Modernism
Edited by Robin Truth Goodman
Understanding Flusser, Understanding Modernism
Edited by Aaron Jaffe, Rodrigo Martini, and Michael F. Miller
Understanding Marx, Understanding Modernism
Edited by Mark Steven

Understanding Barthes, Understanding Modernism
Edited by Jeffrey R. Di Leo and Zahi Zalloua
Understanding Kristeva, Understanding Modernism
Edited by Maria Margaroni
Understanding Žižek, Understanding Modernism
Edited by Jeffrey R. Di Leo and Zahi Zalloua
Understanding Nancy, Understanding Modernism
Edited by Cosmin Toma
Understanding Bakhtin, Understanding Modernism
Edited by Philippe Birgy
Understanding Badiou, Understanding Modernism
Edited by Arka Chattopadhyay and Arthur Rose
Understanding Sade, Understanding Modernism
Edited by James Martell
Understanding Cavell, Understanding Modernism
Edited by Paola Marrati
Understanding Lacan, Understanding Modernism
Edited by Thomas Waller and Sinan Richards (forthcoming)
Understanding Cixous, Understanding Modernism
Edited by Peggy Kamuf (forthcoming)

Understanding Cavell, Understanding Modernism

Edited by
Paola Marrati

BLOOMSBURY ACADEMIC
NEW YORK • LONDON • OXFORD • NEW DELHI • SYDNEY

BLOOMSBURY ACADEMIC

Bloomsbury Publishing Inc, 1359 Broadway, New York, NY 10018, USA
Bloomsbury Publishing Plc, 50 Bedford Square, London, WC1B 3DP, UK
Bloomsbury Publishing Ireland, 29 Earlsfort Terrace, Dublin 2, Ireland

BLOOMSBURY, BLOOMSBURY ACADEMIC and the Diana logo are
trademarks of Bloomsbury Publishing Plc

First published in the United States of America 2026

Copyright © Paola Marrati, 2026

Each chapter copyright © by the contributor, 2026

Series design by Louise Dugdale
Cover design by Olivia D'Cruz
Cover image: © Ivan Vukelic / Getty Images

All rights reserved. No part of this publication may be: i) reproduced or transmitted in any form, electronic of mechanical, including photocopying, recording, or by means of any information storage or retrieval system without prior permission in writing from the publishers; or ii) used or reproduced in any way for the training, development or operation of artificial intelligence (AI) technologies, including generative AI technologies. The rights holders expressly reserve this publication from the text and data mining exception as per Article 4(3) of the Digital Single Market Directive (EU) 219/790.

Bloomsbury Publishing Inc does not have any control over, or responsibility for, any third-party websites referred to or in this book. All internet addresses given in this book were correct at the time of going to press. The author and publisher regret any inconvenience caused if addresses have changed or sites have ceased to exist, but can accept no responsibility for any such changes.

Library of Congress Cataloging-in-Publication Data
[tk]

ISBN: HB: 978-1-5013-1363-9
ePDF: 978-1-5013-1365-3
eBook: 978-1-5013-1364-6

Series: Understanding Philosophy, Understanding Modernism

Typeset by RefineCatch Limited, Bungay, Suffolk

For product safety related questions contact productsafety@bloomsbury.com
To find out more about our authors and books visit www.bloomsbury.com
and sign up for our newsletters.

Contents

Series Preface ix
List of Abbreviations x

Introduction *Paola Marrati* 1

Part 1 Conceptualizing Cavell

1 *Must We Mean What We Say?* and the (Re)Birth of Ordinary Language Philosophy *Sandra Laugier* 7

2 Modernism in *The World Viewed* *Hugo Clémot* 29

3 *The Senses of Walden*: Thoreau's Exemplary Act *Paul Standish* 43

4 *The Claim of Reason*: On Finding a Voice of One's Own in Philosophy *Paola Marrati* 67

5 Democracy as a Way of Life and An-archic Perfectionism: Rereading *Conditions Handsome and Unhandsome* *Naoko Saito* 95

Part 2 Cavell and Aesthetics

6 Philosophy, Literature, and the Romantic Response *Andrew Brandel* 113

7 Measuring the Value of Human Life According to a Perfectionist Philosopher *David LaRocca* 143

8 Modernism: Notes Toward a Philosophical Approach *Piergiorgio Donatelli* 167

9 Modernism and Film at Criticism: Rethinking the "Aesthetic Possibilities" of the Medium *Élise Domenach* 189

10 Cavell and the Modernity of Film *Eli Friedlander* 199

Part 3 Glossary

11 Claim *Sandra Laugier* 215

12 Criteria *Martin Shuster* 227

13 Skepticism *Jeroen Gerrits* 241

Notes on Contributors 251
Index 255

Series Preface

Sometime in the late twentieth century, modernism, like philosophy itself, underwent something of an unmooring from (at least) linear literary history in favor of the multi-perspectival history implicit in "new historicism" or, say, varieties of "presentism." Amid current reassessments of modernism and modernity, critics have posited various "new" or alternative modernisms—postcolonial, cosmopolitan, transatlantic, transnational, geomodernism, or even "bad" modernisms. In doing so, they have not only reassessed modernism as a category, but also, more broadly, rethought epistemology and ontology, aesthetics, metaphysics, materialism, history, and being itself, opening possibilities of rethinking not only which texts we read as modernist, but also how we read those texts. Much of this new conversation constitutes something of a critique of the periodization of modernism or modernist studies in favor of modernism as mode (or mode of production) or concept. Understanding Philosophy, Understanding Modernism situates itself amid the plurality of discourses, offering collections focused on key philosophical thinkers influential both to the moment of modernism and to our current understanding of that moment's genealogy, archaeology, and becomings. Such critiques of modernism(s) and modernity afford opportunities to rethink and reassess the overlaps, folds, interrelationships, interleavings, or cross-pollinations of modernism and philosophy. Our goal in each volume of the series is to understand literary modernism better through philosophy as we also better understand a philosopher through literary modernism. The first two volumes of the series, those on Henri Bergson and Gilles Deleuze, have established a tripartite structure that serves to offer both accessibility to the philosopher's principle texts and to current new research. Each volume opens with a section focused on "conceptualizing" the philosopher through close readings of seminal texts in the thinker's oeuvre. A second section, on aesthetics, maps connections between modernist works and the philosophical figure, often surveying key modernist trends and shedding new light on authors and texts. The final section of each volume serves as an extended glossary of principal terms in the philosopher's work, each treated at length, allowing a fuller engagement with and examination of the many, sometimes contradictory ways terms are deployed. The series is thus designed both to introduce philosophers and to rethink their relationship to modernist studies, revising our understandings of both modernism and philosophy, and offering resources that will be of use across disciplines, from philosophy, theory, and literature, to religion, the visual and performing arts, and often to the sciences as well.

Abbreviations

Works by Stanley Cavell

CHU   *Conditions Handsome and Unhandsome: The Constitution of Emersonian Perfectionism.* Chicago: University of Chicago Press, 1990.

CR   *The Claim of Reason: Wittgenstein, Skepticism, Morality, and Tragedy.* Oxford: Oxford University Press, 1999. First edition published 1979.

CT   *Contesting Tears: The Hollywood Melodrama of the Unknown Woman.* Chicago: University of Chicago Press, 1996.

CW   *Cities of Words: Pedagogical Letters on a Register of the Moral Life.* Cambridge, MA: Harvard University Press, 2004.

DK   *Disowning Knowledge in Seven Plays of Shakespeare.* Updated edition. Cambridge, MA: Harvard University Press, 2003. First edition published 1987.

ETE   *Emerson's Transcendental Etudes*, ed. David Justin Hodge. Stanford: Stanford University Press, 2003.

IQO   *In Quest of the Ordinary: Lines of Skepticism and Romanticism.* Chicago: University of Chicago Press, 1988.

LDIK   *Little Did I Know: Excerpts from Memory.* Stanford: Stanford University Press, 2010.

MWM   *Must We Mean What We Say?: A Book of Essays.* Updated edition. Cambridge: Cambridge University Press, 2015. First edition published 1969.

NYUA   *This New Yet Unapproachable America: Lectures after Emerson after Wittgenstein.* Chicago: University of Chicago Press, 1989.

PDAT   *Philosophy the Day after Tomorrow.* Cambridge, MA: Harvard University Press, 2005.

PH   *Pursuits of Happiness: The Hollywood Comedy of Remarriage.* Cambridge, MA: Harvard University Press, 1981.

PPh   *A Pitch of Philosophy: Autobiographical Exercises.* Cambridge, MA: Harvard University Press, 1994.

SW   *The Senses of Walden: An Expanded Edition.* Chicago: University of Chicago Press, 1992. First edition published 1972.

TS   *Themes out of School: Effects and Causes.* Chicago: University of Chicago Press, 1984.

WV   *The World Viewed: Reflections on the Ontology of Film.* Enlarged edition. Cambridge, MA: Harvard University Press, 1979. First edition published 1971.

Other Works

CF   *Cavell on Film*, ed. William Rothman. Albany: State University of New York Press, 2005.

PI   Ludwig Wittgenstein, *Philosophical Investigations*, trans. G. E. M. Anscombe, 3rd ed. Oxford: Basil Blackwell, 1967.//**or**//trans. G. E. M. Anscombe, P. M. S. Hacker, and Joachim Schulte, ed. P. M. S. Hacker and Joachim Schulte, revised 4th ed. Oxford: Wiley-Blackwell, 2009.

PP   J. L. Austin, *Philosophical Papers*, ed. J. O. Urmson and G. J. Warnock. 2nd ed. Oxford: Clarendon Press, 1970. First edition published 1961.

W   Henry D. Thoreau, *Walden*, ed. J. Lyndon Shanley. 150th anniversary edition. Princeton: Princeton University Press, 2004.

Introduction

Paola Marrati

The work of Stanley Cavell is a particularly interesting case for the study of the relations between philosophy and modernism. Cavell, undoubtedly one of the most singular and influential voices in contemporary philosophy and culture at large, has written extensively on modernist art—particularly on painting, photography, music, and literature; he has also dedicated an impressive body of work to cinema, whose complex and nuanced status in regards to modernism constitutes one of Cavell's main concerns.

However, Cavell's importance for understanding modernism is not exhausted by his interest in, and analyses of, modernist art and literature. Equally significant, and perhaps even more original, is his understanding of ordinary language philosophy as a modernist enterprise in its own terms. Deeply influenced by J. L. Austin and Wittgenstein's *Philosophical Investigations*, Cavell interprets their works along very different lines than those of logical positivism and dominant currents in analytic philosophy. Rather than identifying philosophy with logic or quasi-scientific factual inquiries, Cavell sees Austin's method of elucidating "what we say when" and Wittgenstein's investigations of the grammar of language as an attempt to clarify the meaning of what we say for ourselves and to one another. Such an endeavor is made both possible and necessary in his view by the absence of any universal or a priori foundations of language that could guarantee objectively the meaning of our words. Contrary to other scholars, Cavell does not believe that Wittgenstein replaces a priori universals with conventional rules as an explanation for how language is learned and used. What Wittgenstein shows, as Cavell puts it in his seminal essay "The Availability of Wittgenstein's Later Philosophy," is rather that:

> We learn and teach words in certain contexts, and then we are expected, and expect others, to be able to project words into further contexts. Nothing insures that this projection will take place (in particular, not the grasping of universals nor the grasping of books of rules), just as nothing insures that we will make, and understand, the same projections. That on the whole we do is a matter of our sharing routes of interest and feeling, modes of response, senses of humor and of significance and of fulfillment, of what is outrageous, of what is similar to what else, what a rebuke, what forgiveness, of when an utterance is an assertion, when an appeal, when an explanation—all the whirl of organism Wittgenstein calls "forms

of life." Human speech and activity, sanity and community, rest upon nothing more, but nothing less, than this. It is a vision as simple as it is difficult, and as difficult as it is (because it is) terrifying.

MWM 52

Cavell emphasizes that no external authority can settle our misunderstandings and disagreements when interests and feelings diverge and hence are no longer "ours," but only mine or yours. He considers such a situation as similar to the logic of aesthetic judgments in general and suggests that the analogy is further accentuated in modernism. As Kant already pointed out in the *Critique of Judgment*, the specificity of aesthetic judgments consists precisely in their claim to a universal validity that is not founded in any objective property. In Cavell's terms, their universality is not given, but called for, and the fact that it may never be achieved does not undermine its logical necessity. When the conventions and the tradition of an art become problematic, as is the case in modernism, the absence of objective criteria to guide our judgments is revealed in an exemplary manner: I am called upon to judge not only the value of a work, but also and foremost whether it counts as a work of art. When it comes to the works of modernist artists such as Anthony Caro, John Cage, or Samuel Beckett—to name just a few of Cavell's examples—to acknowledge the value of their sculptures, music, and plays implies in the first place to claim that they *are* sculptures, music, and plays, that *they are works of art*, although of a previously unknown kind. The nature of modernist works is thus inseparable from a crisis in the authority of certain conventions and the attempt to establish new forms of conviction in the expressive power of art. In this regard, Cavell sees modernism as a continuation of the same tradition that it contests rather than an ironic distancing from it.

The same can be said, in Cavell's view, of Austin, Wittgenstein, Nietzsche, Emerson, Thoreau, and others, who pursue a *philosophical critique of philosophy* that contests not only the contents and arguments of a given doctrine, but the very idea of *what counts as philosophy*, what modes of expression, ways of writing, choice of objects can lead philosophy away from its recognizable paths without losing the internal connection with its own tradition, that is to say without ceasing to be philosophy. And as with art, the answer to the question of what is (still) philosophy can never be known in advance.

Needless to say, Cavell's own works belong to this modernist vein in philosophy: his singular style of writing (which many find "obscure" or "literary," depending on their taste, but few have actually studied); the insistence of the autobiographical voice; and the choice of dedicating the same serious attention to philosophers and canonical authors such as Shakespeare, Kierkegaard, and Beckett alongside Hollywood comedies and other instances of "popular culture" invite a reassessment of what we call philosophy. Cavell's ongoing concern with the current divide in philosophy between its Anglo-American and European traditions, with what is included or excluded in the accepted philosophical canon in a given historical period or region, is one aspect of this problem. Another related but more general aspect is that of the audience of philosophy: whom does philosophy speak to or for? Who needs philosophy and when? The answer to these questions remains naturally and essentially open: it may well be the case that one day there will no longer be an audience for what we call philosophy; then perhaps our culture will have undergone such a profound transformation that many of our present concepts and assumptions will have become unrecognizable. But for now, Cavell strongly believes, like Socrates, that philosophy is for everyone, or no one:

> What I take Socrates to have seen is that, about the questions that were causing him wonder and hope and confusion and pain, he knew that he did not know what no man can know, and that any man could learn what he wanted to learn. No man is in any better position for knowing it than any other man—unless *wanting* to know is a special position. And this discovery about himself is the same as the discovery of philosophy, when it is the effort to find answers, and permit questions, which nobody knows the way to nor the answer to any better than you yourself. Then what makes it relevant to know, worth knowing? But relevance and worth may not be the point. The effort is irrelevant and worthless until it becomes necessary to you to know such things. There is the audience of philosophy; but there also, while it lasts, is its performance.
>
> MWM xvi

Its professionalization notwithstanding, *philosophy finds its audience whenever the urgency of questions no specialized knowledge or science can answer or even permit holds us*. The nature of Cavell's works, which constantly challenge disciplinary boundaries and established genres and conventions, is faithful, I believe, to Socrates's discovery and it is not surprising then that Cavell's reception and legacy are as unpredictable and surprising as his own texts.

The essays collected in this volume study the main themes and multiple aspects of Cavell's thought from a variety of disciplinary lenses: philosophy, of course, but also literary and film studies, anthropology, and political theory. They reflect the complexity of Cavell's works and its importance for contemporary debates in the humanities across and beyond narrowly construed disciplinary fields. The first part, "Conceptualizing Cavell," introduces the readers to some of the most influential books by Cavell in a chronological and systematic manner. Together these chapters describe the general outlook of his philosophy: how moral and aesthetic problems are intimately connected to one another and reshaped by his novel interpretation of what is at stake in skepticism, ordinary language philosophy, perfectionism, romanticism, and modernism. The contributions to the second part, "Cavell and Aesthetics," study more specific aspects and problems within Cavell's conception of aesthetics and its moral and political implications. A Glossary concludes the volume: Cavell mostly refrains from using highly specialized philosophical concepts; however, he redefines and gives new depths to familiar terms such as skepticism and tragedy while investing others like claim or acknowledgment with unprecedented philosophical weight. For this reason, the Glossary is particularly important for understanding Cavell. A summary, even brief, of the essays collected in this volume would require too lengthy an introduction and would not do justice to their value and interest: I simply want to express my deep gratitude to all the colleagues and friends who have agreed to contribute and a special thanks to Nils F. Schott for his invaluable help in the preparation of this volume.

Part One

Conceptualizing Cavell

1

Must We Mean What We Say? and the (Re)Birth of Ordinary Language Philosophy

Sandra Laugier

> *Yet no intervention in philosophy more clearly than Austin's prompted an awareness of our apparent failures to mean what we say.*
>
> —Stanley Cavell, *Little Did I Know*, 360

Stanley Cavell's entire work has its starting point in two essays, one on Austin and the other on Wittgenstein, that constitute the opening of *Must We Mean What We Say?* and express a defense and illustration of the philosophy of ordinary language to which Cavell had been converted during a series of lectures given by Austin at Harvard in 1955. Cavell was teaching the new material and method he had discovered; he was an activist of ordinary language philosophy. As he recalls in his autobiography, *Little Did I Know*,

> I had been invited the early spring of my first year of teaching at Berkeley—ordered was more like it—to participate in a panel some eight months later for that year's Christmas meetings of the Pacific Division of the American Philosophical Association, to be held at Stanford University. My insistence on the treasures I was finding Austin to have brought to philosophy was getting on the nerves of some accomplished teachers in and around my senior colleagues in the Berkeley department and it was their idea, whose point it was not hard for me to appreciate, even agree with, that it was time for me to justify my confidence before a public of professional colleagues.
>
> LDIK 360

The occasion was a reply to a paper to be prepared by his Berkeley colleague Benson Mates that criticized the procedures of the "philosophers of ordinary language" and "the appeal to ordinary language as such." The presentation actually went very well; the exchange was published in the newly founded journal *Inquiry* and later led to the publication of the essay "Must We Mean What We Say?" as the first chapter of the 1969 book.

In the days after the papers were delivered, during the break between semesters, ideas for expanding the thoughts I had arrived at in the paper began coming at a greater pace than I had ever before experienced with any philosophical material. For some days it seemed that I could hardly sit still for ten minutes without beginning to scribble down further suggestions. Many came to nothing; some found their way into work years later; some went immediately into new or expanded paragraphs of the talk.

LDIK 360–61

The paper is the start of Cavell's involvement with philosophy. Until then, he was hesitant about his career. "The perplexity resolved itself when Austin appeared halfway through that year, the spring term of 1955, to present the William James Lectures at Harvard" (*LDIK* 257). There is a form of revelation here, as if Cavell finally found a form of expression and realization of his desire for philosophy, after the first shock of the meeting with Austin. In Cavell's brief first summary of his life at the very beginning of *Little Did I Know*, the meeting with Austin is mentioned as a founding event—one that will take him away from his initial destiny, from his first talent, music. Cavell mentions "The crisis precipitated by Austin's appearance on the scene" (*LDIK* 187); his work in philosophy "had yet again to begin again" (he had started, and discarded, half a dissertation):

> Austin's presence opened lines of thought I recognized almost at once that I had no choice, or wish, but to take essentially into consideration but which, on seriously putting them into practice, left me once again with no body of work of my own to draw on in which I placed confidence.

LDIK 227

The examination of ordinary language is a starting point that leads to aesthetics. The aim is

> to get free in aesthetics of an obsession with the beautiful and the sublime and attend to the dainty and the dumpy, to get a list of words . . . that articulate attractive and unattractive qualities of objects, natural and crafted (concepts such as delicate, monumental, stark, gaudy, cluttered, neat, trite, boring, repellent, etc.) and of humans and other animals (cute, frisky, majestic, repulsive), including ones that are not perceivable merely through the plain and healthy exercise of the five senses (as with bright, loud, heavy, tall, smooth).

LDIK 337

The attention to the ordinary detail of words and world becomes a new, revolutionary method Cavell decides to follow. In this he is methodologically faithful to Austin, who calls philosophy of language "a promising site for field work, taking, as it were, an *anthropological view* of the human as such"—often read today into Wittgenstein (*LDIK* 337, my emphasis). The main concepts in Austin, the performative and excuses, are as early as *Must We Mean* seen not only as propositions, utterances, but "ways we encounter . . . each other" (*LDIK* 337). So Cavell in his teaching at Berkeley was trying to communicate his own experience of Austin's method, in the way it had communicated itself to him; hence the invitation by his colleagues to develop and justify his passion.

Must We Mean What We Say? is a development of this encounter with ordinary language philosophy. It contains most of the themes that Cavell developed in exciting ways throughout his philosophy. These include the establishment of the foundations of a radical reading of Wittgenstein in the essay "The Availability of Wittgenstein's Later Philosophy" (which launches the main themes of *The Claim of Reason*); the exploration of connections between skepticism, acknowledgement, and Shakespearean tragedy (in *Disowning Knowledge* and in *Pursuits of Happiness*); reflections on ordinary language as voice, a theme that appears throughout his later works (for instance, *In Quest of the Ordinary* and *A Pitch of Philosophy*); and the original aesthetic approach that defines Cavell's work, through his objects, which range from William Shakespeare to Samuel Beckett and pass through Hollywood comedies and melodrama, as well as opera.

But everything starts from this passionate expression of the *importance* of Austin. Of course we can retrospectively draw the essence of Cavell's work out of these first writings. The particular importance of *Must We Mean* lies in bringing together essays that, simply by being brought together in a *book*, reveal a radical, original problematic that is then thematically (and, in each case, brilliantly) developed. It is a book that is not only of historical importance, but of utmost *actual* importance.

Must We Mean is indeed not an ensemble of "collected writings." Claiming it as a *book* meant, for Cavell, claiming the necessity to write and to publish books at a moment when analytic philosophy was establishing itself as a conversation and polemic between articles and arguments. Cavell meant to prove that inheriting analytic philosophy (the works of Frege and Wittgenstein, and the power of logic, which were his first discovery in philosophy and played an important role in his education) could be something else, or rather: to show that the project of analytical philosophy, getting closer to the world by examining language, could only be accomplished if it were possible to find the conditions of truth or validity of ethical or aesthetic statements as well as of conversations, of all that we say about what actually matters to us, of, in short, what in *Must We Mean* Cavell calls *the ordinary world*: "I mean, of course, the ordinary world. That may not be all there is, but it is important enough: morality is that world, and so are force and love; so is art and a part of knowledge (the part which is about the world); and so is religion (wherever God is)" (*MWM* 40). The ordinary world is not everything there is in the world, "but it is important enough": it is the world of what matters—Cavell's world and the world we inherit from him.

The Importance of the Early Cavell

Must We Mean can be integrated into a first part of Cavell's work, which we may see now as the "early Cavell." It is moving to study it, because even if many later works are remarkable (of course *The Claim of Reason*, but also *Pursuits of Happiness*, *This New Yet Unapproachable America*, *A Pitch of Philosophy*), this early period is certainly the most exciting because it expresses the moment when Cavell begins to make his philosophical voice heard in the midst of violent doubts (almost worries of fraudulence) about his ability to continue philosophizing and the validity of his approach, completely new in fact. The books that follow may be seen as founded on this first work—and on the comfort of an early tenured position at Harvard obtained thanks to these early papers and the dissertation that grew from them. But this first work, as well as the parallel early works (*The World Viewed* of 1971 and *The Senses of Walden* of 1972), were exploring new territory. The two articles that constitute the point of discussion, Austinian and Wittgensteinian, of *Must We Mean* were written in uncertainty and controversy, and in an intellectual outburst motivated, first, by the defense of Austin and his method in philosophy and, second, by the irritation at conformist readings of Wittgenstein.

> In the months before I showed up to teach in Emerson Hall, the philosophers J. Fodor and J. Katz attacked the two articles I had submitted (in addition to my dissertation) as evidence in the case for my tenure appointment to Harvard, asserting (I believe I recall the exact words) that the articles were "deleterious to the future of philosophy." . . . When *The World Viewed* appeared two years after *Must We Mean What We Say?* one of the two reviews that came my way declared that the book was sickening, the other granted that my friends might like talking with me about movies but that this should not be grounds for publishing what was said privately.
>
> LDIK 442

This is where the philosophy of ordinary language really comes into being. Still, ordinary language philosophy is a name Wittgenstein never claimed centrally, and even Austin never did; Cavell himself uses the term with caution, well aware that his work is not part of the Oxford school of "conceptual analysis" either. It is significant that his exchanges with Austin took place entirely in the United States and that he was seldom in contact with British philosophy—which very quickly buried Austin. Today, there is very little discussion or study of Austin in England, while Wittgenstein studies are flourishing. Ordinary language philosophy is less an official domain of philosophy than a polemical term, and *Must We Mean* is somehow a work of activism. Indeed, the 1960s were also the moment that ordinary language philosophy bashing began. For the rest of the twentieth century, calling a thinker an "ordinary language philosopher" was typically an insult. The very name, in fact, began as a term of derision coined by detractors. It is probably time for us to claim the term and turn it around, just as others did with other disparaging words.

At the same time as Cavell's articles were published, Ernest Gellner in his 1959 book *Words and Things: An Examination of, and an Attack on, Linguistic Philosophy* had launched an attack on ordinary language philosophy that was so contemptuous and also so poorly argued that no real discussion followed. But for the space of a year or two it was the most widely discussed book in Anglophone philosophy. The book is nicely dismissed in *Must We Mean*—in what may have been the first genuine response to it. The fun fact is that the central allegation of Gellner's monograph was that ordinary language philosophy is essentially politically conservative. Neither the fact that there was no basis for this accusation, nor the fact that most advocates of ordinary language philosophy were and still are philosophizing with an eye to advancing politically radical endeavors, kept the charge from sticking.

Must We Mean is actually the first and only work of contemporary philosophy to carry the project of ordinary language philosophy through to its end. This philosophy of language has little to do with what has been called linguistic philosophy, or with Oxford philosophy as a method of analysis. It is a philosophy that goes back to Wittgenstein's first question in the *Blue Book*, and to Austin's questions in his first essays: What is the meaning of a word? What is it to speak, and how do we talk?[1] What are the implications of this activity for our account of what it is to be human? We still do not have answers to these questions, and *Must We Mean* focuses on these crucial issues of contemporary philosophy and metaphysics. When Cavell published what he deliberately called a "book of essays" in 1969, he knew he was upsetting analytic philosophy as it had emerged out of the arrival on the American philosophical scene of Vienna Circle philosophers, epistemologists, and logicians fleeing Nazism.[2] In *Must We Mean*, analytic philosophy was called into question *from within* and for the first time in America, where it had become dominant.

Relevance

Both the title essay, "Must We Mean What We Say?," which develops a theory of *meaning* in opposition to propositional sense and to psychological intention, and "The Availability of Wittgenstein's Later Philosophy" are articles of historical importance that provoked discussion at the time of their publication.[3] They not only contain the seed of all of *The Claim of Reason*, including the later parts; they exhibit the radicality and simplicity that characterizes Cavell's approach. This approach reflects an important displacement: one must not only attend to analyzing the empirical content and logical structure of statements, one must also look at what we say—to explain who "we" are and what "saying" is. That is, we must ask ourselves what we do with our language, and how what we do in a situation is part of what we say. And this is not merely contextualism. *Must We Mean* was the first work to put *human encounters* at the core of philosophy of language and to ask questions about the *relevance* of our statements *to ourselves* by drawing from various domains and by turning to unexpected sources such as Beckett, Shakespeare, Kierkegaard, or music criticism. This notion of relevance has since been absorbed into a mentalist philosophy of communication, but we must not let that prevent us from seeing the importance of the model that Cavell, with great fidelity to the Austinian model, proposes here. The central question of *Must We Mean* is not the question of a proposition's objective, semantic, or empirical content, but rather of the fortunes and misfortunes of ordinary expression. The issue is no longer what propositions *mean* or even what they *do* but to *mean what one says*.

For Wittgenstein, as for Cavell, language is always *ours*, we are born into it. This is an ethical truth, one difficult to accept: all our words are learned, they are the words of others, have already been spoken. Language is our form of life and there is no other. Cavell puts this in very clear terms: "[F]or those creatures for whom language is our form of life, those who are what 'Experience' entitles 'victims of expression'—mortals—language is everywhere we find ourselves, which means everywhere in philosophy" (*NYUA* 118). The limits of language are the limits of my world, and hence of my life: to recognize my form of life in language is to recognize my finitude, to understand my situation in language, and it is an education in death, as in life, the limits of which are the limits of my world.

Cavell takes a watchword from Wittgenstein to describe bringing words back from their metaphysical to their ordinary use: to *bring them home*. But he goes further than Wittgenstein, because, as Dorothy says in *The Wizard of Oz*, "there's no place like home." Cavell maintains in *Must We Mean* that we know neither what we think nor what we mean, and that the task of philosophy is to bring us back to ourselves, that is, to bring words back to their everyday use and to bring knowledge of the world back to our knowledge of or proximity to ourselves. The "voice of the ordinary" is a response to the risk of skepticism, that loss of or distancing from the world, which is also explored by film, as Cavell shows in a book from the same period, *The World Viewed*.

The appeal to the ordinary and to "our" uses of words is not obvious; it is shot through with skepticism, with what Cavell defines as the "uncanniness of the ordinary" (*IQO* 153–78). Thus, the ordinary is neither the common sense that empiricist philosophy sometimes claims for itself, nor does it have anything to do with a rationalized and descriptive version of ordinary language philosophy or with a semantics of ordinary language. For Cavell, the ordinary is lost or distant.

Cavell's originality in *Must We Mean* thus lies in defining the ordinary on the basis of a redefinition of ordinary language. It is his reading of Austin that makes such an approach possible—Cavell was the first to bring out Austin's realism. To talk about language is to talk about what language talks about. As Cavell says, "the philosophy of ordinary language is not about language, anyway not in any sense in which it is not also about the world. Ordinary language philosophy is about whatever ordinary language is about" (*MWM* 95). What is at stake in ordinary language philosophy is, as he will later put it in *Pursuits of Happiness*, "the internality of words and world to one another" (*PH* 204). It is this kind of neat fit between language and the world that will give us back the world—not the search for metaphysical adequacy. This search for the right tone, the *pitch*, gives ordinary language realism its musical dimension. For Austin, "true" designates one of the possible ways of expressing the harmony between language and the world. "Fitting" for him designates a concept no longer of correspondence or even of correctness, but rather the appropriateness of a statement within the circumstances. "The statements fit the facts always more or less loosely, in different ways on different occasions" (*PP* 130).

What Cavell introduces—already in *Must We Mean* and later as the object of his reflection on voice in *A Pitch of Philosophy*—is the connection of rightness of tone, adequacy of expression to knowledge of self (and self-reliance). Hence Cavell's interest in the "aesthetic" problem understood as a theory of meaning that connects ethics and aesthetics, along the lines of the *Tractatus*, while returning to the truth of the later Wittgenstein: "What is true or false is what human beings *say*" (*PI* §241). Examining ordinary language allows us to "sharpen our perception of . . . phenomena" (*PP* 182). It is this sharpening of visual, tactile, and auditory perception that Cavell seeks in *Must We Mean*. The reciprocal "internality of words and world" is an intimacy that cannot be demonstrated, or posited by a metaphysical thesis; it can only be brought out by attending to the differences traced by language.

In exploring the uses of words, Austin is searching for the natural or, as he calls it, "boring" relation between words and the world. He opposes arguments (even Wittgensteinian ones) that would validate this relation in terms of a structure common to language and the world: "[I]f it is admitted *(if)* that the rather *boring* yet satisfactory relation between words and world which has here been discussed does genuinely occur, why should the phrase 'is true' not be our way of describing it?" (*PP* 133, second emphasis added). That is why Austin mentions "linguistic phenomenology" as a "less misleading name" for "this way of doing philosophy" than "'linguistic' or 'analytic' philosophy or 'the analysis of language.'" He explains:

> When we examine what we should say when, what words we should use in what situations, we are looking again not *merely* at words (or "meanings" whatever they may be) but also at the *realities we use the words to talk about*: we are using a sharpened awareness of words to sharpen our perception of, though not as the final arbiter of, the phenomena.
>
> *PP* 182, second emphasis added

The relationship between language and the world is characterized by Austin in terms of a *given*. The problem is not agreeing on an opinion but agreeing on a point of departure, a *given*. This given is *language*—conceived of not as a body of statements or words but as *agreement* on what we should say when. Austin explains: "For me, it is essential at the beginning to come to an agreement on the question of 'what we should say when.' To my mind, experience proves amply that we do come to agreement on 'what we should say when' such or such a thing, though I grant you it is often long and difficult."[4] Here, the agreement Austin is talking about concerning what we should say and what we mean is normative. This *normativity of the ordinary* is also the main theme of *Must We Mean*. It is normative because ordinary language "embodies all the distinctions men have found worth drawing, and the connections they have found worth marking" (*PP* 182). This capacity to mark differences is Cavell's obsession; in order for us to have something to say and mean, there must be differences that hook onto us and *are important* to us: "[T]he world must exhibit (we must observe) similarities and dissimilarities (there could not be the one without the other): if everything were either absolutely indistinguishable from anything else or completely unlike anything else, there would be nothing to say" (*PP* 121). Austin's realism consists in this conception of differences and resemblances. In the chapter "Austin at Criticism," Cavell insists on the reality of the distinctions in Austin, in contrast with the distinctions usually established by philosophers.

Consequently, one form his investigations take is that of repudiating the distinctions lying around philosophy—dispossessing them, as it were, by showing better ones. Better not merely because finer, but because more solid, having, so to speak, a greater natural weight; appearing normal, even inevitable, when the others are luridly arbitrary; useful where the others seem twisted; real where the others are academic; fruitful where the others stop cold.

MWM 103

For Austin, "true" designates one of the possible ways of expressing the harmony between language and the world. "Fitting" for him designates a concept not of correspondence or even of correctness, but rather of the appropriateness of a statement within the circumstances—the fact that it is proper, *right*. This moral dimension of language use is probably the strongest strand in *Must We Mean*'s inheritance of Austin.

Wittgenstein also has a say in formulating what proved to be Cavell's obsession throughout his work: the search for the right, fitting tone[5]—conceptually, morally, and perceptually—that Cavell mentions in his autobiographical writings with regard to his mother's musical talent and his father's jokes. It is a matter of finding a fine sensitivity to things and the fit of words at the heart of ordinary uses. In this agreement between what is "achieved through mapping the fields of consciousness lit by the occasions of a word" (*MWM* 100), Austin registers the possibility of finding an ordinary adequacy to the world.

Saying

Austin in *How to Do Things with Words* mentions the tradition of rhetoric: the fact that language is used in a world of feelings, actions, and attitudes is an old story. But Austin, and Cavell after him, are the firsts to explain that these affects and agency are part of language *by saying and in saying*.

What Cavell introduces in *Must We Mean* and expands on later as the object of his reflection on voice, is the connection of rightness of tone, of the adequacy of expression, to knowledge of self (an early form of his obsession with self-reliance). He navigates adroitly between the Austinian critique of psychologism on the one hand, and, on the other hand, caricature forms of emotivism that separate the content of our words from the emotion associated with them. What interests Cavell is *what we say* as human beings. "What is true or false is what human beings *say*" (*PI* §241).

Cavell answers the need expressed by Wittgenstein and Austin to take into account what is said when determining meaning. What pertains to expression and what pertains to description cannot be separated within a statement, as if one could break statements down into stabilized propositions and some "additional" force—some psychological stand-in, as pitiful to Cavell as pounding a table or one's chest to legitimate or reinforce a contestable or insincere affirmation. Turning to literature and to the stage, where ordinary language is brought to life, goes directly against this approach. The problem is semantic, ethical . . . and also political; in one of the rare mentions of politics in *Must We Mean*, Cavell denounces the "Manichean conception" of a "moral philosophy which distinguishes between the assessment of individual actions and of social practices" (47). This is a transparent critique of John Rawls's 1955 article "Two Concepts of Rules," very influential at the moment Cavell composed these essays included in *Must We Mean*. Rawls aimed at distinguishing between agreement to, or following, a rule or principle internal to a practice and general agreement to a practice. Committing to a practice leads to learning the rules that define it and to recognizing that "its rules define it"; it means following the appropriate rules. For Rawls, "it doesn't make sense for a person to raise the question whether or not a rule of a practice correctly applies" as long as "the action he contemplates is a form of action defined by a practice . . . the only legitimate question concerns the nature of the practice itself."[6] Cavell's point is not only, first, that not all practices are governed by rules (*MWM* 52) but also, furthermore, that agreement to a practice is never *given* but always under discussion. We have not agreed to everything, in language use and in political practice. This makes *Must We Mean* a work of political philosophy, an early heterodox criticism of analytical political thought.

Cavell makes it his goal to "reinsert . . . the human voice in philosophical thinking" (*CT* 63). The goal of ordinary language philosophy is indeed to make it understood that language is *spoken*, pronounced by a human voice within a "form of life," a concept central to *Must We Mean* (84). It then becomes a matter of shifting away from the question of the common use of language to the new question of the relation between an individual speaker and the language community. For Cavell, this leads to a reintroduction of the voice into philosophy, and to a redefinition of subjectivity in language precisely on the basis of the relationship of the individual voice to the linguistic community: the relation of voice to voices. Voice is the place of subjectivation and our condition is *con-diction*, diction together. This extension of the semantical and social meaning of "forms of life" to the organic "whirl" of *lifeforms* is essential to the emergence of forms of life as a concept.

The philosopher's task, to bring our words back to earth, is neither easy nor obvious, and the quest for the ordinary is the most difficult of all, even if (and precisely because) it is available to anyone. "No man is in any better position for knowing it than any other man—unless *wanting* to know is a special position. And this discovery about himself is the same as the discovery of philosophy, when it is the effort to find answers, and permit questions, which nobody knows the way to nor the answer to any better than you yourself" (*MWM* xlii, Cavell's emphasis). Ordinary language philosophy responds to skepticism not with new knowledge or beliefs, but by acknowledging our condition, which, to quote one of Cavell's puns, is also our diction together. Skepticism, far from dissolving in this community of language, takes on its most radical sense here: what allows me to speak in the name of others? How do I know what *we* mean by a word or world, to take up another of Cavell's puns? *Must We Mean* explores our form of life in language in all its diversity; as Cavell will later say, "language is everywhere we find ourselves, which means everywhere in philosophy (like sexuality in psychoanalysis)" (*NYUA* 118).

Ordinary Realism

The philosophical interest of turning to what we say appears when we ask ourselves not only what it is to *say* but what this *we* is. For Cavell, this is the question at the beginning of the *Philosophical Investigations*. But it is also Thoreau (and Emerson, who takes on considerable importance in Cavell's later work), through his attention to the ordinary and the common, who underwrites the practices of Wittgenstein and Austin. Without Thoreau, there would not be this need for a radical change in how we listen to language, a change in our sensitivity to what is said. This is the task Thoreau set for himself in *Walden*: to make us better speakers. "Our reading, our conversation and thinking, are all on a very low level, worthy only of pygmies and manikins" (*W* 104). The falsity, the hopeless inadequacy of our tone and our language, are left unexplained both by the analytic notion of truth and by the correspondence to reality that semantic approaches (continued today by contemporary representationalism) emphasize. Against these approaches Cavell proposes his own version of realism, which is *realistic* in the sense Cora Diamond uses the word: grounded in a survey of the details of expressions and in attention to the adequacy or inadequacy of our expressions to ourselves.[7]

It is again a matter of replacing or complicating truth with relevance, with our perception of what is relevant to us, of what counts. Cavell takes up the discovery of one's own relevance and one's relation to the real, with regard to cinema, in his later essay "What Becomes of Things on Film" (1978). There, he says that the *ontology of film* is defined by "the appearance and significance of just those objects and people that are in fact to be found in the succession of films, or passages of films, that matter to us" (*TS* 183). Importance is the criterion of reality and determines how our concepts apply to it.

The starting point of Cavell's investigation in *The World Viewed* at the same moment as *Must We Mean* is to reiterate the gesture by which Tolstoy substitutes the question of the essence of art for that of its importance. Importance is not a supplement to essence. Mastering a concept implies knowing what role the word can play in our uses, which means knowing its role, its importance in our lives, in the real. Mastering a concept is therefore knowing its importance: our criteria for use state what is important to us, in the double sense of what is identified as falling under the concept (counting for) and of what arouses our interest and presents value to us, stands out.

For Cavell, there can be no definition of relevance and truth without an examination of what is important. Here, the risk of subjectivism arises: what is relevant for me is not, or is not always, relevant for others. But this is the whole combined argument of *Must We Mean*, *The Senses of Walden*, and *The World Viewed*: to show how importance for me and importance for others are *logically* connected. The early Cavell marks the theoretical moment of a conceptual connection between ordinary language (sensitivity to what we should say when) and aesthetic judgment. No relevance without importance, without an investment in what counts. "But relevance and worth may not be the point. The effort is irrelevant and worthless until it becomes necessary to you to know such things. There is the audience of philosophy; but there also, while it lasts, is its performance" (*MWM* xlii). That is why criticism is, necessarily, an enterprise in self-knowledge. According to Cavell, this is a defining characteristic of "writing the modern." The modern is defined by the claim of the importance of how the writer, artist, filmmaker, *and* audience want things to be, regardless of tradition or good taste. "The . . . exercise of criticism is not to determine whether the thing is good that way but why you want it that way." He proposes a conception of criticism and objectivity according to which "these questions are always together" (CR 95). By radically associating "the scrupulous exactitude" of artistic desire with "a moral and intellectual imperative," Cavell redefines meaning (intention) through the conjunction of desire and importance.

> When in earlier writing of mine I broach the topic of the modern, I am broaching the topic of art as one in which the connection between expression and desire is purified. In the modern neither the producer nor the consumer has anything to go on (history, convention, genre, form, medium, physiognomy, composition . . .) that secures the value or the significance of an object apart from *one's wanting the thing to be as it is*.
>
> CR 94–95, emphasis added

Life Forms and Rules

What, then, are the criteria for what is important or significant? Our words and concepts are *dead* without their criteria for use. Wittgenstein and Austin look for these criteria on the basis of their perception of uses. Cavell asks: how can one claim to accomplish this? It is this question—of the essential lack of foundation to this claim—that defines the sense of *criteria* and the task of criticism:

> Why are some claims about myself expressed in the form "We . . ."? About what can I speak for others on the basis of what I have learned about myself? . . . Then suppose it is asked: "But how do I know others speak as I do?" About some things I know they do not; I have some knowledge of my idiosyncrasy. But if the question means "How do I know at all that others speak as I do?" then the answer is, I do not.
>
> MWM 67

Ordinary language philosophy thus consists in searching for means to recognize and find one's voice, to find agreement in language and the right, fitting expression—but also to find means of expressing inadequacy and disagreement. On what is the appeal to ordinary language based? All that we have is *what we say* and our agreements in language. The agreement Austin and Wittgenstein speak of is in no way an intersubjective agreement. It is as objective as an agreement can be. But where does this agreement come from? In "The Availability of Wittgenstein's Later Philosophy," Cavell makes the following remark about Wittgenstein, which would go on to have great resonance for other philosophers, including Hilary Putnam, John McDowell, Cora Diamond, and Veena Das:

We learn and teach words in certain contexts, and then we are expected, and expect others, to be able to project them into further contexts. Nothing insures that this projection will take place (in particular, not the grasping of universals nor the grasping of books of rules), just as nothing insures that we will make, and understand, the same projections. That on the whole we do is a matter of our sharing routes of interest and feeling, modes of response . . . of when an utterance is an assertion, when an appeal, when an explanation—all the whirl of organism Wittgenstein calls "forms of life." Human speech and activity, sanity and community, rest upon nothing more, but nothing less, than this. It is a vision as simple as it is difficult, and as difficult as it is (and because it is) terrifying.

MWM 52

That our ordinary language is founded on nothing but itself is not only a source of disquiet about the validity of what we do and say, but also the revelation of a truth about ourselves. The fact is that I am the only source of such validity. This is an understanding of the fact that language is a form of life—which Cavell defines as "the absence of foundation or guarantee for creatures endowed with language and subject to its powers and weaknesses, subject to their mortal condition."[8] As early as *Must We Mean*, Cavell suggests that we understand *forms of life* not only in the social (ethnological) sense, but also in the natural (biological) sense, as *lifeforms*.[9]

[T]here is a pervasive and systematic background of agreements among us, which we had not realized, or had not known we realize. Wittgenstein sometimes calls them conventions; sometimes rules . . . The "agreement" we act upon he calls "agreement in judgments" (§242), and he speaks of our ability to use language as depending upon agreement in "forms of life" (§241). But forms of life, he says, are exactly what have to be "accepted"; they are "given."

CR 30

It is sometimes feared that the "ordinary" approach could lead to a new and perverse form of conservatism: one would rely on customs and traditions rather than on argued principles. That we agree in language means that language—our form of life—produces our understanding of one another just as much as language is a product of agreement, that it is natural to us in this sense, and that the idea of convention is there simultaneously to imitate and disguise this necessity. At this point, the criticism mounted by Cavell of usual interpretations of the concept of "form of life" becomes relevant. Cavell opposes these interpretations by his use of the formulation "form of *life*," or *life* form, by contrast with "*form* of life." What is given is our forms of life. What leads us to want to violate our agreements, our criteria, is the refusal of this given, of this form of life in not only its social but also its biological dimension. It is this second (vertical) aspect of form of life that Cavell insists on in *This New Yet Unapproachable America* while at the same time recognizing the importance of the first (horizontal) dimension, i.e., social agreement. What discussions of the first sense (that of conventionalism) have obscured is the strength of the natural and biological sense of form of life, which he picks out in evoking what Wittgenstein calls "natural reactions" and "the natural history of human beings" (*PI* §415).

What is *given* in forms of life is not only social structures and various cultural habits, but everything that can be seen in "the specific strength and scale of the human body and of the human senses and of the human voice" (*NYUA* 42) and everything that makes it the case that, just as doves, in Kant's phrase, need air to fly, so we, in Wittgenstein's phrase, need friction to walk (*PI* §107).[10]

For Veena Das, the idea of lifeform involves not a banal distinction between natural and conventional but a *naturalness of* the acts of eating, instead e.g. of pawing or pecking, as *belonging to our lives as humans*, as distinct from what is natural for other animals or birds, and as distinct from ethnological variation. What the notion of form of life involves, then, is the mutual implication of the natural and the social.

> In being asked to accept this, or suffer it, as given for ourselves, we are not asked to accept, let us say, private property, but separateness; not a particular fact of power, but the fact that I am a man, therefore of this (range or scale of) capacity for work, for pleasure, for endurance, for appeal, for command, for understanding, for wish, for will, for teaching, for suffering.
>
> *NYUA* 44

Ordinary voice is part of the human form of life: to acknowledge this is to redefine what we understand by "grammar." Conformist readings of Wittgenstein lead to focusing on the *rules* that would constitute grammar: a grammar of the norms of language's functioning and its "normal" uses, to be acquired like a form of knowledge. Cavell, on the other hand, proposes a reading of Wittgenstein in which learning language is initiation into a form of life, into the "relevant forms of life." "In learning a language, you do not merely learn the pronunciation of sounds, and their grammatical orders, but the 'forms of life' which make those sounds the words they are, do what they do" (*CR* 177–78).

From the beginning, Cavell positioned himself against a reading of Wittgenstein (institutionalized at the time and dominant ever since) that is based on a false separation between Wittgenstein's early philosophy (notably, the *Tractatus*) and his later philosophy—a first Wittgenstein, a realist metaphysicist, and a second Wittgenstein, an anti-realist and "normativist." Cavell was the first to unseat this dogma of Wittgensteinism. In "The Availability of Wittgenstein's Later Philosophy," Cavell tells us that where Wittgenstein speaks of rules or language he does not give a *thesis* or explanation, but rather describes what we do; we learn how to use words in certain contexts, from our elders, and all our lives we must use them in new contexts and without any safety net, without any guarantee, without universals; we must project them and create new meanings, or improvise these meanings in the background of a form of life.[11]

With his first systematic study of the philosopher's work, Cavell found the future tone for his reading, which would go on to revolutionize, still today, the field of Wittgenstein studies. In "The Availability," Cavell subverts the recourse to the notion of a rule, replacing it with the notion of criteria and forms of life—the fabric, texture, or whirl of human existence. We agree in forms of life, but this agreement neither explains nor justifies anything. To agree *in* language means that language—our form of life—produces our understanding just as much as it is the product of an agreement. Cavell's (and today Das's) insistence on reading the concept of forms of life as *life*forms is a way to enhance the "natural," fatal sense of lifeforms, the casual/fatal character of the ordinary that Wittgenstein evokes in his mention of "the natural history of human beings"—realities of ordinary life, of the living, to which the beautiful epigraph to the chapter from Jean Giraudoux also refers:

> For there is no theatre which is not prophecy. Not this false divination which gives names and dates, but true prophecy, that which reveals to men these surprising truths: that the living must live, that the living must die, that autumn must follow summer, spring follow winter, that there are four elements, that there is happiness, that there are innumerable miseries, that life is a reality, that it is a dream, that man lives in peace, that man lives on blood; in short, those things they will never know.
> qtd. in *MWM* 44

This allows us to understand—beyond any banalities about a "Wittgensteinian therapeutic"—how reading Wittgenstein can transform us, how it is revolutionary. Beyond Cavell's now incontestable influence on heterodox studies of Wittgenstein, we must note his critical innovation, mother of all the others: for Cavell, Wittgenstein's text is *written*, and its statements are not a group of theses. They establish the author's paradoxical position (even in the *Tractatus*), the estrangement gap between himself and his writings and voice. This represents a new subjectivity, no longer foundational but skeptical, which emerges in ordinary use of language. In reading a sentence by Wittgenstein one must be attentive to his tonality, and to the sensitivity of meaning to the use and practice of language. Reading Wittgenstein—or for what it's worth, any philosopher—as a *writer*, just like reading Emerson, Thoreau, etc. as *thinkers*, is somehow a *transgression*.

The originality of *Must We Mean* is its reinvention of the nature of language, and the connection he establishes between the nature of language and *human nature*. In this sense, the question of agreement in language reformulates ad infinitum the question of the human condition, and acceptance of the latter goes hand in hand with acknowledgement of the former.

The Universal Voice

The philosophical problem raised by the philosophy of ordinary language is hence double. First, by what right do we base ourselves on what we say ordinarily? Next, on what or on whom do we base our determination of what we ordinarily say? But—and here lies the genius of Cavell's questioning in *Must We Mean*—these two questions are but one. The central enigma of rationality and community is whether it is possible for me to speak *in the name of others*. This extends the shift in Wittgenstein from the paradigm of description to that of confession, and accounts for the particular autobiographical tone of the *Philosophical Investigations*. In *Must We Mean* and in its method, the idea that all philosophy is autobiographical is born, and it is certainly here that Cavell's later project to realize this idea by writing an autobiography begins. In the later Wittgenstein, as in Jean-Jacques Rousseau, Kierkegaard, and Thoreau, the genre of autobiography replaces the genres of philosophical treatise, argued essay, even poetry and aphorism. As Cavell puts it in the contemporaneous *Senses of Walden*:

> The writer has secrets to tell which can only be told to strangers. The secrets are not his, and they are not the confidences of others. They are secrets because few are anxious to know them; all but one or two wish to remain foreign. Only those who recognize themselves as strangers can be told them, because those who think themselves familiars will think they have already heard what the writer is saying. They will not understand his speaking in confidence.
>
> SW 92

This remark, typical of the early Cavell, brings us back to the notion of voice and the question of the foundations of agreement—the *I* as the ability to speak in my own name.

It is important for the early Cavell that Wittgenstein says we agree *in* language and not *on* language. This means that we are not agents of the agreement; language precedes this agreement just as much as it is produced by it, and this very circularity constitutes an element of skepticism. The answer will not be found in convention, for convention is not an explanation of language's functioning but rather a difficulty within it. The idea of convention cannot account for the practice of language. Our agreement—with others, with myself—is an agreement of voices; for Wittgenstein our *Übereinstimmen* is a "harmonic" agreement. Cavell defines an agreement that is neither logical, nor semantic, nor psychological, nor intersubjective. Instead, it is founded on nothing more than the validity of a voice. Claiming is what a voice does when it founds itself on itself alone in order to establish universal agreement—a claim that, as exorbitant as it already is, Cavell asks us to formulate in an even more exorbitant manner: in place and stead of any condition of reason or understanding. My individual voice claims to be a "universal voice"; this is what a voice does when it bases itself on itself alone, instead of on any condition of reason, in order to establish universal agreement. This discovery of *The Claim of Reason*—"That a group of human beings *stimmen* in their language *überein* says, so to speak, that they are mutually voiced with respect to it, mutually *attuned* top to bottom" (*CR* 32, Cavell's emphases)—is already explicit in *Must We Mean*. "Aesthetic Problems in Modern Philosophy" puts the question of the foundation of language in these Kantian terms, showing the proximity of Wittgenstein's and Austin's methods to a paradox inherent in aesthetic judgment: basing oneself on *I* in order to say what *we* say. Cavell refers to the well-known passage in §8 of the *Critique of Judgment*. Kant leads us to discover in aesthetic judgment "a property of our faculty of cognition that without this analysis would have remained unknown": the "claim to universality" proper to judgments of taste. Kant distinguishes the agreeable from the beautiful, which claims universal agreement, in terms of *private* versus *public* judgment. How can a judgment that has all the characteristics of being private claim to be public, to be valid for all? Kant notes the strange, "disconcerting" nature of this fact, whose *Unheimlichkeit* Wittgenstein took to the limit. The judgment of taste demands universal agreement, and it "ascribes this agreement to everyone."[12] It is what Kant calls the universal voice that supports such a claim; it is the *Stimme* heard in *übereinstimmen*— the verb Wittgenstein uses when speaking of agreeing. The question of the universal voice is in *Must We Mean* the question of the voice itself and of its arrogation. The universal voice expresses our agreement and thus our claim to speak in the name of others—to speak, *tout court*.

What is, then, the status of the voice? This question receives a full response in *A Pitch of Philosophy* and in the essay "Passionate and Performative Utterance"—in the "later" Cavell of the late nineties and in *Little Did I Know*. Still with the help of Austin.

The philosopher speaks with ordinary words, and nothing says that others will accept these—though the philosopher claims to speak for all. By what right? "Who is to say whether a man speaks for all men?" (*MWM* xl). Here we may think again of *Must We Mean* as pursuing one of the things at stake in Austin and in the method of ordinary language philosophy. It is difficult not to notice that there is an "unhappy" dimension, a dimension of failure in ordinary language philosophy, which is obsessed—at least in the case of Austin—with instances where language fails, is inadequate, inexpressive. Austin draws attention to the sexual connotations (which he says are "normal") of the terms he chooses to designate the different failures of performatives (*misfires, abuses*). The ever-possible failure of the performative defines language as a human and living activity, felicitous or infelicitous. One of the goals of ordinary language philosophy will thus be to determine the way or ways in which a statement can be infelicitous, failed, inadequate to the real. This can happen in a number of ways, for a statement may fail by being false, certainly, but also by being exaggerated, vague, inadequate, incongruous, inept, etc.

The refusal of expression is also a refusal of the community of language in the sense in which the community would impose or represent the limits and constraints of language. Here again the very idea of a secret or of the unsayable masks this radical inadequacy, this absence of control over our speech, our voices, our lives.

Getting Our Living Together

Cavell's permanent question and anxiety is: how can I know if I adequately project words into new contexts? Austin's classification of "infelicities" in his account of performatives in *How to Do Things with Words* is the background for Cavell's analyses. The ever-possible failure of performatives defines language as a human activity and reality. One of the goals of ordinary language philosophy will be, then, to determine the ordinary ways in which an utterance can be infelicitous. Cavell takes it further in *Must*

We Mean. The ever-present and tragic possibility of the failure of language and action is at the center of Austin's concerns. Skepticism runs throughout our ordinary use of language; I am constantly tempted and threatened by inexpressivity. This is the point of later works on opera and melodrama. In *Must We Mean*, Cavell brings together Freud and Wittgenstein in their shared awareness of the impossibility of controlling what we say.

> Because the breaking of such control is a constant purpose of the later Wittgenstein, his writing is deeply practical and negative, the way Freud's is. And like Freud's therapy, it wishes to prevent understanding which is unaccompanied by inner change.... In both, such misfortune is betrayed in the incongruence between what is said and what is meant or expressed; for both, the self is concealed in assertion and action and revealed in temptation and wish.
>
> *MWM* 72

The examination of our statements does not give us any greater mastery over our lives or words. This is the radical shift Cavell makes in *Must We Mean*. In asking how *to mean* what I say, Cavell, far from reestablishing subjectivity by defining it as voice, turns the question of private language around. The problem is not my ability to express what I have "inside" me—thinking or feeling something without being able to say it— but rather the opposite; it is to *mean what I say*. To say, as *How to Do Things with Words* demonstrated, that language is also action does not mean I control language (for, as is clear from the central role excuses play in our lives, I do not control my actions any better). The impossibility of speaking the world masks a refusal to know oneself and to mean. "What they had not realized was what they were saying, or, what they were *really* saying, and so had not known *what they meant*. To this extent, they had not known themselves, and not known the world" (*MWM* 40, Cavell's emphases). Our (deliberate) distance from the world creates a fantasy: the fantasy of the private, of inexpressiveness— which becomes the very anxiety of the weight of expression. The question of privacy is transformed and becomes that of my "fatedness" to signification, to meaning. The problem is thus not meaninglessness or the impossibility of "making sense" but rather the fatality of expression. "The question, within the mood of the fantasy is: Why do we attach significance to *any* words and deeds, of others or of ourselves?" (*CR* 351, Cavell's emphasis). To understand that, as Wittgenstein said, language is a lifeform means accepting the naturalness of language, the fatality of signification. This is not easy to achieve. It is here that skepticism in its various forms is born: the impossibility of accessing the world is a mask for my own refusal to bear signification, meaning, expression. And here, realism in its various forms is born—my claim to know or theorize the real is a mask for my refusing agency, contact, proximity with things. To mean, or to know what one means, would be first and foremost to place the sentence, to quote Wittgenstein, back in its "country of origin" (*PI* §116), to recover the naturalness of language. This was the task of the ordinary language philosopher; as Wittgenstein says, "to bring words back from their metaphysical to their everyday use" (*PI* §116). But the idea of life form goes beyond this imagery of a return to home.

We are not agents of our language, but "victims of expression." In *A Pitch of Philosophy*, Cavell spells out in precise terms what in *Must We Mean* he sketched out concerning the essential passivity of the relation to the voice. "It is in recognizing this abandonment to my words, as if to unfeasible epitaphs, presaging the leave-taking of death, that I know my voice, recognize my words (no different from yours) as mine" (*PPh* 126). To be thus abandoned to language is indeed the opposite of what the concept of speech (active, living, etc.) would seem to imply. I am as active (and also as passive) in my voice as in, for example, my breathing or my exhalation, and the question is then no longer being able to access language, the community of speakers, or one's voice (horizontal forms of life); it is being able to bear precisely "*the (inevitable) extension* of the voice, which will always escape me and will forever find its way back to me" (*PPh* 126, Cavell's emphasis). And thus what is unbearable is not the inexpressible or the impossibility of being expressive; it is *expression* itself as life form, a life that is not mine anymore. The phantasm of the private disguises our fear of being public, "the terror of being expressive beyond our means" (*PPh* 126–27), as a symmetrical fear of inexpressiveness (the idea of "private language") that is at the core of the seminal reading of *King Lear* in "The Avoidance of Love." "I am led to stress the condition . . . [of] the terror of absolute inexpressiveness, suffocation, which at the same time reveals itself as a terror of absolute expressiveness, unconditioned exposure; they are the extreme states of voicelessness" (*CT* 43).

The subjectivity of language is then the impossible adequacy between a speaker and her voice or voices. This dissociation or dislocation of voice and agent starts from ordinary language philosophy, and it is at the heart of the different forms of expression in the human form of life that Cavell will successively analyze in his further work—theater, film, opera:

> [O]n film the actor is the subject of the camera, emphasizing that this actor could (have) become other characters (that is, emphasizing the potentiality in human existence, the self's journeying), as opposed to theater's emphasizing that this character could (will) accept other actors (that is, emphasizing the fatedness in human existence, the self's finality or typicality at each step of the journey). In opera the relative emphasis of singer and role seems undecidable in these terms, indeed unimportant beside the fact of the new conception it introduces of the relation between voice and body, a relation in which not this character and this actor are embodied in each other but in which this voice is located in—one might say disembodied within—this figure, this double, this person, this persona, this singer, whose voice is essentially unaffected by the role.
>
> *PPh* 137

One may also note that such a dislocation of the voice, begun and audible in *Must We Mean*, is at the heart of Cavell's autobiographical project in *A Pitch of Philosophy* and *Little Did I Know*. Cavell's idea in *Must We Mean* is that it is also up to philosophy to make room for life and—going beyond its classical tendency to want to leave the everyday behind—to *become ordinary*. This becoming is of the order of revolutionary change. Hence the definition of the ordinary proposed by Cavell, that covers more or less what matters for us in philosophy: "That may not be all there is, but it is important enough" (*MWM* 40).

Thoreau, maybe better than Wittgenstein, knew that his book—*Walden*, a book on which Cavell wrote a marvelous book at the same time as *Must We Mean*—would only revolutionize those who truly want to understand what he says; those who will see that the answers to the questions we ask ourselves are not to be looked for very far away; the things we believe are ineffable have already been spoken, are there before us, at our feet, in the ground. It is this—finding the right expression—that Thoreau sees as a solution to "lives of quiet desperation." "I desire to speak somewhere *without* bounds . . . for I am convinced that I cannot exaggerate enough even to lay the foundation of a true expression. . . . The volatile truth of our words should continually betray the inadequacy of the residual statement" (*W* 324–25, Thoreau's emphasis). We are thus brought back to the aim of politics: to find an adequate expression, to avoid those "words that chagrin us," that ring false. Thus, Thoreau seeks to accomplish "the exploit of obscurity" in order to attain true clarity: "I do not suppose that I have attained to obscurity, but I should be proud if no more fatal fault were found with my pages on this score than was found with the Walden ice" (*W* 325).

Attaining to obscurity in order to *mean what we say*. A few months after finishing *Must We Mean*, Cavell writes about Thoreau: "We have yet 'to get our living together.'" This of course means that we must be whole, one community, and that is the problem of politics. "We are not settled, we have not clarified ourselves; our character, and the character of the nation is not . . . transparent to itself" (*SW* 79).

Self-Knowledge and Politics

Cavell's first reading of Wittgenstein's *Philosophical Investigations* shows that "the nature of self-knowledge—and therewith the nature of the self—is one of the great subjects of the *Investigations* as a whole" (*MWM* 68). *The Claim of Reason* later masterfully develops this line of thinking. But "The Availability of Wittgenstein's Later Philosophy" nonetheless established, on its own, the principles of an unorthodox reading that continues to inspire various fields and styles of thought. By exploring our relevance to ourselves, *Must We Mean* reveals the connection between the words we pronounce and hear, the truth we search for, and the life we want to lead–which was revolutionary in the philosophy of the 1960s and remains so today. In fact, "revolutionary" is the word Cavell uses in his first Foreword to describe "Wittgenstein's and Austin's sense of their tasks" as "a recognizable version of the wish 'to establish the truth of this world' . . . wherever there really is a love of wisdom—or call it the passion for truth—it is inherently, if usually ineffectively, revolutionary; because it is the same as a hatred of the falseness in one's character and of the needless and unnatural compromises in one's institutions" (*MWM* xxxix).

This revolutionary character, which Cavell attributes to Wittgenstein and Austin, to their capacity to transform us, is that of *Must We Mean*.

There have been signs recently that ordinary language philosophy might be reasserting itself. Following what has been dubbed the "death of ordinary language philosophy," this approach, which many have thought (and still think) antiquated, is starting to reemerge.

In *Must We Mean*, we find discussions of ordinary language, theater, skepticism, modernism in art, etc.—but not of politics. By the time of the publication of the book, in 1969, Cavell, already a professor of Aesthetics and Theory of Value at Harvard, was engaged alongside his students (through what he calls in his autobiography "ordinary fidelity"). Three hundred of them had occupied the offices of the president of their university in protest against its support for the Vietnam War, and had been evacuated with unprecedented brutality (tear gas and beatings) by the police. As a result, the entire campus went on strike. Cavell also accompanied students' struggles for civil rights in the 1960s, travelling with them to Tougaloo College, in Jackson, Mississippi, for a Student Nonviolent Coordinating Committee summer school in the tragic Freedom Summer of 1964, as he recounts in *Little Did I Know*.

In April 1969, Cavell and his colleague John Rawls carried a motion that provided for the creation of a department of African-American Studies at Harvard—relaying a student campaign launched after the assassination of Martin Luther King Jr. The philosopher Cornel West recalled this at Stanley Cavell's funeral in 2018. Stanley Cavell had helped him through his difficult beginnings by having him recruited as a Harvard lecturer.

The political question is again that of the philosophy of language—that of saying and wanting to say, and of actually meaning; the philosophical force of using "what we say" appears when we ask ourselves, not only what is said, but what this *we* is. How do I know what we are saying in this or that circumstance? In what way is the language, inherited from others, that I speak my own? How can I *mean what I say*? In the 1960s, Cavell in *Must We Mean* thus raises the question of our capacity for thought as constantly related to our judgment of what counts, as never being able to be delegated to others, as being our responsibility. And without the real conditions (material, moral, and political) that allow us to say and express what matters to us, we are reduced to conformity—to hollow words and indifference to others or, worse, to the hateful crowd that some want to sell us under the name of democracy.

Thus, already *in Must We Mean*, finding the real conditions of *truth* in politics and in ethics is the most urgent question. And that is what makes this book of essays the starting point of a specific political inheritance of philosophy of language. Ordinary language philosophy is alive and well; its rebirth began fifty years ago.

Notes

1 Ludwig Wittgenstein, *The Blue and Brown Books* (Oxford: Blackwell, 1969), 1, and J. L. Austin, *PP*, 55–75, esp. 56, and 134–53.
2 For a historical perspective on this, see my *Recommencer la philosophie: La Philosophie americaine aujourd'hui* (Paris: Vrin, 2014).

3   See Cora Diamond, *The Realistic Spirit: Wittgenstein, Philosophy, and the Mind* (Cambridge, MA: MIT Press, 1995) and John McDowell, "Non-Cognitivism and Rule-Following," in *Wittgenstein: To Follow a Rule*, ed. Steven Holtzman and Christopher Leich (London: Routledge, 1981), 150, as well as Hilary Putnam, *Jewish Philosophy as a Guide to Life: Rosenzweig, Buber, Levinas, Wittgenstein* (Bloomington: Indiana University Press, 2008); *Pragmatism: An Open Question* (Oxford: Blackwell, 1995); and "Rethinking Mathematical Necessity," in *Words and Life*, ed. James Conant (Cambridge, MA: Harvard University Press, 1995), 245–63.
4   J. L. Austin, *Sense and Sensibilia* (Oxford: Oxford University Press, 1962), 5.
5   "Just think of the expression (and the meaning of the expression) 'mot juste' [*das treffende Wort*]" (*PI* 527; *Philosophical Investigations*, trans. G. E. M. Anscombe, P. M. S. Hacker, and Joachim Schulte, ed. P. M. S. Hacker and Joachim Schulte, rev. 4th ed. [West Sussex, UK: Blackwell, 2009], §266, p. 226). In French, *juste* and *justesse* connote rightness, fittingness, and accuracy as well as fairness and justice. See my *Why We Need Ordinary Language Philosophy*, trans. Daniela Ginsburg (Chicago: University of Chicago Press, 2013).
6   John Rawls, "Two Concepts of Rules," *The Philosophical Review* 64, no. 1 (Jan 1955), 26.
7   See Diamond, *The Realistic Spirit*.
8   Stanley Cavell, "Préface . . .," *Les Voix de la raison: Wittgenstein, le scepticisme, la moralité et la tragédie*, trans. Nicole Balso and Sandra Laugier, xx–xx (Paris: Seuil, 2012), 3.
9   See my "Voice as Form of Life and Life Form," in "Wittgenstein and Forms of Life," ed. Danièle Moyal-Sharrock and Piergiorgio Dontelli, special issue, *Nordic Wittgenstein Review* (October 2015): 63–82, and Veena Das, *Textures of the Ordinary: Doing Anthropology after Wittgenstein* (New York: Fordham University Press, 2020).
10 See my "Wittgenstein and Cavell: Anthropology, Skepticism, and Politics," in *The Claim to Community: Essays on Stanley Cavell and Political Philosophy*, ed. Andrew Norris (Stanford, CA: Stanford University Press, 2006).
11 See Ludwig Wittgenstein, *Zettel*, trans. G. E. M. Anscombe, ed. G. E. M. Anscombe and G. H. von Wright (Berkeley: University of California Press, 1967), §567:99.
12 Immanuel Kant, *Critique of the Power of Judgment*, trans. Paul Guyer and Eric Matthews (New York: Cambridge University Press, 2000), §8:99.

2

Modernism in *The World Viewed*

Hugo Clémot

Introduction

Stanley Cavell's second book, *The World Viewed*, was published in 1971. Almost half a century later, the first book devoted to cinema by a great philosopher has lost none of its boldness and relevance.

It was and still is daring to use popular films and ordinary language to think about cinema and the experience we have of it, as daring as the project of introducing voice in philosophy in order to gain recognition for the necessarily autobiographical dimension of philosophical writing. It is imperative to read or reread the work of a philosopher who, working under "the threat of skepticism" (*WV* 165), knew that the condition of philosophy, not to mention art as a whole, was already much like that of modernism, that is, the situation of a practice where it is no longer possible to rely solely on traditional conventions and methods to contribute to its living history, to ensure its continued importance. We could extend to philosophy what Stanley Cavell writes here of Tolstoy's "concern" about art: "Tolstoy knew its saving importance; that is how he knew that whatever importance the rich are likely to attach to art, it is not the true importance of art; and why he cared that the poor (most people) attach no importance at all to it." About serious contemporary philosophers, we can indeed write today what he writes elsewhere in this book about artists: they "have virtually no audiences any longer, except in isolated or intermittent cases." In 1971 this was not the case with cinema: "rich and poor . . . all care about movies, await them, respond to them, remember them, talk about them, hate some of them, are grateful for some of them" (*WV* 4–5).

Cinema counts in everyone's life: this is what makes it possible to say that it then had meaning and importance. To help us get to know ourselves better so that we can become a better version of ourselves and thus accomplish the therapeutic task of philosophy, the project of finding "words I could believe in to account for my experience of film" (*WV* xxiii) seemed and therefore still seems relevant to a modernist philosopher.

The Ordinary of Film and the Philosophy of Ordinary Language

Cavell defends his choice to speak of ordinary, popular cinema on several occasions in his book. *The World Viewed* is one of the rare works on cinema to fall within the approach of "the philosophy of ordinary language" as practiced by J. L. Austin and Ludwig Wittgenstein. Applied in an exemplary way in the chapter devoted to the "physical basis" of the cinematographic medium, this method justifies Cavell's gesture at the beginning of the first chapter: quoting the title of Tolstoy's book *What Is Art?*, he proposes to replace the statement with the question "What is the importance of art?" This approach is similar to the first paragraph of the *Blue Book*, where Wittgenstein recommends replacing the question "What is the meaning of a word?" by the question "What does the explanation of a word look like?"[1] This substitution should indeed encourage us to remember what uses we can make of a term such as meaning, its mode or criteria of use or what Wittgenstein calls its "grammar," thus avoiding the "mental cramp" and "philosophical error" that arise from our tendency to take words for nouns and therefore always seek the object that the word seems to mean.

To ask the question of the importance of art is to recall the requirement to have to describe the uses or roles of art in our lives. As we have seen, Cavell finds that traditional art forms generally play no role in people's lives, except for serious artists who are "devoted to the making of objects meant as the live history of their art." In 1971, film "is the one live traditional art," that is, the only art still in use, whether we are rich or poor, whether "we care about no (other) art" or whether "we live on the promise of art" (*WV* 15, 4, 5).

This exceptional status invites us to reflect ontologically on the essence of film. But the question "What is film?" must itself be replaced by the question "What is the importance of film?" In other words, what are the contexts that reflect the role that film can play for us, or what uses do we make of film in our lives?

Film, Philosophy, and Autobiography

To conduct this investigation into our uses of cinema, Cavell chooses to rely on his own experience so that "to write a study of movies" is in a sense to "write my autobiography" or "a kind of metaphysical memoir" (*WV* xix). This idea of a right for everyone to speak out on cinema is, of course, hampered by the problem of a lack of expertise. A similar objection had been raised by Benson Mates against the philosophy of ordinary language:[2] If it is a question of starting from the ordinary use we make of words, how can the philosopher allow himself to talk about them without having conducted an empirical and statistical survey to determine majority use? Should he not keep quiet and yield the floor to others, linguists and statisticians, who are better informed than he is?

Cavell's answer, the essay "Must We Mean What We Say?" (*MWM* 1–43), consists in particular in showing that the recommended empirical investigation, insofar as it presupposes mastery of language and therefore of the ordinary meaning of words, could not take place unless each competent speaker of a given mother tongue were already the best possible source of information on the subject. Ordinary use is less a matter of knowledge than of know-how observed together, by agreement in practice as when individuals seek to agree on the steps of a dance or to be "in agreement throughout, being in harmony, like pitches or tones, or clocks, or weighing scales, or columns of figures" (CR 32). People who speak their mother tongue therefore do not need any more evidence to talk about cinema than they do to recount their dreams: they are the source of all possible evidence. This also means that in terms of film experience, everyone's judgment and memories have a claim to universality based on agreement in practice.

However, agreement in language is never definitively guaranteed, and Cavell's private experience will resonate with us only if we recognize ourselves in it and are able to use it to establish criteria for our own purposes:

> The establishing of criteria makes the process of judging more convenient, more open, less private or arbitrary. One might say: here establishing criteria allows us to *settle* judgments publicly—not exactly by making them certain, but by declaring what the points are at issue in various judgments, and then making them *final* (on a given occasion). That is a practice worth having; human decisions cannot wait upon certainty.
>
> CR 31, Cavell's emphases

The ontological investigation of film is an adventure that requires self-confidence while remaining aware that disagreement is a constant possibility, a—skeptical—possibility which one must learn to live with.

Film Grammar and the Priority of Reading Particular Films

To say that ontological investigation is grammatical is to say that we must start, not from the concept of cinema or "cinematography" and then decide what is or is not "cinema," but rather from our uses, from what we tend to say when we refer to particular films. In his excellent book on Cavell, Stephen Mulhall describes the principle of this approach as follows: "rather than imposing our general preconceptions about objecthood on to a given object, we bring ourselves to consider what our everyday experiences of and with that object . . . can teach us about its specific, distinct nature."[3] If it is indeed a methodological consequence of the philosophy of ordinary language, it can also be modeled on the critical practice of one of "the two continuously intelligent, interesting, and to [him] useful theorists [he had] read on the subject," André Bazin (WV 16).[4] According to his biographer, Dudley Andrew, Bazin's approach in his reviews was typically to elaborate the film's successes and difficulties before discussing its genre or the nature of the genre and the place of these laws in the context of global film theory.[5] Cavell also uses specific film readings to determine what possibilities of the medium of film have made his experience possible.

"Film is a Moving Image of Skepticism"[6]

Living and thinking under the threat of skepticism means recognizing that we can never know with certainty that the world we believe we are experiencing is not the projection of a disposition of the mind, of what Emerson called a mood or a "lord of life,"[7] that is, a category so deeply rooted in our minds as a premise of all our possible reasoning that it is immune to all the denials of experience as it constitutes an indelible coloration of it: to acknowledge with Wittgenstein that, for this reason, "the world of the happy man is a different one from that of the unhappy man"[8] is to take seriously the hypothesis that the world could be only a view of the mind. In this perspective, the task of philosophy cannot consist in a desperate effort to know the world, but rather, first of all, in an act of acknowledgment of our being separated from the world or of that our condition is one of loss. To find the world, there is no other way than to seek to identify these moods, what Cavell in "More of *The World Viewed*" (*WV* 177–78) calls those myths according to which we live, which hinder our relationship to the world and prevent us from having an experience, in order to separate us from it. In this sense, philosophical work is analogous to the work of mourning as Freud sees it, namely as the effort to break the bonds that emotionally connect us to the lost "object," which implies revisiting each of the memories and expectations that still bind us to it despite its disappearance.

The Cavellian enterprise of philosophizing by means of film in *The World Viewed* is therefore justified in at least three ways: First of all, it is a matter of living more fully by thinking of the experience of losing his past relationship as a regular moviegoer, in order to find the world and his place in it thus lost.[9] Then it is a question of finding in the experience of the cinematographic projection of the world an opportunity to recognize our skeptical condition, we who doubt a world of which we fear that it is only a projection of our mind, that is, as in solipsism, that it exists for us, that it is only present to us, at the cost of our absence in it. Finally, it is a question of experiencing particular films that matter to us, in order to find in them not only the myths according to which we live, but also the dimensions of our ordinary experiences that most of the time escape us.

The Structure of *The World Viewed*

The plan Cavell follows is both logical and chronological and can be broken down into three main parts. The first part consists of the first five chapters, which can be summarized roughly as follows: Cavell first makes a methodological shift from the ontology of film to film criticism (chapter 1), before making an ontological shift that favors the idea of transcription over representation when he questions what we say when we speak of the "physical basis," i.e. photography (chapters 2 and 3) and the screen (chapter 3), of the film medium. Discovering the subject of cinema in stars and in types (chapter 4), Cavell, in a very original and too often ignored way, renews reflection on the notion of a "medium" to the point that we can say of the types and cinematographic genres that welcome them that they are media of the revelation and celebration of the myths according to which we live (chapter 5).

If we understand that these first five chapters reflect Cavell's past filmic experience, we can, more or less artificially, say that the second part of the book, guided by Baudelaire's *The Painter of Modern Life*, will explore these types, genres, and myths conceived as a reservoir of filmic obsessions (chapters 6 to 9) and seeks to understand how these media could have lost their power over him by the time Cavell writes his book (chapter 10).

The eleventh chapter, for its part, is a transitional chapter in which Cavell summarizes the main results of the previous ten chapters before asking the question the rest of the book will try to answer: if the Hollywood classic film media have lost their power, what media, what possibilities of the medium can replace them? Rejecting some false answers, Cavell proposes his famous heuristic definition according to which the material basis of film media is "a succession of automatic world projections" (*WV* 72) whose analysis will lead him to study not only the possibilities relating to the world (chapters 12 and 13) and automatism (chapter 14), which will result in a very important chapter on "an aspect of modernist painting" (chapter 15), but also those concerning projection, i.e. "the phenomenological facts of vision" (chapter 16) and "the continuity of the camera's movement as it ingests the world" (chapter 17), as well as the other techniques mentioned in the definition in chapter 11 (chapter 18). The last is a concluding chapter in which Cavell questions the possibility of recognizing the silence of nature and the unspeakable with the help of cinema, that is, precisely what constitutes the project of *The World Viewed*: finding the words in which he can believe to express his lost and present experience of cinema (chapter 19).

Modernism's Importance for Cavell

Historically, artistic modernism is that moment in the history of art that can be described as

> a response to the fact that the impersonal certainties and general principles that partly constituted the classical traditions in, for example, architecture and painting seem no longer able to elicit conviction from artists, critics, or audiences; as a consequence, individual art works cannot presuppose agreed conventions but rather embody intensely personal concerns whose claim to intersubjective intelligibility and power might none the less be granted by critics and audience and thereby become the ground of new conventions and so of a new aesthetic community.[10]

Stephen Mulhall rightly notes here that Stanley Cavell's interest in modernism in the arts is part of a broader interest in (liberal) modernity, artistic modernism being conceived as a reaction to the problem of modernity as it emerges in the aesthetic field. Indeed, the word "modernity" appeared in the nineteenth century to designate a historical consciousness of self that makes it impossible to imitate the classics and tradition in a pure and simple way. In Cavell's terms, modernity in the life of an art is

> a moment in which history and its conventions can no longer be taken for granted; the time in which music and painting and poetry (like nations) have to define themselves against their pasts; the beginning of the moment in which each of the arts becomes its own subject, as if its immediate artistic task is to establish its own existence.
>
> *MWM* xxxvi

Quoting this excerpt, Élise Domenach notes in her book on Cavell, cinema, and skepticism that the "categories of 'modern' and 'modernism' make the link between the Cavellian defense of the new philosophical procedures of Austin and Wittgenstein and his thinking of film."[11] We understand that Cavell's interest in the philosophy of ordinary language is itself part of this interest in modernity since it is not difficult to see how this philosophy can be in his eyes the paradigm of "modern" philosophy. One could indeed say, by strictly applying the previous definition, that the works of modern philosophers such as Wittgenstein's *Philosophical Investigations* "cannot presuppose agreed conventions but rather embody intensely personal concerns whose claim to intersubjective intelligibility and power might none the less be granted by [other philosophers and readers] and thereby become the ground of new conventions and so of a new [philosophical] community."

More specifically,

> [a] philosophy which grounds itself upon modes of self-knowledge through which the individual can speak for others and discover surprising depths of community without sacrificing her right to speak for herself, a philosophy which does not impose or presuppose uniformity between individuals but which holds out the hope of establishing that individuals are deeply, internally related to one another— such a philosophy might have been expressly designed for the predominantly liberal culture of which it is a part.[12]

Modernism in *The World Viewed*

Given the above, it is therefore not surprising to note the omnipresence of modernism in *The World Viewed*. This theme is present from the preface when Cavell argues that "art now exists in the condition of philosophy" (*WV* 14). It means that the artist, like the philosopher, knows that modern spectators and readers, affected as they are by skepticism, no longer accept conventions, rules, and genres by tradition. They can only accept them by a singular adherence, punctually obtained when the artist manages to work seriously, but without naivety, in a way that reaches the spectator and incites him to recognize that something has happened that consisted in a revelation of a beauty that was not alien to him, in short that he has had an aesthetic experience.

Film, the Only Modern Art? (Chapter 1)

In the first chapter, the evocation of the condition of artistic modernism leads Cavell to comment on the commonplace according to which cinema is the only modern art in the sense that it is the art to which modern humans would react most naturally. There are two reasons to be suspicious of such an idea. The first is that it presupposes, without justification, that other arts are not capable of making a modern human being react, without specifying what way this modern human would distinguish himself from humans of the past who nevertheless reacted in their time to other arts. Indeed, this reference to the modernity of contemporary humans seems condemned to be meaningless or contradictory since modern human beings are characterized by skepticism towards the outside world and others, which condemns them to considerable efforts to regain the meaning and the possibility of a "natural" reaction. The second reason is "the blatant fact about film," namely that, "if it is art, it is the only live traditional art, the one that can take its tradition as granted" (*WV* 15). He thus agrees with Erwin Panofsky's observation in his text on "Style and Medium in the Motion Pictures" that "[t]he 'movies' have re-established that dynamic contact between art production and art consumption which ... is sorely attenuated, if not entirely interrupted, in many other fields of artistic endeavor."[13] This, however, means that it would be necessary to explain how cinema has been able to avoid the fate of artistic modernism. The designation of cinema as the only "modern art" therefore seems either empty, or false, or incoherent, because artistic modernity is not only a matter of chronology but depends on a certain relationship to tradition, an interrogative relationship for the modernist, a parodic and blind relationship for the "modernizer" (*WV* 15):

> I believe that philosophy shares the modernist difficulty now everywhere evident in the major arts, the difficulty of making one's present effort become a part of the present history of the enterprise to which one has committed one's mind, such as it is. (Modernizers, bent merely on newness, do not have history as a problem, that is, as a commitment...)
>
> *MWM* xxxvi

In *Art and Objecthood*, Michael Fried develops a similar distinction between "modernism" and "literalism," the former being characterized by the search for ways of doing art in which one could "believe," "the discovery of conventions capable of eliciting conviction—or at least of dissolving certain kinds of doubts,"[14] the latter aiming at objectivity, knowledge, and novelty without regard to the question of conviction or success.

The fact that film is the only traditional living art means that it is based on "its presuppositions and successes," its "conventions," without questioning its definition, its modalities, and its aims, without questioning itself. The pleasure he offers us is linked to the ease with which cinema is comfortable with its tradition. But it is perhaps naive to explain this ease and lack of questioning by naivety. Moreover, a mystery remains:

how could a system run by individuals considered corrupt and stupid produce films that are not only exceptional, but also ordinary and equally important to us?

The End of Myths and the Modernism of Film (Chapters 1 to 11)

The first chapters up to the tenth, entitled "End of the Myths," are therefore devoted to clarifying this mystery. To say that the myths of cinema are coming to an end at the time when Cavell writes means that audiences have stopped trusting them to give them a sense of presence in the world. In other words, cinema has joined the other arts in the modernist world. However, the end of Hollywood myths does not mean the end of the film medium, but the end of "certain possibilities, particular directions within the medium" (*WV* 61).

The question that deserves to be asked, and is indeed asked by Cavell in chapter 11, is that of knowing which media, which possibilities of the medium can replace the old Hollywood myths. In order to answer this question, Cavell returns to the definition of the material support of film media as

> a succession of automatic world projections. "Succession" includes the various degrees of motion in moving pictures: the motion depicted; the current of successive frames in depicting it; the juxtapositions of cutting. "Automatic" emphasizes the mechanical fact of photography, in particular the absence of the human hand in forming these objects and the absence of its creatures in their screening. "World" covers the ontological facts of photography and its subjects. "Projection" points to the phenomenological facts of viewing, and to the continuity of the camera's motion as it ingests the world.
>
> *WV* 72–73

While the previous chapters have clarified a number of these facts, it is understandable that further study is still possible from which some decisive elements could emerge to determine the possibilities to which contemporary modernist works can still give meaning and importance today. This deepening will be carried out in the following chapters, but it is in chapter 14 that the notion of modernism will reappear in the connection with the concept of automatism.

Automatism and Modernism (Chapters 12 to 14)

In chapter 12, to justify the idea that the fundamental question in film aesthetics, that of whether the essence of cinema is to use editing or to insist on its power to record reality in its continuity, is not a question, Cavell asks his readers to first follow the developments devoted to the categories of "world" and "automatism." Chapter 14 is the place where new considerations on automatism are developed. The notion has already been mentioned at the beginning of the book, in chapters 2 and 3, and is repeated further on in chapter 6, where it is associated with a desire to see the whole world without being seen. Cavell introduces here an interesting expression to reflect this desire: since modern philosophers have taught us that we could not know the world itself, either because our finiteness prevents us from reaching the thing-in-itself (according to Locke, Hume, or Kant) or because reaching reality would mean changing our way of life (for Hegel, Marx, or Kierkegaard), we "look out at it, from behind the self" (*WV* 106). This image refers to the passage in the second chapter in which Cavell writes that "the unhinging of our consciousness from the world interposed our subjectivity between us and our presentness to the world" (22). In other words, we, as modern people, are aware that the content of our representations is always likely to be influenced by our sensitivity, feelings, and subjective values and thus to be the pure and simple projection of our subjectivity. For this reason, we wish to "view the world itself" independently of our subjectivity, that is, of our "fantasies": "It is our fantasies, now all but completely thwarted and out of hand, which are unseen and must be kept unseen. . . . So we are less than ever in a position to marry them to the world" (102).

One of the satisfactions offered by the automaticity of film recording would be to allow us to come into contact with the world without the risk of making a mistake by confusing our "fantasies," our subjectivity, with the world. Indeed, films "are reliefs from private fantasy and its responsibilities; from the fact that the world is already drawn by fantasy" (102). If the filmic image were automatically of the world, it would keep us from having to make efforts to match our desires to the world or the world to our desires: it would be enough to keep our fantasies to ourselves, in a private way, and to open our eyes on the screen to obtain the fulfillment of our wish. In this respect, filmic automaticity has something of a magical power.

These reminders give Cavell an opportunity to clarify the nature of his approach when compared to that of other film theorists. To recognize that "what enables moving pictures to satisfy the wish to view the world is the automatism of photography" is not to claim "that film which is not used photographically, to reproduce the world, cannot be used for the purpose of art." Indeed, this does not mean "that art cannot be made without this power, merely that movies cannot so be made." In other words, Cavell's remarks are not prescriptive, since he does not claim to deduce from the ontology of the filmic medium artistic prescriptions, but descriptive: "what has made the movie a candidate for art is its natural relation to its traditions of automatism." Being descriptive by nature, Cavell's discourse is open to historical change: "we may have to forgo this power; it may lose its power for us" and bring cinema into the condition of modernism (102–3).

The question that has been asked since the first chapter is therefore how cinema has been able to avoid entering this modernist condition for so long and to maintain our adherence to its traditions.

To answer, Cavell proposes to use the term "automatisms" to refer to "broad genres or forms in which an art organizes itself (e.g., the fugue, the dance forms, blues) and those local events or *topoi* around which a genre precipitates itself (e.g., modulations, inversions, cadences)." Cavell intentionally uses the term "automatism" to refer both to the material or physical basis of cinema and to "artistic discoveries of form and genre and type and technique" in order to draw attention to a difficulty that needs to be thought of rather than bypassed by introducing new labels. This difficulty is the same as the one that makes him use the term "medium" to designate both the physical basis of an art and the artistic achievements that give it its meaning and importance. It is due to the fact that the use of the term is no less justified in one case than in the other and "it could also be said that modernist art is itself an investigation of this confusion, or of the complexities of this fact" (104–5).

These complexities are both historical and philosophical. From a historical point of view, there was indeed a time when arts such as poetry or painting shared a common purpose, that of describing events, which allowed Lessing, in his *Laocoön*, to recommend to each individual art to "be faithful to its own way, dictated by the nature of its medium, of doing the common thing," but this time is over: there is no longer an obvious common purpose and there is therefore no specific way for each art to fulfill this function. For example,

> [a] description of the styles and genres of classical music would be a description of the media of classical music. In a modernist art, to which the concepts of style and genre lack clear application, the concept of a medium loses touch with ideas of manner and ordonnance, and seems to separate out for denotation the physical materials of the art as such.
>
> 106

However, this reduction of the concept of artistic medium to the sole material basis poses a real philosophical problem: that of knowing what the medium of an art as such can be. Indeed, it is not enough to answer that the medium of painting will be painting as such, the medium of music, sound as such, etc., because there is a logical priority of artistic success over the identity of the medium. In other words, painting and sound are not primarily artistic media, but above all means of expression for mankind which may, in some of their dimensions, not be means of artistic expression. For example, the use of throat-cleansing in non-Western music, a use that is generally absent or even prohibited in Western classical music, clearly shows how the identity of the medium is not decisive for artistic practice, but on the contrary determined by it. Indeed, it also means that nothing is the medium of an art as such, because, for example, "[a] medium of painting is whatever way or ways paint is managed so as to create objects we accept as paintings. Only an art can define its media" (107).

In other words, the media of an art can only be defined by an art and the identity of a medium is a function of artistic success.

One could read in this observation what motivates the injunction of Noël Carroll to "forget the medium."[15] Since nothing can constitute the medium of an art as such, it is better to renounce the notion. However, it would seem to Cavell that this would short-circuit the problem and prevent us from seeing what it has to teach us about our relationship to art and, more generally, to meaning. Thus, the following laudatory description of modernist art would also apply to the philosophy of ordinary language as the philosophy of liberal modernity:

A modernist art, investigating its own physical basis, searching out its own conditions of existence, rediscovers the fact that its existence as an art is not physically assured. It gracefully accepts our condemnation to meaning—that for separate creatures of sense and soul, for earthlings, meaning is a matter of expression; and that expressionlessness is not a reprieve from meaning, but a particular mode of it; and that the arrival of an understanding is a question of acknowledgment.

107

What a modernist art "rediscovers" is what the first artists discovered when they first created works that established an artistic form, namely that they could not find in the "physical" means of expression at their disposal any "certainty" to guide them in their expressive process. Like them, a modernist art or artist recognizes that it is wrong to say that the discovery of the medium precedes and always determines logically and chronologically the expressive intention. On the contrary, he accepts the difficult task of expressing himself without knowing what to express, or how to express it, of having to determine at the same time what is meaningful to say, what is important to say, and the possibilities of expression endowed with meaning themselves important to say it.

The modernist artist finds the fate of human beings "condemned to signification" as Sartre said that "man is condemned to be free,"[16] that is to say, forced without having chosen it and without being able to escape from it to find the meaning and importance of humanity in what he does and expresses, without this "existence as [a human being] being physically assured" and without being able to escape this fate by the refusal of freedom or expression which would still be a particular way to give meaning to humanity. In any case, the only validation of the meaning and importance of the media of artistic or human expression will be that given by the acknowledgement of others.

However, the proximity of Cavell's use of the terms "medium" and "automatism" could lead to questions about the interest of such a terminological duality. Cavell therefore finally specifies three factors at the origin of his desire to use the term "automatism" in this way. First of all, the term aims to convey the idea that "when such a medium is discovered, it generates new instances [and] calls for them, as if to attest that what has been discovered is indeed something more than a single work could convey." The term then also refers to the strictly artistic power of a work, that is, "what works (what happens of itself)" (107)—in the sense that perhaps Gombrich says in his introduction to his famous *The Story of Art*, that the problem the artist is trying to solve is whether "it goes like that" or whether the clothes you wear go well together or whether the plates are well placed on the table.[17] Finally, the term refers to Cavell's own situation insofar as the philosopher of language or ordinary experience is in the same situation as the modernist artist and he too tries to "free the object from [him], to give new ground to its autonomy" by inventing a new philosophical medium that can free him from the automatisms that his training as an analytical philosopher has imposed on him, which "generates new instances: not merely makes them possible, but calls for them, as if to attest that what has been discovered is indeed something more than a single work could convey" and gives his book the power to "work," that is, to provoke the experience of film that it is a matter of describing (108, 107).

"Excursus: Some Modernist Painting" (Chapter 15)

To illustrate the interest of this concept of automatism, Cavell will propose, in chapter 15, reflections that mobilize it to talk about his experience of several contemporary modernist painters such as Jackson Pollock, Frank Stella, or Morris Louis. It will suffice here to mention the Cavellian reading of Pollock's work and his discovery: the technique of the all-over line. In accordance with his thesis that the identity and importance of a medium depend on the meaning and importance of the works that mobilize it, Cavell wonders what Pollock discovered when he discovered the all-over line that allowed him to produce paintings again, that is, entities that we are ready to call paintings, or, in Michael Fried's words, "paintings whose quality could stand comparison with the art of the museums."[18]

It seems to him that what has been discovered in this way is a fact "as primitive as any" about painting, namely that a painting is flat and of a limited surface and that it "means that it is totally there, wholly open to you, absolutely in front of your senses, of your eyes, as no other form of art is." This discovery is exemplary of the approach of modernist painting, which finds it important to reveal to us what we are aware of without admitting it, what we know without acknowledging it: modernist painting is thus in this sense an "acknowledging of its conditions." However, since this is not something unknown we could be taught, it will not be possible for the modernist artist to demonstrate the importance of his discovery, as could be done in the case of authentic knowledge. He will only be able to teach "this by acknowledgment—which means that responding to it must itself have the form of accepting it as a painting, or rejecting it." In other words, once we have shown how the work is the solution to a problem that the artist has and that he thinks is important and meaningful to painting and others, we can only hope that art "works": "that is where the art comes in." That is to say, one can only hope that the work will succeed in having the viewer acknowledge its importance and meaning, it being understood that, in terms of acknowledging in general, universality is never guaranteed, whether it is to acknowledge a truth about art or about oneself. Indeed, just as there have always been people who refuse to recognize the success of a masterpiece, so "there have always been some men who have been able to acknowledge something that other men accept as true also of them, or that they have to deny" (*WV* 109–10).

It seems possible to thus complete in a decisive way the solution that Noël Carroll brings to the problem of the definition of art.[19] If the idea of conceiving the work as an artist's contribution to the conversation about the history of his art certainly has a Cavellian resonance, it undoubtedly misses the novelty of artistic modernism and comes up against the problem of why art should be reduced to what a group of individuals (artists) have held or still hold as artistic. The role of the "historical narrative," which is supposed to demonstrate the work's belonging to art, would therefore be rather that of a means of bringing the viewer to acknowledge the meaning and importance of the artist's contribution, not only to the history of art, but also to humanity. It would also leave open the possibility that some may not agree to acknowledge this, just as some may not wish to acknowledge others.

Conclusion

This comparison between acknowledgment in art and in general makes it possible to conclude while answering an objection that would be to know why one should be interested in what seems after all to be only one tradition among others, that of an avant-garde or a philosophical current among others. Indeed, rejecting as vain the name of the avant-garde and the conception of the era that accompanied it, Cavell thinks that modernist artists are merely rediscovering another primitive fact, the fact that "acknowledgement is the home of knowledge" (*WV* 110), insofar as any authentic knowledge of the world begins with a self-understanding that is not possible without acknowledgement of what we cannot simply fail to know, in other words, of all that in us can prevent ourselves from acknowledging what we know nevertheless. If this idea seems to find a particularly relevant illustration when we talk about our relationship to language, where we cannot simply fail to know what we are saying when, without this preventing us from making mistakes and being ignorant, it also describes very well the philosophical approach in general, starting with Socratic maieutics, and the Cavellian philosophy of film in particular. Rothman and Keane make the point in enlightening terms:

> Film study could not validly begin by adopting preexisting theories, taking for granted their applicability to film, but only by reflecting philosophically on the testimony of movies themselves, the testimony of our experiences of movies.... To know films objectively, we have to know the hold they have upon us. To know the hold films have on us, we have to know ourselves objectively. And to know ourselves objectively, we have to know the impact of films on our lives. No study of film can claim intellectual authority if it is not rooted in self-knowledge, our knowledge of our own subjectivity.[20]

The effort of modernist artists is therefore similar to that of philosophers who, like Wittgenstein, seek to "unravel purely intellectual difficulties, ways of knotting that have formed in people's minds, as a result of interference or confusion between the various and multiple conceptual 'lines' that each must draw and weave in his mind in order to understand where he stands and what he is doing,"[21] to return to what we always already know of ourselves and the world: it is "an effort, along blocked paths and hysterical turnings, to hang on to a thread that leads from a lost center to a world lost" (*WV* 110).

Notes

1. Ludwig Wittgenstein, *The Blue and Brown Books* (Oxford: Blackwell, 1969), 1.
2. Benson Mates, "On the Verification of Statements About Ordinary Language," in *Ordinary Language: Essays in Philosophical Method*, ed. V. C. Chappell (Englewood Cliffs: Prentice-Hall, 1964), 161–71.
3. Stephen Mulhall, *Stanley Cavell: Philosophy's Recounting of the Ordinary* (Oxford: Oxford University Press, 2006), 160.
4. The other theorist is Erwin Panofsky.
5. Dudley Andrew, *André Bazin* (Paris: Editions de l'Etoile, 1983), 179.
6. *WV* 188.
7. Ralph Waldo Emerson, "Experience," in *The Complete Essays and Other Writings of Ralph Waldo Emerson*, ed. Brooks Atkinson (New York: The Modern Library, 1950), 342.
8. Ludwig Wittgenstein, *Tractatus Logico-Philosophicus*, trans. C. K. Ogden (London: Routledge, 1981), 6.43.
9. "What broke my natural relation to movies? What was that relation, that its loss seemed to demand repairing, or commemorating, by taking thought?" (*WV* xix).
10. Mulhall, *Stanley Cavell*, 70.
11. Élise Domenach, *Stanley Cavell, le cinéma et le scepticisme* (Paris: Presses universitaires de France, 2011), 53.
12. Mulhall, *Stanley Cavell*, 73.
13. Erwin Panofsky, "Style and Medium in the Motion Pictures," in *Film: An Anthology*, ed. Daniel Talbot, 2nd ed. (Berkeley: University of California Press, 1966), 16.
14. Michael Fried, "Jules Olitski," in *Art and Objecthood: Essays and Reviews* (Chicago: University of Chicago Press, 1998), 146n12.
15. See Noël Carroll, *Engaging the Moving Image* (New Haven: Yale University Press, 2003), 1–9.
16. Jean-Paul Sartre, *Existentialism Is a Humanism*, trans. Carol Macomber (New Haven, Yale University Press, 2007), 29.
17. Ernst Gombrich, *The Story of Art*, 4th ed. (New York: Phaidon, 1951), 14.
18. See Fried, "Jules Olitski," 144.
19. Noël Carroll, *Philosophy of Art: A Contemporary Introduction* (New York: Routledge, 1999), 251–67.
20. Marian Keane and William Rothman, *Reading Cavell's* The World Viewed: *A Philosophical Perspective on Film* (Detroit: Wayne State University Press, 2000), 17.
21. Vincent Descombes, "Que peut-on demander à la philosophie morale?," in *Le Raisonnement de l'ours. Et autres essais de philosophie pratique* (Paris: Editions du Seuil, 2007), 432.

3

The Senses of Walden: Thoreau's Exemplary Act

Paul Standish

Stanley Cavell's work is challenging, especially for the reader who comes to it for the first time. There is no obvious way in. This chapter is based on the thought that a good place to start may be with a book that has, on the whole, received less attention than others in the mainstream secondary literature on Cavell: *The Senses of Walden*. While particular ideas have been taken up by various authors, the only major text to give sustained treatment to this work is Andrew Norris's *Becoming Who We Are*.[1] Norris draws out the political significance of Thoreau's text and of Cavell's reading of it, and this is particularly to be welcomed: it provides insight into Cavell's work as a whole.

In part 1 of this essay, I attempt to provide the groundwork for such an introductory reading. In important respects *The Senses of Walden* constitutes a microcosm of a range of themes that recur in Cavell's work, and it does this in a way that is relatively accessible. It is less densely invested in the intricacies of argument against the background of which Cavell's highly original but demanding first set of essays was produced, *Must We Mean What We Say?*; it contrasts with the length and challenging complexity of Cavell's master-work, *The Claim of Reason*; and it anticipates themes that will come to the fore more prominently in his later writings.

In part 2 I extend the discussion more specifically in relation to modernism. Paola Marrati draws attention to the fact that modernist artworks characteristically carry with them a sense of "crisis in the authority of certain conventions and the attempt to establish new forms of conviction in the expressive power of art." In philosophy, this principle is exemplified by Cavell in his critique not only of the arguments of a given philosophy but of what counts as philosophy. This opens questions of expression and style, as well as matters of content, that can lead philosophy away from its recognizable paths but without ceasing to be philosophy. What philosophy is can never be known in advance. My discussion locates *The Senses of Walden* and *Walden* itself in relation to these insights.

Stanley Cavell's *Walden*: An Introduction

> *You only need sit still long enough in some attractive spot in the woods that all its inhabitants may exhibit them to you by turns.*
>
> —Thoreau, *Walden*, 228

> *Light dawns gradually over the whole.*
>
> —Wittgenstein, *On Certainty*, §141

The purpose of this introductory essay is not to explain what Cavell has to say. He will do that for himself. Its aim is to recognize that in *The Senses of Walden* the reader is confronted by a difficult and demanding text, perhaps all the more so in view of the richness and particularity of the range of cultural reference upon which Cavell shows Thoreau to draw. The difficulty is compounded in that a major commitment of Cavell's book is to lead the reader away from certain received notions of what *Walden* is about—specifically, away from the idea that the text is a rejection of society in favor of an escape to a life of rural isolation, and away from the idea that it is the celebration of a kind of individualism, as commonly understood. This requires registering complications in *Walden* that a more superficial reading will pass over. In order to see that this is so it is necessary to attend to less obvious aspects of the text, and to attend to those that are most familiar in new ways. It is part of Cavell's achievement that he makes *Walden* more difficult and that he does this in exemplary ways. Hence, anyone embarking on the text looking for an explanatory commentary in any conventional sense is likely to be stopped in their tracks—and rightly so.

The Senses of Walden is also something more than, and different from, a commentary in a further respect. This is that its purpose is less exegesis than engagement. It rises to the demands of language that the reading of *Walden* exacts: it asserts its authorship, finds its own voice, not in a challenge to Thoreau but in seeking to realize what Thoreau is about. Hence, as we shall see repeatedly below, the question of language—of Thoreau's and Cavell's—is doubly important.

Recognizing that these inherent difficulties in the text are compounded for readers unfamiliar with the cultural context in which Thoreau is writing, I shall proceed by way of the following steps. *The Senses of Walden* is, first, located in the context of Cavell's own work. That work is well-known for its extraordinary range, encompassing Wittgenstein and ordinary language philosophy, American philosophy, John Rawls, music, Shakespeare, dance, film . . . Beyond this remark I make no attempt to address this range but rather wish to acknowledge the specific and obvious relevance to *Walden* of Cavell's subsequent writings on Emerson. When Cavell published the revised edition of *The Senses of Walden*, in 1981, this included two essays on Emerson. Equally important, though perhaps less obvious, are the connections with Wittgenstein. I go on to say something about aspects of the socio-historical context of Thoreau's writing, with particular reference to the New England background of Puritanism. This will perforce lead to some explanation of Biblical themes that are important in *Walden*, themes that are carefully worked out in its imagery or that are presumed to be part of the background knowledge of Thoreau's imagined reader. These religious themes inevitably connect with some of the literature to which Cavell refers—specifically to the seventeenth-century poet John Milton's monumental work, *Paradise Lost*. There are important literary connections also with British Romanticism, a movement that had reached and passed its peak in the decades leading up to Thoreau's "experiment in living."

At a slightly different level, as I have indicated, it is necessary to alert the reader to a range of matters concerning the language of Cavell's own text, including its commentary on and response to features of style in *Walden* itself. Indeed, this is at the heart of the difficulty to which I refer above, and hence crucial to the deeper understanding to which Cavell and, by implication, Thoreau wish to lead the reader.

Let me begin then by identifying some connections with Cavell's work as a whole and so attempt to place this text within his broader philosophical undertaking. The familiarity of *Walden* makes *The Senses of Walden*, for all its inherent difficulties, a fine entry into Cavell's writings: it presents in microcosm themes and concerns that pervade his work as a whole. There is no obvious first step in the understanding of Cavell's work, so why not start, as it were, in the midst of the woods.

Skepticism

The most sustained theme in Cavell's philosophical work as a whole is the engagement with skepticism, and, although not explicit in *Walden*, this is a theme that underlies the experiment in living that is that book's concern. Skepticism is to be understood first and foremost in philosophy, and specifically in Anglophone philosophy, in terms of the concern to find a secure basis for knowledge claims. Indeed this is what has characterized epistemology over the past four centuries, especially, that is, since Descartes. Cavell's interest was shaped particularly by his encounter, in the 1950s, with the "ordinary language philosophy" of J. L. Austin and with the writings of the later Wittgenstein. The *Philosophical Investigations* has been widely read, within Anglophone philosophy, as an attempt to refute the skeptic—that is, to show that the skeptic's questions (Is this a table in front of me? Are there other minds? How do I know that I exist?) always presuppose a background in which, in effect, these items of doubt are taken for granted. In epistemological terms, then, these skeptical questions involve a kind of circularity, with the conclusions of enquiry embedded in the premises. Cavell's reading of Wittgenstein, however, finds rather more to be at stake here, and in the process it exposes the inadequacy of the idea that skepticism is hereby *refuted*. It is not so much that this is wrong as that it misses the point. A key point of emphasis that Cavell will develop is that the skeptic's questions can only be raised where there is a suppression or repression or denial of the background; and, as these terms indicate, and as his subsequent writings richly show, this resonates with forms of denial to which human beings are peculiarly prone. Cavell develops the theme of denial in terms of the failure not so much of knowledge as of acknowledgement, the burden of which is examined especially in his writings on literature, particularly Shakespeare, and on the Hollywood film of the 1930s and 1940s, the principal focus of his attention being genres that he identifies as the "Hollywood comedy of remarriage" and the "melodrama of the unknown woman."

That the *Investigations* is something other than an epistemological refutation can be seen, as Cavell eloquently shows, in the way that Wittgenstein "dissolves" the problem only to allow it to start up again—and this Wittgenstein does repeatedly. The itch returns. The question will not go away. This is tantamount to an acknowledgement not of the truth of skepticism but of the truth *in* skepticism; and this is, as it were, not an epistemological but an existential truth. It testifies to something deep in the human condition: our compulsion to doubt; our inclination to demand a greater reassurance than the circumstances allow or a more robust verification than they could reasonably bear; and, as Cavell—attending to the mild deflation of the Wittgensteinian claim that explanation must come to an end somewhere, that there must be an end to justification in acknowledgement of our "form of life," and hence in acceptance that ultimately "This is what we do"—nicely puts it, our disappointment in criteria. It is such denial that is at the heart of Shakespearean tragedy, as well as being the stuff of our more everyday meanness of spirit.

A part of Wittgenstein's purpose is to undo the knots that develop in our thinking, and these are knots for which philosophy has often itself been responsible. The untying of these knots, sometimes requiring movements more elaborate and more difficult than those that tied them, is part of the "therapy" of philosophy that Wittgenstein seeks to provide. In doing this he repeatedly returns philosophy to the ordinary. In the flights of philosophy to which the sceptic is drawn, language goes "on holiday," suggesting, at a different level, the kind of ineffectuality that Thoreau sees in the lives of his neighbors, for all their ostensible busyness; such thinking spins on ice and can make no progress; it needs to be returned to the rough ground, against which it can gain purchase. In the successful return to the ordinary, we do not achieve a resolution of our doubts; it is rather that we are, for a time, relieved of the compulsion to raise them, and hence that we "know how to go on."

But it is part of Cavell's position that the emphasis on the therapeutic can be overplayed or misconstrued. That Wittgenstein speaks of finding peace yet worries away at these doubts again and again not only testifies to but dramatizes this. To return to the ordinary is to find an economy of living that incorporates and acknowledges this fragility and disturbance in the human condition. One way in which that fragility is apt to be denied is where there is an overemphasis on the robustness of the rules of the community into which the child is inducted. A few paragraphs back I used the phrase "This is what we do," and there have been times when this has been taken as a crucial expression of this authority of the community. That this is not what Wittgenstein writes—he writes "This is what I do"—indicates the prevailing prejudice within which the *Philosophical Investigations* was read by so many, and it is part of his achievement that he resisted that dominant mis-reading.

A part of this economy of living will involve a proper appreciation of the various things we do with language. In J. L. Austin's work, this is elaborated in terms, for example, of the distinction between the constative and performative functions of language—that is, the distinction, respectively, between "She made a promise to him" and "I promise," where the latter statement, unlike the former, does not describe the promise but is itself the act. In spite of Austin's largely dismissive attitude to Wittgenstein (he particularly disliked the tendency amongst Wittgenstein's admirers to regard his philosophy as "deep"), his procedures and purposes are not so far removed, priority being given to the piecemeal study of particular samples of usage or segments of experience, a procedure that is itself a principled defiance of the pressure in philosophy towards larger metaphysical claims. Like Wittgenstein, Austin returns words from their metaphysical to their everyday use, a return demonstrated in various ways, so Cavell will claim, in *Walden* itself.

Cavell is stuck especially by the way that the characteristic procedure of the ordinary language philosopher, its characteristic mode of appeal, takes the form of "When we say . . ., we mean . . ." This is an appeal to ordinary use not as some kind of empirical generalization about the behavior of a particular people; a survey of usage would be beside the point. Two things should be noted especially: the statement is first person, and it is plural. That it is first person shows the significance of voice; the authentication of the statement has to do with the speaker's sincere assent, with how things seem to her, and with her desire or responsibility to express this. That it is plural testifies to her desire or responsibility to speak *for* others, to find community of some kind with them. This is by no means to impose on their views, nor is it simply to align herself with them in terms, say, of shared characteristics (a community of the same); it is rather to offer her assertion as exemplary in some way, testing this against the responses of others, and testing her own responses against what those others themselves say.

That this relation to others does not spring from a fully-fledged personal autonomy is evident in the importance that is attached to reading: reading is a metonym for the ways in which our responses are drawn out and tested in the words of others, and hence to the salience of reception. This then is to see her autonomy as inevitably tied to the political (the creation of the *polis*)—as two sides, so it might be said, of the same coin—and to see it as inextricably tied to the conditions of response within which she finds herself. The political is to this extent internal to language, and literary activity conditions political participation. While these are themes that pervade Cavell's work, he elaborates them in explicit terms in *The Claim of Reason* and develops aspects of them especially in his later writings on Emerson. But it is clear that he finds them also in Thoreau, and in *The Senses of Walden* they are revealed with particular subtlety, where questions of reading and writing are never far from the surface of the text. Cavell's recognition that our words condition our being in these ways explains not only the profound impact that ordinary language philosophy has had on his thought but his acute sensibility to the language of the texts he reads, a sensibility manifest also in his own distinctive style.

Emerson and Thoreau

Cavell's return to Emerson and Thoreau at different stages in his career, which in effect reiterates his stance towards skepticism, is motivated partly by his sense that these writers have in some ways been disparaged by the culture from which they came, the culture that they helped to shape—specifically that they have been shunned by philosophy (that is, by established, institutionalized philosophy) as non-philosophical. This he sees as a particular kind (and maybe a characteristically American kind) of repression or denial. It is surely significant then that *The Senses of Walden* was written at a time when American identity, or what America represents, was exposed in an especially painful way—the last stages of the war in Vietnam. Cavell wrote the book in a matter of weeks during the summer of 1971. Perhaps like Jacques Derrida's *Specters of Marx*, written defiantly against the backdrop of triumphalism over the demise of communism and the "end of history," *The Senses of Walden* is also an "untimely" book. Cavell focuses philosophically on a philosophical work that has come to be denied, on something of America's culture that has been repressed, and reads this in a way that challenges both what has become the conventional reception and celebration of this work, with its convenient placement for some within the genre of the pastoral, and the received understanding of what philosophy itself is. He reads it as a book about politics and education, and about what has gone wrong with the American dream: allusions to the visceral precision of Thoreau's remarks regarding the Mexican war leave little doubt as to Cavell's concerns about American encroachments on East Asia, while the Eastern influences acknowledged in *Walden*—its references to Buddhist stories and to the *Bhagavad Gita*, for example—reflect a hospitality to thought that America has learned to deny.

If one aspect of the pastoral reading of *Walden* has the beneficial effect of showing the possibility of an ecology or environmentalism that would resist the plundering and destructive consequences of booming industry and commerce, its capitalism, this falls well short of the broader terms in which Thoreau seeks a different economy of living. For this would require not only a different relation to the land but a different incarnation of work and rest, of the ways that we house ourselves and our relation to our neighbors, of our connections at home and abroad, of death and birth, and of settlement and departure. The economy of living at issue here is an economy of the words we use and of the thoughts and practices that they condition.

It is not a matter of mere circumstantial detail that this is American philosophy, for what might constitute American philosophy is taken by Cavell to be inextricably linked to the question of what America is or can be. These concerns are perhaps most explicitly played out in Cavell's writings on Emerson, where the repression referred to above has also perhaps led to an underappreciation of the extent to which Emerson's work was influential for Nietzsche. More recently Cavell has written of what it is concerning the relation of land and belonging that separates Thoreau from Heidegger.[2] For all the differences between these thinkers, it is difficult to believe that Thoreau's experiment in living and in writing—and hence, in building, dwelling, and thinking (Heidegger's *Bauen Wohnen Denken*)—did not influence Heidegger, unacknowledged though that influence may remain. It is important, however, that what Cavell finds in Emerson and Thoreau is other than pragmatism, the prime candidate for a distinctively American philosophy, whose honoring of Emerson he shares and towards which he has continually shown respect, but which he has never espoused. Cavell has coined the phrase "Emersonian moral perfectionism"—a perfectionism without final perfectibility—to capture a loose set of features, all related to a kind of cultural conversion, which he draws together along the following lines.

> Each self is drawn on a journey of ascent . . . to a further state of that self, where . . . the higher is determined not by natural talent but by seeking to know what you are

made of and cultivating the thing you are meant to do; it is a transformation of the self which finds expression in ... the imagination of a transformation of society into ... something like an aristocracy where ... what is best for society is a model for and is modeled on what is best for the individual soul.

CHU 7

Far from any crude individualism, this suggests aspiration towards our own best selves. What is aspired to is typically understood in terms of a new reality—the good city, the good society. It involves thinking how our world should be constituted, what words we can find for it, what practices should give it substance, and what standards sustain it; it involves questioning what America might be. That the question of America, of its creation and inauguration, is never far from the preoccupations of *Walden* is made plain enough by the fact that Thoreau began to build his house on the fourth of July.

As may have become clear from the above remarks, Cavell sees a close relation between philosophy and what it is to live a human life, and hence between philosophy and education. As he puts this in a celebrated passage in *The Claim of Reason*, "In the face of the questions posed in Augustine, Luther, Rousseau, Thoreau ... we are children; we do not know how to go on with them, what ground we may occupy. In this light, philosophy becomes the education of grownups" (*CR* 125). It is no surprise then that he finds *Walden* itself—a book that Thoreau wrote for "poor" students—to be profoundly relevant to education; it is a book to be placed alongside Rousseau's *Emile*. Moreover, the recurrence of themes of turning and departure, here and in his readings of Emerson and other texts, also place this text thematically in relation to Plato's *The Republic*, especially with regard to its myth of the Cave and the imperative of turning towards the light, away from the flickering images that the darkness offers. Education is inherent also in the processes of self-discovery evident in the confessional and autobiographical forms of writing exemplified here.

We have seen that Cavell writes against the easy interpretation of *Walden* as an escape to nature, and I have claimed that he makes the book more difficult. I shall shortly provide examples to show how this is so. Cavell goes so far as to say that Thoreau is as difficult as Wittgenstein.

It is an extraordinary feature of Cavell's thought that he reads with the kind of attention to language sometimes associated with the literary critic, and that he writes in a style that tests the boundaries of philosophy and literature as conventionally understood, for such is the quality of some of the texts that most interest him, *Walden* itself being an exemplary borderline text. Philosophers have typically been preoccupied with how their enquiries can lead to conviction, and they have sought to achieve this, in the analytical tradition especially, through the precision of their argumentation. The rigor of this other writing—of which *Walden* is exemplary—is that it leads the reader to certain convictions, "conviction" carrying the sense both of being convinced and of being convicted. And it does this in such a way that the full resonance of this word, beyond its somewhat anodyne significance in terms of logical deduction, impacts on the reader: the reader is tested, tried, put on trial; and conviction by the truth is not a matter of logic alone. So too, philosophers have typically been concerned with necessary and sufficient conditions, and the corresponding rigor here involves seeing, with Emerson and Thoreau, the ways in which, perhaps, our saying (*-dit-*) of things together (*con-*) is embedded in "condition."[3]

Given the turn to questions of literature, confession, and conviction here, it will be helpful if something of the literary and religious—and, that is, the historical and political—context of Thoreau's book is acknowledged, for this inevitably has a bearing on Cavell's concerns in this text in highly important ways.

The Religious Context

The location of Walden, just outside Concord, Massachusetts, and in New England, inevitably opens questions concerned with the founding of something new. New England was the site of the Pilgrim Fathers' first settlement, and the place where, in 1621, their first successful harvest prompted the establishment of Thanksgiving Day. Concord was the battleground that, perhaps more than any other, marked the beginning of the American revolution—the war between the American colonies and Great Britain (1775–83), leading to the formation of the independent United States. It laid the way for the Declaration of Independence in 1776.

The Pilgrim Fathers were Puritan dissenters who had come to North America as a result of their conviction that the ways of Europe had become corrupt and that its religious practices had lost touch with spiritual truth, the word of the Lord. The New World offered the possibility of creating a better, more God-fearing society, where a life of religious faith and simplicity would free them from the fallen state of the Old. In sailing across the Atlantic, into an uncertain future, they also re-enacted the Biblical story of the journey to the Promised Land. In certain respects also—and notwithstanding the harshness of the first year they spent in America, when forty-six of the one hundred and two pilgrims died[4]—this promise, and the abundance of the land to which they had come, became associated with the possibility of a return to the Garden of Eden, or of a Heaven on Earth.

The way that the Puritan settlers understood themselves can be illuminated if, at this point, some quite specific connections with the Bible are drawn out. The Puritans had escaped from religious persecution in England and from what they took to be the corruption and ungodliness of Europe. It was Old Testament prophets such as Ezekiel and Jeremiah, who had warned of the dire consequences of failing to heed the word of a just but wrathful God, and this lesson, it seemed, had not been learned. Let us pause to take note of certain details of their message, for these foreshadow themes in Thoreau. The God of Ezekiel, who is severe and just, is eternally the same, but the ways in which he can be apprehended by the people change. In consequence, it falls to each generation to think of God in new ways. The destruction of Jerusalem and exile to Babylon had left the people to whom Ezekiel ministered traumatized and manifesting anger and denial. Ezekiel responded to this by exposing the people's responsibility for the disaster that had afflicted them, castigating them for their worship of idols and their acceptance of the words of false prophets. He implored them to see that their only hope for recovery was to change. Ezekiel is a key figure in the survival of a Judean identity, and he was a major transitional figure in the move from an Israelite religion to what became the religion of Judaism. He is the prophet who affirms the continued presence of God amongst the people but of God's withdrawal under certain conditions, who challenges the people over their part in the failures of Judah, and who ponders the question of legitimate religious and political leadership in the restored community. In similar fashion and at about the same time, Jeremiah's task was to show the moral necessity of the destruction of Jerusalem and to proclaim this in the ears of the people to be the inevitable result of their moral guilt. In order to arouse the people from their moral lethargy, he preached repentance until it became monotonous. He had not only "to root up, and to pull down," but also to undertake the positive work of salvation, "to build, and to plant" (Jeremiah 1:10).

It was in the light of such ways of thinking that the Puritans saw both their society and their lives as individuals as in need of redemption. Redemption is a process in which loss is a condition of salvation, where ultimately this is to be understood in terms of the renunciation of worldly happiness in favor of an afterlife of heavenly bliss. But redemption also models an economy of living in *this* world, an economy that places importance on frugality, prudence, piety, and the rejection of both material wealth and indulgence in sensuous pleasures in favor of the goods of a simple life, in service of the Lord. The characteristic individualism of such dissenting faiths is to be found in their emphasis on the significance of personal commitment and conscientious testimony, marked especially by the ceremony of adult baptism. In line with the eschatological cast of such faith, with its anticipation of a final Judgment Day, baptism is a once and once only, life-changing event. It is a kind of rebirth, whose enduring influence—considerably debased, to be sure—is seen, incidentally, in the fact that most leading politicians in the United States feel bound to declare themselves "born-again Christians."

Beyond these historico-religious factors, however, the significance of these matters needs to be understood in terms of the extraordinary resonance in Anglophone sensibilities of the King James Version of the Bible—the version that is taken as classic. Echoes of its language recur throughout Thoreau's text.

The Bible is taken to be the word of God, and for the Puritans it was taken to be literally true. The Gospel of St. John begins with "In the beginning was the word, and the word was with God and the word was God," where "word" is the English translation of *logos*, and where *logos* connects etymologically with the idea of a way.[5] This perhaps helps to underline the extent to which these words pointed to a *way* of life, but the translation may fail fully to record the extent to which the words did not merely present certain propositions or stories or commandments as to how to live but themselves constituted the conditions for that life. The words themselves were inseparable from the life, and the religious poetry and hymns that were subsequently generated from such religious faith were an elaboration of this way of life. For all the restraint of the Puritans when it came to matters of art, one rhetorical form flourished particularly, and this was the sermon, with the preacher or minister assuming the mantle of the prophet speaking to a people who are constantly in danger of being deaf to the word of

God. As Cavell will show, such a positioning of the preacher or prophet in relation to the people is re-enacted in Thoreau's text.

The Literary Context

It was said above that a recurrent concern of Cavell's writing has been with the way in which the founding of America is dependent upon its finding its own philosophy. This is not to be separated, especially in Thoreau's time, from the question of America's finding or founding of its own literature, of its establishing itself through its literature. Hence, it is necessary to consider connections between the writing of *Walden* and some background literary sources to which reference is made. The most obvious of these is Homer's *Iliad*, a founding text for what we think of as Ancient Greece, and hence for Europe as a whole. The writing of such a text evidently became a project for John Milton, the English poet who, in 1667, published a work whose title, *Paradise Lost*, declares its epic ambitions for the culture and the English language, and whose theme is no less than the Creation and Fall. *Paradise Lost* narrates the Christian story of the Fall of Man: the temptation of Adam and Eve by Satan and their expulsion from the Garden of Eden. The story is innovative in that it attempts to reconcile the Christian and the Pagan; like Shakespeare, Milton found Christian mythology lacking, and he tried to incorporate pagan and classical Greek as well as Christian references within the poem. The work was written just after the English Civil War (1642–48), and Milton had worked for Cromwell, who had been Lord Protector of England during the period of the Commonwealth (1649–60); hence Milton had first-hand experience of the (short-lived) English revolution. Writing from a Puritanical background, and at a time of religious conflict and contested identity, he sought in this epic poem to "justify the ways of God to men."[6] The failed rebellion and restoration of the monarchy left Milton to explore his own losses in the writing of *Paradise Lost*.

If the writings of Homer and Milton stand as examples of the establishment of a native literature against which Thoreau might in some sense be conceiving his own purpose, and however ironically modest his journal of the time he spent at Walden Pond seems, on the face of it, to be, there are other poets whose work bears more directly on the substance of what he attempts. Hence there are occasional allusions in the text to British Romanticism. William Blake, William Wordsworth, and Samuel Taylor Coleridge—both reacting to the Enlightenment and seeing themselves as products of it—were writing in part out of a horror at some of the effects of recent industrialization and urbanization, but their larger purpose concerned the highly rationalistic, machine-like Newtownian universe that confronted them and the kinds of repression that this had put into effect. In particular, their efforts were directed towards the retrieval or perhaps the (re)creation of the inner life. The relation between subjectivity and objectivity was reconceived, casting the connections between reason and emotion in a new light; at the same time the significance of the imagination across the range of human activity was newly appreciated, with the darker sides of human experience, of reason and madness, more fully acknowledged. They changed English literature by turning their attention to the ordinary lives of people, by finding the epic in the ordinary. Autobiographical and confessional writing featured prominently in this work.

This was a characteristically European reaction, however, and by the time that Thoreau was writing, Romanticism was in any case well past its peak. But the huge influence of this movement constitutes a major part of the cultural backdrop to the age in which Thoreau lived and hence to his undertaking in *Walden*. (Indeed, he begins the book with an allusion to Coleridge's *Ode to Dejection*.) It may also have been a factor in reinforcing the reception of this text as American pastoral, in effect as a homely version of the realignment with nature that was the Romantics' preoccupation, from Rousseau onwards. That such a reading is to be contested—of Thoreau, as of the Romantics themselves—should be abundantly clear.

There are, however, aspects of *Walden* that appear to court such an interpretation, as, for example, in his registering of the character of some of the animals that he encounters in the woods. Cavell relates this to the work, nearly a century later, of the anthropological historian Constance Rourke, whose book *American Humor: A Study of the National Character* (1931) examined such legendary figures as the Yankee, the backwoodsman, and the minstrel singer, as well as the stock identities of familiar animals in the landscape, in order to show the ways in which the popular comic imagination had contributed to American self-awareness. There are indeed comic aspects to Thoreau's text, but a closer look at his imagery will show that this serves to conceal a greater depth and moral seriousness, as well as to dispel any easy assumptions regarding his naturalism.

Indicative Imagery and American Folklore

Much of Cavell's account depends upon drawing the reader's attention to the functioning of various levels of imagery in the text—manifested in metaphor, direct comparison, and symbolism, but also in an implication, in certain respects, of the quasi-allegorical nature of the text. There are also religious connotations here that provide pointers to Thoreau's relation to nature—that is, to a transcendence in the natural and the ordinary. The examples I cite are intended to prepare the reader for the precise elaboration of these matters found in Cavell's attention to the text.

The cockerel (an old name for which is "chanticleer"—that is, one who chants clearly) is introduced at the outset as the bird to wake people up. But the farmyard connotations this has—the bird is raucous and ridiculous—ironically conceal the connections with the Old Testament prophets, whose purpose is also to wake people up. There is also a more subtle religious connection: Jesus's most ardent and in some ways bravest and most outspoken disciple, Peter, when questioned by Roman soldiers in the Garden of Gethsemane, denied his acquaintance with the man three times *before the cock crew*, exactly as Jesus had prophesied. The fox, the natural predator of the cockerel, which appears later in the text, is archetypally associated with cunning and slyness. While the cockerel's brightly colored plumage and loud crowing, and his strutting back and forth in full view, make his presence obvious and direct, the fox proceeds by stealth and indirectness, for the most part out of sight. Thoreau, as Cavell shows, aligns himself in his writing with both forms of approach.

While the animal symbolism, which extends far beyond these examples, tempts, as it were, the interpretation of the book in terms of the rural idyll, there is another, more dominant range of imagery that pulls in a different direction. This is to be found in the array of economic terms—"interest," "means," "profit," etc.—and their doubling as terms with a different sense, pointing to different kinds of economy. So too the multiple uses of "account" and its cognates imply both book-keeping and the keeping of an account or journal in which one might account for oneself; they ask what counting is and what it is that counts. Writing of this kind tests the reader, as Cavell shows, and as Thoreau obliquely acknowledges, in that it puts the reader in the position of having to decide on the way to read a passage, on which meaning predominates, and on the consequences of this. In fact, Cavell shows numerous ways in which such demands are made by the text, so that the nature of reading itself emerges as a motif for the book as a whole.

What we are considering here are features of Thoreau's style but also of the writing of Cavell himself. Such features include plays on words and puns, ironic juxtapositions (the bean-field Thoreau hoes/Hector in the Trojan War; the academic/the domestic; erudition/the vernacular), ironic understatement, self-referentiality (turning the page, *SW* 69), cryptic chapter titles ("Words," "Sentences," "Portions"), and double-genitives (*The Senses of Walden* suggesting, at the least, the meanings of Walden, the meanings of *Walden*, the sensuous experience of Walden and perhaps the senses of inhabitants who may exhibit themselves to you by turns), not to mention variations of rhythm and stress, and contrived ambiguity. Sometimes a family of words is to be discerned in the light of its common etymology: thus, the meanings of "accident," "coincidence," "case," and "occasion" play off one another as a result of their common origin in the Latin "to fall" (*caedo, cadere, cecidi, casum*), all of which resonates again with the Fall. To be sure, all this can be missed readily enough, but for anything beyond a superficial encounter with the text, it deserves the kind of attention that Thoreau gives to the animals in the woods. Such devices and tropes reveal their significance by turns. They put the reader in the position of *having to read*: of deciding which way to take a phrase and of weighing the consequences of this for the book as a whole; of weighing the significance of these words for the economy of living that it depicts. Both Cavell's and Thoreau's words exercise destabilizing effects on our position in relation to language, presenting us with texts whose diverse and dynamic shifts of meanings refuse to be fixed. It is then a very specific purpose of these books that they enjoin us to trust to the autonomy of language. (Wittgenstein speaks of the autonomy of grammar.)

I began this essay with the remark that it is part of Cavell's achievement that he makes *Walden* more difficult and that he does this in exemplary ways. I hope here not only to have provided background knowledge that the reader may not have but also some signposts to indicate the kind of reading that the book requires. Cavell's own style is difficult, and this reflects his thinking about language, the sense and sensuousness of the prose he writes. It is the virtue of this difficulty that it makes us think more. It points to the depth of his work as a whole, a quality so richly demonstrated in his reading of *Walden*.

Theatricalizing experience in the woods

> *I desire to speak somewhere without bounds; like a man in a waking moment, to men in their waking moments; for I am convinced that I cannot exaggerate enough even to lay the foundation of a true expression.*
>
> —*Walden*, 324

The Shop at Walden Pond[7] displays various editions of Thoreau texts and a range of books about Thoreau, some lavishly illustrated, as well as T-shirts, mugs, greetings cards, jewelry, a predictable range of souvenirs. When I visited, I looked for but could not find *The Senses of Walden*. The salesperson was enthusiastic but told me he had not come across it. The pond is a beautiful place to visit, and the place where Thoreau built his hut is duly marked. The railroad is a short distance away, and it is moving to stand on the open track and stare down the lines. That the place is celebrated in this way should surely be no surprise, and indeed it is because of the Thoreau connection that I went there, as opposed to the many other beautiful lakes in New England. Thoreau declares his desire to "speak without bounds, to men in their waking moments," but Walden has become theatricalized. His unflagging criticism of the lives of those who "are said to live in New England" involves the charge that they are living a lie (*W* 324, 4). They are living imitation lives. But here, in celebrating Thoreau's achievement, experience itself has become staged.[8]

For Cavell, "The task of the modern artist, as of the modern man, is to find something he can be sincere and serious in; something he can mean. And he may not at all" (*MWM* 212). But what is it to be serious? How to avoid imitation, fraudulence? How to say what we mean?

Recollecting Romanticism

The Romanticism in the wake of which Thoreau was writing was in part a response to the effects of industrialization and mass culture, as well as to the Newtonian disenchantment of the universe. Modernism, which so significantly provided the cultural context within which Cavell developed his own thought, was a reaction to similar forces. It shares with Romanticism a commitment to what J. M. Bernstein has called cultural renewal via the "transfiguration of meaning":[9] amongst other things, this means rejecting the assumption that the objective order (how things are for everyone) is separate from the subjective (how they look or seem to me). As Romantics and modernists alike have tried to show, those apparently merely subjective aspects of knowing and meaning are, in fact, ingredients in objective knowing and public meaning. Attention to the "jointure of orders of fact with orders of feeling," which reveals the world "an expressive empirical order," restores hope for renewal.[10] In the modern world that order is "hounded," as Bernstein puts it, from three different directions: the growing belief that meaning is a matter of mere convention; a modern reductive naturalism coupled with the belief that the only rational authority is of a form modelled by the natural sciences; and by "'determined society,' say, the consequences for social existence implied by the first two houndings" (123).

Bernstein writes:

> From the outset Cavell has proclaimed an intimacy, at times amounting to a virtual identity, between the *logic* of aesthetic claiming (the logic appropriate to our claims, evaluative and interpretive, about works of art and, by extension, the logic of those works, their claiming) and the *logic* peculiar to ordinary language philosophy ("what we say when" and "what we mean when we say it").
>
> 107

In the engagement of art and art criticism, judgments are offered not as expressions merely of individual preference but as appealing to a putative truth that others might come to see, yet where no proof is possible. In the procedures of ordinary language philosophy, samples of usage are considered in terms of convergences of empirical structure and affective significance in a manner that parallels the production and criticism of artworks: philosophy of this kind provides "a record of our response to such jointures—which is why we say what we do when we do" (116), and they depict what Cavell has called our "conviction and connectedness with the world." They acquire their importance and urgency once "we have discovered that the task of making sense of our standing in the world is somehow wholly up to us" (*WV* 116–17). The implications of this intimacy extend through Cavell's work, especially in his conception of the political, which he develops with particular pertinence through the thematization of voice. In aesthetic judgment, not to speak in one's voice, to mimic another, is not only to accede to a kind of conformism but to render one's judgment void; in politics, it is to undermine the articulation of experience on which democracy depends. In the end this articulation depends upon testimony ("don't you see, don't you hear, don't you dig ... Because if you do not see *something*, without explanation, then there is nothing further to discuss" [*MWM* 93]), but it is important that this is other than that more bland assertion ("Well, I liked it" or "That's what I think") that is a mark of the speaker's withdrawal—denying the responsibilities of criticism, frustrating political discussion, and courting isolation.[11]

Cavell sees the distinct demand of modern art that it take the form of acknowledgement: this requires "my voicing my acknowledgement" and my regarding work and criticism as "exemplary individual performances":[12] "The problem of the critic, as of the artist," Cavell writes, "is not to discount his subjectivity, but to include it; not to overcome it in agreement, but to master it in exemplary ways. Then his work outlasts the fashions and arguments of a particular age. That is the beauty of it." Such performances are moves in resistance against ideas of objectivity emptied of subjective engagement and in undoing "the psychologizing of psychology" (the business of cognitive operations) (*MWM* 94, 91, 93).[13] Let me move in on what this phrasing might mean via two stages, one presented immediately here and the other quite late in my discussion. Exposure of inaccurate or misleading conceptualizations of subjectivity and objectivity, as of the inner and the outer, is close to the heart of Cavell's ambitions. Thus—to begin the First Stage—in the opening paragraph of part 4 of *The Claim of Reason*, Cavell writes: "I have suggested that [Wittgenstein's] teaching is in service of a vision that false views of the inner and of the outer produce and sustain one another, and I would be glad to have suggested that the correct relation between inner and outer, between the soul and its society, is the theme of the *Investigations* as a whole" (CR 329). Wittgenstein remarks of his investigation that it "compels us to travel criss-cross in every direction over a wide field of thought" (*PI*, "Preface," 3). Bernstein draws attention to the echo of German Romanticism in the fragmentary structuring not only of the *Investigations* but of part 4 of *The Claim* itself, where the names Cavell lists on the contents page ("Embryos," "Slaves," "Soul-blindness," . . .) are to serve not as headings for discrete sections but as road-signs (viii). Cavell describes the genesis of this part of his book in terms of his keeping of "a limited philosophical journal," remarking that in such writing "the autonomy of each span of writing is a more important goal than smooth, or any, transitions between spans" (xxiii). There are affinities here with the sentence style and essay form that Emerson adopts and develops, as with the non-chronological and uneven sections of the "journal" that is Thoreau's *Walden*. The journal form defeats itself if it does not engage the author in writing that is serious. But the avoidance of fraudulence or artificiality will sometimes require giving up on the idea of proceeding from one subject to another in a direct linear argument: Wittgenstein found that his "thoughts were soon crippled" if he tried "to force them on in any single direction against their natural inclination." Hence, his collection of remarks is "really only an album" (*PI*, "Preface," 3).[14] The notion of the philosophical fragment in Cavell is intended, Bernstein writes, to "cover a variety of discontinuous forms of philosophical presentation and writing: aphorism, aside, entry, reading, remark, parenthesis, digression, introduction, sentence, and so on. What all these have in common is their relative autonomy or independence."[15] It defies subordination from first premises or from an ideal method or procedure—the "purely rational authority of the ideal-type analytic philosophy."[16] Hence, Emerson's sentences are democratically styled as "collections of equals rather than hierarchies of dependents" (*PDAT* 244).[17]

The fragment's autonomy but openness of connection are something other, however, than indeterminacy of meaning. Fear that our words may not mean what we intend has fueled anxiety about fraudulence. Cavell sees Pop art and deconstruction alike as acquiescing in indeterminacy, and it is against this that he affirms the importance of seriousness. That, at least, is the provocative starting-point for Gordon Bearn's "Staging Authenticity: A Critique of Cavell's Modernism."[18] Bearn lights on Cavell's emphasis on perfection and on the figure of the return home, both facets of Cavell's engagement with skepticism. Our words can go astray, being understood in ways other than we had intended, or perhaps we find that we cannot say what we mean. "The way back home," the way to seriousness, as Bearn paraphrases Cavell, "is through the 'perfect acknowledgment' of the contingent conditions of being able to mean what we say"; only in this way can one make "one's sense present to oneself":[19]

First, we begin at home in our language, quite able to mean what we say, that is, we are able to make our sense present to ourselves. But then, second, something happens, and we find ourselves no longer able to mean what we say, alienated from the words of our language, choked by the skeptical anxiety that perhaps we know nothing at all, not even what we meant to say. Finally, third, we are led, with our words, back home, to enjoy Wittgensteinian seriousness. It will not last. Words brought home wander away again. But while it lasts, we will have made our sense present to ourselves—enjoying, momentarily, peace.[20]

Wandering away (the theme of skepticism) then contrasts with the return home (the theme of acknowledgement) (305-6). And this third phase, the stage of seriousness, enables escape, momentary as this may be, from the threat of fraudulence: "perfect acknowledgment" of contingent conditions serves to "get us over our anxiety about the conditions of meaning anything at all" (299).

In modern art a quality that Cavell emphasizes is candor, taking the view that this can overcome the controlling power of the beholder of the work of art and achieves the defeat of theatricality (*MWM* 333n16). "In Cavell's dialect," Bearn writes, "theatricality is a form of nonseriousness, inauthenticity, endlessness. Since theatrical expression is continuously aware of itself and its effect on its audience, it is always divided between itself and its audience. In this divide, the endlessness of interpretation, the endless play of possible significations, opens up" (302).

Bringing words home so that they are "pure and serious, uncontaminated by the endless nonserious semantic forces they might convey" is based on the idea that it is possible to eliminate "all possible significances of a word except one serious significance." But, Bearn claims, this is simply not possible. Such an elimination would deprive words of the condition of their meaning anything at all: "Thus, even at home, our words must be energized by the nonserious significances which we might have hoped were contextually excluded" (306). Bearn glosses Derrida's argument as follows:

> To be a meaningful mark is just to be able to be used in various situations, so if words could not wander away from home, again, even after Wittgenstein led them back, they would not be words. But if they can still wander away, then this possibility must be inscribed in them, even at home. Thus Cavell cannot achieve authentic seriousness, all he could ever do would be to stage it.
>
> 306

Cavell's thinking is drawn by vertical forces, whether towards depth or upwards, towards the sublime. Bearn wants to redirect this orientation, towards horizons of connection and intensity that preoccupation with candor and total thereness is apt to be deny. Rather than appeal to vertically charged faith, grace,[21] and the sublime, Bearn emphasizes the laterally extending "immanent endlessness of beauty: purposiveness without a purpose, and without end."[22] In a bravura passage, which I shall quote at length, he explains what he has in mind.

The arts are crafts, and the craft of intensifying may be modeled on the caress. The caress aims at nothing, or everything. The hand is famous for its opposable thumb. It is a fine instrument, able to type, to drive, to perform the minute maneuverings required for cutting edge, key hole surgery. But if it is to caress, all of this must be left behind. The hand must be deprived of its glorious instrumentality. To caress is not to beat, nor to rub, nor to clutch, nor to hold, nor even to pet, as we pet a dog. The caressing fingers of the hand are made to dangle, like things, and these dangling things are turned around, for fingers caress not with the fingertips, their business side, but with their backs, their useless side. And these dangling things, turned backwards against their design, are dragged by their arm against the chest of your lover. The caress has no point, not because it has no purpose, not because it has many different purposes: neither one nor many, the caress swarms with innumerate intensities. The caress is pointless, in a positive sense. The caress is Yes. Every sensation counts. On the side of the fingertips while we are typing, only some of the world gets in. QWERTY. Typing, like all instrumental action, says No. No to what is not intended. But the caress says Yes to every sensation. In life, in art and in philosophy, beyond authenticity and inauthenticity, is intensity.

Seeking seriousness, Cavell anaesthetized aesthetics. What if, coming to our senses, aesthetics were sensualized?

308-9

Typing, type, mark, category, taxonomy, *Schlag, Geschlecht*[23]... No to what is not intended. But the caress says Yes. What can be said in response?

Coming to Cavell's Senses

Part of the strength of Cavell's writing is that he has been prepared to leave himself open to criticism at times.[24] But attention to context should perhaps mitigate to some degree the force of the criticisms above. Some of the remarks for which Bearn takes Cavell to task date from the 1960s, when talk of genuineness and authenticity was less jaundiced than it has since become. This is not, of course, to make the sanguine assumption that there was a lack of pretentiousness then! Moreover, the audience for which Cavell probably imagined himself to be writing would not itself have imagined or entertained the pertinent Derridean—indeed Deleuzean—lines of response that Bearn brings into view. The present discussion of Bearn's response is necessarily schematic and does not extend to the many other writings in which Bearn has refined his sympathetic yet demanding and disturbing critique.[25] But let me pursue three points.

First, Bearn's criticism of perfection seems to presuppose a particular sense of perfection, a sense that has its origins in the idea of perfect *form*. This reinforces the implication that the problem with Cavell's position is its latent metaphysical underpinning, elaborated, as we saw above, with reference to height and depth. But perfection can be given a more dynamic sense. Consider, for example, the idea of the perfective verb, which refers not to states of affairs but to actions, as complete bounded events. In Cavell's later development of the idea of Emersonian moral perfectionism, it is action that is to the fore, the improvement of the hour. When Emerson writes, in "Circles," that around every circle another can be drawn,[26] this does not refer to a progressive consolidation of identity, the increasing rings of the tree-trunk, but to the fact that the action of drawing a circle comes to an end. You find yourself already outside the circle by which you have defined yourself, and you have to draw again. We find ourselves on a stair, we take steps on the way, and these are little perfections of action. Our words are little steps, not undifferentiated flow. This sense is absent from what Bearn finds in Cavell's usage.

Second, this dynamism connects with the account of meaning in the "Excursus on Wittgenstein's Vision of Language" in part 1 of *The Claim of Reason*. The section called "Projecting a Word" throws emphasis on the way that a word does not exist in a fixed correlation with a thing but is projected into new contexts. That this possibility inheres in the very nature of a word stands in tension with the idea that a singular meaning can be found as its rightful home. Acknowledging this involves seeing home not as a final resting place, but as a state whose very condition will be disturbed. One version of this pattern is to be found in Cavell's elaboration of the idea of the ordinary, where the actual ordinary contrasts with the eventual ordinary, the ordinary that we, as it were, come back to, weighted by our self-consciousness, burdened by a kind of alienation, exiled as it were from the pure presence enjoyed by animals or in Eden. Bearn's fable of wandering words prompts associations of a different kind in Thoreau's eulogy to "Walking," where wandering connects with sauntering and, hence, etymologically with pilgrimage ("'There goes a *Sainte-Terre*,' a Saunterer, a Holy-Lander") and with, after the Knight, the Walker Errant.[27] Iterations of this thought are found in *Walden* itself. The home that Thoreau makes in the woods is not a fixed home but a place to sojourn. In the end he leaves the woods for the same reason he went there: it was time to try something new (*W* 323). The iterations of this thought are there in Cavell's discussion of *Walden*—most graphically in the idea of the "father tongue" ("a reserved and select expression, too significant to be heard by the ear"), associated especially with the indirectness of the written word, and the process of reading itself, indirectness being figured in the bent arm of the reader. Such thoughts are expressed most eloquently in the final chapter of *Walden*: "The volatile truth of our words should continually betray the inadequacy of the residual statement. Their truth is instantly *translated*: its literal monument remains" (*W* 325, Thoreau's emphasis)—words that anticipate the distinction between the *saying* and the *said* in Levinas, and the idea of translation as occurring not just inter- but intra-lingually, developed so richly in Derrida.

Third, Cavell draws a contrast between seriousness and theatricality, and although his use of "theatricality" may be stipulative, the contrast remains problematic: our real actions are not neatly separated from what actors do on a stage; fictions are part of our real world. Bearn provides a deft illustration of this in his discussion of Roy Lichtenstein's *Eddie Diptych* from 1962:

> In gigantic cartoon format, we are presented with a moment of a love story. The blonde girl has apparently been told by her parents to stop seeing Eddie because

it just made no (common) sense to continue... Feeling bad about causing such heartache, her mother says "I have something for you to eat in the kitchen, dear ... ," but the girl is not hungry and just wants to be left alone in her room. Cavell almost says that such art "burlesques the condition of high art, as the lows of culture generally do."[28]

But in moments when our lives are emotionally wrecked, we may find we are living the comic book story "I'm not hungry, please I just want to be alone. Authentic experiences following comic scripts."[29] The point is wittily made, but perhaps it is not so original, and in fact it is understated. It is difficult to believe that romantic love could exist without the background of the art of courtly love or, say, contemporary popular love songs. The extensive attention that Cavell has given to popular cultural forms should make it clear that he would be sympathetic to this point. (Popular cultural forms are not the lows of culture.) The good point that Bearn makes here also risks obscuring the fact that Liechtenstein's picture and script is *not* a comic strip and, hence, perhaps does *not* supply the script for our real experience: "I just want to be alone" relives the comic strip, not the script of the Pop artwork.[30]

The insight that the real is realized with the benefit of fictions, and hence is "staged" in this way, however, is fully live in *Walden*. When Thoreau hoes the weeds amongst his lines of beans, he is fighting the Battle of Troy: "Many a crest-waving Hector, that towered a whole foot above his crowding comrades, fell before my weapon and rolled in the dust." When he exaggerates that he "cannot exaggerate enough even to lay the foundation of a true expression," this is an acknowledgement that foundations cannot be achieved nor truth be found by looking down, as it were, to some rock-bottom matter-of-factness but must be drawn by possibility, the imagination, excess. And when he writes that you only have to sit for long enough at some attractive spot in the woods, "all its inhabitants may exhibit them to you by turns," he is implying that each animal does its turn, puts on its display, and has its characteristic self-expression (*W* 162, 324, 228). Such expression is staged in the way that the writing of a diary might be—or the providing of an example in an academic paper, or ordinary language philosophy's sampling of speech, or the making of your life experiment. These human doings depend upon a range of possibilities of acting and pretending, of honesty and deceit, of seriousness and fraudulence, that provide registers of expression or vocabulary out of which their meaningfulness is constructed.

I am inclined to suggest that significant stretches of Wittgenstein's late remarks on psychology are in service of a vision that false views of seriousness and theatricality produce and sustain one another. And I would like to say that the correct relation between seriousness and theatricality, between seriousness and pretense, and pretense and deception, are recurrent themes in those remarks as a whole. If, as Wittgenstein tries to show, there were beings to whom pretense was unknown and to whom lying was not just morally wrong but incomprehensible, where perhaps nothing was hidden, their form of life would be of a kind totally different from our own: they would not be human at all. That there is necessarily a degree of indeterminacy and unforeseeability to what people intend indicates something of what "mental" means,[31] and this connects with the "endless multiplicity of expression."[32] The possibility of revealing one's inmost heart is tied to the possibility of hiding it. Revealing and hiding are played out within the range of expression. The presence of ambiguity and the possibility of pretense drive the inclination to speak of the inner and the outer, and it is a condition of the human.

What would it be like if this ambiguity were arrested? "Imagine," Wittgenstein writes, "that people could observe the functioning of the nervous system in others. In that case they would have a sure way of distinguishing genuine and simulated feeling."[33] But questions of genuineness and fraudulence could not arise, because genuineness depends upon the possibility that one might deceive. An expression, to be an expression, must contain this possibility. Hence, insofar as we can speak of a perfection of speech, it must incorporate this.

In elaborating on these matters, Wittgenstein has recourse to ideas of playing a role and of being an actor on a stage, and he comments: "That an actor can represent grief shows the uncertainty of evidence, but that he can represent *grief* also shows the reality of evidence."[34] I want—now the Second Stage—to see the actor's experimenting with forms of expression as on a continuum with the range of experimentation, the testing of expression and response, that constitutes the fabric of our ordinary lives and experience. Our lives are not just contrived performance, but the performative is there in what we say and do. We must feel our way in this. In testing out our words—in shading what we say with gentle sarcasm or as a mild rebuke, with a withering glance, the raised eyebrow of disapproval, with affectionate teasing or dead-pan irony, with bold encouragement or the reassurance of a smile—we are not so much conforming those expressions to pre-existing intentions but finding what those intentions and meanings might be. And enacting them. There is no plottable line that divides the serious from the theatrical in these matters, or sincerity from fraudulence, or pretense from deception. The actor in rehearsal exemplifies what we do in ordinary life; and that life includes its forms of play-acting.

At the memorial gathering for Cavell, at Harvard University in November 2018, David Cavell recalled a recent occasion when he had visited his father at the family home. As he left, his father had said to him: "Well, don't do anything I wouldn't do." And then with a wry smile: "That should leave you plenty of latitude." This familiar joke depends upon a shift in tone from the pinched propriety of the first sentence to the license of the second. It works in part through its predictability, like the quoting of a phrase from a song or film. Would it have been better if Stanley had said goodbye with words such as those of Polonius to his departing son ("This above all things: To thine own self be true")? Would it have been more serious? How else are the bonds of affection, the fabric of relation, sustained? Seriously.

In exposing the false metaphysical conception of the inner (that is, the psychologizing of psychology), Wittgenstein writes: "The 'inner' is a delusion. That is: the whole complex of ideas alluded to by this word is like a painted curtain drawn in front of the scene of the actual word use."[35] Psychologized psychology is this painted curtain, a glossy but lifeless draping of technical jargon that hides the reality of what we say and do, and concentrates instead on a backstage of cognitive operations. The psychologist is like a theater critic who explains the machinery of the backdrops, the cold tea used for whiskey, the ketchup for blood, and the trapdoor through which the genie escapes. But to understand the backstage is not to understand the play![36] The action on the stage, the scene of actual word use, is like the reality of our lives, and the actor's experimentation with word and gesture analogizes the way we find ourselves— muddling through those multiple habitual little failures (where words fall short or are bombastic or hollow, where a gesture lacks grace, where the tone does not ring true) and instead trying to find something closer to what Cavell has called perfect pitch. Cavell was a gifted musician, and his mother an outstanding pianist. He envied her perfect pitch. But perfect pitch, it turns out, is not quite what it seems. Atmospheric conditions can cause the instruments of an orchestra to vary very slightly in pitch. This is a condition to which most musicians naturally adjust, perhaps without awareness of what they are doing. But for the person with perfect pitch, it is a potential problem, drawn as she will be to find a note slightly out of tune with her fellow players. It is as if perfect pitch attunes its bearer to an ideal form, whereas those without can seamlessly and intuitively adjust to the sound and sense they are making together. It is in the end the latter accommodation that Cavell's philosophy expresses, as illustrated richly in *The Senses of Walden* and in Thoreau's exemplary act.[37]

Notes

1 Andrew Norris, *Becoming Who We Are* (Oxford: Oxford University Press, 2017).
2 Cavell, "Thoreau Thinks of Ponds, Heidegger of Rivers," in *PDAT*, 213–35.
3 The etymology here is pertinently and rather delightfully ambiguous. Modern dictionaries tend to suggest that "condition" derives from *con-dicere* (to say together), but older sources identify the connection with *condire* (to prepare, preserve, oil, season). Either way this accords happily with the insights of ordinary language philosophy. I am grateful to Anne-Marie Eggert Olsen for her clarification of the twists and turns of possible connection here.
4 Those who survived would not have done so had it not been for the help of the people who were already there.
5 The standard Japanese translation of the Bible translates *logos* as *tao*.
6 John Milton, *Paradise Lost*, ed. Gordon Teskey (New York: Norton, 2005), bk. 1, line 25.
7 See www.shopatwaldenpond.org.
8 Cavell's discussion of the Henry James short story "The Birthplace" is apposite here: "Fred Astaire Asserts the Right to Praise," in *PDAT*, 61–82.
9 J. M. Bernstein, "Aesthetics, Modernism, Literature: Cavell's Transformations of Philosophy," chap. 5 in *Stanley Cavell*, ed. Richard Eldridge (Cambridge: Cambridge University Press), 109.
10 Ibid., 122. Bernstein writes: "So aesthetics concerns, speaking crudely and indiscriminately, the sensible conditions of knowing and meaning, which is to say, sensuous or material meaning, the sensuous element of perceptual claims, and the perceptual element of objective cognitions, the subjective but not private conditions for objective knowing, what can be known only in sensing (['Music Discomposed'], 191) or only known in or by feeling (['Music Discomposed'], 192)" (111). For "Music Discomposed," see Stanley Cavell, "Music Discomposed," chap. 7 in *MWM*.

11 But, as Bernstein also recognizes, it is appropriate also to allow that such responses can be given a different inflection. When the critic stops arguing, what is left can be seen as her testimony.
12 Bernstein, "Aesthetics, Modernism, Literature," 124.
13 For a thoughtful brief discussion of the background to this idea, see Arata Hamawaki, "Undoing the Psychologizing of the Psychological," *Conversations: The Journal of Cavellian Studies* 7 (2019): 83–87, https://uottawa.scholarsportal.info/ottawa/index.php/conversations/issue/view/490.
14 Bernstein's discussion extends into passing consideration of Cavell's "The World as Things," in *PDAT* 236–80. On collecting and curiosity, with reference to Emerson and Cavell, see also my "Curiosity, Collecting, Ways of Knowing," in *Curious about Curiosity*, ed. Marianna Papastaphanou (Cambridge: Cambridge University Press, 2019).
15 Bernstein, "Aesthetics, Modernism, Literature," 132–33.
16 Ibid., 132.
17 For further discussion of the essay "The World as Things," see my "Curiosity, Collecting, Ways of Knowing."
18 Gordon C. F. Bearn, "Staging Authenticity: A Critique of Cavell's Modernism," *Philosophy and Literature* 24, no. 2 (Oct 2000): 294–311.
19 Once again there are lines connecting Wittgenstein and the Romantics: "it is true that we do not know the existence of the world with certainty," Cavell writes; "our relation to its existence is deeper—one in which it is accepted, that is to say received, ... acknowledged." Bearn is quoting from *MWM* xxxiii.
20 Bearn, "Staging Authenticity," 296–97; see *PI* §§107, 116, and 133.
21 As Michael Fried puts it, "presentness is grace"; see *Art and Objecthood* (Chicago: University of Chicago Press, 1998), 168, qtd. in Bearn, "Staging Authenticity," 306.
22 Bearn, "Staging Authenticity," 308.
23 See Jacques Derrida, *Geschlecht III: Sexe, race, nation, humanité*, ed. Geoffrey Bennington, Katie Chenoweth, and Rodrigo Therezo (Paris: Seuil, 2018).
24 See *LDIK* 491–92. See also Standish, "The Philosophy of Pawnbroking," in Paul Standish and Naoko Saito, eds., *Stanley Cavell and Philosophy as Translation: The Truth is Translated*, (London: Rowman & Littlefield, 2017), 171–82.
25 See, for example, Gordon C. F. Bearn, *Life Drawing: A Deleuzean Aesthetics of Existence* (New York: Fordham University Press, 2013) and *Waking To Wonder: Wittgenstein's Existential Investigations* (Albany: SUNY Press, 1997).
26 "Our life is an apprenticeship to the truth, that around every circle another can be drawn; that there is no end in nature, but every end is a beginning; that there is always another dawn risen on mid-noon, and under every deep a lower deep opens." Emerson, "Circles," in *Emerson*, selected and with notes by Joel Porte (New York: Library Classics of America, 1983), 403.
27 Thoreau, "Walking," in *The Essays of Henry D. Thoreau*, selected and edited by Lewis Hyde (New York: Northpoint Press, 2002).
28 Bearn, "Staging Authenticity," 303. Bearn is quoting *WV* 121.
29 Bearn, "Staging Authenticity," 304.
30 Of course the artwork may supply scripts of a more sophisticated and different kind.
31 Ludwig Wittgenstein, *Last Writings on the Philosophy of Psychology: The Inner and the Outer*, vol. 2, ed. G. H. von Wright and Heikki Nyman, trans. C. G. Luckhardt and Maximilian A. E. Aue (Oxford: Blackwell, 1992), 63.

32 Ibid., 65.
33 Ludwig Wittgenstein, *Remarks on the Philosophy of Psychology*, vol. 2, ed. G. H. von Wright and Heikki Nyman, trans. C. G. Luckhardt and Maximilian A. E. Aue (Oxford: Blackwell, 1980), #702.
34 Wittgenstein, *Last Writings on the Philosophy of Psychology*, 67.
35 Ibid., 84.
36 In *How to Do Things with Words*, Austin famously invokes the idea of the backstage. Rejecting the suggestion that good intentions (something inner) might excuse a promise (something outer), as classically expressed in Euripides' *Hippolytus*, he translates ἡ γλῶσσ' ὀμώμοχ', ἡ δὲ φρὴν ἀνώμοτος with "my tongue swore to, but my heart (or mind or other backstage artiste) did not" (9–10). Near the end of his discussion, claiming that authenticity and seriousness have nothing to do with the "joyful intensification" of art, life, and philosophy, Bearn alludes to this passage: "The fundamental fact is that without the backstage artist of the sacramental interpretation of seriousness and authenticity, the very idea of authenticity is metaphysically bootless" (Bearn, "Staging Authenticity," 308).

Austin's studiedly theatrical and pointedly inappropriate word "artiste," which Bearn drops, is brilliantly funny. An artiste is not exactly an artist but an entertainer in music-hall (or vaudeville)—a singer perhaps or, quite likely, a comedian, a conjuror, contortionist, juggler, escapologist . . . Austin is exploiting the phony sophistication and pretentiousness of this English usage, within this indecorous though telling insertion of the parenthesis into his "translation." In a footnote he remarks: "I do not mean to rule out all the offstage performers—the lights men, the stage manager, even the prompter; I am objecting only to certain officious understudies, who would duplicate the play" (10n1). This might be read both as a rejection of behaviorism and an acknowledgement of the complex conditions of expression, including the necessity of brain processes. The incisive snub of "officiousness" names a vice that, I take it, may be manifest in a certain seriousness amongst the psychologizers of psychology.
37 An earlier version of the first part of this paper was published in Japanese as an Introduction to *The Senses of Walden*, translated by Naoko Saito (Tokyo: Hosei University Press, 2005). This was the first of Cavell's books to be translated into Japanese. I am grateful to the publishers for permission to publish a major part of the substance of that introduction here. In thinking about questions of seriousness and theatricality, I have gained much from conversations with Adrian Skilbeck. His *Stanley Cavell and the Human Voice in Education: Serious Words for Serious Subjects* (Springer, 2019) extends discussion of these matters with particular style and richness. I would also like to thank Suzy Harris and Paola Marrati for comments on a draft of this paper.

4

The Claim of Reason: On Finding a Voice of One's Own in Philosophy

Paola Marrati

History, Composition, and Themes

The Claim of Reason, first published in 1979, was a long time in the making and as Cavell explains in its Foreword is the result of a series of transformative encounters. First with J. L. Austin, who during his visit at Harvard in 1955 gave a series of lectures on the material that would become *How to Do Things with Words* and a seminar on excuses, whose intellectual impact on Cavell was so profound that he abandoned his dissertation project on human action and decided he had to embark on a new one that would explore the significance of Austin's procedures for moral philosophy. What Cavell learns from Austin, directly or indirectly, are ways in which our capacity as moral agents to justify, excuse, and explain our actions coincides with our capacity to know ourselves. Hence, morality is not limited to issues of public interest and to what is right or wrong to do, but has a more private dimension as well, one of reflection and examination of the self. The idea of an intimate connection between morality and knowledge of the self plays an important role in *The Claim of Reason* and will be further explored and developed in what Cavell will later call moral perfectionism, in particular in his studies of Emerson and in *Cities of Words*.

This new path, however, did not lead directly to the completion of a dissertation, let alone of *The Claim of Reason*. The encounter with Thompson Clarke at Berkeley was equally influential: Clarke's idea that Austin's methods were both supportive and destructive of traditional epistemological problems, namely of skepticism, struck Cavell as a discovery about the possibilities offered by Austin's mode of philosophizing he had not previously perceived and deeply resonated with Cavell's increasing interest in Wittgenstein's *Philosophical Investigations* (*CR* xvi). The sense that the *Investigations* are indeed a response to skepticism, but one that neither affirms nor denies its central thesis, but instead recasts the problem of the possibility of knowing whether the external world and other minds exist in completely different terms, is central to *The Claim of Reason*. The enduring significance and pervasiveness of modern skepticism and the need for new terms of criticism are themes that will continue to guide Cavell's philosophical journey. I do not mention these encounters for the sake of outlining

Cavell's intellectual biography: many other names and works would need to be added, but instead to emphasize that if *The Claim of Reason* is arguably Cavell's most important text it is because it is the result of the convergence, and reciprocal transformation, of such a set of interests and preoccupations which Cavell formulates as the need of reclaiming the centrality of the human voice for philosophy. What skepticism, Wittgenstein, and Austin's ordinary language philosophy have to do with the human voice is certainly not obvious, nor for that matter what Cavell means by "human voice." In what follows I will attempt to elucidate how these themes are developed and connected in *The Claim of Reason*.[1]

The Claim of Reason is composed of four parts: the first three parts (entitled, respectively, "Wittgenstein and the Concept of Human Knowledge," "Skepticism and the Existence of the World," "Knowledge and the Concept of Morality") discuss in a rather classic academic manner what vision of language and knowledge Wittgenstein offers in the *Investigations* and what consequences such ideas have for rethinking the problem of skepticism as well as the nature of the moral life. They elaborate and expand on Cavell's dissertation *The Claim to Rationality*, submitted at Harvard in 1961. Part 4, redacted later and entitled "Skepticism and the Problem of Others," focuses on skepticism about other minds and thus thematically complements the previous chapters but sharply diverges in its writing style: traditional continuous arguments are replaced by a series of sketches of arguments, sometimes closer to short stories or parables. The difference in writing is so striking that it's impossible not to wonder what about other minds compels Cavell to search for new forms of philosophical expression, at times in the proximity of literature, as he himself suggests at the very end of *The Claim of Reason*. What is at stake, however, is more crucially the relation of philosophy to its own writing and tradition rather than its kinship with literature.

Philosophy has its own genres—the treatise, the essay, the dialogue, the meditation, etc.—and in this respect the relation between "form and content" has always been as intrinsic to it as to novels, poems, or tragedies.[2] If something has changed, if the writing of philosophy has become more difficult and problematic, it is not simply because ideas and concepts are not independent from their form of expression—they have never been—but rather because philosophy, some philosophy, has encountered the same predicament as other modernist arts. Modernism, as Cavell understands it, is that moment when the established conventions of a form of art have lost their power of conviction for us, when we do no longer know a priori what will count as a new instance of that art and in this sense every work redefines *what* that art is or what counts as *art*.[3] Modernism, then, is not the rejection of tradition, but the attempt to remain faithful to tradition by reinventing its conventions, by making it relevant for us anew. Cavell never affirms that *The Claim of Reason* is a modernist work, but the novelty of the style of part 4 and the problem of how and whether it fits with the rest of the book opens the question of what counts as philosophy, of what modes of arguments, expression, and coherence it allows or call for. I take this set of issues, and the impossibility of any simple answer to them, to be a central feature of *The Claim of Reason* as well as Cavell's way of inheriting Wittgenstein's lesson in the *Investigations* which is the explicit theme of most of the book.

It should be noted that the *Philosophical Investigations* is for Cavell one of the major modernist works of the last century (*CR* xx): its obscurity is not intentional, as if Wittgenstein had not made the effort of making himself understandable, but the result of the difficulty of expressing new thoughts and the modes of inquiry appropriate for them. Hence there are no traditionally reliable ways to approach such a text: situating it historically would presuppose one already knows how to situate it philosophically; considering the *Investigations* as a criticism of the *Tractatus* would similarly imply one knows what that criticism consists of (*CR* 3). Cavell finds his way into the text through the notion of criteria, which, while pervasive, had previously received little attention. The importance criteria play in Cavell's reading cannot be overstated: they guide both Cavell's understanding of Wittgenstein's conception of knowledge and his redefinition of the problem of skepticism. For the sake of clarity of exposition, I will first briefly sketch how Cavell understands modern skepticism and then turn to a discussion of criteria.[4]

Redefining Modern Skepticism

Cavell has profoundly reshaped our understanding of skepticism, which he finds expressed as much in Shakespearean tragedies and Hollywood films as in traditional epistemological problems. In his view, skeptical attitudes largely exceed epistemological concerns and are in fact pervasive in the moral life, as if skepticism, arguably the philosophical position most removed from everyday life, would bring us into that region of thought where the questions of how to live in the world, with oneself, and with one another would become explicit and urgent. While ancient skepticism was indeed inspired by ethical concerns, the tradition of modern skepticism, which is the one Cavell focuses upon, does not invite any explicit connection between the problems of the foundation of knowledge and those of the moral life. What defines modern skepticism is a quest for certainty that gives to knowledge a very specific outlook and grants to epistemological inquiries an absolute autonomy. Distrust of traditional disciplines such as philosophy or theology leads Descartes to develop his method of the generalization of doubt by which, step by step, all the sources and domains of knowledge are shown to rely upon shaky foundations. The chair I sit on, the fireplace I contemplate, this very body which is my own may be the deceptive illusions produced by madness; mathematical truths may be false beliefs induced by an evil genius who takes great pleasure in deceiving my mind.[5] Both the most concrete sensible knowledge and the most abstract intellectual one fail to meet the standard of absolute certainty. It is unlikely that I am mad, it is unlikely that an evil genius exists, but their possibility cannot be ruled out and thus the whole of our knowledge is cast in the shadow of doubts.

The quest for absolute certainty leads Descartes from what could be called local doubts to general ones, from being suspicious of traditional scholastic knowledge to questioning the reliability of everyday experience and mathematical calculus alike. Epistemological inquiries go beyond specific fields and objects to invest the whole of reality. It is at the same time, and for the same reason, that certainty becomes the only sufficient ground for knowledge and that knowledge becomes knowledge in general, *knowledge as such*. And that a chair, my body, that man in the street are as good candidates for knowledge as the circulation of the blood or the movements of the planets. Needless to say, questions about anatomy or astronomy are of a very different kind than questions about the reality of my body, or about the possibility that what looks like a man in the street could actually be an automaton. The latter are questions about reality, or existence: but the quest for certainty as the ground for knowledge leads, in the Cartesian framework, to raise questions about existence that knowledge must be able to answer. A link is established between certainty, knowledge, and existence that gives rise to the two defining questions of modern skepticism: how can we know with certainty that the external world exists? How can we know with certainty that other minds exist?

The "true" skeptic, the skeptic in the strict sense of the term, will give a negative answer to those questions and will claim the impossibility of knowing beyond any doubt that the world or other minds exist. Hume is probably the best example of the "true" skeptic; Descartes, who uses hyperbolic doubt as a method to reach with the *cogito* a ground for certainty upon which to reconstruct on sound foundations the entire system of knowledge, is hardly a skeptic in the restricted sense of the term. But if one can talk about a tradition of modern skepticism, it is because the haunting power of questions about the existence of the external world and/or of others runs through authors as different as Descartes, Hume, Kant, Moore, and Heidegger. Feeling *compelled* by those questions is what truly constitutes the skeptical attitude, an attitude shared both by those who deny and those who affirm our possibility of knowing the existence of the world and of others. Cavell's ongoing interest in skepticism is directed precisely toward the assumptions implied by the skeptical attitude:

> I do not, that is, confine the term [skepticism] to philosophers who wind up denying that we can ever know; I apply it to any view that takes the existence of the world to be a problem of knowledge. . . . I hope it will not seem perverse that I lump views in such a way, taking the very raising of the question of knowledge in a certain form, in a certain spirit, to constitute skepticism, regardless of whether a philosophy takes itself to have answered the question affirmatively or negatively.
>
> CR 46

Rather than focusing on divergent answers to the skeptical questions, Cavell is concerned with the explicit and inexplicit assumptions about knowledge that make those very questions possible in the first place, and impose them upon philosophers who, strictly speaking, do not hold "skeptical views." To put it differently, Cavell aims at understanding why both the skeptic *and* her critics come to ask the question of the existence of such peculiar "objects" as the world and others. For those who believe that philosophical problems hold regardless of their origins and the concerns that shaped them, skeptical questions just belong to the canon of philosophy, and the inquiry about what sustains skeptical doubts and the attempt to refute them is at best a psychological or historical analysis. But those who dismiss skepticism in the name of common sense, or on the ground of ordinary language philosophy, are equally uninterested in what drives the battle of arguments and counterarguments about the existence of the world or of others. For Cavell, though, these two stances are deeply unsatisfactory: philosophical problems are not disconnected from human needs, desires, uneasiness, or aspirations and, as a consequence, are not the expression of a peculiar kind of lunacy; madness, it is true, is not totally foreign to philosophy, but madness is a threatening human possibility that does not haunt philosophy alone.

There is a seriousness of philosophy (its professionalization notwithstanding) that Cavell is committed to honor: skepticism with its extraordinary doubts and strange problems is no exception. Its very insistence and pervasiveness in modern philosophy call for a better understanding of its stakes. But such a better understanding cannot be reached by focusing only on the structure of the arguments, their different strategies, the examples typically chosen, and so on. Such an analysis is necessary, but much more is needed. According to Cavell, to truly grasp what is at stake in skepticism, one has to uncover the presuppositions that shape a specific conception of knowledge and certainty as well as the desires and fears that motivate those conceptions.

Given the aim and scope of Cavell's approach to skepticism, it becomes more intuitive why his readings and analysis are not confined to the canon of philosophy, but include Shakespearean tragedies, Hollywood comedies, and a host of other topics and authors quite unusual for academic philosophers to engage with. The fact is that the significance of the skeptical attitude, for Cavell, invests all the fields of human life, from morality to conversation, from politics to aesthetics and religion. Or to be more precise, skepticism defines an essential aspect of modernity, and one that has not yet been sufficiently explored, let alone overcome. Philosophy certainly plays an important role in what we call, without much agreement on the meaning of the term, "modernity," but so do Shakespeare and cinema.

One can grant to Cavell, without entering too much into the detail of his arguments, that skeptical doubts and attitudes exceed philosophy as a discipline; still the question remains as to how Cavell understands the link between strictly epistemological inquiries about the possibility of knowledge on the one hand, and moral or existential concerns about the possibility or impossibility of reaching out to one another, or to oneself, that make up the fabric of tragedies and comedies, of morality and everyday life on the other hand. His reading of Wittgenstein in *The Claim of Reason* provides some answers to such a question.

Wittgenstein's New Form of Criticism

The pervasiveness of skepticism in modern culture needs to addressed, but the response cannot consist in refuting its thesis. Trying to prove against the skeptic that we can in fact know beyond any doubt that the world and other minds exist is a hopeless pursuit. Cavell's insight is that even if such a "proof" could be established, skepticism would not be defeated because what constitutes its own internal dynamic is precisely to turn the world and others into "objects" of knowledge. All efforts to refute skepticism are doomed to fail since they accept its very premises, without even beginning to question their necessity or inescapability. The response to skepticism, to be effective, has to take a different path: it has to make explicit its implicit assumptions, weigh the image of knowledge it presents us with, uncover the reasons why it has such a grip on us, reveal what obsessions, fears, or desires it so powerfully resonates with. For Cavell, the only possible response is to provide a new interpretation of skepticism that transforms its self-interpretation (*CR* 28). The importance of Wittgenstein's *Philosophical Investigations* consists precisely in opening the path for such a different form of criticism.

From the early reception of the *Investigations* onwards, readers of Wittgenstein have pointed out that his conception of the public nature of language and the emphasis on the examples of pain, sensations, and states of mind seem to be directed by skeptical problems. Many interpreters have concluded that Wittgenstein's analysis of language constitutes an explicit refutation of skepticism. According to this line of reading, Wittgenstein's original contribution to skeptical debates would have been to shift the weight of the argument to *language* rather than, say, sensations, thus making of "grammar" the ground for certainty of knowledge.

Criteria and Judgments

Of particular importance for Cavell's argument are Norman Malcolm and Roger Albritton's early essays on the *Investigations* insofar as they lay out an influential interpretative framework against which Cavell defines his own project.[6] Malcolm and Albritton are the first to read the *Investigations* as a response to skepticism and to emphasize the decisive role of the notion of criteria in such a response. In their view, Wittgenstein, in his remarks on the use of language, uncovers criteria that can establish with certainty the existence of something or other, for instance criteria of pain are the means by which we can know with certainty that someone is in pain. Where symptoms offer mere probability, criteria provide certainty on the double account that being "grammatical" they function as a "sort of definition," and that being "outward" and shared, they undermine skeptical doubts about what is or is not "really going on" inside someone else's mind. Fully embracing the idea that Wittgenstein's answer to skepticism depends on the notion of criteria, Cavell nevertheless parts company with Malcolm and Albritton's interpretation of what criteria are and are meant to do:

> The permanent value of this view lies in its awareness that Wittgenstein's teaching is everywhere controlled by a response to skepticism, or, as I will prefer to say, by a response to the threat of skepticism. The view takes Wittgenstein's motivation with respect to skepticism as that of showing it to be false.... I might put it as the first phase of my argument to show that criteria cannot do this, and on my reading of the *Investigations*, are not meant to. On the contrary, the fate of criteria, or their

limitation, reveals, I should like to say, *the truth of skepticism*—though of course this may require a reinterpretation of what skepticism is, or threatens.

CR 7, emphasis added

However, the answer to the question of what criteria are or are meant to do is not an easy one. True, Wittgenstein describes his investigations as grammatical ones, and eliciting or describing criteria is an essential feature of his method, but as Cavell points out, the rare explicit remarks by Wittgenstein on what he means by "grammar" and "criteria" are rather obscure, and do not offer the best entry into the matter.[7] Cavell finds that a more promising approach is offered by a comparison of the ordinary use of the term with Wittgenstein's: both the similarities and differences between the two help to highlight some essential aspects of Wittgenstein's take on language and grammar.

Using a list of examples that ranges from criteria for the stability of a government set up by American officials to Anna Freud's evaluation of infantile neurosis and to Radcliffe's criteria of excellence for freshman admissions, Cavell remarks that in the ordinary use of the term criteria are a set of conditions, defined by a person or a group, on the basis of which to judge whether something or someone has a particular status or value: for instance, what counts as a stable government under certain circumstances, what are the essential qualities required to be an outstanding college freshman, or what we should call neurotic behavior in a child (*CR* 8–9). All these examples resonate with Wittgenstein's talking about criteria as what is shared, or adopted by certain persons or groups; as what provide a "kind of definition," or show what "count as" something, or what something "consists in." In sum, be it in ordinary language or in the *Investigations*, criteria function as a set of specifications by means of which we can judge whether an object belongs to a certain category. But if the analogy brings us to this point, the disanalogies are equally very telling and bring us a step further.

In the ordinary use of the term, criteria leave an open space for different degrees at which they are satisfied: a government is more or less stable, a child more or less neurotic. We judge whether a child is neurotic according to certain criteria and at the same time we evaluate how neurotic he or she is according to certain standards: the two processes are intimately related but different in principle (*CR* 11). Depending on the context, the reciprocal importance of clarifying either standards or criteria vary dramatically. There are cases, like diving competitions, in which criteria are just straightforward and the discretion of the judge consists only in applying standards: judges may disagree on how well a candidate enters the water but not about the fact that entering the water is the criterion of a dive. In other cases, though, like assessing the stability of a government, standards and criteria are equally decisive: the degree to which a given government is "stable" may be so low that one may judge that, after all, it doesn't fit the criteria of political stability. In any case, the distinction between standards and criteria is a clear and pertinent one. This is not true, though, for Wittgenstein's use of the term:

> In no case in which he [Wittgenstein] appeals to the application of criteria is there a separate stage at which one might, implicitly or explicitly, appeal to the application

of standards. To have criteria, in his sense, for something being so is to know whether, in an individual case, the criteria do or do not apply. If there is doubt about the application, the case is in some way "non-standard." This means that we have no decisive criteria for it, as we haven't for "all eventualities."

CR 13

The reason why Wittgenstein's criteria do not admit degrees in their application is explained by a second difference Cavell draws attention to: in ordinary cases, criteria are applied to objects whose status or ranking clearly require evaluation, and the whole point of establishing criteria is precisely to help arrive at a judgment that is as rational and objective as possible. It is because the value of some objects is manifestly difficult to assess that we set up criteria. But Wittgenstein's objects are not of this kind: he appeals to criteria to determine things such as "'whether someone has a toothache, is sitting on a chair, is of an opinion, whether it's raining'" (*CR* 13). The entire range of familiar activities, from reading to following a rule, from thinking to expecting someone, from believing to meaning, to copying an ellipse, are the "objects" that Wittgensteinian criteria are meant to determine. No wonder then that Wittgenstein never considers the application of standards at a separate stage: someone may have the qualification to apply for a job and nevertheless not be a good enough candidate, but either I am sitting on a chair or I am not. What is puzzling in Wittgenstein's cases is that something has to be judged at all when it comes to these kinds of "objects."

Although Wittgenstein's and ordinary criteria have the same function, that of assessing what "counts as something," the nature of their objects is so dramatically different that one may wonder what Wittgenstein needs criteria for. If some special feature is required to determine what counts as sitting on a chair, then we may think we need criteria for everything we say, for all the concepts and the objects of our world. And indeed, according to Cavell, this is precisely Wittgenstein's insight: that we do need criteria for everything we say, that criteria are the means by which we learn what our concepts are and without which we would not know how to apply our concepts to the objects of the world. Cavell's analysis of criteria aims at making explicit this insight as well as the specific conception of knowledge and language that sustains it.

Two Concepts of Knowledge

To situate Wittgenstein's position, Cavell sketches out two different traditional approaches to the problem of knowledge. One way of asking the philosophical question of what is knowledge, is to focus on the grounds of certainty, on what counts as evidence for our statements, on truth conditions, and the like. Along these lines, knowledge is understood as the sum of true statements, and the limits of knowledge are defined by the amount of true statements about the world we have not yet gathered. The second approach asks a different question, and it is less concerned with evidence and verifiability than it is with how we come to know, how we learn to identify and discriminate different things and objects; it thus focuses on *judgments* rather than on *statements*. In this view, knowledge is first of all a way of mapping out the world conceptually, of establishing the categories, the conceptual schemes, without which there would be neither objects in the world, nor the world itself (for us). The limits of knowledge are accordingly also understood along very different lines: they coincide with the limits of our concepts at a certain time rather than with all the true statements we have not (yet) discovered. The first approach is oriented towards epistemology and thinks of knowledge mainly or paradigmatically as scientific knowledge; the second one is more interested, one could say, in what it takes to become a human. Here is how Cavell describes it:

> The focus upon judgments takes human knowledge to be the human capacity for applying the concepts of a language to the things of a world, for characterizing (categorizing) the world when and as it is humanly done, and hence construes the limits of human knowledge as coinciding with the limits of its concepts (in some historical period). The philosophical task in this case will be to provide an organon which will bring those limits to consciousness – not to show the confinement of our knowledge . . . but to show what in a given period we cannot fail to know, or ways we cannot fail to know in.
>
> CR 17

Wittgenstein clearly belongs to this second line of thought: his emphasis on judgments and criteria is the emphasis on the question of how we come to know, on how we learn to apply the concepts of our language to the objects of the world. His different twist from previous philosophers consists in looking at language rather than, say, at the categories of the understanding, in order to explore how we conceptualize the world, but his investigations of "language games" have the same purpose: to elucidate what makes knowledge possible. According to Cavell, it is this level of questioning that Wittgenstein sets up for himself when he writes that "grammar tells what kind of object anything is" (*PI* §373), making explicit that grammatical investigations are an attempt at elucidating the ways in which we experience the world and categorize objects as we do. If we consider that this is the kind of question about knowledge Wittgenstein wants to address, we can then understand why the "objects" of his analysis are the most common ones. Wittgenstein has no interest in highly specific objects like those we apply criteria to in ordinary cases, something we can do only once the world already has a shape for us; Wittgenstein is interested in things like sitting on a chair, following a rule, or having a toothache because he believes that without criteria, although of a different kind, not even the simplest things could be determined, because he believes that *we need criteria in order to know anything whatsoever*. Rather than focusing on epistemological questions about the verifiability of our (scientific) knowledge, Wittgenstein wants to know what makes a world possible for us in the first place, what criteria we use to elucidate "what kind of object anything is" (*CR* 16–17).

Cavell sees in this regard a strong Kantian strand in Wittgenstein's thought that is important to outline. If the aim of the *Critique of Pure Reason* is, rather traditionally, to foreground the objectivity of knowledge, the way in which Kant thinks the task can be achieved is quite novel. Kant sidesteps the old problem of how to ascertain the correspondence between subjective knowledge and objective reality—which he believes is a deadlock—and moves in an entirely different direction, that of establishing the necessary and universal conditions of the possibility of experience for the kind of beings we happen to be. The subjectivity of knowledge cannot be overcome, but Kant's powerful idea is that subjectivity is not bound to be contingent and relative: reason—which defines subjectivity—is an active faculty, capable of giving to experience the necessary and universally valid contours without which a consistent world could not appear to us.

Crucial to his "Copernican revolution" is Kant's famous introduction of a new kind of judgment: synthetic judgments *a priori*. Traditional logic distinguished two kinds of judgments: analytic and synthetic ones. The first are true independent of experience, by virtue of the meaning of the concepts that they contain; the second are true or false depending on experience, because they affirm something of the subject that is not a matter of definition or meaning. Judgments like "every effect has a cause" or "every widow had a husband," for instance, are analytic because they affirm nothing that is not implied by the meaning of the terms they contain; judgments like "every woman has a husband," on the contrary, require that we check up on reality to assess their truth value. They have opposite virtues: while analytic judgments are necessarily true (*a priori*, in Kant's terminology), they do not teach us anything about the world; synthetic judgments, on the contrary, are informative, but they hold no necessity (they are *a posteriori*, in Kant's terminology). Kant's third kind of judgments, those that are synthetic *a priori*, are defined as combining the precious qualities of being *both* necessarily true *and* informative about experience. Kant's idea that some judgments are simultaneously synthetic (informative) and *a priori* (universally necessary) conveys his central insight that reason is an *active faculty*, capable of establishing *by itself* the conditions of possibility of experience. Obviously, synthetic judgments *a priori* don't legislate upon the *content* of what we experience, but they lay out a conceptual framework that gives to experience consistency, and hence makes it possible, that is to say thinkable and knowable. A judgment like "every event has a cause" is a helpful example to grasp Kant's point. Unlikely the analytic judgment "every effect has a cause" —which is a matter of definition: we call "effect" what is produced by a "cause"—it informs us of something that is not a matter of meaning only, hence has to be considered synthetic, both for Kant and traditional logic. But Kant, against the tradition, would argue that "every event has a cause" is not a judgment that is true *a posteriori*, once we have repeatedly observed that events do in fact have causes; according to him, it is true *before* experience, in the sense that it does not depend upon what we encounter in experience but, rather, it structures experience, it categorizes the way in which the facts of the world make sense for us, enabling something like a world to exist for us.

Cavell sums up Kant's new logic of judgments as a response to the traditional problem of the objectivity of knowledge by highlighting that for Kant: "judgments can be true *of the world* (of anything we can call a world) *necessarily*, before our experience of the world, necessary to our experience of the world" (*CW* 123, Cavell's emphases). To say it otherwise, without the capacity of making a specific kind of non-empirical judgment, there would be no experience at all; the world would not appear to us as a world. This new kind of judgment belong to what Kant calls the *transcendental* logic, a logic that is not concerned with truth conditions but, rather, with establishing the categories that make experience as such possible and without which nothing could be either true or false.

Wittgenstein's *Investigations*, in Cavell's reading, also aim at understanding the conditions of possibility of a world, as some of his remarks that echo Kant's terminology suggest, for instance:

> We feel as if we had to *penetrate* phenomena: our investigation, however, is directed not towards phenomena, but, as one might say, towards the *"possibilities"* of phenomena.
>
> PI §90, Wittgenstein's emphases

Like Kant, Wittgenstein is not concerned with facts or phenomena, but with what makes the facts and phenomena of the world possible, with the "essence of everything empirical." Wittgenstein's grammatical investigations, though, also have striking differences with Kant's transcendental logic. Wittgenstein's criteria, like Kant's categories, tell us what our concepts are, and hence what kind of object anything is (*PI* §373), but, unlike Kant's categories, they do not frame in advance any possible experience. Wittgenstein's criteria are not *a priori* available for all eventualities: if they frame a world, *it is a world open to change, and a world that we do not necessarily share*, as we will discuss shortly. Cavell's Wittgenstein has a strong transcendental vein, an ongoing interest in what makes knowledge possible in the first place, rather than in methods to increase our knowledge or procedures to verify it. Yet his "transcendentalism" is a very peculiar one, one that does not aim at, or believe in, uncovering the conditions of possibility of everything that may or may not occur. Wittgenstein wants rather to reveal or make explicit the conditions of what we actually say and do, and what we actually say and do does not cover the logical space of "all eventualities." In this regard, Wittgenstein's method of imagining different language games is very significant: it highlights, among other things, the contingency of our words and actions, it explores alternative possibilities, and it invites us to consider the open-ended nature of our language.

Wittgenstein's Objects

Before discussing further the importance Wittgenstein's difference from Kant has for Cavell, more needs to be said about how grammar and criteria accomplish their quasi-transcendental function of telling 'what object anything is.' A passage from *The Blue Book* gives a fairly striking example of Wittgenstein's use of grammar and criteria:

> It is part of the grammar of the world "chair" that *this* is what we call "to sit on a chair," and it is part of the grammar of the word "meaning" that *this* is what we call

"explanation of a meaning"; in the same way to explain my criterion for another person's having a toothache is to give a grammatical explanation about the word "toothache" and, in this sense, an explanation concerning the meaning of the word "toothache."[8]

As a way of approaching what Wittgenstein wants to suggest in this passage, as in so many others, Cavell emphasizes the role of the expression "what we call" and engages in an attempt to further sketch out the grammar of the word "chair." His exercise deserves to be quoted at length:

> That you use this object *that* way, sit on it *that* way, is our criterion for calling it a chair. You *can* sit on a cigarette, or on a thumb tack, or on a flag pole, but not in *that* way. Can you sit on a table or on a tree stump in that (the "grammatical") way? Almost, especially if they are placed against a wall. That is you can *use* a table or a stump as a chair (a place to sit; a seat) in a way you cannot use a tack as a chair. But so you can use a screw-driver as a dagger; that won't make a screw-driver a dagger. What can *serve as a chair* is not a chair and nothing would (be said to) serve as a chair if there were no (were nothing we called) (orthodox) chairs. We could say: It is part of the grammar of the word "chair" that *this* is what we call "to serve as a chair."
>
> The force of such remarks is something like: If don't know all this, and more, you don't know what a chair is; what "chair" means; what we call a chair; *what* it is you would be certain of (or almost certain of, or doubt very much) if you were certain (or almost certain of, or doubt very much) that something is a chair.
>
> CR 71

In expanding and giving some content to Wittgenstein's pure outline of what a grammatical description is, Cavell succeeds in highlighting some important aspects of Wittgenstein's vision of language. Namely, that in order to know what a chair is, we need to know many other things, and that the difference between what a thing is, and what it is called, is sometimes, *but not always*, an obvious one. In order to unpack these points, let us return to the comparison between Wittgenstein's and ordinary criteria.

Both Wittgenstein's and ordinary criteria are marks of identification or recognition, and in both cases learning what a thing is called is an essential part of our capacity to identify and recognize objects, but the ways in which they relate names and things are very different. If I do not know the name of a specific tree, I can ask someone who is more knowledgeable than I am in these matters, or pick up a book, or google and learn that that specific shape and color of leaves characterize a silver birch. I have learned now what is the name of that tree in the back of the garden, I have learned what it is. Ordinary criteria provide a set of specifications that tell us what a particular thing is, or is called: they *relate a name to an object*. Wittgenstein's criteria, on the other hand, describe a field of relations, show that learning what an object is (called) takes more than learning a word, that naming is neither the only nor the primary function of language. Wittgenstein's criteria, or grammatical criteria, as Cavell also suggests calling them, tell us what an object is by showing how *different concepts are related to the concept of an object*, by sketching the conceptual framework that is relevant.

The difference in the ways in which ordinary and grammatical criteria identify objects corresponds to the difference in the kind of objects they aim at. Wittgenstein's "objects" are the most common ones, the kind of objects no one needs a special training to be acquainted with: Cavell calls them "generic objects" as opposed to the "specific objects" of ordinary criteria.[9] To know what a generic object is, a chair, a bird, the meaning of a word, is very different from knowing what a specific object is, a Louis XVI chair, a goldfinch, or the meaning of "moose" in English. The first kind of knowledge requires that we possess various concepts, that we have learned which concepts are relevant in different contexts, and that we know how to use them in relation to the concepts of different kinds of objects. We learn what a specific object is by relating a name to a thing, but only because we already have a conceptual space to situate this new object in (*CR* 73). Wittgenstein's criteria describe a conceptual landscape in which empirical experience becomes possible, in which we can learn new things and their names because we already have the concepts of what names and objects, words and meanings, chairs and trees, are. In summarizing the difference of level at which grammatical and ordinary criteria operate, Cavell makes the Kantian tone of the *Investigations* resonate strongly:

> The general relation between these notions of a criterion is roughly this: If you do not know the (non-grammatical) criteria of an Austinian object (can't identify it, name it) then you lack a piece of information, a bit of knowledge, and you can be told its name, told what it is, told what it is (officially) called. But if you do not know the grammatical criteria of Wittgensteinian objects, then you lack, as it were, not only a piece of knowledge, but the possibility of acquiring any information about such objects *überhaupt*; you cannot be told the name of that object, because there is as yet no *object* of that kind for you to attach a forthcoming name to: the possibility of finding out what it is officially called is not yet open to you. (To *what* does the child attach the name <Nyuw York>? The child's world contains no cities.) This is, I take it, part of what Wittgenstein wished to suggest in saying that "Essence is expressed by grammar": You have to know *certain* things about an object in order to know *anything* (else) about it (about *it*).
>
> CR 77, Cavell's emphases

But how does the child, that is to say all of us, acquire the capacity to conceptualize the world? What opens for us the possibility of acquiring knowledge as such, and hence of asking what a specific thing is, or is called, of adding bits of information to those we already possess? Such questions mark the difference between Wittgenstein's and Kant's approach at the very point of their proximity. From a strictly Kantian perspective, this kind of question cannot even arise: it is reason in its universality and necessity that gives to experience a conceptual shape. How a child becomes, or fails to become, a reasonable being is of no interest for transcendental philosophy, although it can be a legitimate topic for psychology or some other discipline. Wittgenstein, though, is not committed to any transcendental or transhistorical notion of reason, is not committed to the idea of a universal foundation, logical or otherwise, of knowledge: for him the question of how we learn to conceptualize the world is an urgent one, and replying that it is language that "does the job" is simply missing the point. True, Wittgenstein does not believe that we could think without or outside language, nor that language is a mere translation of ideas, thoughts, and emotions that have no need for words to be formed, but only to be communicated and remembered. But assuming that it is "language" rather than "thought" or "reason" that provides the conceptual framework for the world, is not as such an answer to the question of how we learn to speak, and particularly not for Wittgenstein, who takes language to rest upon the most fragile foundations, as we shall discuss shortly. To put it differently: replacing the universality of reason with language, when language itself has no universality of its own, turns the question of how we learn to speak into a *philosophical problem*, and brings the figure of the child to the center of the stage.[10]

The Child

Cavell, indeed, sees the question of the child, of how language is inherited and acquired, as central to Wittgenstein's vision of language. Wittgenstein famously opens the *Philosophical Investigations* with a quote from Augustine's *Confessions* that provides a condensed picture of most of the assumptions about language that he considers deeply misleading, like the idea that all words are names, that learning a word is being told its meaning, or that learning a language is a matter of learning new words. In this passage, Augustine recounts how he learned to speak from his elders by repeatedly watching them uttering words and moving towards objects, thus gradually understanding what objects those words signified, and later training himself to form the same sounds to express his own desires.[11] What strikes Wittgenstein in this passage is that Augustine describes the child as an adult who ended up in a country of which he doesn't know the language while being already familiar with everything else: the existence of human meanings, expressions, desires, words, actions; as if coming into language for the first time would be no different than learning a foreign language for an already speaking human being. In other words, Augustine forgoes the child altogether:

> Someone coming into a strange country will sometime learn the language of the inhabitants from ostensive definitions that they give him; and he will often have to *guess* the meaning of these definitions; and will guess sometime right, sometimes wrong.
>
> And now, I think, we can say: Augustine describes the learning of human language as if the child came into a strange country and did not understand the language of the country; that is, as if it already had a language, only not this one. Or again: as if the child could already *think*, only not yet speak. And "think" would here mean something like "talk to itself."
>
> PI §32, Wittgenstein's emphases

A comprehensive discussion of Wittgenstein's criticism of traditional assumptions about language and of the alternative views he proposes is obviously beyond the scope of this essay, but some points need to be highlighted. Construing the child as a little adult, ignoring the difference of childhood, has several consequences, one of the most important being that it leads to ignore the fact that learning how to speak, being initiated into language, is being initiated into a whole form of life to which language belongs but which it does not exhaust. Traditional philosophers explain how language functions by appealing to intellectualized notions like universals, rules, and the like, thus obscuring basic facts about human language that the figure of the child helps to emphasize but that are true of all speakers, regardless of age: namely, the fact that we learn words in *certain* contexts, not in all possible ones, because no such thing exists, and that after a while we are expected to project those words appropriately in *different* contexts, and the fact that this capacity is neither explained nor guaranteed by the philosophical notion of universals (*CR* 168–69; *PI* §73).

Let us take Cavell's example of a child learning a new word. The situation is familiar enough: we point to the kitty and tell the child in an inviting way, "This is a kitty"; after some time she looks at the kitty and says, "Kitty," and we smile and kiss her, we rejoice because she has learned a new word. The day after, the example more or less goes, the child points at a fur and says, "Kitty"; we are disappointed: maybe she has not learned the word after all, she does not yet understand what a kitty is, or maybe she means something that we should translate as "It looks like a kitty," "Look at the funny kitty," or "Aren't soft things nice?" (*CR* 172). How can we know, how can we decide? Is there a point in deciding at all? Certainly not for Cavell, who sees the moral of the little story to be of a different order altogether. What the child has learned is to pronounce the word about a soft, warm, furry kind of object: she has learned to make a leap from one context to another, and the capacity of making such leaps is what will allow her to "walk[] into speech" (*CR* 172).

If we compare this with Augustine's narrative, the differences couldn't be starker. Cavell's child does not exactly learn the meaning of the word "kitty" any more than what a "kitty" exactly is, she does not learn the specific name of a specific object, and even more importantly, she is not left alone, looking at her elders. She is addressed, smiled at, encouraged in making the leaps necessary to learn how to speak: she is introduced and accompanied in her steps into speech. Thinking, as Augustine suggests, that learning a language is a matter of learning new words, and that learning a word is a matter of being told what it means, or of "grasping an universal," is an overly intellectualized picture that fails to recognize that language is *inherited*, that the child learn *from us*, and that learning "words" and "meanings" is being introduced into a *form of life* (*CR* 177). Cavell emphasizes the importance of acknowledging that the child does not merely learn "the names of things," but also what names and things are, what words are and do, what calling, pointing at an object, expressing a wish or an emotion are in the world we inhabit and share:

When you say "I love my love" the child learns the meaning of the word "love" and what love is. *That (what you do)* will *be* love in the child's world; and if it is mixed with resentment and intimidation, then love is a mixture of resentment and intimidation, and when love is sought *that* will be sought. When you say "I'll take you tomorrow, I promise", the child will begin to learn what temporal durations are, and what *trust* is, and what you do will show what trust is worth.... Of course the person, growing, will learn other things about these concepts and "objects" also. They will grow gradually as the child's world grows. But all he or she knows about them is what he or she has learned, and *all* they have learned will be part of what they are. And what will the day be like when the person "realizes" what he "believed" about what love and trust and authority are? And how will he stop believing it? What we learn is not just what we have studied; and what we have been taught is not just what we were intended to learn. What we have in our memories is not just what we have memorized.

CR 177

All of this and much more is implied in learning to speak, and this is why Cavell suggests that rather than imagining that we teach children the meaning of words, or what things are, we acknowledge that we initiate them into a form of life, asking them to follow us in what we do and say, in sharing with us the sense of what comfort or pain are, of what expresses love and what reproach, of what is funny or sad. For such an initiation to "succeed" we have to respond to and accept what the child tentatively says and does, not shun away from her when she makes an "inappropriate leap" as well as the child must want to follow us "naturally," liking a smile better than a slap, or looking at our finger point when we point out to an object rather than the other way round (*CR* 178).[12]

In an important sense what is true of the child, for Cavell, is true of grown-ups as well: learning is never over. The figure of the child dramatically highlights the fact that the use of language is nowhere fully directed by rules or secured by universals: if we learn words in certain contexts and after we have to use them in different contexts, there is no reason to assume that there are pre-established limits to what can or cannot be said, to what projections, or "leaps," can or cannot be made. New contexts, new affects, needs or desires, new objects and perceptions can always emerge: our words are open, and have to be open, to a new life, capable of expressing new experiences, of disclosing the world differently. Wittgenstein's notion of grammar, in Cavell's reading, conveys the sense of how intimately related our concepts are among themselves and with the "objects" of our world, hence the idea that language belongs to a form of life. But Wittgenstein's vision of language, and of forms of life, does not take the relatedness of words and things as being sustained by any logical or transcendental ground; on the contrary it underlies the lack of meta-foundations and the open-ended character of what we say and do. In his early essay "The Availability of Wittgenstein's Later Philosophy," Cavell openly and forcefully sums up his view:

> We learn and teach words in certain contexts, and then we are expected, and expect others, to be able to project them into further contexts. Nothing insures that this

projection will take place (in particular, not the grasping of universals nor the grasping of books of rules), just as nothing insures that we will make, and understand, the same projections. That on the whole we do is a matter of our sharing routes of interest and feeling, modes of response, senses of humor and of significance and of fulfillment, of what is outrageous, of what is similar to what else, what a rebuke, what forgiveness, of when an utterance is an assertion, when an appeal, when an explanation—all the whirl of organism Wittgenstein calls "forms of life." Human speech and activity, sanity and community, rest upon nothing more, but nothing less, than this. It is a vision as simple as it is difficult, and as difficult as it is (and because it is) terrifying.

MWM 52

Like Kant, Wittgenstein seeks to uncover the conditions of possibility of knowledge and experience but, unlike Kant, he sees those conditions as *human*, nothing more and nothing less than human. The grammatical criteria he describes do not have the normative force of transcendental or universal rules that all reasonable beings (should) share no matter how different from us they might be—living on faraway planets, with alien bodies or with no bodies at all.[13] Their force is to point out how intertwined and pervasive our concepts are—and in this sense they are "grammatical"—but they rely on nothing else than shared human attitudes and responses, on what Cavell calls our *attunement*. In this respect, Wittgenstein's insistence on the human sets him apart from the later Heidegger's conception of language to whom he is often compared; true, none of us creates his or her own language, we inherit it and in this sense language precedes us, as well as it is essential to our inhabiting the world, but these similarities should not hide a deeper difference: for Wittgenstein, contrary to Heidegger, it is always *us* who speak, language as such does not have the power of opening the world, it emerges *from within* a form of life:

> It is what human beings *say* that is true or false; and they agree in the *language* they use. That is not agreement in opinions but in form of life.[14]

Criteria do not explain—let alone prove—that the possibility of human language rests on the immanence of a form of life rather than on a transcendent set of universals: they are a *description* of this fact, the reminder of the presence of the human in what is said, done, and known. For Cavell, to understand why such a description is necessary at all, or how it comes about that the presence of the human has to be recalled constitutes Wittgenstein's true response to skepticism and its power to reinterpret the very terms of the problem, as we are about to see.

Wittgenstein's Response to Skepticism: The Problem Has Changed

Cavell's analysis of criteria brings him to highlight their descriptive character: rather than providing a foundation or even an explanation of our agreement in language, they merely describe this fact; they show how we apply our concepts, how we learn words in certain contexts and later we project them in new contexts. But the fact that we agree in language to a surprising extent is nothing but a fact: criteria give no guarantee, they are necessarily open to repudiation, having no power to define in advance what projections will be accepted, and what will not. But if criteria cannot even provide a secure foundation for language, if they constantly redirect our attention from the sublime realm of logic to the fact that it is we, humans, who speak, what can they do, if anything, against skeptical doubts? What is the relation between skepticism and criteria understood along these lines? And, more generally, what response to skepticism can Wittgenstein offer from the perspective of such a vision of language so unrestrainedly exposed to human contingencies?

From everything we have discussed so far, it should be apparent that criteria cannot refute skepticism by proving with certainty that something or other, this hand, your pain, the outside world, "really" exists. But we can also begin to see for what reasons Cavell can argue that they are not meant to: if his reading of the *Investigations* is correct, if criteria do indeed expose the absence of transcendental or logical foundations of language and describe how it rests only on a shared form of life, it is highly unlikely that Wittgenstein aimed at any refutation of skepticism along traditional lines. What remains to be discussed, though, is in what sense Wittgenstein's vision of language provides a reinterpretation of skepticism capable of transforming the problem, which is, let us remember, the most important point Cavell wants to make.

Cavell's argument in this regard relies on a further exploration of two ideas we have already encountered in the discussion of criteria: namely, that the presence of the human cannot be overcome in the use of language by sets of rules or universals on the one hand, and that the concept of knowledge Wittgenstein is interested in deals with the possibility of conceptualizing the world, with the conditions upon which something like a world can be experienced by us, on the other hand. This second idea implies that Wittgenstein's engagement with the problem of knowledge is situated at the same level as that of the skeptic: what is at stake, in both cases, is the possibility of knowledge in general, of knowledge as such, rather than procedures to verify the truth value of statements or the discovery of new facts. The spirit in which Wittgenstein addresses this question couldn't be more different than the skeptic's, but sharing the level at which the question is raised allows Wittgenstein to take skepticism seriously, to engage with its problems and provide a different picture of what they are about rather than simply dismissing it or attempting to refute it. The first idea, on the other hand, will sustain what I would like to call a symptomatic or therapeutic reading of skepticism: a way of bringing to the fore the implicit assumptions of the skeptic's position along with what motivates them, the threats, fears, and wishes that keep skepticism alive. Needless to say, the two ideas are deeply interconnected and the coherence and persuasiveness of Wittgenstein's position depend on how the one completes the other. For the sake of exposition, though, I will discuss in the first place in what sense for Cavell Wittgenstein and the skeptic address the problem of knowledge at the same level.

Knowledge as Revelatory of the World

To clarify this point, Cavell compares Austin's and Wittgenstein's very different attitudes towards skepticism and the role of criteria in countering it. Austin shares with Wittgenstein the mistrust of a traditional style of philosophical speculation and the insistence on the necessity of a context for making sense of what we say, but these similarities only highlight the striking difference of their positions on what counts as an answer to skeptical doubts depending on how one envisions the problem of knowledge.

Cavell focuses in particular on Austin's influential essay "Other Minds," where the latter undertakes to refute skeptical arguments from the perspective of ordinary language philosophy and its methods. His strategy is to discuss what we say in ordinary contexts to either support or contest claims to knowledge to show the emptiness of the skeptical attitude. The examples Austin discusses are assertions like "there is a goldfinch in the garden," of which he sketches grounds for doubt as well as possible justifications, drawing a typology of what constitutes pertinent answers to the question "How do you know?" depending on the context. In the case of the goldfinch, for instance, one may doubt my identification because of some features of the bird (the color of the head, the size, etc.), or because it is very dark and my vision at night is far from perfect and the like. Austin thus describes several ways of doubting my statement depending on the circumstances to which correspond plausible ways of justifying it, but, he argues, when all the alternative competitive identifications of the bird are ruled out, the conversation has to stop because "enough is enough," and for "all practical purposes" we know that the bird in the garden is a goldfinch.[15]

Obviously, Austin is aware that the traditional philosopher will want to insist that I cannot be absolutely certain that the creature in the garden is a "real" goldfinch because it may turn out to be stuffed, or a mirage, or I may be dreaming or hallucinating, etc. But the problem with such familiar arguments, in his view, is that they mistakenly assume that "real" has a single meaning, one that is absolutely defined regardless of any context, where the truth is that "real" has a variety of different meanings depending on what it is opposed to and means nothing whatsoever without some specification. A "real" goldfinch is a goldfinch which is not stuffed, or hallucinated, but in all these cases there are specific procedures to distinguish "real" from "not real": we know how to distinguish dreaming from waking, mirages from hallucinations or perceptions. The skeptic fails to see this plurality of specific meanings and, as a consequence, her doubts are empty because there is no context, ordinary or extraordinary, to make them plausible; not even the unlikely event of a miracle would do justice to the skeptic's suspension of certitude:

> "Being sure it's real" is no more proof against miracles or outrages of nature than anything else is or, *sub specie humanitatis*, can be. If we have made sure it's a goldfinch, and then in the future it does something outrageous (explodes, quotes Mrs. Woolf, or what not), we don't say we were wrong to say it was a goldfinch, *we don't know what to say*. . . . When I have made sure it's a real goldfinch (not stuffed,

corroborated by the disinterested, &c.) then I am *not* "predicting" in saying it's a real goldfinch, and in a very good sense I can't be proved wrong whatever happens. It seems a serious mistake to suppose that language (or most language, language about real things) is "predictive" in such a way that the future can always prove it wrong. What the future *can* always do, is to make us *revise our ideas* about goldfinches or real goldfinches or anything else.[16]

The argument is compelling, but it is compelling only if we think of knowledge as identification or recognition, as Austin does in his analysis of the pertinent ways to answer the question "How do you know?," which are all meant to provide features, or marks of identity, and justify the speaker's competence to recognize those marks. What is at stake for Austin, as Cavell observes, are criteria for recognition in the ordinary sense of the term: sets of features that allow us to name and identify a specific object, learn what it is or what it is called: that this bird is a goldfinch and not a bittern for example (*CR* 50). Under such a conception of knowledge as identification, the question of reality or existence plays no role: criteria are meant to identify, categorize objects by means of some marks or conceptual features, but existence or reality has no feature whatsoever. From Kant's refutation of the ontological proof of the existence of God to Frege's logic, modern philosophy has recognized that existence is not a predicate and that nothing in the concept of an object can determine whether it exists or not. As Cavell writes:

> There are (can be) no criteria for something being a real X over and above the criteria for its being an X. Or to repeat: There are no criteria for a thing *being* so over and above the criteria for its being *so*.
>
> CR 51

For Cavell, Austin's analysis helps to see that *criteria as such*—be it in the ordinary, Austinian, or Wittgensteinian sense of the term—have *in principle* no power whatsoever to settle skeptical doubts because these doubts concern the "real existence" of something and not its identification, but existence or reality have no specific qualities or aspects that could be identified or recognized with appropriate criteria. But for that very same reason Austin's argument misses its target because the skeptic is *not* concerned with knowledge as identification.

The skeptic knows like anyone else that for "all practical purposes enough is enough," in a sense she knows it even better than anyone else. Her worries are not about goldfinches that may turn out to recite Ms. Woolf; she is not afraid of miracles or freaks of nature any more than she is preoccupied with English birds. What drives skeptical doubts is the fear that the most familiar objects, in the most ordinary contexts—where precisely no question of identification can arise—may be deceitful. I cannot even know with certainty that I am sitting in front of my fireplace dressed in a nightgown, that this body is mine, or that I have a body at all. Remarks about goldfinches cannot answer these doubts, and more importantly they cannot even begin to ask where these kinds of questions come from, what motivates them, what makes make them sound interesting, let alone compelling.

The skeptic is concerned with—or haunted by—the possibility of the *failure of knowledge as such*. She worries about some intrinsic unknowability of the world and not about specific domains of reality that one may happen to ignore or misrecognize: what's at stake for her is the *possibility of knowing in general, not the possibility of knowing something in particular*. This is why the objects chosen by the skeptic as exemplary are always and necessarily the most common and generic ones: chairs, hands, fireplaces, someone's pain—all sort of objects about which we can feel that if we do not know *this*, then we cannot be sure of anything else. Austin's very choice of examples, on the other hand, shows his unwillingness or incapacity to seriously engage with skepticism: specific objects—like particular birds, flowers, or antique chairs—could never trigger a truly skeptical doubt because in order to be identified, named, or recognized they require some specific knowledge or training. My failure to identify a goldfinch speaks to my ignorance of birds, or to my lack of interest in even basic ornithology, but it does not speak to the possibility of the *failure of knowledge as such*, just as my correct identification does not prove the reliability of knowledge. The level at which Austin takes the problem of knowledge is so different from the skeptic's that his remark that 'enough is enough' lacks any power of conviction for anyone who has ever come to feel the temptation of skepticism.

Wittgenstein, on the other hand, shares with the Cartesian tradition the problem of understanding the general relation of knowledge to the world. The two approaches are certainly different, but they both think of knowledge in the first place as *revelatory of the world*, rather than as procedures for the identification of particular things (*CR* 224). This is why, in Cavell's reading, Wittgenstein's criteria are about the very same common, generic objects that constitute the skeptic's paradigmatic objects of inquiry. If what is at stake in knowledge, prior to any scientific or otherwise specialized pursuit, is the possibility of relating to the world as such, then what has to be investigated in the first place are the most basic categories and objects of experience. Questions of identification of specific objects, like those discussed by Austin and by ordinary criteria, are made possible by the fact that something like a world is available, they can occur only when a world is already open to us and, in this regard, they are irrelevant for Wittgenstein as well as for the skeptic.

The common ground between Wittgenstein and the Cartesian tradition, though, stops at this point: Wittgenstein's problem is to bring to light how our knowledge can be *of* the world, not to establish beyond any possible doubt whether the world and its objects are *real*. This is why his criteria, like Austin's, are about identification and not about reality or existence even though, unlike Austin's, they aim at identifying *generic* objects and not *specific* ones. In this sense Wittgenstein not only renounces the quest for a proof of the existence of the world and of other minds, but he even grants the skeptic that such a proof is impossible, and by doing so shifts the terms of the debate:

> Wittgenstein's appeal to criteria, though it takes its importance from skepticism, is not, and is not meant to be, a refutation of skepticism. Not, at least, in the form we had thought a refutation must take. *That is, it does not negate the concluding thesis of skepticism, that we do not know with certainty of the existence of the external*

world (*or of other minds*). *On the contrary, Wittgenstein, as I read him, rather affirms that thesis, or rather takes it as undeniable, and so shifts its weight.* What that thesis now means is something like: Our relation to the world as a whole, or to others in general, is not one of knowing, where knowing construe itself as being certain. So it is also true that we do not *fail* to know such things.

CR 45, first emphasis added

By granting the skeptic his "concluding thesis," Wittgenstein shifts its weight because he challenges the very premises of the argument: if the existence of the world and of others cannot be proved it is not because of a failure or limitation of knowledge, but because the world and others are not "objects" of knowledge. The problem with skepticism is precisely that it construes the world and others as objects of an epistemic quest for certainty, and the problem with any attempt to refute it is that it necessarily has to concede, hence reaffirm, these very premises. It is at this point that Wittgenstein's conception of knowledge as revelatory of the world radically parts company with the skeptic's in so far as it constantly recalls the unavoidable presence of the human in any and all acts of knowledge.

Presence of the Human or Metaphysical Solitude

Wittgenstein's elucidation of criteria presents an alternative—and competitive— picture of the relation of knowledge to the world, one in which the investigation of "what object anything is" proves to be inseparable from the human form of life. Wittgenstein's insistence on the necessary connection between knowledge and the human counters, in Cavell's reading, a fundamental—albeit unnoticed—presupposition of skepticism, namely that knowledge not only tolerates, but rather demands a *metaphysical solitude*.

To put it in other terms, the Cartesian framework has produced a quest for certainty that is pervasive, that cannot be satisfied unless it covers the possibility of knowledge as such, and hence gives to questions of existence or reality their haunting power and to skepticism its *raison d'être*: it will never be enough to know *what* something is unless I can prove that it *really* is, that it *exists*. No argument along Austinian lines, affirming that we do in fact have grounds to know *what* something is, can challenge the power of this picture of knowledge because it does not even try to undo the link between certainty and reality that makes it compelling. But what could satisfy a quest for certainty bound to be a quest for reality? What is the skeptic, knowingly or unknowingly, hoping for? What would her dream look like if it were to come true?

The desire to prove that the outside world exists, that this is really my hand, that I have a body and you have a soul, is the desire to establish an absolute firm connection with a world that has become an object rather than the place we dwell in, and an *outside* object, one that we are sealed off from. The Cartesian cogito can achieve a fragile ground of certainty in its "I think, I am," but only at the prize of losing any connection with the outside and everything that inhabits it—be it my own body, or anyone else's mind: the truth of the cogito is a metaphysical solitude. What saves Descartes is the idea of God, an idea that not only allows the reconstruction of the whole system of knowledge on sound bases, but also ensures that I am not alone, that the divine Other is there and because of his presence I can trust my fellow human creatures to really be what they look like: other humans, and not just soulless machines. But when the existence of God himself becomes impossible to prove with Hume, and even more with Kant, or otherwise lacks any power of conviction, the Cartesian picture of knowledge cannot escape an absolute solitude (*CR* 220). Descartes's insistence in the *Meditations* on the need to be alone to pursue his philosophical enterprise may be considered a narrative device, but, regardless of Descartes's intentions, it expresses a necessary condition of his philosophy and of the tradition he inaugurates. The skeptic is by necessity, if not in fact, alone: sealed off from the world and from others, she attempts to look at the outside from her interiority, to escape from it and gain the vision and the knowledge of a world of objects as they are in themselves, indifferent to and unmoved by her presence (*CR* 224).

Such demands imposed upon the conditions of knowledge express, for Cavell, the dream or the desire to escape from the burden of being human and the responsibilities that come with it:

> The wish underlying this fantasy [of necessary inexpressiveness] covers a wish that underlies skepticism, a wish for the connection between my claims of knowledge and the objects upon which the claims are to fall to occur without my intervention, apart from my agreements. As the wish stands, it is unappeasable.[17]

The modern skeptic states her problem in purely epistemic terms, but Cavell's diagnosis, sustained by his reading of the *Philosophical Investigations*, is that more is at stake than epistemology. The concept of knowledge that foregrounds skepticism implies the wish for an absolute transparence of the world and its objects that has as its counterpart the equally absolute irrelevance of human agency, procedures, interests, and motives. The certainty that the skeptic is aiming at could only be achieved if human knowledge would vanish and be replaced by the pure gaze of an indifferent spectator, a spectator without a body or soul, who looks at the world from an unbridgeable distance. Such a wish is a denial of the human condition, of the fact that we humans have bodies and souls, live in a world, are separate from each other, are born and will die. The skeptic's quest, for Cavell, thus expresses a denial of human finitude that is not triggered by disinterested epistemological concerns only, but also and more deeply by the wish to escape the responsibility that comes with the human condition. If the certainty of knowledge can only be secured without my intervention, it may never be secured but, by the same token, I am not responsible for what I know or fail to know; to say it otherwise, the standards are so high that they cannot be met, but then whatever I do or do not do does not really matter: I am powerless but *innocent*.

What disentangles knowledge from the quest for certainty about reality in Wittgenstein is the constant reminder that knowledge is a *human* pursuit, that language is shared, that criteria are *ours*. Maybe nothing is more human than the desire to escape the human condition, but the force of Wittgenstein's philosophy is precisely to bring to light what implicitly motivates skepticism as an attempt to deny the human conditions of knowledge and hence explain both its significance as a human temptation and the impossibility of either proving or disproving its thesis in a purely epistemic mood. Wittgenstein's insistence on the shared nature of language does not imply, though, that the possibilities of solitude or radical disagreement are ruled out: quite to the contrary, Wittgenstein is permanently aware that criteria can fail or be repudiated, leaving us exposed to the loss of words we can share. But the solitude that the failure of criteria may produce is altogether different in nature from the skeptic's metaphysical isolation and points in the direction of a different concept of reason.

Agreement and Its Limits: the Possibility of Tragedy

For Cavell's interpretation of Wittgenstein, it is of the utmost importance to realize that the notions of attunement or agreement in a form of life do not replace transcendental or logical foundations of language with some notion of a "human nature" that would guarantee the same kind of (presumed) stability. If it is true that the elucidation of criteria always appeals to what "we" say, where "we" refers to human beings in general, it does not follow that the "we" in question is not endowed with any nature or substance but is instead as precarious as attunement itself. This is a point Cavell analyzes in his comparison between the use of criteria in ordinary contexts and in the *Investigations* that we haven't discussed yet. To the different kinds of objects criteria are applied to in the two cases, corresponds a complementary difference in the source of authority that establishes the criteria. Unsurprisingly, the need to assess specific objects and situations calls for an equally specific source of authority endowed—in principle if not in fact—with some required competence (the US military, Anna Freud, etc.). But Wittgenstein's generic objects do not call for any qualification other than being a speaking human: criteria are upheld by "us" only. Then the question obviously arises of what justifies Wittgenstein's analyses, of what gives him the right to speak for everyone else, of affirming that what *he* says "we say" is indeed what humans in general say. This objection, though, presupposes that Wittgenstein proceeds by *generalization*, in which case his analyses would indeed be preposterous, when in fact for Cavell Wittgenstein's method is to advance instances or samples of criteria, "invitations" for others to see whether they have the same uses (*CR* 19). Wittgenstein's procedure is thus more akin to the case of the modernist artist who can never be assured her work will be recognized as art than to that of a linguist collecting data.

Not only is Wittgenstein acutely aware that other groups or humans may in fact *not* agree with what "we say," but he also shows that no instance can refute another, that what *I* say has no more normative power than what *you* say, that we are all authoritative in this domain and, as a consequence, no one is in principle in a better position than anyone else to establish what counts as the "true" grammar of "our" language.

Contrary to many readers of Wittgenstein who insist on the publicity and conventionality of language as a secure device to achieve agreement, Cavell remarks that the possibility of disagreement is as fundamental a topic in the *Investigations* as the elucidation of criteria. Indeed the two are inseparable: if there is no foundation for language other than our attunement, nothing can insure that we will understand each other in all possible circumstances, that interests and feelings will always take the same route. To put it differently: claiming that there is nothing "beyond us" to guarantee that we share a language does not imply that "we" become the ultimate ground for the certainty and stability of meaning; it implies, and it is a very different claim, that whenever agreement cannot be reached, there is no "us" at all, and "we" cannot speak for one another. As Cavell writes:

> But if the disagreement persists, there is no appeal beyond us, or if beyond us two, then not beyond some eventual us. There is such a thing as intellectual tragedy. It is not a matter of saying something false. Nor is it an inability or refusal to say something or to hear something, from which other tragedies may spring. . . . At such a crossroads we have to conclude that on this point we are simply different; that is, we cannot here speak for one another. But no claim has been made which has been disconfirmed; my authority has been restricted. Even if Wittgenstein had (and it is significant he did not) introduced the ungrammatical wish by saying "We would like to say . . .", then when it turns out that I should not like to say that, he is not obliged to correct the statement in order to account for my difference; rather he retracts it in face of my rebuke. He hasn't said something false about "us"; he has learned that there is no us (yet, maybe never) to say anything about. What is wrong with his statement is that he made it to the wrong party.[18]

Wittgenstein's vision of language is open to the possibility of tragedy, to solitude as the disappearance of any eventual "us," to the loss of words that could be shared; but tragedy and solitude appear as *human* possibilities, not as a denial of the human as in the case of the skeptic.[19] The skeptic needs metaphysical isolation to sustain her conception, or fantasy, of knowledge; Wittgenstein envisions solitude as a possible outcome of the human condition of speakers. The difference is stark.

Wittgenstein's constant reminder of the presence of the human that the tradition of modern skepticism denies does not amount to the affirmation of some kind of human nature or essence, nor to the celebration of the established authority of society; it is rather a call to change our perception of what knowledge and reason are about that has bearings on the very meaning of *community*:

> The philosophical appeal to what we say, and the search for our criteria on the basis of which we say what we say, are claims to community. And the claim to community is always a search for the basis upon which it can or has been established. I have nothing more to go on than my conviction, my sense that I make sense. It may prove to be the case that I am wrong, that my conviction isolates me, from all others, from myself. That will not be the same as a discovery that I am dogmatic or egomaniacal. The wish and search for community are the wish and search for reason.
>
> CR 20

Community and society do not come to occupy the place once reserved for logical or transcendental foundations as what guarantees the universality of reason and meaning. No social norms, established values, or ordinary beliefs come to play the role of the judge in a new version of the Kantian tribunal of reason. Obviously, Cavell is well aware that in fact social norms largely define what counts as reason and normality, that they have the power to exclude, and worse, those who do not "agree." But this fact is not the philosophical and moral lesson that can be learned from Wittgenstein. Wittgenstein's lesson is an altogether different one: reason as well as community have always to be achieved over again, they are a task and not a given, and a task that is assigned to any and all of us, but can never be accomplished alone (in isolation).[20] There is no reason, meaning, or even quest for the self outside of the horizon of some actual or eventual conversation and companionship.[21]

The lesson of Wittgenstein, in Cavell's reading, is to uncover the *truth* of skepticism, namely that what is at stake in apparently purely epistemological questions is not so much the existence *of* the world and *of* others as existence *in* the world and *with* others, a problem to which epistemology can offer no answers. If the *temptation* of skeptical doubt can resurface at any moment as is the case in modern philosophy, literature, and cinema, if no logical argument however compelling can quell it once and for all, it is because it does not originate from a problem of knowledge. This is why, for Cavell, skepticism should not be taken as a transcendental illusion of pure reason: to use the Kantian terminology, it is closer to a transcendental illusion of *practical* reason. What hovers behind the pursuit of an unattainable proof of the existence of the world and of others is the fear of accepting our condition in the world, the fear of being exposed to the world, or to love, or to finitude.[22] These are not matters of knowledge but, rather, of *acknowledgement*: accepting the separation between one another may not be an easy task, but without the recognition of this human fact that philosophy calls finitude, there is no hope for learning how to bear the responsibility to express oneself or not to avoid someone else's expression.[23] As for the world, the problem is symmetrical: what has to be overcome is the modern feeling of separation, the sense of being sealed off from the outside. Cavell's abiding concern with the everyday speaks to the difficulty of relating to the world precisely when the horizon of transcendence seems to have faded away, when *this* world appears to be the only one we inhabit. If skepticism still matters to us, it is because it expresses in a poignant way something about modernity that most of the time is overlooked while continuing to haunt our present.

Notes

1 A complete and detailed reading of *The Claim of Reason* would require a far more extensive study than the one I can present in this volume. I hope, however, that the themes I decided to present will offer a useful introduction to readers interested in engaging more in-depth with the text.
2 Philosophy, for Cavell, is a set of texts and not of problems: see *CR* 3.
3 See for instance *CR* 123–24; *MWM* 187; *WV* 127.

4   For a discussion of skepticism and criteria from different angles, see, respectively, Jeroen Gerrits's and Martin Shuster's essays in this volume.
5   René Descartes, *Meditations on First Philosophy*, trans. D. A. Cress (Indianapolis: Hackett, 1983), 14–17.
6   Norman Malcolm, "Wittgenstein's *Philosophical Investigations*," *The Philosophical Review* 63, no. 4 (1954): 530–39; Roger Albritton, "On Wittgenstein's Use of the Term 'Criterion,'" *The Journal of Philosophy* 56, no. 22 (1959): 845–57.
7   Cavell thinks of remarks like "Grammar tells what kind of object anything is" (*PI* §373) or "Essence is expressed by grammar" (*PI* §371), of which he says: "Such obscurity may be a fault in a philosopher. But the greater the attachment to a concept (as to a person, or to a god), the harder it may be to explain either the attachment or the concept; *or perhaps it should be said that everything one does is, or could be, the only explanation of it*" (*C* 6, emphasis added).
8   Ludwig Wittgenstein, *The Blue Book*, quoted in *CR* 67.
9   Stephen Mulhall, in his extensive discussion of criteria in Wittgenstein and Cavell, rightly emphasizes that such a distinction is not about different *kinds* of objects, but about different *problems* of knowledge that may arise depending on the context. See Mulhall, *Stanley Cavell: Philosophy's Recounting of the Ordinary* (Oxford: Oxford University Press, 1994).
10 The figure of the child is of crucial philosophical importance for Wittgenstein, contrary to a long tradition of philosophers who either ignore childhood altogether or evoke it as a sad and unfortunate fact about the human condition in the manner of Descartes or Spinoza, who see in childhood, the age in which reason is not yet fully developed, the origin of all sorts of mistakes, false knowledge, and superstitions that it will be the burden of adulthood to get rid of.
11 It's worth giving the full quotation from Augustine that opens the *Investigations*: "When they (my elders) named some object, and accordingly moved towards something, I saw this and I grasped that the thing was called by the sound they uttered when they meant to point it out. Their intention was shewn by their bodily movements, as it were the natural language of all peoples: the expression of the face, the play of the eyes, the movements of other parts of the body, and the tone of voice which expresses our state of mind in seeking, having, rejecting, or avoiding something. Thus, as I heard words repeatedly used in their proper places in various sentences, I gradually learnt to understand what objects they signified; and after I had trained my mouth to form these signs, I used them to express my own desires." *Confessions*, I:8.
12 It's important to notice that Cavell does not endow "nature" with the power of determinism; he thinks of it more as a range of attitudes or inclinations that are followed more often than not, but that do not entail necessity, let alone causality: "Most people do descend from apes into authorities, but it is not inevitable" (*CR* 178).
13 In his extensive discussions of Cavell's and Wittgenstein's notions of criteria and grammar, Stephen Mulhall follows Cavell's idea that criteria play no foundational role in the *Investigations*, and that they do not provide a logical, transcendental, or conventional ground for our agreement in language. He disagrees, though, with Cavell's insistence that criteria are not some kind of rule: Wittgenstein, in his view, demystifies an impersonal, calculus-like conception of rules, but not rules as such. Mulhall further argues that criteria are indeed rules of grammar and, as a consequence, that Wittgenstein's vision of language is essentially normative. See

"Cavell's Vision of the Normativity of Language," in *Stanley Cavell*, ed. Richard Eldridge (Cambridge: Cambridge University Press, 2003), in particular 91–93.
14 *PI* §241. It is because there is no transcendental ground for what we say and do that language cannot be separated from a specific form of life: a point Wittgenstein often reaffirms in the *Investigations*.
15 J. L. Austin, "Other Minds," in *PP*, 76–116.
16 "Other Minds," 88, Austin's emphases. See also *CR* 240.
17 *CR* 352. Cavell makes these remarks in the context of a discussion of the fantasy of inexpressiveness that underwrites the idea of a private language.
18 *CR* 19–20. On this set of issues, see also Stanley Cavell, "The Argument of the Ordinary: Scenes of Instructions in Wittgenstein and Kripke," in *CHU*, 64–101.
19 Cavell certainly acknowledges that the denial of the human is a *human* possibility: the pervasiveness of skepticism in modern culture is rooted precisely in the temptation to deny the human condition, a temptation nobody should claim to be sheltered from.
20 Cavell interprets along these lines also theories of the social contract, and Rousseau's in particular. The idea of a contract implies in the first place the recognition of the principle of consent, that is to say of political equality, and in the second place, that each member of the society is not only responsible *to* it, but also *for* it. Consent to society goes along with responsibility and accountability: to ask why I should obey society means to ask whether the present state of society, with its specific injustice and inequalities, is one I should withdraw my consent from. In other words: theories of the social contract have a critical function and teach us to ask ourselves what we can and cannot consent to and what the consequences of our consent or withdrawal therefrom are. But all these questions of consent, dissent, disobedience, accountability, etc. cannot be separated, for Cavell, from the question of who "we" are: "That is the question the theorists of the social contract teach us to ask, and the beginning of an answer is *to discover whom I am in community with, and what it is I am obedient to*" (*CR* 24, emphasis added).
21 The term "conversation" is as significant for Cavell as some conceptual or technical terms are for other philosophers. It indicates the willingness of expressing oneself as well as of accepting someone else's expression; it is the opposite of the avoidance of others that motivates, consciously or unconsciously, skepticism about other minds. The promises and difficulty of conversation are explored everywhere in Cavell's works but particularly in his analyses of the comedies of remarriage in *PH*.
22 Othello and King Lear are for Cavell exemplary figures of the tragedies that stem from the fear of loving and of accepting love. See *CR* 439–40 and Stanley Cavell, "The Avoidance of Love: A Reading of *King Lear*," in *MWM*, 287–89.
23 The concept of acknowledgment is critical in Cavell's response to skepticism about other minds: "[T]he concept of acknowledgment is evidenced equally by its failure as by its success. It is not a description of a given response but a category in terms of which a given response is evaluated. (It is the sort of concept Heidegger calls an *existentiale*.) A 'failure to know' might just mean a piece of ignorance, an absence of something, a blank. A 'failure to acknowledge' is the presence of something, a confusion, an indifference, a callousness, an exhaustion, a coldness. Spiritual emptiness is not a blank." "Knowing and Acknowledging," in *MWM*, 263–64.

5

Democracy as a Way of Life and An-archic Perfectionism: Rereading *Conditions Handsome and Unhandsome*

Naoko Saito

Introduction

In the documentary film *Fahrenheit 11/9* (2018), director Michael Moore criticizes politics in the United States, epitomized by the election of Donald Trump as president. Beginning with the unexpected defeat of Hillary Clinton in the election of 2016, the film is not simply a criticism of Donald Trump: rather, it describes how the silenced voices of people, their frustration, their distrust of politicians—both Republican and Democrat, on the right and on the left—have helped the election of Trump. Behind its apparently "just0" political slogans, democracy always harbors injustice. Democracy as a political system never guarantees democracy at the level of people's daily lives. It is fragile, always on the verge of destruction. The film illustrates this with vivid images: angered, underpaid teachers; the despair of people in Flint, Michigan, now addicted because of toxic water; and the grief and outrage of young students over the gunning down of a fellow student. Such negative political emotions of fear, anxiety, and hate are stirring beneath the sanitized political discourse. At the same time, the film depicts the way in which the voices of grassroots activists provide hope for change. It is a reminder that the resources for healthy democracy rest on the *voice* of the people—of the marginalized, of the inaudible, of the silenced; and that democracy must always be resuscitated from within, and, hence, criticized from within.

As one of the historians in the film comments, democracy is always on the way, still to come. This reminds us of John Dewey's idea that democracy is both an ideal and a fact—created and recreated in people's daily lives. He writes:

> Regarded as an idea, democracy is not an alternative to other principles of associated life. It is the idea of community life itself. It is an ideal in the only intelligible sense of an ideal: namely, the tendency and movement of some thing which exists carried to its final limit, viewed as completed, perfected . . . The idea or ideal of a community presents, however, actual phases of associated life as they are

freed from restrictive and disturbing elements, and are contemplated as having attained their limit of development.[1]

In another article, "The Creative Democracy—The Task Before Us" (1939), Dewey declares that democracy is not so much a political mechanism as people's personal ways of living. Its energizing source lies in conversations among people at the dinner table, on the street. He writes:

> To cooperate by giving differences a chance to show themselves because of the belief that the expression of difference is not only a right of the other persons but is a means of enriching one's life experience, is inherent in the democratic personal way of life.[2]

Here Dewey indicates that, in the midst of tension and hostility, we human beings can be open to the possibility of reconciliation *if* we learn from our enemies as from "friends" (Ibid.). That is to say, one's moral life and experiences can be shared with others through mutual respect and mutual learning from difference. Dewey writes that "[t]he more unlike the two [countries] are, the more opportunity there is for learning."[3] Dewey is in a way a precursor for the politics of recognition today. Much as Dewey's American hope for democracy is called for, when recognition is urgently needed in the face of worldwide tensions, conflicts, and atrocities, its viability today is severely tested. Our age encounters a greater difficulty than did Dewey's times in that the spirit of mutual learning is blocked by fear and anxiety: the rise of militant Islam, the theatrical tensions surrounding North Korea, and the different threats posed by cyberwarfare are examples of a changed geopolitical landscape.

In an interview about the aforementioned film, Moore remarks that Americans are afraid of other people, indicating that Donald Trump's politics takes advantage of such a psychology of fear.[4] Perhaps as much as in Dewey's times, and perhaps in a more complicated way, we need today to take into consideration the negative power of those political emotions that determine the fate of democracy. In the face of such new challenges, how can we achieve democracy as a personal way of living, as Dewey envisioned nearly eighty years ago? What kind of political education is needed?

In response to this question, and especially in response to the negative political emotions that threaten democracy at the level of people's ways of living, this chapter reexamines Stanley Cavell's idea of Emersonian Moral Perfectionism, which is presented in his book *Conditions Handsome and Unhandsome: The Constitution of Emersonian Perfectionism* (1990). It attempts to reread this particular text of Cavell as a testament to—and enrichment of—Dewey's idea of democracy as a way of life: democracy as inseparable from human transformation and from the "education of grownups" (*CR* 125). As a text from an ordinary language philosopher, *Conditions* can be read as a text on political education—an education inseparable from our engagement with language. Emphasizing "the criticism of democracy from within," Cavell reinvigorates Emerson's idea that "the inmost in due time becomes the outmost,"[5] bridging the personal and the political, the private and the public. He says that

"Emerson's version of perfectionism [is] essential to the criticism of democracy from within" (*CHU* 3). Cavell's Emersonian idea of the cultivation of the self-reliant individual and of the first-person voice provides hope for a way of creating democracy from within, by transcending negative political emotions.

Much as this resembles Dewey's democracy as a way of life; attention must be paid, however, to the fact that, in *Conditions*, Cavell warns against the assimilation of Emerson's perfectionism into Dewey's pragmatism. One of the goals of this chapter, then, is to elucidate Cavell's persistent sense of the distance between him (and his Emerson) and Dewey. In particular, I shall argue that attention to his idea of *acknowledgment* can enrich the understanding of *Conditions* as a *political* text. I shall characterize Cavell's Emersonian moral perfectionism as *an-archic perfectionism* and show how such perfectionism is needed today.

Along these lines, I shall, first, examine some key features of Cavell's Emersonian moral perfectionism as depicted in *Conditions* and indicate its apparently common spirit with Dewey's democracy as a way of life. Second, I shall pay attention to the more skeptical tone of Cavell's "What's the use of calling Emerson a pragmatist?," which is echoed in *Conditions*—his growing sense of the distance between Emersonian perfectionism and Dewey. Third, to untangle Cavell's ambivalence toward Dewey's pragmatism, I shall consider the ideas of acknowledgment and skepticism in Cavell's ordinary language philosophy and try to show how this can change the reading of *Conditions*. It is his unique approach to skepticism that provides means strong enough to respond to the contemporary crisis manifested in the negative political emotions identified above. Based upon these observations, I shall read Emersonian moral perfectionism as an *an-archic perfectionism*. In conclusion, I shall claim that Cavell's sustained commitment to the idea of creating democracy from the inmost to the outmost is especially needed in order to replenish the spiritual vacancy of democracy today: hence, there arises the need for political education for human transformation.

Emersonian Moral Perfectionism

> *Happiness . . . Cheerfulness, in a democracy, is what I call a political emotion. Your democracy requires that morale be kept up. It's difficult.*
>
> —Stanley Cavell[6]

Cavell's Emersonian Moral Perfectionism in Response to Rawls

Cavell says that Emersonian perfectionism is not only "compatible with democracy," but is its "prize" (*CHU* 28). But how can the apparently elitist tone of perfectionism be compatible with democracy? Emersonian perfectionism is provocative in the following senses. First, as *Emersonian* (by implication, American) perfectionism, it is distinguished from traditional strains of Western perfectionism. Unlike the teleological forms of Plato's and Aristotle's perfectionism, Emerson's is *a*teleological, or, in Cavell's words, "goalless" (*CHU* xxxiv). Perhaps the most distinctively Emersonian aspect is the idea that "the self is always attained, as well as *to be* attained," that "'having' 'a' self is a process of moving to, and from, nexts" (*CHU* 12), and that "the human self... is always becoming, as on a journey, always partially in a further state" (*CW* 26). If there is anything final, "each state of the self is," he says, "final" (*CHU* 3). The goal of perfection is not decided by "anything picturable as the sun" but by "the way of the journey itself" (*CHU* 10). In Emerson, in contrast to Kant, the place of "the ideal occurs at the beginning of moral thinking, as a condition, let us say, of moral imagination, as preparation or sign of the moral life" (*CHU* 62). The reader of Emerson is challenged, then, to be perceptive to this "perpetual moral aspiration to an 'unattained but attainable self'" (*CW* 247). "The self is always attained, as well as *to be* attained" (*CHU* 12).

Second, Emersonian *moral* perfectionism requires a reconsideration of what it means to be moral. It is a precursor of Nietzsche's *antimoralism* (*CHU* 46). For Emerson, morality is not a matter of "ought" (as it is for Kant) but of the "soul's 'attraction'" (*CHU* 10)—whether we "*are* drawn beyond ourselves" or not (*CHU* 59). For Emerson morality hinges not on theoretical justifications (Kantianism and utilitarianism) but on words (*how we say what we mean*). Cavell quotes Emerson's "every word they say chagrins us and we know not where to begin to set them right" (*CHU* 24). Here "'every word' is not a generalization but bespeaks an attitude toward words as such, toward the fact of language" (*CHU* 22).[7] Writing is the perfectionist task of "authorship" (*CHU* 22). Re-possession of language, re-turning it to the language community, is participation in the "city of words" (*CHU* 8). It is this idea of speaking for oneself, of "representativeness" (*CHU* 9), that adds a *narrative* dimension to the moral life.

Third, the self oriented toward perfection must "speak with necessity" and "stand for humanity" (*CW* 31–32). "My" voice is my own, and yet is not just "mine": it is already implicated in the words of others. This is a unique feature of Emerson's self-transcendence. Cavell hears also in Emerson a Kantian call for speaking with a "universal voice" (*CW* 31). This again reflects the political, say democratic, facet of Cavell's ordinary language philosophy—the idea of "myself and my society being in conversation, demanding a voice in each other" (*CW* 68). This is an idea of "assent," as Paul Standish explains, "something like membership in a polis, a common world in which judgments are shared, in which (together) we find things the same, in which we project things (together)."[8] The voice, the "I" that speaks, must be particular and yet universal. And this voice of the "I" is conditioned by the voice of the "we." Cavell writes: "As representative we are educations for one another" (*CHU* 31). Perfectionism's issue is "whether the voice I lend in recognizing a society as mine, as speaking for me, is my voice, my own" (*CHU* 27). In Emersonian perfectionism, "my liberty" is a matter of "my voice" (*CHU* 26). Hence Cavell says that Emersonian perfectionist claims can join the "conversation of justice" (*CHU* 27)—the idea of conversation presented by Rawls in his *Theory of Justice* (*CHU* 23).

But two aporias persist. The first is to be found in the paradoxical aspects of *anti-foundationalist* perfectionism. How far is it possible to maintain the idea of perfection as goalless? More specifically, what does it mean to say that "*each state of the self is, so to speak, final*" (*CHU* 3, emphasis added)? The second aporia is concerned with the dual nature of the self, its being personal (partial) and universal (impartial). Cavell contends that the main difference between Emerson's self and Kant's lies in the former's refusal of "selflessness," "the absence of self"—a position that is derived from Kant's idea of the "noumenal self" (a "true self") (*CHU* xxxiv). In Emersonian perfectionism, the "partiality" of the self should be retained throughout, in the passage from the inmost to the outmost. In this figuration of the transitory nature of human being, Emerson sustains both particularity (and hence, partiality) and universality. As Cavell says, "Emerson's turn is to make my partiality itself the sign and incentive of my siding with the next or further self, which means siding against my attained perfection (or conformity), sidings which require the recognition of an other—the acknowledgment of relationship—in which this sign is manifest" (*CHU* 31). As this quote indicates, the presence of the other as a friend is a crucial driver of Emersonian perfectionism. The "friend (discovered or constructed) represents the standpoint of perfection" (*CHU* 59).

The implications of this apparent paradox in Emerson's democratic-perfectionist stance can be further elucidated by way of his idea of *genius*. Genius, Cavell says, should be distinguished from the elitist idea of "talent." Genius is the matter of the "capacity of self-reliance," which is universally distributed (*CHU* 25–26). Emerson says: "I shun father and mother and wife and brother when my genius calls me."[9] And yet, this provocation should be read to imply neither that this is merely selfish self-affirmation nor that what is at stake is the genius of the exceptional individual, the person with remarkable talents: by contrast, genius is an element in everyone. The point of Emerson's phrasing, we can surmise, is to defy the understanding of the human being as a genus, while alluding to the kind of genie, the guiding spirit, that might properly characterize the "active soul"—a property, perhaps like Socrates's *daimon*, that we might imagine to be equally distributed, if unequally accessed.[10] As Emerson says, genius is not the privilege of here and there a favorite, but the "sound estate of every man."[11] It refuses to be subject to comparative measure. On another account, genius here is related to Emerson's idea of greatness. In "The Over-Soul," an essay whose spirit and motive resonates through Nietzsche's *Übermensch*, Emerson writes: "I am born into the great, the universal mind. I, the imperfect, adore my own Perfect. I am somehow receptive of the great soul."[12] Emersonian perfectionism might be called a form of aristocracy whose appeal is not to noble birth, class, or comparative distinction but to the greatest possibility within each self. Hence, this might be called "an aristocracy of the self."[13]

It is through this Emersonian perfectionism that Cavell presents us with a sense of democracy always to be perfected, with a strong focus on its process of perfecting here and now, with no final state of perfectibility—an idea that sounds as if it is very close to Dewey's idea of democracy as a way of life. There is a strong sense of imperfection here. Cavell positions his account of Emersonian moral perfectionism in part as a response to Rawls's theory of justice (*CHU* 3). Against Rawls's criticism of Nietzsche's perfectionism as elitist, and on the strength of ample evidence of Emerson's influence on Nietzsche, Cavell argues that Rawls misreads Nietzsche (*CW* 248). Emersonian moral perfectionism raises a "different concern at a different point in the system," different from "the image of justice's sword" (*CW* 172): it is epitomized by the idea that the "higher person is *you*."[14] The point is that we are all equally placed, equally unique, when it comes to the fact that, whoever we are, there is some next, best possibility within ourselves: it is incumbent on each of us to find that. In Cavell's moral perfectionism, morality is not comprehended solely by normative measures: perfectionism takes up "the perplexities of human life itself" (*CW* 186). This is the moment when Rawls's "systematicity" (*CW* 168) breaks down, and when we must confront individual "eccentricities of taste" (*CW* 186). Philosophy begins when we lose our way, when "the crises of experience" overtake us. What measures justice is "morality itself, specifically justice itself" (*CW* 186).

What Cavell means by the "political" cannot be fairly understood without close attention to the undercurrent of political emotions in his perfectionism. While the pursuit of happiness is its central theme, the negative emotions of shame and guilt are driving forces for perfecting democracy. He says that Emerson's "Self-Reliance" is a "study of shame" (*CHU* 47). "Emersonian Perfectionism requires that we become ashamed in a particular way of ourselves, or our present stance, and that the Emersonian Nietzsche requires, as a sign of consecration to the next self, that we hate ourselves, as it were impersonally" (*CHU* 16).[15] This sense of shame, Cavell calls "aversion to ourselves in our conformity" (*CHU* 58). Moreover, "[i]n a democracy," he writes, "happiness is a political emotion, as depression is; each is a contribution, oppositely, to the general mood in which our joint faith in our enterprise is maintained" (*CW* 185). When you "take the sins of society upon you," Cavell writes, you can never say you are "above reproach."[16] As Cavell says, "happiness must always be found in the face of imperfect justice" (*CHU* 32), and we are engaged in "the public pursuit of happiness" (*CHU* 28). In Emersonian perfectionism, positive and negative emotions cannot be separated but rather are entangled: "To figure that my voice is called for in the social formation is to figure both that I participate in a structure that produces unaccountable misery and that my participation is to be expressed as happiness, even Emersonian joy. Call this the paradox of (continued) consent" (*CHU* 29).

In the account of political emotions, there is emphasis on the creation of democracy *from within*. Following Mill rather than Kant, Cavell extols "the expression of desire to be included within what is justly mine, as part of what makes society worth consenting to and defending."[17] Echoing Emerson's remark that "the inmost in due time becomes the outmost," Cavell delves into what Emerson calls the "privatest considerations" in order to achieve the public.[18] His political task is to retain this sense of privacy not as confinement but as "the conditions necessary for freedom" (*IQO* 120).

In the face of these features of Emersonian moral perfectionism, one may be struck by its apparent common grounds with Dewey's democracy as a way of life. They include the idea that democracy is a matter not solely of political systems but fundamentally of the human soul; that democracy as a personal way of living is created from *within*; that the ideal of a perfected state cannot be finally fixed; and that friendship and conversation among friends is a crucial condition for creative democracy. Indeed, Cavell includes Dewey's *Experience and Nature* in his list of perfectionist writings (*CHU* 5). As a matter of fact, Dewey does appear from time to time in *Conditions*. For example, Cavell acknowledges a kind of antimoralism as a common feature of the two writers, and yet he does not do this without reservation: "I found myself just now thinking of Dewey in connection with his tireless combating of two forms of moralism. So important is the feature of antimoralism that this alone constitutes Dewey as some sort of perfectionist—*though surely not an Emersonian one*. Tocqueville captures the sense of Deweyan perfectionism" (*CHU* 15, my emphasis). What does he mean by saying that Dewey is perfectionist but "not an Emersonian one"? Why does he label the differences in this way?

What's the Use of Calling Emerson a Pragmatist?: The Point of Seeing a Difference

Hilary Putnam once said, "Dewey was never just a social engineer. I see Dewey himself as a moral perfectionist, if there ever was one."[19] And Richard Bernstein finds common ground between Dewey and Cavell."[20] By contrast, the Dewey that appears in *Conditions* is someone who is *not* an *Emersonian* moral perfectionist. I would like to examine Cavell's words closely, and to explore why it matters to him to show difference instead of commonality.

In *Conditions*, Cavell says that while he had been attracted to Dewey, once he had read the later Wittgenstein, he did not go back to Dewey.

> It was not until the force of Wittgenstein's *Philosophical Investigations* came over me, in my own reluctant beginning as a teacher of philosophy, that I found the details of the philosophizing I seemed to imagine must exist, a beginning, deferred inventory of what I felt missing in Dewey, whose signature concepts are, to my ear, characteristically eclipsed by *their very similarity to, yet incommensurability with*, Wittgenstein's problematizings of "privacy," "thinking," "knowledge," "use," "practice," "context," "language," and "philosophy.... Not even this work [of Richard Rorty's] . . . has enabled me to find my way back to Dewey's writing.[21]

Here Cavell does not simply elucidate the difference between Dewey and Wittgenstein, but the curious harboring of difference in such apparent similarity. This paradoxical sense of closeness and distance can be said of the relationship between Dewey and Emerson also. Let us see the following long remark by Cavell:

> To see how close and far they are to and from one another, consider just the difference in what each will call "knowledge" and "ignorance" and how each pictures this "difference." For Dewey, representing the international view, knowledge is given in science and in the prescientific practices of the everyday, that is, the learning of problem solving. For Emerson, the success of science is as much a problem for thought as, say, the failure of religion is. Again these words might be true, in a different spirit, of Dewey as well. Then it may help to say: for Dewey the relation between science and technology is unproblematic, even definitive, whereas for Emerson the power manifested in technology and its attendant concepts of

intelligence and power and change and improvement are in contest with the work, and the concept of the work, of realizing the world each human is empowered to think. For an Emersonian the Deweyan is apt to seem an enlightened child, toying with the means of destruction, stinting the means of instruction, of provoking the self to work; for the Deweyan the Emersonian is apt to look, at best, like a Deweyan.[22]

If Deweyans read this passage, they would immediately react by saying that this is not fair to Dewey. Dewey is not an "enlightened child," and his idea of intelligence is far richer than what Cavell represents here as associated with problem-solving and science. Cavell's point, however, is not simply to represent Dewey as a defender of science: his point is to reconsider the nature of our thinking, what it means to be intelligent, and more broadly, the task of philosophy in enriching our ordinary lives. To Cavell, Dewey's idea of and his language of intelligence do not get out of the "picture of thinking as moving in action from a problematic situation to its solution as by the removal of an obstacle." And his idea of intelligence is "to overcome inner or outer stupidity, prejudice, ignorance, ideological fixation," whereas what he finds in Emerson (and in Wittgenstein, and in Heidegger) is the idea of "stopping to think."[23] "Wittgenstein's picture of thinking is rather one of moving from being lost to oneself to finding one's way, a circumstance of spiritual disorder, a defeat not to be solved but to be undone" (*CHU* 21).[24]

There are two more distinctive features that are expressed as the cause of distance between Emerson and Dewey. One is Cavell's sense of Dewey's lack of "the depths of psychoanalytic discovery" (*CHU* 13). It is undoubtedly the case that Dewey contributes to the resistance to introspective psychology in his attempts to go beyond the inner self, releasing the self to the outer world. And yet, in his avoidance of psychoanalysis, his use of language gives the impression that the inner self, as private, is uniformly assimilated into the "public open air";[25] and hence, the nature of the self is kept invisible. In view of this, Cavell's passing and yet apt criticism about not being able to see in Dewey the nature of the human psyche is understandable.

Another criticism is the different concept of or emphasis on experience. In contrast to Dewey's idea of experience, which is based upon the principle of continuity, Emerson's concept and language of experience is characterized by separation. As Cavell puts this: "For Dewey the philosophical interpretation of experience was cause for taking up scientific measures against old dualisms, refusing separation. For Emerson the philosophical interpretation of experience makes it a cause for mourning, assigning to philosophy the work of accepting the separation of the world, as of a child" (*CHU* 40).[26]

Thus, *Conditions*, albeit intuitively and sporadically, manifests Cavell's sense that, beyond the apparent similarities in their thinking and vocabulary, Dewey and Emerson depart from one another. But Deweyans may still wonder, "Why should we opt for separation and loss, not for love and solidarity? Why for psychoanalysis and withdrawal, not for public participation?" In order to respond to such questions, a further examination of Cavell's ordinary language philosophy is needed: to show why it matters so much to keep the line drawn between Deweyan democracy as a way of life and

Emersonian moral perfectionism; and eventually, to make the idea of democracy as a way of life a powerful philosophical appeal in addressing negative emotions in our contemporary political life.

Acknowledgment—a Cavellian Way of Living with Skepticism

In order to see how Emersonian moral perfectionism can *both* attest *and* criticize Deweyan discourse on democracy as a way of life, to do justice to Cavell's sense of distance, let us deviate for a while from the text of *Conditions* and explore a certain feature of Cavell's ordinary language philosophy: skepticism. This can help to shift the focus in reading *Conditions*. Cavell's unique approach to skepticism provides a powerful means of responding to the contemporary crisis manifested by the negative political emotions we considered at the start.

Cavell shares with Emerson the sense of asymmetry in our relationship with others. When you "take the sins of society upon you," Cavell claims, you can never say you are "above reproach."[27] Here is the sense that you owe others what can never be fully returned. Faced with this infinite responsibility to others, one has to go through an experience that is unsettling. Cavell asks us to get deeper into the realm of self-knowledge—much deeper than Dewey—such that we ourselves are radically destabilized in the presence of the other, as a precondition of our responsibility to community. This means that self-knowledge in its deepest sense involves a recurrent unsettlement of one's standpoint, and this becomes a powerful means of affecting the world. It is in such disturbing, anxious experience that Cavell's account of one's relationship with the other is to be found.

Such a sense of disturbance is captured most saliently in his response to skepticism. What Cavell calls "the truth of skepticism" exemplifies the attempt to re-place philosophy—to question what it is for human beings *to know*, and to take the terms of this question beyond those of traditional epistemology (*CR* 241, 448). Our relationship to others is not a matter of re*cognition*: rather to know what it is to know is to learn, in Cavell's words, "correct blindness"—learning how to close your eyes in the face of doubt, as Cavell says: "To live in the face of doubt, eyes happily shut, would be to fall in love with the world. For if there is a correct blindness, only love has it" (*CR* 431). (Obviously Cavell has in mind Wittgenstein's remark: "'But, if you are *certain,* isn't it that you are shutting your eyes in face of doubt?'—They are shut'" [*PI* 224]). Skepticism for Cavell is a matter of the tragic state of one's denial of the ordinary, of one's withdrawal from the world (*CR* 83–84)—the denial of the finite self.[28] This is a state created by "complacency about our knowledge of ourselves" (*CR* 109). In *Conditions*, Cavell indicates that skepticism is a mark of Emersonian moral perfectionism, as in the later Wittgenstein.[29]

> In Wittgenstein's *Philosophical Investigations* the issue of the everyday is the issue of the siting of skepticism, not as something to be overcome, as if to be refuted, as if it is a conclusion about human knowledge (which is skepticism's self-interpretation),

but to be placed as a mark of what Emerson calls "human condition," a further interpretation of finitude, a mode, as said, of inhabiting our investment in words, in the world.

CHU 61

The truth of skepticism is an alternative way of living with fear and anxiety beyond the stability of the self. Such negative emotions are inseparable from a vertiginous "anxiety that our expressions might at any time signify nothing" and a "fear" of "inexpressiveness," the result of which would be that "I am not merely unknown" but that "I am powerless to make myself known" (*CR* 351). Bernstein says that we need both "utopianism and healthy scepticism," and he endorses pragmatism's tendency to "*exorcise* 'the Cartesian Anxiety.'"[30] And yet, in the face of deep incommensurability, the verb, "to exorcise," smacks a little of an evasion of fear and anxiety, a denial of apt acknowledgement of the "secret melancholy" Emerson detects.[31]

What Cavell calls *acknowledgment* (rather than recognition) is a vision of knowing deeply connected with skepticism. There is here the pervasive sense that full understanding is from the beginning blocked in human life. Not solidarity or interdependence, but a thorough realization of "the pain of individuation" and "the pain of separation" (*CT* 212, 211) are at the heart of Cavell's idea of acknowledgment. The following words from Cavell tellingly capture this sense of difficulty and blockage: "In making the knowledge of others a metaphysical difficulty, philosophers deny how real the practical difficulty is of coming to know another person, and how little we can reveal of ourselves to another's gaze, or bear it" (*CR* 90). It is precisely because of this fated human tendency towards denial and avoidance that we have to learn how to live with doubt, "to live in the face of doubt, eyes happily shut" (*CR* 431).

Such a dimension of doubt is characteristically missing from Dewey's discourse on friendship, as it is from the politics of hope that Nussbaum advocates. In contrast to the politics of recognition, Cavell's (and Emerson's) political path might be called *the politics of acknowledgment*—acknowledging the obscure dimensions of human life and the unredeemable debt we owe to others, our endlessly asymmetrical relation to others with an infinite sense of responsibility to others. Cavell's politics of acknowledgment involves the sense of shame and the negative emotions that we experience when we live with dissent, exposing ourselves to voices that are not simply different but discordant and dissonant. In Cavell's and Emerson's antifoundationalism, there is a sense of confronting and delving into bottomlessness and uncertainty that is stronger than anything found in Dewey. And still (or because of this) the politics of acknowledgment points towards a perfectionist striving for community—democracy always still to be achieved. The sense of loss, groundlessness, silence, and doubt adds gravity to creative democracy in the face of negative political emotions.

Norris says that tragedy and skepticism in Cavell are "two sides of a single coin" and that "the possibility of such tragedy is always present, and no appeal to rules or practices can effectively dispel it, or provide a foundation for our responses independent of those responses."[32] If so, how can we move beyond doubt? How can a "passion for critique," as Bernstein puts it, be ignited when we are faced with an unbridgeable gap, the sense of doubt and the reality of incommensurability? What, then, would be the Emersonian and Cavellian way of achieving such moments of acknowledgment, beyond the avoidance of the other, beyond the denial of the world? The issue here is the practical task of how to convert negativity to affirmation.

Emerson says: "I grieve that grief can teach me nothing, nor carry me one step into real nature."[33] Emerson here makes the claim that we should not only not render the tragic absolute, but also not make absolute the act of despairing itself. Cavell says: "Despair is not bottomless, merely endless; a hopelessness, or fear, of reaching bottom" (*SW* 76). This is Emerson's evocation of "the sacred affirmative" (Emerson, qtd. in *SW* 133) combined with the sense of humility. In "Rebuking Hopelessness," Paul Standish suggests that Cavell sees despair not as "a recognition of the tragic facts of life, but rather [as] a fear, an avoidance, of life."[34] Based upon this, Standish claims that Cavell's and Emerson's thinking is best characterized as a "rebuking of hopelessness."[35] This is "to move beyond nihilism, or beyond the curse of the charge of human depravity and its consequent condemnation of us to despair" (*SW* 133). To think in this way is to "stand on tiptoe,"[36] between affirmation and negativity.[37] The crucial imperative in Emersonian perfectionism is, first, to keep converting silent melancholy to mourning, to a self-reflective state of facing the tragic, and then to turn from mourning to morning (*CT* 221, 212)—to move from doubt to recovery, from darkness to light (*CR* 102). What is at stake here is the very experience of standing at the "threshold" and at the "crossroads" (*CR* 19). Emerson's focus is on the affirmation of human power on the very verge of the fragility and transience of the human condition—a power only possible from within a rift, over an abyss, from within darkness, and a power that is manifested only in and after action. This will be the most resilient way of confronting and living with fear, doubt and anxiety. Emerson's thinking is thoroughly antifoundationalist with its focus on turning away, on the gaining of a "*point d'appui*" (Thoreau, qtd. in *SW* 71). There is no pre-given answer to *how* one can achieve this turning: for "power seems to be the result of rising, not the cause" (*SW* 136). All we can do, here and now, is to "set up the strong present tense against all the rumors of wrath, past or to come."[38] In order to accept and acknowledge, and contest "sleep within sleep" (a wrong kind of blindness), we must acquire "correct blindness."[39] This simultaneously means learning the correct way of gradually shedding light on the world, of learning what to see, what to make reappear in the world. This is a Cavellian and Emersonian pursuit of happiness, bringing forth the moment of reunion with the world, despite and because of human finitude. Our anxieties will never dissipate, our negative emotions never fully disappear. To contest tears, to resist negative emotion, is not to negate the significance of mutual understanding itself: rather it means to explore an indirect route to a deeper sense of reconciliation, through the unlimited possibility of affirmation. Instead of culminating in the perception of evil and suffering, an Emersonian way of dealing with suffering accepts the poverty of life, the "unhandsome" human condition, and then leaves and abandons its poverty (*SW* 137). As Emerson says, "I simply experiment, an endless seeker with no Past at my back."[40]

Achieving mutual understanding from within incommensurability, especially when one suffers from the political emotions of fear and doubt, is difficult. Emerson's and

Cavell's sense of asymmetry and imbalance is in tune with this difficulty, and this is at the heart of their moral perfectionism—not the perfectionism of unity and integrity, but perfection without perfectibility, with a strong sense of imperfection. Unlike the idea of harmony and integrity that is usually associated with the idea of perfectionism, Cavellian and Emersonian perfectionism keeps the space of *disequilibrium*, in contrast to Rawls's idea of "reflective equilibrium" (*CHU* xxv)—a space in which a disturbing element of society is always a crucial factor in sustaining a communal life.

Although the politics of acknowledgment involves instability and dissonance, it points towards a perfectionist striving for community. Different from relativism and licentious anarchism, Cavell's anti-foundationalist perfectionism might be called an *an-archic perfectionism*—a perfectionism that seeks always a better state and yet without relying on any transcendental (or, that is, foundational) ground, the original sense of an-archism.

It is here that Cavell's an-archic perfectionism has implications for the cultivation of political emotions—thus Cavell's Emersonian moral perfectionism can now be seen as a call to transcend negative political emotions and as a language to fill the spiritual void of democracy.

Political Education for Human Transformation

In *Conditions*, Cavell says that "[a]s representative we are educations for one another" (*CHU* 31). He also says that Emersonian moral perfectionism is a matter of "the transforming of oneself and of one's society" (*CHU* 2), and of the soul's journey. Thus, education for mutual transformation is an essential task of Emersonian moral perfectionism. In order to respond to the peculiar manifestation of negative political emotions, to fill the spiritual void of democracy, we need a kind of education that enables teachers and students to learn to face such negative emotions as hate, indifference, and shame, and to acknowledge human finitude. Teaching "how to respond to [the inevitable failures of democracy], and to one's compromise by them otherwise than by excuse or withdrawal," is the task of Emersonian perfectionism, to learn how to be engaged in the "criticism of democracy from within" (*CHU* 18).

Following Cavell's ordinary language philosophy, education for language is crucial for the cultivation of political emotions—learning how to find one's voice as the void of the "I" and how to test it and share it with others. The challenge to an-archic perfectionism is *how* we learn to attest to and to stand within the critical moment of conversation, from negativity to affirmation, to create the moment of conversion from fear and doubt to openness for mutual understanding. How can one come to the point of mutual learning beyond fear, to such an extent as to say: "my participation is to be expressed as happiness, even Emersonian joy" (*CHU* 29)? Here silence, in the face of the unsayable, in people's "quiet desperation," will provide a crucial momentum towards remembering one's *desire to speak*. This is what Cavell calls "passionate utterance"[41]—a type of language that responds to the "political emotions" of depression, cynicism, and irony (*CW* 185). As Cavell says: "A performative utterance is an offer of participation in the order of law ... A passionate utterance is an invitation to improvisation in the disorders of desire" (*PDAT* 185). The cultivation of political emotions in Emersonian perfectionist education is geared towards affirmation, not *ressentiment*. Passion and desire are the sources of our "search for reason" (*CR* 20), and they ask for "residence in the shared realm of reason" (*PDAT* 188).

Concerning *how* to kindle affirmative emotions for our political life, Emerson's idea of expanding circles of conversation offers the suggestion of a way forward.

> Conversation is a game of circles. In conversation we pluck up the *termini* which bound the common of silence on every side ... When each new speaker strikes a new light, emancipates us from the oppression of the last speaker to oppress us with the greatness and exclusiveness of his own thought, then yields us to another redeemer, we seem to recover our rights, to become men.[42]

"In the mode of passionate exchange," Cavell writes, "there is no final word, no uptake or turndown, until a line is drawn, a withdrawal is effected, perhaps in turn to be revoked" (*PDAT* 183). Unlike a Rawlsian "social project," where society is seen as "a field of fairness for individual projects" (*CW* 173), the point of Emerson's *conversation of justice* is to retain space for "a residuum unknown, unanalyzable,"[43] a space for disequilibrium—in Cavell's words, "the opacity, or non-transparence, of the present state of our interactions, cooperative or antagonistic" (*CW* 173). Hence, its virtues are "those of listening, the responsiveness to difference, the willingness for change" (*CW* 173–74).

Resisting the "flattening of the self" (*CR* 386) behind the normalized and standardized measures of equality and fairness, what is at stake here is the kind of vulnerability the "I" exposes in confronting the other—exposure to what threatens "my" stability, the state of equilibrium. There is no pre-existing measure independent of conversation that assures you of your conviction about your moral standing. It is from such precarious ground that one learns to stand on one's own feet. There passionate utterance is a mode of speech in which, in disorder, one's standpoint is at stake: "I declare my standing with you and single you out, demanding a response in kind from you, and a response now, so making myself vulnerable to your rebuke, thus staking our future" (*PDAT* 185).

Our voices are tested in conversation with others who are *to be discovered to be friends*. We cannot tell what our motive is until we learn to speak out, to leave "the oppression of the last speaker" (*PDAT* 184). It is to be discovered *a posteriori* when each of us learns to strike "a new light." The other is a crucial resource for finding the measure of the authority of one's words. For the self to learn to speak again, for a person to "regain his tongue"[44] in conversation and simultaneously the passion for commitment, a friend is needed who attests to the moment when the secret is translated into the public. Such a mode of conversation, with its everlasting residuum and with its disturbing asymmetry, does not call for reciprocity in communication, where language's importance is taken to be primarily functional: rather, it requires a use of language in which one suffers from the pain of separation with this unbridgeable gap. This Cavell and Emerson would call the sincerest way of mutual understanding.

Notes

1. John Dewey, *The Public and Its Problems*, in *The Later Works of John Dewey*, vol. 2, ed. Jo Ann Boydston (Carbondale: Southern Illinois University Press, 1984), 328.
2. John Dewey, "Creative Democracy—The Task Before Us," in *The Later Works of John Dewey*, vol. 14, ed. Jo Ann Boydston (Carbondale: Southern Illinois University Press, 1988), 228.
3. John Dewey, 1983a. "Some Factors in Mutual National Understanding," in *The Middle Works of John Dewey*, vol. 13, ed. Jo Ann Boydston (Carbondale: Southern Illinois University Press, 1983), 262.
4. Interview with Michael Moore, broadcast on November 5, 2018.
5. Ralph Waldo Emerson, *The Essential Writings of Ralph Waldo Emerson*, ed. Brooks Atkinson (New York: The Modern Library, 2000), 132.
6. Stanley Cavell and Paul Standish, "Stanley Cavell in Conversation with Paul Standish," *Journal of Philosophy of Education* 46, no. 2 (2012): 155–76, 172.
7. "Emerson's return of words may be said to return them to the life of language, to language and life transfigured, as an eventual everyday" (*CHU* 21).
8. Paul Standish, "In Her Own Voice: Convention, Conversion, Criteria," *Educational Philosophy and Theory*, 36, no. 1 (2004): 94.
9. Emerson, *Essential Writings*, 135.
10. Nigel Blake, Richard Smith, Paul Smeyers, and Paul Standish, eds., *Education in an Age of Nihilism* (London: Routledge, 2000).
11. Emerson, *Essential Writings*, 47.
12. Ibid., 250.
13. Blake et al., *Education*, 62.
14. Cavell and Standish, "Stanley Cavell in Conversation," 161.
15. As Cavell says, the consent of the relatively advantaged "is subject to an oppressive helplessness—I have described its signs as a sense of compromise and of cynicism—Emerson calls it being ashamed—that distorts or blocks their participation in the conversation of justice" (*CHU* 30).
16. Cavell and Standish, "Stanley Cavell in Conversation," 162.
17. Cavell and Standish, "Stanley Cavell in Conversation," 182.
18. Emerson, *Essential Writings*, 53. Cavell says in the interview: "One way to start thinking about it," he remarks, "is that I want to make both the private and the public problems. Another is to make each of them tasks" (Cavell and Standish, "Stanley Cavell in Conversation," 157).
19. Hilary Putnam, Naoko Saito, and Paul Standish, "Hilary Putnam interviewed by Naoko Saito and Paul Standish," *Journal of Philosophy of Education* 48, no. 1 (2014): 19.
20. This was Bernstein's response to Saito's paper, "Pragmatism, Analysis, and Inspiration," delivered at the conference "Pragmatic Themes in the Philosophy of Hilary Putnam," New School for Social Research, November 18, 2016.
21. *CHU* 14, my italics. Cavell adds: "I was not moved to look again at what Dewey had actually said" (*CHU* 14).
22. *CHU* 15-16. And he continues: "In part Dewey's fine essay on Emerson reads this way; but in part it also reads like a poignant wish to find something in Emerson's achievement that he could put to use in his own work" (*CHU* 16).
23. "So thinking [for Emerson] may present itself as stopping, and as finding a way *back*, as if thinking is remembering something" (*CHU* 55).

24 "Dewey's repeated forcing of his attentions on me has also, I think, to do with having recently and repeatedly heard Wittgenstein's view of language described as pragmatism, one whose certainty between words and world is based on action, opposed to, I guess, something mental" (*CHU* 21).
25 John Dewey, *Human Nature and Conduct*, in *The Middle Works of John Dewey*, vol. 14, ed. Jo Ann Boydston (Carbondale: Southern Illinois University Press, 1983), 9.
26 Cavell also expresses a sense of difference with regard to the idea of the ordinary between Dewey and Emerson. "It will help to remark that for Dewey the philosophical appeal of the ordinary is present but intermittent, as when he relates esteeming to estimating or relates objects to what it is that objects, or mind to minding" (*CHU* 23).
27 Cavell and Standish, "Stanley Cavell in Conversation," 162.
28 Andrew Norris, *Becoming Who We Are: Politics and Practical Philosophy in the Work of Stanley Cavell* (Oxford: Oxford University Press, 2017), 93.
29 Emerson's perception of the dispossession of our humanity, the loss of ground, the loss of nature as our security, or property, is thought in modern philosophy as the problem of skepticism" (*CHU* 61).
30 Richard Bernstein, *Pragmatic Encounters* (New York: Routledge, 2016), 103, 32.
31 Emerson, *Essential Writings*, 401.
32 Norris, *Becoming Who We Are*, 93, 81.
33 Emerson, *Essential Writings*, 309.
34 Paul Standish, "Rebuking Hopelessness," in *Stanley Cavell and Philosophy as Translation: The Truth Is Translated*, ed. Paul Standish and Naoko Saito (London: Roman & Littlefield International, 2017), 61–72. Standish here alludes to *CHU* 130.
35 Cf. *PPh* 189.
36 Ralph Waldo Emerson, *Selections from Ralph Waldo Emerson*, ed. Stephen E. Whicher (Boston: Houghton Mifflin Company, 1957), 344.
37 Cavell's approach to hope(lessness) is radically different from Nussbaum's call for "a politics of hope" as a remedy to rampant fear in democracy. Unlike Nussbaum's based upon an "inclusive" metaphor" and the principle of reciprocity and "mutual respect," there is more of the sense of disturbance and imbalance in Cavell's idea of hope(lessness) precisely because of his take on skepticism. See Martha Nussbaum, *The Monarchy of Fear: A Philosopher Looks at Our Political Crisis* (New York: Simon & Schuster, 2018), 233, 227.
38 Emerson, *Essential Writings*, 316.
39 Ibid., 317.
40 Emerson, *Essential Writings*, 288.
41 See *PDAT*, esp. chap. 7.
42 Emerson, *Essential Writings*, 256–57.
43 Emerson, *Essential Writings*, 254.
44 Emerson, *Essential Writings*, 210.

Part Two

Cavell and Aesthetics

6

Philosophy, Literature, and the Romantic Response

Andrew Brandel

> *People nowadays think scientists are there to instruct them, poets, musicians, etc. to delight them. That these have something to teach; that never comes to their mind.*
> Ludwig Wittgenstein, *Vermischte Bemerkungen*

This chapter examines Cavell's most sustained writing on the place of romanticism in his philosophy, written during the period that follows the publication of *The Claim of Reason*. We have occasion in the course of such a reading to touch on a number of themes that emerge again and again throughout his oeuvre, including the thought of philosophy as therapy, the approach to skepticism as it appears in the texture of everyday life, and the characteristic "American belatedness" to philosophical questions. But it is this last point, the particularly American quality of a certain pitch of philosophy, that Cavell says in the preface to *In Quest of the Ordinary* accounts for his initial opening into romanticism as standing in the wake of Kant. Romanticism, he writes, "it is habitually said . . . is a function of (whatever else) how we conceive the philosophical settlement proposed in the achievement of Kant" (*IQO* 29). But if the German romantics, by way of France, had begun their response to the Kantian settlement with "the weakening of the subject," American romanticism, by contrast, sets off from the "legacy of the thing in itself" (*IQO* xii). It is concerned, in other words, with a response to Kant's having bargained away the possibility of knowing the world in itself, in order to secure the possibility of metaphysics, and which concedes, at the same time, that the things to which the subject's concepts refer really stand outside of the reference. In this way, the question of romanticism is a variation on the Cavellian theme of the response to skepticism.

Kant imagined that critical philosophy could guard us against the threat of skepticism (and its double in dogmatism) through a critique of reason. But the settlement he proposed required drawing a firm line between the subject, her language, and the world, a salve we might say for the temptation of the inexpressible, the noumena. The cost was our conviction in the animacy of the world, save for its appearances. In this way, metaphysical answers to skepticism denied the child's (and the poet's) animism, denied life to the world by relegating it to a supersensible substratum, a separation that despite (or perhaps because of) its stability proves tormenting. Informed by his reading of

Wittgenstein, Cavell argues that what is at stake is not the outcome of our search for the expressive limits of language, the limits of reason, but the fact of our desire for the inexpressible. Other commentators had understood romanticism's response to the Kantian refutation of skepticism as an attempt to provide a more felicitous alternative to his ideal language[1] (e.g., by reclaiming and uniting the fantastic, the mythic, and the ordinary), one that could reach finally the other shore, resolve these tensions, and bring nature back to life. But for Cavell, romanticism holds no promise of overcoming skepticism, no cure for our disquiet, and it affirms no place outside of language that a special class of statements helps us to reach. Its poetry reminds us, instead, of something we knew as children and to the fact of our having been educated out of it. It points to a "route back to our conviction in reality" (*WV* 70), what he calls our recovery from the noumenal, from the thing in itself, from metaphysics. It recognizes, as Wittgenstein says, that the "limits of my language mean the limits of my world,"[2] while affirming the truth of skepticism, that I live this antagonism.

In his earlier work, Cavell had already invoked romanticism as "the discovery, or one rediscovery, of the subjective; the subjective as the exceptional; or the discovery of freedom as a state in which each subject claims its right to recognition, or acknowledgment; the right to name and assess its own satisfaction" (*CR* 466). Its dream, Sandra Laugier writes instructively, is the "re-appropriat[ion] of the ordinary world through individual expression";[3] a quest, in other words, for the "right tonality" in which inner and outer worlds come into alignment, where an individual voice claims "universal validity," where an expression simultaneously "expresses me" and "exposes me."[4] Put more simply, the problem that is shared by Kant and Wittgenstein and that interests Cavell is the intimacy of our language and the world. Unlike Kant, however, Wittgenstein recognizes the "impossibility of *grounding* [this] relation [between my words and the world] . . . what Cavell calls the truth of skepticism."[5]

The romantic interpretation of Kant reformulates the problem by asking what is at stake in the claim of reason, the desire for foundations. The claim, Cavell had already shown, signals a pretense to speaking in the name of a community, a form of life, with others who share criteria that determine what it is that we say in a particular context. The claim therefore purports to speak in the name of other humans, others with whom I share a language, who lend the claim authority in virtue of my belonging. But that belonging is not, as in Kant, the human as such in virtue of a general rule. My membership is vulnerable. Contrary to metaphysical settlements that propose to stand once and for all, Cavell writes that we are in *quest* of the ordinary, because the work of returning to life is ongoing.[6] Romantic works do not "enable us either to escape our fantasies or to accept our governance by empirical generalizations," but rather, as Richard Eldridge articulates, to:

> bring us to ongoing awareness . . . of a practical situation we continue to make . . . [that] it requires ongoing re-accomplishment, since consent to one's present state can be accomplished only . . . as one experiences it, not once and for all. To think the contrary is to persist in the skeptic's and anti-skeptic's shared fantasy of completeness, intactness, and freedom from responsibility.[7]

"One can think of romanticism," Cavell says, "as the discovery that the everyday is an exceptional achievement. Call it the achievement of the human" (*CR* 463). This task of returning to our conviction in reality, to abiding the uncanniness of the ordinary, requires a different picture of thought for our striving after cultivation within a *human* form of life, tantamount perhaps to the (re)discovery of an anti-Platonic *paideia*.

I follow these insights as they unfold primarily in the lectures that make up *In Quest of the Ordinary*, but my interpretation is informed as well by his extension of his initial thoughts in *This New Yet Unapproachable America*, published the following year. I begin by tracing Cavell's description of the Kantian bargain, and the very different picture of "conditions" of experience he develops through his reading of Wittgenstein and Emerson's replies to Kant. I then turn to the expressions of this response—this interpretation of the Kantian bargain—in poetry and in particular in Coleridge and Wordsworth. This theme shows up in theater as well, and Cavell uses the example of *The Winter's Tale* to elaborate the torment teetering on madness that comes from the separation insinuated by metaphysical settlements. In the character of Leontes, for instance, we see how the skeptic seeks to revenge themselves on the world for the fact of their separation, and in Hermione, how theater offers something like a route to recovery. The final parts of this essay examine Cavell's characteristically romantic account of the expulsion of poetry (and philosophers like Thoreau and Emerson) from professional philosophy, and how this follows from different views on reading.

With Regards to Kant

Cavell glosses the Copernican Revolution as the claim that the form of experience, constituted essentially by appearances, can be known in its entirety through synthetic a priori judgements like the categories of the understanding, and these appearances we cannot help but think are appearances of something other than themselves, but which cannot be known, abiding as they do in a supersensible substratum. Reason reveals itself to itself in the necessity of being "drawn to think about this unknowable ground of appearance" (*IQO* 30), the setting right of which is the purpose of a *critique*—in the case of pure reason as a withdrawal back to safe ground, and for practical reason as extension. For Kant, the noumenal realm, insofar as it refers to something which is not itself an object of sensible intuition, can only have a negative meaning (*bloß negative Bedeutung*). Our mode of intuition is objectively valid, therefore, only with regards to objects of our senses. If we were to posit a special faculty of intuition outside of sensibility—an intellectual intuition—the noumenal would have a *positive* meaning, but this capacity Kant reserves for God. Since for humans the deployment of the categories can never exceed the objects of experience (what is given in sensible intuition), we are limited to this negative meaning of things-in-themselves—that is, they play a merely regulative function. I can't help but think it, though about it in itself I can say positively nothing.[8]

This limitation of knowledge thus secures it, purportedly, against both skepticism and dogmatism—a settlement that proves remarkably stable. The price of this settlement, however, is a weighty disappointment. The resultant human is split between two worlds, one restricted, the other free. There are romantic uses for this idea of two worlds; for example, in that it provides us with an account of the "human being's dissatisfaction with itself" (*IQO* 32). It also gives rise to the insight that the human "now lives in neither world ... we are, as it is said, between worlds." But the distaste expressed by professors of philosophy for romantics like Emerson and Thoreau—a point to which I will return later on—ushers in part from the fact that the romantic sees the world as capable of being remade, "or I in it, that I could *want* it, as it would be, or I in it" (*IQO* 35). As with Marx, or with Nietzsche, the recognition that the world has been made (perhaps by me) and thus that it is conceivable that I might wish it to be undone and remade, can take on a maddening quality, "if kept green"; that is, as a "continuous rebuke to the way we live compared to which, or in reaction to which, a settled despair of the world, or cynicism, is luxurious" (*IQO* 35-36). Kant's two worlds are thereby resolved into *perspectives* on the world—Cavell calls them hope and despair. The dismissal of romanticism as youthful optimism, or its cheeriness, misses the embeddedness of this essential polarity. In other words, romanticism responds to the fact that we "live" this antagonism.

When Emerson uses the phrase "the mysteries of the human condition," assuming, as Cavell does, that this is not simply an error in his formulation, it is not to reify something like *the* human condition but instead to point out the awkwardness of *conditions* in human life. It recalls the assertion that "the history of the individual is always an account of his condition" and that this involves "[knowing] himself to be a party to his present estate."[9] If Kant was interested in the conditions of possible experience (at least in the B edition), the issue of how synthetic a priori judgments— that is, concepts of objects in general—are possible, Emerson turns the formulation on its head by foregrounding the concept of condition itself. If the former wanted to understand "the behavior of the world by understanding the behavior of our concepts of the world," the world itself only in the negative sense, the latter responds by calling for a transcendental deduction of "every word in the language." As Laugier puts it:

> [E]ach word of ordinary language, each bit of ordinary experience, each aspect of the ordinary require a deduction to know its use: each one must be retraced in its application to the world, by the criteria of its application. The ordinary, then, is what escapes us, what is distant precisely because we seek to appropriate it to us rather than letting ourselves go to the things, and to insignificant encounters.[10]

Conditions, on these terms, are about "talking together," they are the *terms* of agreement, irresistible, criterial.[11] For Wittgenstein, and for Cavell, "the relationship between me (my words) and the real (our world)" is "the question of our criteria." Once again, Laugier's gloss is instructive: "agreements in language [that is, in form of life] ... determine and are determined by criteria: We share criteria by means of which we regulate our application of concepts and through which we establish the conditions of conversations."[12] And, she quotes from Cavell, "the wish and search for community are the wish and search for reason."[13] In other words, the Kantian claim on reason is transfigured by a question of how it is that we are able to speak *in the name of others*. "Self-Reliance," in contrast to self-knowledge qua conditions of objects in general, Cavell will later argue, "may accordingly be understood to show writing as a message from prison."

> The idea is that we have become permanently and unforgettably visible to one another, in a state of perpetual theatre . . . [if] there were Lethe for our bondage to attention of others, to their sympathy or hatred, we would utter opinions that would be "seen to be not private but necessary" . . . that is, my visibility would then frighten my watchers, not the other way around, and my privacy would no longer present confinement but instead the conditions necessary for freedom. But as long as these conditions are not known to be achieved, the writer cannot know that I am known in his utterance, hence that he and I have each assumed our separate existence.
>
> *IQO* 119

Kantian conditions are shaped by schemata, products of the imagination that unite the categories and the manifold of intuition. They connect the realm of sensibility with the realm of concepts, as if one stands outside the other (however necessary their congruence). Schematism models the rule for the *application* of the concept, just as logic prescribes the form of pure concepts and the structure of representational content (*Inhalt*). The schemata thus provide Kant with the solution to the problem of generating rules for the application of rules. They allow us to see something as something, and they give us pleasure because through them we are able to "[grasp] and [articulate] a world."[14] In contrast grammar, for Cavell, "through its schematism in criteria, is given in the ordinary."[15] Schemata, from this perspective, furnish us with an "intuitive horizon" of ordinary uses in which the concept feels right in context. In other words, they "reflect back on our understanding of the concept and rediscover its form by way of the singular new instance."[16]

> In each word we utter we emit stipulations, agreements we do not know and do not want to know we have entered, agreements we were always in, that were in effect before our participation in them. Our relation to language—to the fact that we are subject to expression and comprehension, victims of meaning—is accordingly a key to our sense of our distance from our lives, of our sense of the alien, of ourselves as alien to ourselves, thus alienated.
>
> *IQO* 40

Agreements in language reflect criteria that regulate the use of concepts and which in turn entail our agreements as conditions of conversation. They refer not to objects in general, then, as per Kant, but to grammatical objects. But a grammatical investigation should not, however, be misunderstood to treat them as mere conventions, conventionally conceived; rather, as other contributions to this volume will show in greater detail, what is at stake is the naturalness of our language.

Coleridge and the Spirit of Kant

In his *Biographia Literaria*, Samuel Coleridge chastises the philosophical elite for the insinuation of a speculative limit to science that could never be transgressed, lest they be branded fanatics and phantasts. In the history of philosophy, he writes, "the true depth of science, and the penetration to the innermost center from which all the lines of knowledge diverge to their ever distant circumference was abandoned to the illiterate and the simple."[17] Of these latter mystics like Jacob Behmen, De Thoyras, and George Fox, those "uneducated [men] of genius,"

> [their] meditations are almost inevitably employed on the eternal or the everlasting ... need we then be surprised that under an excitement at once so strong and so unusual the man's body should sympathize with the struggles of his mind; or that he should at times be so far deluded as to mistake the tumultuous sensations of his nerves, and the co-existing spectres of his fancy, as parts or symbols of the truths which were opening on him?[18]

Coleridge uses this aside to introduce a distinction familiar to readers of German idealism between the letter and the spirit of Kant. For Coleridge, Kant's mysticism requires interpretation, because there were some thoughts the "illustrious sage of Königsberg... did not think it prudent to avow, or which he considered as consistently left behind in pure analysis, not of human nature *in toto*, but of the speculative intellectual alone," in part because such thoughts would land him in danger of persecution in Prussia.

> In spite therefore of his own declarations, I could never believe it was possible for him to have meant no more by his *Noumenon*, or Thing in Itself, that his mere words express; or that in his own conception he confined the whole plastic power to the forms of the intellect, leaving for the external cause, for the *materiale* of our sensations, a matter without form, which is doubtless unconceivable.[19]

The two Kants run deeply throughout Coleridge's poetry and his biographical reflections, but Cavell is particularly struck by the following sentiment:

> [T]he writings of these mystics acted in no slight degree to prevent my mind from being imprisoned within the outline of any single dogmatic system. They contributed to keep alive the heart in the head; gave me an indistinct, yet stirring and working presentiment, that all the products of the mere reflective faculty partook of death, and were as the rattling twigs and sprays in winter into which a sap was yet to be propelled from some root to which I had not yet penetrated, if they were to afford my soul either food or shelter.[20]

While Cavell does not explicitly reference the fact that the two positions are, for Coleridge, internal to Kant, we can read this as implicit in romanticism's responsiveness.

Cavell's reading of the phrase "the mere *reflective* faculty partook of death" involves the sense that the conventional reading of the letter of the Kantian bargain requires we say nothing at all about the world, save what conforms to the forms of the intellect—thus that the world is nothing without us, or as in Hegel's idealism, that the limit is the Absolute.

It is the *world* that appears dead against the liveliness of Kant's categories. Dead objects in a merely negative world "made in our image," or at least in the image of our faculties (*IQO* 44). Nature is passive, and when it moves, it is unpurposive, mechanistic. But if this is the case, it means we carry "the death of the world in us, in our very requirement of creating it, as if it does not yet exist."[21] Philosophical skepticism entreats you to doubt the existence of the world and chides the romantic for imagining that the world could die. In the grip of this threat, it seeks to overcome skepticism, at the sober cost of the world itself. "The romantic," by contrast, "will want you to see that his vision expresses the way you are living now" (*IQO* 34). This, Cavell teaches us, seems a rather sensible, even urgent undertaking—to give the world back, to bring it back, as to life. When he describes romantic works as texts for recovery, therefore, it means a recovery of the world; a recovery from the thing-in-itself, from the noumenal, and from merely negative meaning of things.

In the third of his Beckman Lectures, Cavell writes that the "beginning of skepticism is the insinuation of absence, of a line, or a limitation, hence the creation of want, or desire: the creation, as I have put it, of the interpretation of metaphysical finitude as intellectual lack." This is the same compulsion to discover a special class of statements the truth about which we can be free of doubt (*IQO* 51). Austin's assault on such skepticism, through the painstaking notation of errors of such statements, teaches us not only that the world is given to exceeding our expectations and overthrowing our knowledge (of course it is). The idea, rather, is that:

> [F]or all our human liability to error, the world is Eden enough ... and what is more, all the world there is: risk and error are inherent in the human, part of what we conceive human life to be ... and this condemnation to an unsurveyable freedom is not well described by saying that we can never, or can only in a certain class of cases, be certain. If the earth opens and swallows me up, this need not prove my trust in it was misplaced. What better place for my trust could there be? (The world *was* my certainty. . .).
>
> IQO 52, Cavell's emphasis

The Enlightened among us might justly retort that we romantics respond only to the threat of skepticism and ignore Kant's refusal of dogmatism. The romantic gives us back too much (everything in fact) through animism (as in, bringing back to life).[22] "Not ideas about the thing," Wallace Stevens observes, "but the thing itself"—"a scrawny cry from outside / Seemed like a sound in his mind ... it was like / A new knowledge of reality."[23]

Cavell reads four texts in succession as a mode of reply to these charges against romantic animism. His primary example, however, is Coleridge's *The Rime of the*

Ancient Mariner, and his reading focalizes the crucial scene where the Mariner kills the Albatross, and which critics had read as a "species of motiveless malignity . . . meant to establish one's own identity" (*IQO* 55). Inspired by Robert Penn Warren, Cavell reads the lack of motive as the "key to the poem's work" (*IQO* 57). If the seascape stands for the conventional limit of knowledge and our temptation to go beyond it, then the killing of the Albatross could be read, by analogy to the Kantian response to skepticism, "as an issue of the human denial of the conditions of humanity for which there is no (single) motive" (*IQO* 57). The motivelessness of the killing would suggest an "understanding the motive as the horror of being human itself—but then the fate of denying this condition, hence denying the possession of such a motive, would be the point of the motive." Now compare this with Kant's categorical imperative and its demand that we respect human Reason ("of which the horror of the human is an opposite, a denial, a parody"): "the denial of the human signals not the absence of motive but the presence of a particular kind of motive" (*IQO* 57).

We might be tempted to read the Mariner's killing of the Albatross as, in this sense, perverse. But this, Cavell says, would not go far enough. Why not? And in what sense *does* the Mariner's act cross the line? For one, the transgression is always derivative of an earlier transgression, as though the first step has "always already been taken" (*IQO* 48). The desire to get *out* of language, to put the matter differently, has always been there. Kant would dismiss this gesture as a dialectical delusion, as fanaticism, or what we had been just calling animism. To decry it as perverse, however, ignores its casualness—the casual tendency we have to wish we could "escape the human"—and which Cavell associates with the "fear of inexpressiveness" (*IQO* 59). The poet, like the Mariner, is not alone in their fear of being misunderstood, but is somehow more "radically incommunicado" (*IQO* 59). When Coleridge writes that the bird loved his killer, this seems to suggest to Cavell that the bird's killing is a denial of a claim made on the Mariner. Firing his cross-bow attempts to silence the claim to human responsibility, and splits that attempt off from its consequences (namely, the death of the bird, or nature, or the world). Here is Cavell drawing the analogy to language:

> The dissatisfaction with one's human powers of expression produces a sense that words, to reveal the world, must carry more deeply than our agreements or attunements in criteria will negotiate. How we first deprive words of their communal possession and then magically and fearfully attempt by ourselves to overcome this deprivation of ourselves by ourselves, is a way of telling the story of skepticism.
>
> *IQO* 60

The skeptical doubts that pervade everyday life often take the form of this drive to repudiate the social, "as if my reaction to the discovery of my separateness is to perpetuate it, radicalize it."[24] The Mariner's human connections are "dead to him before he shoots, as if just possibly the shooting should bring them back to life" (*IQO* 60). The poet may likewise worry that their art is fatal and that it might require a selfsame splitting off from the consequences. The Mariner is guilty chiefly of being self-absorbed.

"[W]hatever else the Albatross may signify, to the Mariner it must present itself as a manifestation of himself" (*IQO* 61). And so in this way, it is an allegory of philosophical self-reflection in the Kantian mode.

Cavell does not see the Mariner as, in the end, reconciled with society. The Mariner asks the Hermit to hear his confession—that is, he asks the Hermit to ask him to speak—and his penance takes the form of the retelling of his story. He invites us to recall at this juncture Thoreau's notion that the philosopher does not speak first. The ambiguity in who speaks first in this scene tells us that the Hermit is no philosopher, or at least no philosopher of that kind. When the Mariner meets the Wedding-Guest, he similarly prompts the latter to ask a question, but it proves no real "invitation to dialogue" (*IQO* 63). The Mariner, the gloss tells us, is meant to teach by example of his life, but the lesson he offers the Wedding-Guests is that union with God far outweighs, and supersedes, the wedding. Posing the wedding as standing in competition with the union with God, the Mariner's tale stuns his audience: they are left to embrace "either aloneness or else society in its totality [over] the splitting or pairing contracted in marriage" (*IQO* 64). The tale can stun but rescue no further.

The lesson, Cavell argues, is that a romantic quest for "genuine publicness" requires the survival of privacy until the ground is properly laid. The marriage alone does not suffice to secure us from privacy (say, from the fantasy of private language); marriage is nothing but a further investment in our self-absorption, a substitution for the real thing. "If marriage is the name of our only present alternative to the desert-sea of skepticism, then for that very reason this intimacy cannot be celebrated, or sanctified; there is no outside of it. You may describe it as lacking its poetry; as if intimacy itself, or the new pressure upon it, lacked expression."[25] The Mariner's tale is a romantic affirmation of a larger sense of intimacy, a genuine publicness, to which poetry gives expression in making our common lives interesting, whereas the equivalent of the marriage in language only allows us to express our intimacies in a "*search* for expression, not in assurances of it" (*IQO* 65).

The Theme of Separation and the Skeptic's Revenge

The figure of the child, or rather, the adult who struggles in the "debris" of childhood's aftermath, is the point of departure for the final Beckman lecture, the pivot point of *In Quest of the Ordinary*. The theme of the lecture is a familiar one: the denial of separation through its radicalization.[26] The child sees the liveliness of the world. She talks to plants. Her education requires, however, that she put away such things, and accept that she stands apart from the world, that is, is separated from it. The adult is a metaphysician. Cavell notes that in the final stanza of Wordsworth's "Intimation of Immortality from Recollections of Early Childhood," the "earth appears as an omen, open to interpretation." This idea seems easier to accept (for "us English-speaking metaphysicians") than the thought, expressed in stanzas 4 and 6, that the Earth (note the orthographic shift) is animate. "But in favor of what is this overcome?" Cavell asks, "and why is it so hard? I mean, why is it, or why was it, when we were children, *natural* to us: an ordinariness which a new ordinariness must replace?" (*IQO* 71). What does Wordsworth mean by "communicating with objects"? Does it matter whether it is us, or nature, who does the talking? And who speaks first?

When the poet "speaks to things, what he speaks to them about is their speaking" (*IQO* 72). Take the line "Our birth is but a sleep and a forgetting," and by a forgetting (and recollecting) and a birth, we mean not only my own, but also the birth of the human, our coming into language. We recover from the loss of childhood (we recover its forms of recovery), Cavell wants to argue, by imitating it, "as it imitated us ... by participating in what it participated in, for instance in remembering what it remembered, and in forgetting what it forgets ... so imitating ourselves, or what we might become" (*IQO* 73). We learn from childhood also what it means to have had a childhood, to forget and to recollect, to acquire language, to be brought into a form of life. Putting away childish things is an achievement of intellect, Cavell says, but Wordsworth is calling on us to remember childhood, which is to say, the animacy of things, but also the whole affair of human life, of becoming a human, of entering into a life in language. It remains to be said just how we are meant to "replace the ordinary in the light in which we live it," replace it with birth (*IQO* 75). Faced with the cost of this intellectual achievement, there are those who would lash out, seek revenge against the world for our separation from it. If Wordsworth provides a way of picturing recovering, it is Shakespeare who best captures the skeptic's maddening pursuit of revenge.

Cavell turns our attention to *The Winter's Tale*, particularly its comedic end, which despite its comedy nevertheless leaves a young boy's death unaccounted for. The child's presence appears to organize the unfolding of every major event in the play: Hermione's pregnancy leads to the eruption of suspicion (Leontes's of his paternity), Paulina has faith that the sight of the child will turn Leontes's heart, Leontes orders the child abandoned (only later to be named), the Apollonian Oracle at Delphos declares Hermione innocent and pronounces Leontes will have no heir until the child is found, at which moment Leontes's older son and presumptive heir is discovered to have died (seemingly from sickness brought on by the suspicion of his mother, and which in turn leads to her death from agony), and finally, the child returns after sixteen years, bringing her mother back to life. Given the comedic re-marriage, which is to say, the reconciliation and return to ordinary life, perhaps even the retributive acquisition of a son-in-law, it is not immediately clear what is to be made of the unaccounted-for death. It is suggested (that is to say, Leontes himself suggests) that the boy dies "[c]onceiv[ing] the dishonour of his mother," while the servant who reports the boy's death says he has perished from anxiety over his mother's situation.[27] But the boy has already left our sight for good after his father sees him whispering with his mother seated in her lap, purportedly sharing a winter's tale, which causes the father to fly into a rage, reminded seemingly both of the threat of her seduction (and disloyalty) and the threat posed by whispers, especially those of rumors of his cuckoldry. Cavell proposes a strikingly original reading of this scene.

> We are by now so accustomed to understanding insistence or protestation, perhaps in the form of rage, as modes of denial, that we will at least consider that the

negation of this tale is the object of Leontes' fear, namely the fear that he *is* the father. As if whatever the son says, the very power of his speaking, of what it is he bespeaks, is fearful; as if his very existence is what perplexes his father's mind.

IQO 77–78

If it is the case that Leontes fears of his paternity, then his jealousy of Polixenes is derivative of this desire to disown his son. This would certainly explain why Leontes's "diseased opinion . . . vanishes exactly upon his learning that his son is dead," and not only after the death of both son and wife, unsettled as he might have been from the shock that issues from the discovery that his disbelief has the power to kill. Since it is the scene of mother and son whispering, and the mother's confession that such whispering makes her feel full, that is the proximate cause of Leontes's jealousy, "the son's death reads like the satisfaction of the father's wish" (*IQO* 79). So when Leontes declares, upon learning that his wish has been fulfilled, that "Apollo's angry, and the heavens themselves / Do strike at my injustice" (as cited in *IQO* 78), it stands to reason that Apollo's anger stems not only from Leontes's disbelief of the oracle, but instead from having been outsmarted by the king's performance of jealousy toward Polixenes—Leontes has, in effect, tricked Apollo into exacting his revenge for him against his son. It is at this point that Leontes orders Hermione removed that she might recover, saying he has "believed too much mine own suspicion" (*IQO* 79). But what, Cavell asks, would be the right amount to have believed? How else are we to respond to our doubts? Here is the passage from Leontes' speech that returns us to the theme with which we have been otherwise occupied in this chapter:

> There may be in the cup
> A spider steeped, and one may drink, depart,
> And yet partake no venom, for this knowledge
> Is not infected; but if one present
> Th'abhorred ingredient to his eye, make known
> How he hath drunk, he cracks his gorge, his sides,
> With violent hefts. I have drunk, and seen the spider.

Winter's Tale, 2.1.39–45, qtd. in *IQO* 79

This "poisonous knowledge"[28] is the inability of Leontes to acknowledge his son as his own. Shakespeare has given us a way of returning to the point with which we began: language's power to word the world, as well as its repudiation of that power. The instability of Leontes's condition mirrors the skeptic's sense of "knowing more than his fellows about the fact of knowing itself, in having somehow peeked behind the scenes, or say conditions, of knowing" (*IQO* 80). We can read *The Winter's Tale*, therefore, "as a study of skepticism—that is, as a response to what skepticism is a response to. Recall that we had said at the outset that skepticism calls for a response, or an effort at recovery, and that "skepticism's own sense of what recovery would consist in dictates efforts to refute it" *(IQO* 80). But to respond to these doubts with knowledge only leads us to the demand of further proof (since it aims at eliminating skepticism). "True recovery lies in reconceiving [skepticism], in finding skepticism's source," to creatively re-inhabiting the ordinary, full of doubt though it remains (*IQO* 80).

If *The Winter's Tale* itself constitutes the telling of a *tale*—a word that is invoked throughout the play to describe claims that would be hard to believe in the absence of first-person experience—whether it is Leontes's or Mamillius's (after all, this Oedipal dilemma in reverse seems to be the central conflict, but whose story is it that is narrated?), it is a reflection of this order of response; the play is itself a meditation on our *capacity* to tell a tale. Two ideas are connected by its telling: ideas about relating ideas and ideas about reproduction. The language of the play, Cavell points out, is saturated with terms in this domain of counting, recounting, telling, and relating, words that are shadowed by the economic or the computational, and which seem to imply a sense "that the very purpose of language is to communicate . . . which is to say, to tell. And you can always tell more and tell less than you know" (*IQO* 83). Our "most human predicament" is this ambivalence of wanting to express more than our words can bear, and wanting to avoid telling altogether.

This formulation also brings us back to the question of romantic animism. Actually, it connects fully the various threads that have arisen out of our disappointment with Kant's response to skepticism. (The reader will recall that we carry the death of the world itself inside our categories.) In response to doubts, one might claim to know something in virtue of being able to tell it ("you can for instance tell a goldfinch from a goldcrest because of their differences in eye markings"). In this case, a certain piece of expert knowledge is at stake, one theoretically available for anyone's possession. But there are also things I claim to know in virtue of seeing, and in which case I claim to know something because I myself have seen it ("to know a hawk from a handsaw—or a table from a chair—you simply have . . . to be able to say what is before your eyes") (*IQO* 84). In the latter case, my competence as a knower is on the line. This is the conventional expression of foundationalist epistemology. How do I know that I know that a thing really exists, when I might as well be dreaming, or mad, or deceived by a malevolent being? The epistemological question, of course, turns out to be a question about existence (of things in the external world, things-in-themselves, or other minds, or of the Cartesian *res extensa* in general). And this is precisely what Cavell takes Leontes's "perplexity" over this issue to be. When Leontes first wonders whether Mamillius is his son, he tries to answer this doubt by comparing certain of their shared features. Nothing, he can tell, seems to suffice to answer his suspicions, and he rules out anyone else's testimony (his is a particularly masculine form of skepticism). No *knowledge* suffices to disabuse him of his doubts. The only cure, Cavell says, would be for Leontes to acknowledge his son as his, whatever the "truth" of the matter. Even the truth of the oracular testimony fails to bring him back to sanity, or to the world.

> This is confirmed as a matter of this drama's competition [the concluding drama of revelation and resurrection, the reconciliation of the family] with narrative romance, by making the finding of a child who has been empirically lost, in *fact* rejected and abandoned, a matter swiftly dealt with by simply narration.
>
> *IQO* 86

It is easy for Leontes to believe the otherwise fantastic story of the daughter's return. Hermione's return to life is a return from *transcendental* loss, by contrast, in the sense that Leontes has been blind to her. Cavell says that in this way, one sees in theater a contestation of the distinction between saying and showing (perhaps this is also why so many Shakespeare scholars find it so difficult to agree on the genre of *The Winter's Tale*). The final scene of reconciliation—of returning what we earlier called a conviction in reality—relies on a *re-constitution* of knowledge, and with it, the world, and not a telling of something already known. The poetic (re)founding of the world reveals to us that "to speak is to say what counts" (*IQO* 86). By *counting*, Cavell means the manner whereby we take interest in something, and in terms of what Wittgenstein calls establishing a grammatical kind of object—to say that an instance counts as something (a chair, or a table, or a hawk), as we noted earlier, is to say we intuit a feeling of rightness, or aptness, in the situation before us. *Telling* in this way seems to cover both relating a story and that something counts, in one gesture. Cavell here builds on Wittgenstein's ingenious example of what it means to learn to count—we simultaneously learn to recite the numbers, and to count things by means of them. When I count by numbers, I recount events already fixed, but when I tell a story (or a tale), things are worked out in the telling. I *re*count them. When Leontes is unable to convince himself, by means of any criteria, of his son's belonging to him, he concludes he must disown his son. Put otherwise, he must make him not count as his own and in so doing loses his capacity to speak—his capacity to use language, which is his attunement with others. What is at stake is not ignorance, Cavell writes, but ignoring, not "opposable doubt" but "unappeasable denial" (*IQO* 88).

> The Shakespearean portraits lets us see that the skeptic *wants* the annihilation, that it is his way of asserting the humanness of knowledge, since skepticism's negation of the human, its denial of satisfaction in the human (here in human conditions of knowing), is an essential feature of the human, as it were its birthright.
> *IQO* 88

Leontes wants to turn his defeat into a victory, not unlike Nietzsche's slave revolt, though Nietzsche imagines an overcoming of this condition by saying *yes* to one's self, a possibility of becoming more-than-human. Like Thanatos, "Leontes is quite logical, in wanting there to be nothing, to want there to be no separation" (*IQO* 88). He is both fanatic (dogmatic) *and* skeptic. Counting implies a splitting up, a parting of ways, a marking of distinction, an unbearable separation. But a journey into nothingness—suicide—would likewise only destroy his individual experience, not return him to a whole. So perhaps his desire is to have never been born? This it seems would be the only solution to his simultaneous desire "neither to exist nor not to exist, neither for there to be a Leontes separate from Polixenes and Hermione and Mamillius nor for there not to be, neither for Polixenes to depart nor for him not to" (*IQO* 90).

This moment in his reading is strikingly similar to an episode from Cavell's own childhood, recounted some thirty years later in *Little Did I Know*, and which he describes as the moment in which he realized his father wished him not to have existed. I recall it here just briefly because it so powerfully captures the absolutely mundane quality of the gestures and expressions that his mother relates that part of his father's rage was borne of jealousy. It was evident, for example, once while they were watching contestants on *Information Please* brag about their knowledge of Shakespeare, and which led the father to call out "they are the aristocracy!"—a statement which his young son recognized may well have also been addressed to him. The family decides to move to the north side of Atlanta—a catastrophic event for the child, for whom it signaled that his own fate was different from that of other children—and dismayed at the unfamiliar new house, he finally recognizes a purple, ornamental box that was filled with sweets when company came over. And as he realizes his father is also with him in the semi-dark room, that they are alone together, he also realizes he knows his father less well than anyone else who was in their old familiar house. To break the silence, the son says to his father, "I didn't know we had these here," meaning the little speckled wafers that filled the purple bowl, to which his father replies, "And you still don't know it!" (*LDIK* 18).

If this were another case of mundane displaced affect, why should it affix itself to his own son, "an innocent bystander who had intercepted his rage"? (*LDIK* 19). Upon reflection, it occurs to the now adult Stanley that the boy, releasing his "numbness," crying for himself after this episode, was also crying for his father, who was as much a target of the son's hatred (for being hated) as the reverse. I cite here a rather lengthy passage in which Cavell analyzes this memory because it so deftly captures the charge invested in exchanges of this kind and their relevance to philosophical questions:

> It is as if I knew then that I would one day find a way out of the devastation he could make of his island, and knew that such a day would never come for him. (Don't tell me no man is an island.) Not of course that I escaped it entirely, but I have made headway in keeping, as it were, my knack of adopting his powers of devastation separate from my own causes for despair. . . .
>
> Yet I know that without a certain caution I could take on at this moment a version of his murderous melancholy, not fully sure whether it would be in response to him or in identification with him. How could I have failed to be suspicious, no matter how many years later, when I found philosophers asking such questions as, "Do I know your pain the way you do?" My principal problem was not that of doubting my knowledge of the feelings of others but rather of standing apart from them, or failing to. Not to know them would require exorcism. . .
>
> Wittgenstein recognizes that "our investigation" "seems only to destroy everything . . . important" but insists that he is "destroying nothing but houses of cards" (§ 118). Read more persistently, however, the moment conveys a recognition of inner devastation, expressed explicitly in a phantasm of the rubble of a destroyed city ("leaving behind only bits of stone and rubble"). (I recall that Thoreau shows himself to have acquired wood for his new cabin by demolishing an old shack.) I do not leap to the conclusion that my attraction to philosophy was as to an intellectual region from which I might avert or provide reparation for scenes of inner devastation.
>
> *LDIK* 19–21

Is any redemption to be had from such devastation? What of Leontes? And why the economistic language if the play is really about overcoming revenge, asking for and receiving forgiveness? The debt that sets off the accounting, the exchanges, with which the play is occupied, Cavell wants to say, is for "the fact of separation, for having one's own life," a debt for the condition of indebtedness (*IQO* 92). Leontes wants to settle accounts and "annihilat[e]" debt "in a world without counting." If a debt is repaid, this would only affirm indebtedness. Exchange implies multiplication, of debt (Polixenes for having stayed so long?), of one's issue (a son, for example), of words, all seemingly out of control. This double bind of our indebtedness, "for so to speak the gift of life, produces a wish to revenge oneself upon existence, on the facts, or facts, of life as such," and on Time.[29] Leontes's jealousy of Polixenes, we said a moment ago, is derivative of his desire for overcoming separation. In this sense, it is posed as "the solution of a problem in computation or economy" (*IQO* 94). "It is a place ... within which to investigate psychic violence, or torture, as a function both of skepticism's annihilation of the world and of the wounded intellect's efforts to annihilate skepticism," to which romanticism offers its own response, a mode of recovery, through the "buying back" of the thing-in-itself, through animism, at the price, at least potentially, of the "autonomy" of poetry and philosophy (*IQO* 95).

Cavell sees in the final scene, we have said, a wedding ceremony, and thereby, a study in theater itself. Hermione, awoken back to life, *is* the play, *is* the creation that reconceptualizes knowledge, *is* acknowledgment. The ceremony, and Hermione's resurrection, testify to the poet's capacity to bring "words to life, or vice versa."[30] Put another way, the scene theatrically enacts a resurrection of language for the audience, not just before them; they are transformed into participants. Is it safe to say this is a reconciliation, though? Do we go on using words just as we have done before? Is Leontes reconciled with his wife? Is he forgiven? Forgiveness seems to require that one allows oneself to be forgiven, much as we said earlier that the philosopher allows themselves to be read, and in so doing, accounts for themselves. Shakespeare has one of Leontes's advisors suggest to the dismayed king, "do as the heavens have done, forget your evil; / With them, forgive yourself."[31] It seems as though he has indeed forgotten his desired revenge against life, his will to nothingness, which for Nietzsche constitutes a critical act of creativity. If, as Cavell argues, the romantics saw this revenge, this psychical desire to destroy the world, as our "carrying the death of the world in us, in our constructions of it ... the final scene of issuing in *The Winter's Tale* shows what it may be to find in oneself the life of the world." The responsibility for bringing the world to life, Cavell continues, is the same as our responsibility for the "life of our words" that we see in Emerson and Thoreau (*IQO* 101). *This* then is what it means to say that Hermione is the play, and Paulina the director, *and* what it means to see in romanticism's response to the Kantian bargain a bringing back of the world to life, by resurrecting our words. Poetry achieves a creative re-inhabitation by moving us to allow ourselves to be expressed, to creatively forget our metaphysical flights and indulgence, and so to word the world again, vulnerable as that may be. We allow ourselves to be read in the play, without merely returning to the way things were, as if nothing has happened. Something has moved.

Reading and Response

At the outset of *In Quest of the Ordinary*, the answer to the question, *to what does romanticism respond?*, involves, at least for the American philosopher, the severance of philosophy from literature. The kernel of this thought is captured in the very opening lines of Cavell's Beckman Lectures, where he describes his return to Berkeley as suffused by an "uncanny feeling that I could say anything here and be understood completely," despite the fact that "no utterance of mine could be acceptable simultaneously to all those by whom I desire understanding"—in this case, at the hands of philosophy and literature respectively (*IQO* 3). Cavell describes his own practice, informed by the late Wittgenstein and by Austin, as well as the Transcendentalism of Emerson and Thoreau, as concerned primarily with a response to skepticism—a response, that is, rather than a *refutation* in *defense* of ordinary beliefs against skepticism, and which itself seems to run counter to our ordinary use of "belief." But why *these* figures in particular?

The argument between the skeptic and the anti-skeptic had left him "disappointed," Cavell tells his audience, a parallel of the "life-consuming" disappointment we read in the mode of literary tragedy—a "human disappointment with human knowledge" (*IQO* 87). In response, *The Claim of Reason* had tried to understand skepticism as an argument "of language with itself (over its essence)" (*CR* 34). The picture of language at work there was as "the thought that we share criteria by means of which we regulate our application of concepts, means by which, in conjunction with what Wittgenstein calls grammar, we set up the shifting conditions of conversation" (*IQO* 5). These conditions had to remain "open to repudiation"—in fact, this is what it means to possess language.

> Here my thought was that skepticism is a place [he calls Nowhere] . . . in which the human wish to deny the condition of human existence is expressed; and so long as the denial is essential to what we think of as the human, skepticism, cannot, or must not, be denied.
>
> *IQO* 5

For Cavell, Wittgenstein's signal contribution was tied to the re-conception of skepticism as "a standing threat to, or temptation of, the human mind—that our ordinary language and its representation of the world *can* be philosophically repudiated and that it is essential to our inheritance and mutual possession of language" (*CT* 89). Or we could describe it as the danger that our words might fail, that language's "power to word the world" (*IQO* 154) might abjure, that I might be misunderstood. When I express myself—for example, when I express to you that I am in pain—this is a public affair. It is not meant to express something inexpressible (for example, the private, inner state of my pain). Instead, it makes a claim on the addressee, it demands their acknowledgment, though it might not receive it.[32] But if this is what it means to possess a language, then the task of our response could not be the *defeat* of skepticism by means of a guarantee that the communicative act will work out in the end, but must entail instead the preservation of the essential vulnerability that inheres in the meaning of our life in language. It follows that ordinary language cannot be understood as "a special philosophical language," a better replacement for metaphysical language. At most, we can say positively that the ordinary is whatever is at stake in skepticism, "as if the ordinary is best to be discovered ... in its loss" (*CT* 90). If conventionally philosophers have sought to repudiate skepticism, to secure us from its threats, by producing arguments for the grounds of definitive *knowledge*, a response that seeks to preserve skepticism against this gesture requires something more like *acknowledgement*, where the latter is understood as an interpretation of the former. We give the name of romanticism to those gestures that respond to, and are motivated by, these efforts (philosophical and otherwise) to secure knowledge and thereby overcome skepticism.

Where critics have misread Cavell's romanticism as mere sentimentalism, it is because they have understood him to be proposing in acknowledgment just such an "alternative" to knowledge (just as ordinary language might be misread as constituting an alternative to metaphysics), and much in the way they had caricatured Novalis or Schlegel earlier as merely opposing Passion to Reason. But for Cavell, acknowledgment does not ford another route along which skepticism might work itself out. Rather, it allows those doubts to remain "alive in us," to acknowledge that they saturate our everyday existence. "This means that an irreducible region of our unhappiness is natural to us but at the same time unnatural ... To find what degrees of freedom we have in this condition ... is the romantic quest." Call it a quest after the uncanniness of the ordinary, the extraordinary in the low and the common, the "surrealism ... of what we accept, adapt to, as the usual, the real" (*IQO* 9).

There is another side to this coin, which, in *The Claim of Reason*, Cavell posed this way: "how can I fail to believe in my expression of myself, in my capacity to present myself for acknowledgment?" (*CR* 383). Surely, I cannot *simply* express my inner self, because the response my expression produces in the other will be directed toward the expression, rather than to me myself. So alternatively, I might wish to let myself matter to the other. And indeed, that is the advice he offers to Hamlet:

> To let yourself matter is to acknowledge not merely how it is with you, and hence to acknowledge that you want the other to care, at least to care to know. It is equally to acknowledge that your expressions in fact express you, that they are yours, that you are them.
>
> *CR* 383

It is against this backdrop—the thought of ordinary language as a site both threatened by skeptical doubt and capable of bearing its preservation, its acknowledgement—that one is struck by claims like Wordsworth's, that poetry is what makes "the incidents of common life interesting."[33] "To find what degrees of freedom we have in this condition, to show that it is at once needless yet somehow, because of that, all but necessary, inescapable, to subject its presentation of necessity to diagnosis, in order to find truer necessities, is the romantic quest I am happy to join" (*IQO* 9). Cavell's attraction to Wordsworth, or to Coleridge, or Poe (or to Emerson and Thoreau for that matter), his attraction to romanticism, is tied up precisely with what is involved in the words "making" and "interesting." We might from time to time come to doubt that there is anything to the liveliness of things, and so the world becomes rather dull. But poetry makes something happen for those to whom it speaks, by responding to our boredom. That selfsame boredom to which a certain fantastical response is issued in the form of metaphysical desires—a "false excitement," or a "longing for the transcendent," says Wittgenstein—that torments us by its very inexpressibility.[34] Compare with the 1802 Preface to *Lyrical Ballads*, in which Wordsworth was responding to suggestions that he provide a "systematic defense of [his] theory," but which he refused to indulge, either in the register of what he calls *reasoning* or by providing arguments. Instead, he introduces his poems as *experiments* in the "language of conversation," drawing a stark contrast with the "gaudiness and inane phraseology of many modern writers."[35] His principal object, he writes,

> was to choose incidents and situations from common life, and to relate or describe them, throughout, as far as was possible, in a selection of language really used by men; and, at the same time, to throw over them a certain colouring of imagination, whereby ordinary things should be presented to the mind in an unusual way; and further, and above all, to make these incidents and situations interesting by tracing in them, truly through not ostentatiously, the primary laws of our nature.[36]

Cavell of course recognizes that such a view is not exactly that of professional philosophy, and neither is the suggestion that this sort of poetry responds to the same kinds of problems as does philosophy. But inasmuch as they "quarrel" for instance with metaphysics, he suggests, we ought to acknowledge the kinship therebetween. And this is after all how Cavell reads Thoreau's sentiment in *Walden* that "there are nowadays professors of philosophy but not philosophers" (as cited in *IQO*, 9). *Walden* certainly lays a claim to philosophy, which Thoreau understands as living admirably. But philosophy, as a discipline, had cast out such efforts, and instead offers a dream of mastery in the form of this compulsion to metaphysics.[37] Philosophy had disqualified Thoreau and Emerson, and this disqualification led Cavell to ask, in his earlier work, whether therefore America had ever expressed itself philosophically. The splintering of literature from philosophy had called into question that America could take for granted culture in common, i.e. that we might share a cultural inheritance, a fact that would be the case for philosophers like Kant or Hegel. Rationalization split culture apart.[38] Let me make this point another way. The inaugural moment of philosophy as a discipline, as a practice distinct from what Thoreau calls the admirable "economy of living"—a moment Cavell associates with the "defeat" or excision of the Transcendentalists at the hands of religion's defenders among "Harvard philosophers"—amounts to a profound cultural amnesia. American life seemingly forgets its own founding. And this erasure of Emerson and Thoreau on behalf of disciplinary philosophy seems to be "justified" among the vaulted professoriat because they lack "arguments." But then again, why should that concern us?

"I can imagine," Cavell writes, "a number of responses to what may appear as my wish for the participation of philosophy and literature in one another" (*IQO* 12). The problem, we might be tempted to say, originates with Plato and his defensive expulsion of poetry from the republic of philosophy because of the competition it offered. But professional philosophy does not remain "slavishly" beholden, for example, to the philosophical obligation to therapy. And there are good reasons for rejoicing in its having done so, but for Cavell, if we are unable to see these options as in competition with one another, then we have "given up something I take as part of the philosophical adventure . . . That nothing of high culture is common to us means that for us no text is sacred, no work of this ambition is to be preserved at all costs" (*IQO* 12-13). This is the premise, in fact, that Emerson and Thoreau begin with and with which they conclude.

What Thoreau and Emerson offer is a practice Cavell describes as reading. One can think of philosophy as solving problems, or analysis. But we could also think of philosophical interpretation as a mode of reading. If, for example, by argumentation we meant accepting responsibility for one's discourse, then surely one would have to grant the title of philosopher to Emerson and to Thoreau, in virtue of their reading (would not Wordsworth's Preface also count?). Professional philosophy, however, proceeds via a myth of philosophizing, or what Cavell calls "myths of the role of reading in philosophical writing" (*IQO* 15). According to this myth, "philosophy begins only when there are no further texts to read, when the truth you seek has already been missed, as if it lies behind you" (*IQO* 15). Following Wordsworth, we might think of this emptying out by a claim to totality as a state of being empty of interest. Let's call it boredom. It cuts life out of the picture, renders it altogether boring. And one way of securing this domain is by circumscribing the kinds of texts that count as philosophical. But how is this to be avoided? What ought we to read? And for how long?

Here is the startling claim: by reading, Cavell takes Thoreau to mean "a process of *being read,* as finding your fate in your capacity for interpretation of yourself" (*IQO* 16). Reading thus resides in the interplay of reading and writing. "Reading is a variation of writing, where they meet in meditation and achieve accounts of their opportunities; and writing is a variation of reading, since to write is to cast words together that you did not make, so as to give or take readings" (*IQO* 18). For one, this extends the domain of reading philosophy out into the world, well beyond the reading of books. Conventional books of philosophy are especially to be avoided because they are premised on suspense, on how it works out in the end. Instead, we should aim for books with "no forward motion . . . Either we are able to rethink a thought that comes our way, to own and assess it as it occurs, or we must let pass, it is not ours" (*IQO* 18-19). "Words come to us from a distance," Cavell writes elsewhere, "they were there before we were; we are born into them" (*SW* 64). But if this is the case, how is it that I can mean them?

> Meaning them is accepting that fact of their condition. To discover what is being said to us, as to discover what we are saying, is to discover the precise location from which it is said . . . Speaking together face to face can seem to deny that distance, to deny that facing one another requires acknowledging the presence of the other, revealing our positions, betraying them if need be. But to deny such things is to deny our separateness. And that makes us fictions of one another."
>
> *SW* 64-65

If there is no philosophy "until the philosopher is *being* read," then by the same token, each and every claim to, or for, philosophy must come to (ac)count for itself. It cannot point us elsewhere. We will return to the economistic valence of this language below. But for now, Cavell names this recovery *edification*, in the double sense of also building a home in which to dwell, and it is in this sense that the "house being built in *Walden* is *Walden*"—it begins, like any beginning in language, with borrowing from others.[39] "You only need sit still long enough in some attractive spot in the woods," Cavell reads out from Thoreau, "that all its inhabitants may exhibit themselves to you by turns" (*IQO* 21). The moral of *Walden,* he writes later, is comparable to the guiding thought of Heidegger's famous essay on dwelling—that the dwelling comes before building. The difference is that "in *Walden* the proof that what you have found you have made your own, your home, is that you are free to leave it" (*IQO* 175). Reading requires allowing, even inviting, the other to speak first. Waiting and silence. No great surprise that there is no room for such seduction in university classrooms, he notes.

> If every one of our words is implicated in the conformity to usage [that is, is lacking in self-reliance], then evidently no word assures a safe beginning; whether a given word will do must accordingly depend upon how it allows itself to be said.
>
> *IQO* 23–24

Professors are often tempted (are they not?) to think of reading as an act of deciphering the author's intention in writing the text. But what if, instead, we waited, and were attentive to hearing what called their words into being? Or where it is that I find myself feeling at home (in language). This latter option leads us to an investigation closed off by reading for intention: namely, how is it that we are capable of expressing something we ourselves do not know, or that someone else might know us better than we know ourselves (or worse)? Or, to return to the formulation in *The Claim of Reason*, that it might express us, too? It follows that when we express ourselves to one another, or to ourselves even, our words threaten to betray us.[40] This "gesture of waiting" returns us to our ordinary experience, to our everyday ways of speaking and acting, and the skeptical doubt that lines our life in language. There is a well-known moment in the *Philosophical Investigations* where Wittgenstein says, "if I have exhausted justifications I have reached bedrock, and my spade is turned. Then I am inclined to say: This is simply what I do" (*PI* §289). Recalling these lines, Veena Das responds, in an especially moving passage, that "in this picture of the turned spade as indicative of a turned pen, we have the picture of what the act of writing may be in the darkness of this time ... when I reach bedrock I do not break through the resistance of the other, but in this gesture of waiting I allow the knowledge of the other to mark me."[41] These lines capture so well what Cavell means when he speaks of responsiveness, or our capacity to be called by a text, or even just a word, for which we can give no justification.[42] For the romantics among us, this might present itself as "the quest for a return to the ordinary, or of it, a new creation of our habitat [as in Wordsworth and Coleridge]; or as the quest, away from that, for the creation of a new inhabitation [Blake and Shelley]" (*IQO* 53), though in the end these might also amount to the same thing.

The Fantastic and the Ordinary

Until now, I have tried to provide an account of Cavell's understanding of language, the persistent danger that it might repudiate itself, and the Kantian and romantic responses to this situation respectively. The former bargains everything away in hopes of avoiding boredom. One destroys the world by making oneself into its creator. The latter responds to this bargain by allowing one's self to be expressed in someone else's words. Through this acknowledgement, we bring the world back to life. In *Quest of the Ordinary* comes to a close where it began—no forward motion after all—with the idea that

> what in philosophy is known as skepticism . . . is a relation to the world, and to others, and to myself, and to language, that is known to what you might call literature . . . in uncounted other guises—in Shakespeare's tragic heroes, in Emerson's and Thoreau's "silent melancholy" and "quiet desperation," in Wordsworth's perception of us as without "interest," in Poe's "perverseness." Why philosophy and literature do not know this about one another—and to that extent remain unknown to themselves— has been my theme it seems to me forever.
>
> *IQO* 154–55

We might get a feel for what is at stake for Cavell in this crossing, he himself tells us, through his recounting of the discovery of the phrase "uncanniness of the ordinary," and which he had originally thought must have appeared in Freud's famous essay on Hoffmann, but in fact occurs in Heidegger's "Der Ursprung des Kunstwerkes." Of course, Heidegger's sense of the ordinary is not Cavell's: "For him the extraordinariness of the ordinary has to do with forces in play that constitute our common habitual world . . . Whereas for me the uncanniness of the ordinary is epitomized by . . . the capacity, even desire, of ordinary language to repudiate itself, specifically to repudiate its power to word the world" (*IQO* 154). Nevertheless, Cavell detects what might be an "affinity" or "mutual derivation" of their views, and which pertains to a response to the "fantastic in what human beings will accustom themselves to . . . as if to be human is forever to be prey to turning your corner of the human race . . . into some new species of the genus of humanity, for the better or for the worst" (*IQO* 154).

Now for Freud, as everyone knows, the uncanniness (*Unheimlichkeit*, un-homedness) we find in Hoffman's "Der Sandmann" pertains to the threat of castration and not (Cavell says, uncannily) to the incapacity to distinguish the animate from the animate. We might have expected Freud, inheritor of poetry that he is, to think of the castration complex as a "new explanation or interpretation of the particular uncertainty in question," in which one recognizes that there no resolution to be had for underlying Oedipal drama until it is worked out "under the threat of castration," and, which is to say, that one does not, until that point, acknowledge the other as human (*IQO* 156). That Freud does not in fact take up this opening, and instead denies it repeatedly, Cavell diagnoses as a symptom of "the dissociation of psychoanalysis from philosophy"— "Freud seems to me to be protesting too much" (*IQO* 156). Perhaps here then too is a way of reading the denial of literature in Plato's philosophic republic.

The evidence for this reading comes by way of Cavell's noticing of a slight misreading of the Hoffmann text that Freud indulges at a crucial moment. Freud describes an important scene in which Clara's attention is drawn to a figure in the street. Nathaniel, looking through the spyglass after Clara, falls into a fit of madness, at which point Coppelius emerges from the crowd. One expects, Cavell says, indeed Nathaniel himself likely expects, that, looking for whatever caught Clara's attention, he will see his father. But what happens instead in Hoffman's text itself is that Nathaniel catches a glimpse of Clara through the looking-glass, not the figure below, and this is the vision that sends him into a fit. Freud reads the father as coming between the boy and the object of his desire, even as it seems to be that a woman has come between the boy and his father. We recall that the looking glass has the power to turn the inanimate animate (that is to say, to turn Olympia animate) for Nathaniel peering through. Cavell reminds us of an earlier explosive encounter where Clara rejects Nathaniel's poetry, prompting him to call her a "damned lifeless automaton." Cavell interprets this as evidence of a Heideggerian kind of romanticism, marked by an impatience with the ordinary and with Clara's refusal of higher and lower realms—or perhaps, we might say, with transcendence. In this light, we might read her appearance in the looking-glass as bringing her to life in her ordinariness, "together with the knowledge that he could not bear this ordinariness ... since it means bearing her separateness, her existence as other to him, exactly what his craving for the automaton permitted him to escape" (*IQO* 157).

Here the parallel with Leontes's situation is plain. "The glass," Cavell writes, "is a death-dealing rhetoric machine, producing or expressing the consciousness of life in one case (Olympia's) by figuration, in the other (Clara's) by literalization, or say defiguration."[43] Contrast the glass with Hermione's testimony (the play itself) with the poet's capacity to awaken the world (that is, without a resolution to the problem of substantive knowledge, but instead its interpretation. As a "machine of incessant animation," the glass is "the parody of a certain romantic writing." The moral, so to say, is that

> there is a repetition necessary to what we call life, or the animate, necessary for example to the human; and a repetition necessary to what we call death, or the inanimate, necessary for example to the mechanical; and there are no marks or features or criteria or rhetoric by means of which to tell the difference between them.... [T]he difference is the basis of everything there is for human beings to know, or say decide ... on no basis beyond or beside or beneath ourselves. Within the philosophical procedure of radical skepticism, the feature specifically allegorized by the machine of the spyglass is skepticism's happening all at once.
>
> *IQO* 158

So why, in the end, is it that a strand of psychoanalytic literary criticism, like Heidegger, and also like Nathaniel, is so "antagonistic" to the ordinary, to our everyday language? And how is it that the two positions seem to come so close, share an affinity or even a mutual derivation, and yet, one finds the other so threatening?

Take, for example, Lacan's reading of "The Purloined Letter," intended to demonstrate the repetition compulsion, by analogy to the displacement of signifiers. But Poe's tale might also be read, Cavell suggests, as an allegory of ordinary language philosophy, insofar as "The Purloined Letter" identifies itself, for him, as a study in mind-reading.[44] And this claim to mind-reading powers, he continues, seems to be one reason for a persistent irritation with ordinary language philosophy. The objection to such claims emanates, on his reading, from the desire of writers like Austin or Wittgenstein or Cavell himself to repudiate a Platonic hierarchy of (access to) knowledge, in which philosophy proper resides at the top, and proceeds by means of a special class of operators. So when Austin argues that saying "I know" involves a different, though not deeper, stance to what I communicate than the statement "I believe," it is taken to be a direct strike against the entrenched idea in professional philosophy that there are degrees of knowledge and thereby to pose a challenge to the security of their authority (their bargain). This gesture moves us (casually, Cavell notes) from our "use of the words 'belief' and 'knowledge' to, perhaps I can say, the nature of belief and of knowledge" (*IQO*, 162). This Cavell takes to be a move toward Wittgenstein's motto "Grammar says what kind of object something is,"[45] and which reminds of the importance of what we described earlier as literature's (or theater's) contestation of the distinction between showing and saying. At the same time, it goes a long way toward explaining their expulsion from (the offense or threat they are seen to signify to) philosophy.

Philosophy, as it were, seems unable to bear the separation, and falls into madness, insisting on some form of emptiness. By insisting on the fact that it alone has access to the truth of the matter, at least to some higher degree thereof, philosophy not only "underestimates" but takes pains to "falsify" the body—"it is as though I, in philosophizing, *want*... to place the mind beyond reach, want to get the body inexpressive, and at the same time find that I cannot quite want to, want to without reserve" (*IQO* 163). Wittgenstein's diagnosis of this self-torment evidenced in the drive to metaphysics as a way out of boredom, we are now prepared to see, to come full circle, is linked to this antagonism—his method is a way of pursuing what it is in language that makes this torture "seem necessary" and "makes it possible" (*IQO* 163–64).

A philosopher like Wittgenstein and a philosopher like Heidegger are both liable to be attracted to Poe's story of a letter hidden in plain sight, to the image of something *too* ordinary to attract notice—it is, after all, an apt allegory of *Zuhandenheit*, or of Dasein's everyday (*alltäglich*) existence, our inauthentic (*uneigentlich*) Being as the Being of the they (*das Man*) self. But the allegorical pivot specific to the ordinary language philosopher's reading, Cavell writes suggestively, is the "tale's repetition of the idea of the *odd*, and specifically its associating this idea ... with the consequence of laughter" (*IQO* 165). And we can connect this idea of laughter with Emerson's picture of reading in the following way. Cavell writes that the gag of "Self-Reliance" is the sentiment that "man dares not say ... but quotes." This line condenses a number of thoughts, which should by now be familiar:

> First, language is an inheritance. Words are before I am; they are common. Second, the question whether I am saying them or quoting them ... is the same as the question whether I do or do not exist as a human being and is a matter demanding

> proof. Third, the writing, of which the gag is part, is an expression of the proof of saying "I," hence of the claim that writing is a matter, say the decision, of life and death, and that what this comes to is the inheriting of language, an owning of words, which does not remove them from circulation but rather returns them, as to life. . . .
>
> The point I emphasize here is only that the life-giving power of words, of saying "I," is your readiness to subject your desire to words . . . to become intelligible, with no assurance that you will be taken up.
>
> IQO 113–14

The gag is, in a sense, on Descartes (and Kant, and Marx, and Freud), and the epistemological or intellectual response to skepticism, as a compulsive drive to knowing existence. Emerson diagnoses that the philosopher's need—that is, for a proof of self-authoring—arises at "particular historical moments in the life of the individual and in the life of the culture" (*IQO* 111). And he writes in "Fate" that "the history of the individual is always an account of his condition, and he knows himself to be party to his present estate." (As cited in *IQO* 136) "To make sense of this turn," Cavell writes, "Emerson needs a view of the world, a perspective on its fallenness, in which the *uncreatedness* of the individual manifests itself, in which human life appears as the individual's failure at self-creation, as a continuous loss of individual possibility in the face of some overpowering competitor" (*IQO* 111). And we are ashamed of this failure. In responses to the situation, that one cannot, or can no longer, offer Descartes's proof of self-authoring (and that we are embarrassed about it), Emerson offers what we been calling a recovery—that we come to inherit words in such a way that does "not remove them from circulation but rather returns them, as to life" (*IQO* 114). By refusing an "unnecessary acquiescence" (*IQO* 112), and antagonizing conformity, the "uncreated life" (*IQO* 111), we start down the road of adopting a good posture, which is to say, taking the decision to believe in the "promise that the private and the social will be achieved together, hence of the perception that our lives now take place in the absence of either" (*IQO* 114). Or, to put it another way, that expressing myself is also allowing myself to be expressed by another, and conversely, that my personal expression simultaneously "portrays [my] fellows and that [I am] writing on their behalf" (*IQO* 115). I become, in this way, ashamed of my shame.

"The sound of Poe's prose," Cavell continues, "is uncannily like the sound of philosophy as established in Descartes, as if Poe's prose were a parody of philosophy's" (*IQO* 121). What is so odd, we might say, is that we do not know for certain, for example in the *Philosophical Investigations*, whether an "expression is remarkable or casual, where this turns out to be a function of whether we leave the expression ordinary or elevate it into philosophy, an elevation that depends on escaping our sense, let us say, of the ridiculous" (*IQO* 166). In calling attention to oddity, in using laughter philosophically, Wittgenstein,

> speaks to us quite as if we have become unfamiliar with the world, as if our mechanism of anxiety, which should signal danger, has gone out of order . . . The

return of what we accept as the world will then present itself as a return of the familiar, which is to say, exactly under the concept of what Freud names the uncanny. That the familiar is a product of a sense of the unfamiliar and of the sense of a return means that what returns after skepticism is never (just) the same. . . . [Philosophy] turns out to require an understanding of how the seriousness of philosophy's preoccupations . . . its demand for satisfaction, its refusal of satisfaction—how this seriousness is dependent on disarming our sense of oddness and non-oddness, and therewith seeing why it is with the trivial, or superficial, that this philosophy finds itself in oscillation, as in an unearthly dance.

IQO 165–67

"The Purloined Letter" itself, its having been put in my hand, is an "artifact, in a contested play of mind-reading, that is openly concealed in and by the hand" (*IQO* 168). On the one hand, the letter, which is in a sense meant for me, the reader, is also invisible to me (as it is to the King), at the same time that, as it is meant for me, its contents are shown to me (in this sense "I am the Queen from whom it is stolen, as well as the pair of thieves who remove it and return it, therapeutically to me"). So at once I am meant to read the mind of the person into whose hand it is placed, and of the person who wrote it; "it is also to be read as the work of one who opposes me, challenges me to guess whether each of its events is odd or even, everyday or remarkable, ordinary or out of the ordinary" (*IQO* 168). Thus Poe captures what Cavell calls an urgent methodological issue—"an account for the fact that we are the victims of the very words of which we are at the same time the masters" (*IQO* 169). Cavell's great insight—one that he credits to Wittgenstein—is that this double fact of our relation to words, the "drift" it enables toward skepticism, amounts to the *discovery* of the everyday, that which skepticism would deny. And yet, "this recurrent failure in our possession by or of language," he says,

hardly accounts for such a crossroads as the emptiness of the word "only" . . . [or why] the odd is laughable, for what it is we are laughing at philosophically, anxiously . . . Thoreau's guiding vision of the oddness of our everyday . . . produces a response, that is, a texture of prose, lining the border between comedy and tragedy . . . The everyday is what we cannot but aspire to, since it appears to us as lost to us.

IQO 169–71

This, it seems, is precisely what philosophy, in its drive to emptiness, wants by its very nature to deny. The question is, how do we respond? For Thoreau, Cavell argues, one way of responding is through a certain joy in the knowledge of loss—a conjunction of mourning and morning. Or, we might say, to accepting our fate, that the existence of the world is not something we know or do not know, but which we can acknowledge—we acknowledge, that is to say, its separateness from me. Heidegger offers a competing response, a different inheritance of Kant, a response motivated by a desire to answer this separation—to answer violence with violence. A response, nevertheless, to the same threat.

Let me conclude, like I began, where Cavell does, with literature and philosophy and their relationship in America:

> [Claiming] Emerson and Thoreau as the origin in America, not alone of what is called literature but of what may be called philosophy, is to claim that literature is neither the arbitrary embellishment nor the necessary other of philosophy. You can either say that in the New World, distinctive philosophy and literature do not exist in separation, or you can say that the American task is to create them from one another, as if the New World is still to remember, if not exactly to recapitulate, the cultural labors of the Old World.
>
> *IQO* 182

A return, we have said, is never just a return to the same. One way of thinking of the fantastic in the ordinary, or of this task between literature and philosophy, is by returning to what Cavell describes as reading—reading, that is, understood as the

> reader's willingness to subject himself or herself to taking the eyes of the writer, which is in effect yielding his or her own, an exchange interpretable as a sacrifice of one another, of what we think we know of one another, which may present itself as mutual castration, in service either of our mutual victimization or else our liberation.
>
> *IQO* 187

This is an altogether different sort of relation than one that moves by demanding proof of their existence. The capacity, Cavell writes on the final page of *In Quest of the Ordinary*, to "let fact and fantasy interpret one another is the basis at once of the soul's sickness and of its health" (*IQO* 188). The domesticity of this situation, the fact that this is how it is at home, tells us a great deal about what it means to have a life in language.

Notes

1. This is, for instance, how Rorty reads ordinary language philosophy. See, however, Sandra Laugier's devastating reply to his charge in *Why We Need Ordinary Language Philosophy*, trans. Daniela Ginsburg (Chicago: University of Chicago Press, 2013).
2. Ludwig Wittgenstein, *Tractatus Logico-Philosophicus* (London: Anthem Press, 2021), 5.6
3. Sandra Laugier, "The Ordinary, Romanticism, and Democracy," *Modern Language Notes* 130, no. 5 (2015): 1041.
4. Ibid., 1048.
5. I owe my reading of this point to Laugier, *Why We Need Ordinary Language Philosophy*, 83.
6. This is a sentiment common to romanticisms German and American, and which as mere conventions since circulate–Coleridge, Wordsworth, Thoreau, and Emerson figure most prominently in this regard and may be considered the origin of this question of what it is to have a heritage.

7   Richard Eldridge, *The Persistence of Romanticism* (Cambridge: Cambridge University Press, 2001), 199, 201–2.
8   Immanuel Kant, *Kritik der reinen Vernunft* (Leipzig, 1787), 307–11. The distinction between real and logical possibility becomes relevant, because the real possibility of the object cannot be given merely by the fact that its form is in accordance with the catalogue of synthetic a priori judgments, but only insofar as it is supported by a corresponding intuition. For one interesting account of this question, see Nicholas Stang, *Kant's Modal Metaphysics* (Oxford: Oxford University Press, 2016).
9   Emerson, "Fate," quoted in *IQO* 37.
10 Laugier, "The Ordinary, Romanticism, and Democracy," 1047.
11 By criterial he means to mark that "while criteria provide conditions of (shared) speech they do not provide an answer to skeptical doubt. I express this by saying that criteria are disappointing, taking them to express, even to begin to account for, the human disappointment with human knowledge" (*IQO* 87).
12 Laugier, *Why We Need Ordinary Language Philosophy*, 85.
13 Ibid.
14 Andrew Bowie, *From Romanticism to Critical Theory* (London: Routledge, 1997), 58. For a detailed account of rule-following in this vein, see John McDowell's well-known series of essays on non-cognitivism, including "Wittgenstein on Following a Rule," *Synthes* 58, no. 3 (1984): 325–63 and "Non-Cognitivism and Rule-Following," in Steven Holtzman and Christopher Leich, eds., *Wittgenstein: To Follow a Rule* (London: Routledge, 1981), 141–62, and Eli Friedlander's excellent essay on rule-following vs. projection via examples, "Meaning Schematics in Cavell's Kantian Reading of Wittgenstein," *Revue International de Philosophe* 65, no. 256 (2011): 187. For recent anthropological engagement with this notion, see Andrew Brandel and Marco Motta, eds., *Living with Concepts: Anthropology in the Grip of Reality* (New York: Fordham University Press, 2021).
15 Friedlander, "Meaning Schematics," 184.
16 Ibid., 187.
17 These citations are to the 1965 edition, chap. 9.
18 Samuel Coleridge, *Biographia Literaria* (New York: Leavitt, Lord & Co, 1834), 88.
19 Coleridge is himself moved to remark on the closeness of his interpretation of Kant and the one offered by German romantics Schelling and Schlegel.
20 Coleridge, *Biographia*, 89.
21 *IQO* 44. A related argument appears in Horkheimer and Adorno's *Dialektik der Aufklärung* (1947).
22 The discussion of animism is one of the key moments where Cavell takes a step beyond *The Claim of Reason*, a point he himself articulates at some length. The intuition there of twin threats—two routes of skepticism, one being solipsism—being roughly equal in measure here is an exchange of one "craziness" for another "as if this answer to skepticism has gone further than it meant to" (*IQO* 46).
23 Wallace Stevens, *The Collected Poems of Wallace Stevens* (New York: Vintage Books, 1990), 534.
24 Freud is a shadow interlocutor throughout, and explicitly toward the end of the book, but here we might sense a resonance with the account of Eros and Thanatos as responses to the problem of splitting off of the ego qua reality principle and the desire for a return to non-separation evidenced in the oceanic feeling.

25 *IQO* 65. In his work on film, Cavell develops this opposition by juxtaposing the genre of the "comedy of remarriage" with the "melodrama of the unknown woman."
26 The figure of the child for Cavell is totally distinct from its usual treatment as a figure of redemption, as in Benjamin, or as signaling natality, as in Arendt, and instead pertains especially to that famous opening scene in *Philosophical Investigations* of the inheritance of language. In this way, "having been a child" is, as Paola Marrati brilliantly elaborates, "a condition that none of us . . . can ever overcome, grow out of. "Having been a child" is not a fact from the past that we may indifferently recall or forget, but rather an internal aspect of our existence that will last as long as we do." See Marrati, "Childhood and Philosophy," *MLN* 126, no. 5 (2011): 957. For recent perspectives on these issues in other fields, see Yves Érard et. al., eds., "Education and the Figure of the Child in the Works of Wittgenstein and Cavell," special issue, *A Contrario* 25, no. 2 (2017).
27 Shakespeare, *The Winter's Tale* (London: Arden Shakespeare, 2010), 2.3.12, quoted in *IQO* 77.
28 Veena Das, *Life and Words: Violence and the Descent into the Ordinary* (Berkeley: University of California Press, 2007), 77–78.
29 *IQO* 92. Throughout the lecture, Cavell compares this revenge against Time with Nietzsche's.
30 *IQO* 99. Cavell writes suggestively in *Little Did I Know*, "ceremony in human existence is no more measurable by its utility, though philosophers sometimes seem to argue otherwise, than the possession of language is, or living in common; you might as well argue the utility of possessing a human body" (*LDIK* 15). It is, we will recall, for Cavell, the negation of ceremony in *Lear* that leads us into madness.
31 Shakespeare, *Winter's Tale*, 5.1.5–6, quoted in *IQO* 101.
32 See Das, *Life and Words*, on the claim that it bodies forth.
33 Wordsworth, Preface to *Lyrical Ballads*, quoted in *IQO* 6.
34 See Juliet Floyd, "Wittgenstein and the Inexpressible," in *Wittgenstein and Moral Life*, ed. Alice Crary (Cambridge, MA: MIT Press, 2007), 177–234, for an excellent discussion of the stakes of interpreting the question of inexpressibility in Wittgenstein's work.
35 William Wordsworth, *The Major Works* (Oxford: Oxford University Press, 2008), 596–97.
36 Ibid.
37 I owe this turn of phrase to Barbara Cassin, whom I heard use it in a debate with Alain Badiou while a graduate student at Johns Hopkins. Cassin's debt to romanticism is an interesting point of comparison with Cavell's: her employment, for example, throughout her work of Novalis's term "logology," a discourse principally interested in itself, to oppose the Platonic claims to absolute truth. The "relativism" she endorses is thereby one that makes a claim to being only in virtue of what it can bring into being through its performance, and thereby remains similarly open to its own repudiation. See Barbara Cassin, *L'effet sophistique* (Paris: Gallimard, 1995).
38 Cavell invokes Weber's famous lecture on *Science as Vocation* at this juncture to point to a particularly American divorce of professional philosophy and poetry. Suffice it to say that for Weber, the process of cultural rationalization dooms the value spheres to be sundered one from the other, each following their own warring god, and so whatever affinity was borne between art and science inevitably will fall by the wayside.

The commitment of the modern to their vocation cannot be rejoined to another, though they may, from time to time, coexist in the body of a person.
39 *IQO* 20. The sense of "edifice" and "association" is also there in the domain of the German *Wissenschaft*.
40 On this point, see David Greenham, *Emerson's Transatlantic Romanticism* (New York: Palgrave Macmillan, 2012).
41 Das, *Life and Words*, 17.
42 Contrast this "democratization of philosophy" with the rarefied compulsion to philosophical authority evident in the writing of a philosopher like Heidegger. "The view that everything is effable," Emily Apter notes, "implies a faith in the limitless capabilities of rationalism to appropriate (aligned with what Heidegger would insist is the capacity to turn the earth into a world)" (Emily Apter, *Against World Literature* [New York: Verso Books, 2013], 19). Emerson and Thoreau, by contrast, are given to a kind of self-repression, and in so doing, "play . . . Hölderlin to their own Heidegger" (*IQO* 29). The refusal of communication between philosophy and literature, Cavell suggests, causes romanticism, or the kind of writing in which romantics express themselves. In this way, the way to their repression is laid by their self-repression, which Cavell links with their authority as founders of a culture, bound to offering a sacrifice.
43 *IQO* 157. I note here a potentially fascinating comparison with Lacoue-Labarthe's well-known critique of Heidegger on figuration, and what Marrati calls "the lure of demiurgic mimesis." See Paola Marrati, "The Difficulty of Experience," *MLN* 132, no. 5 (2017): 1225–35.
44 I say "in" mind-reading and not "of," as Cavell initially writes, so as to indicate his sense that the tale is, in virtue of its being a study, also an act of mind-reading.
45 *IQO* 162; *PI* §373, quoted in *IQO* 162. And hence the necessity of a grammatical investigation into a form of life. See *CR* 172–77, 184–85.

7

Measuring the Value of Human Life According to a Perfectionist Philosopher

David LaRocca

What if the history of Western moral philosophy were reconceived without regard for chronology (say, causation, intellectual history, the history of ideas), or the established protocols of inherited canons, or the criteria for what has traditionally counted as a legitimate contribution to evaluative thinking about normative experience? In short, what if Greek philosophers of the fifth century BCE, Plato and Aristotle, formed a conclusion while the nineteenth-century American philosopher and essayist Ralph Waldo Emerson lay at the beginning? And to add to the extra-experimental provocation, what if black-and-white Hollywood comedies and melodramas from the first half of the twentieth century supplied roughly *half* of the conversation—along with brightly underlined offerings from Shakespeare, Ibsen, Shaw, Henry James, Freud, and the French filmmaker Éric Rohmer? The answer to these unexpected (unasked for?) questions is Stanley Cavell's 2004 book *Cities of Words: Pedagogical Letters on a Register of the Moral Life*. A reader who wonders, "What is a city of words, much less what are cities of words?," who queries what a "pedagogical letter" might be, or for that matter who asks what a "register of the moral life" might entail, should find some orientation in what follows. No doubt, with a title and subtitle that call for such analysis, a prospective reader may be intimidated—yet, as with so many works by Cavell, there is much to glean from studying the names he gives to his projects (most of them drawn from ordinary language instead of a rarefied glossary of technical jargon). In due time, the ambitions of the project as a whole will come into view. Yet before such comprehension may dawn, a word about how his book is being read on the present occasion.

My central claim, or less insistently, my recommendation for our conversation underway in this volume, is that *Cities of Words* should be treated as a literary-philosophical performance emerging from a modernist sensibility, one that is distinctively informed by moral perfectionism. The book is, put tersely, a modernist work of art (in the form, or guise, of moral philosophy). Understanding Cavell's relation to and contribution to modernism—such as we are collectively undertaking in this volume—is beautifully, compactly (even at 450 pages), and persuasively enacted in this estimable, inimitable document. The book is one record—Cavell's record—of a class, "Moral Reasoning: Moral Perfectionism" (Humanities 34), which he taught at Harvard

University, as part of the College's Core Curriculum, on and off for the better part of two decades. Like all personal impressions of events, it is condensed (how *could* one capture the varieties of classroom experience from year to year, decade to decade, with their lapses and contradictions?) and distorted or perspectival (like the best of letters and diaries must be—attending as they do to the "gleams of light" and "lustres" that make themselves evident in a given season, and for whatever reason not in another).[1] If one wanted mere accuracy of representation, one could listen to the audio files (if they existed), but such a desire for fidelity belies the modernist impulse—in a perfectionist vein—that animates this book and makes it a propulsive force: namely, that it is a thing aware of its movement across time and place to some other thing. Or as Cavell stated it in *The World Viewed: Reflections on the Ontology of Film*, his half-century-old, now canonical book on the ontology of film: "the fate of modernist art generally" is that "its awareness [of] and responsibility for the physical basis of its art compel it at once to assert and deny the control of its art by that basis" (*WV* 105). Since I am claiming *Cities of Words* is a work of modernist art, it will be said how the book shares in this fate—and the reflexive attributes it exhibits and encodes.

William Rothman reminds us that "[b]y characterizing his own writings as *modern* philosophy, Cavell, who was then in regular conversation with Michael Fried, also declared his affinity with modernist artists, declaring himself to be writing from within what he called the 'modernist situation.'"[2] The self-declared and self-defined assignation for his predicament becomes a signature trait for how we read *Cities of Words*. As Cavell said of Ludwig Wittgenstein's *Philosophical Investigations*, so we can see in Cavell's work, including *Cities of Words*, a similar "incessant and explicit self-reflection," an awareness of "manner, the sheer sense of the deliberateness and beauty" of writing "as internal to the sense of his philosophical aims."[3] Similarly, Arthur Danto said: "Wittgenstein's *Philosophical Investigations* has, rather rare among philosophical works, a claim as a work of literary art, not so much because of its vivid and compelling imagery—its 'fervor,' to use Cavell's expression—but because it somehow embodies what it is about."[4] Intriguingly, such issues of style resolve themselves in the question of seriousness, namely, how and what can be (any longer) taken seriously as philosophy/philosophical.[5] We are launched, therefore, into a crisis of criteria. Does poetry count for (or as) philosophy? What of literature, religion, psychoanalysis, theater, opera, music, and cinema? Indeed, anything that is not prescribed analytical epistemology and the philosophy of science? These are questions Cavell replies to, as it were, in every sentence—and in the historical predicament he finds himself in, what Cavell, Rothman, and now we wish to claim as modernist. Since I will be at pains, if with pleasure, to distinguish between modernist/modernism and modern/modernity (the former being a part or expression of the latter), I wish to invoke and then rely upon thereafter a definition and a distinction supplied by Cavell. By the middle of the twentieth century (and we can safely assume continuing to the present day with these bequeathed issues perhaps having become even more vexed), we encounter "two states":

> [O]ne I called the *modernist* (in which the present wishes to maintain the artistic quality, say the greatness, of the past, despite the differences in the look and the

sound of the art, as it were, must discover precisely to preserve its status), and the other, doubtless showing my prejudices, or commitments, I called the *modernizing* (in which the present would forget the past by, so to speak, embracing the fact of the present, in its transience, its fashionableness, its distrust of, even contempt for, greatness.[6]

To underscore the obvious, then, Cavell is—according to his own terms—a modernist, and it is in this sense, his sense, that I will employ the term. I wish to situate Cavell's broader, if still nuanced and decisive, claims for modernist works in an intimate reading of *Cities of Words*. In this way, the book's perfectionist attributes can speak to the more general/generic condition of modernist philosophy (and art). To this end, I begin with a close reading of the front matter to the book, since Cavell himself had to begin at the beginning in order to attempt (or achieve) a translation: namely, from the classroom to the philosophical tract. Unlike the collected classroom notes made by students (drawn from sketchy jottings or even sketchier memories), say as in the many "books" attributed to Wittgenstein, Cavell himself undertook to provide what might be called, in an everyday sense, his "lecture notes." Yet any pedagogue with a gift will know there is a chasm between the sound of the classroom and the sound of written prose. One question to hold in mind, then, is to what degree we should want to have the experience of being in a classroom led by Cavell (and who is to say those same words would hold our interest if we were merely reading them as dictations from a transcript?). Thus, we ask to what extent we should reasonably hope he could successfully undertake a translation of the classroom (sound, cadence, charge) that would make that experience legible, intelligible, and audible in consecutive prose?

When you are handed a book entitled *Cities of Words: Pedagogical Letters on a Register of the Moral Life*, what would you say it is about? Urban planning? Language analysis? Lexicography? Epistolary studies? Musical theory? Ethics? Well, in a sense, yes to all, but also, to be sure, there is need for some elaboration. In the singular, the phrase "city of words" is mentioned in the third epigraph that appears at the beginning of the book (between the Preface and the Introduction, unnumbered pages, xii–xv), drawn from an exchange between Glaucon and Socrates in Plato's *Republic* (592a–b), who speak in that order:

> I understand, he said, you mean in the city which we were founding and described, our city of words, for I do not believe it exists anywhere on earth.
> Perhaps, I said, it is a model laid up in heaven, for him who wishes to look upon, and as he looks, set up the government of his soul. It makes no difference whether it exists anywhere or will exist.[7]

Of the many ways of describing Plato's *Republic*, these few lines do much, first by reminding us that the project of the ancient Greek book is the discovery of what a just city (or *polis*) might be or look like, and second, by drawing a relationship between the political regime of such a place and the nature of the interior lives of those who inhabit it. If the just city is, in fact, a no-place (in Thomas More's inventive notion of *utopia*), such a status is acceptable for Socrates and also for Cavell's reading of the *Republic* as a work of moral perfectionism. That is to say, the ambition of moral perfectionism, contrary to its misleading name, is not perfection, but we might say onwardness to some next self or future state of affairs. As Cavell notes, Emersonian perfectionism "specifically sets itself against any idea of ultimate perfection" (*CW* 3). Can we speak frankly and say that "perfectionism" is an odd (ironic, oxymoronic, perverse) name for an outlook that acknowledges that we "perpetually fail to attain" the state it insinuates (*CW* 18)? Bracketing that lexicographical worry, we might take up William James's sentiment: "I am willing to accept almost any name" (*CW* 17). So, in trying to call things by their right names, we may have fallen short. Yet this is the name we have, and it did not originate with Cavell, nor with Emerson before him. Perhaps the ironic or oxymoronic nature, or perversity, and for that, misunderstanding encoded in the name, is a further fact of the theory's modernist credentials, since it is not saying what it means, but drawing a reader and student in closer for supplementary investigation. Unlike deontology or consequentialism or utilitarianism, moral perfectionism does not include its own explanation, but demands a continual accounting of its nature by others. In this way, moral perfectionism reminds us of the "estrangement of philosophy from theology" in our own era and "expresses the sense that a transcendental element is indispensable in the motivation for a moral existence" (*CW* 18).

For those looking for (moral) "improvement," and the variations of "self-help" that have come to be associated with one approach to Emerson's legacy (call them "debased perfectionisms"[8]), Cavell's reading of Emersonian perfectionism may be bracing for its lack of concern for "individual cultivation" (*CW* 18). As the films Cavell has selected show us time and again, self-knowledge, if we want to call it that, does not happen in isolation, but rather in communion with others—individuals who, in turn, rely on us. For this reason, theories and thoughts about marriage and friendship occupy the core of moral perfectionism, while the turn to societies and cities radiates out from there (inklings of Aristotle's pertinence avail themselves at such moments when the micro indicates the fates and fortunes of the macro). Yet even here, a student of moral perfectionism expecting "results" in the way that deontology, utilitarian, and especially varieties of self-help promise, may be stunned to learn that progress is not an ambition of this trade; hence Cavell's suspicious relationship to the (moral) meliorism so often associated and espoused by pragmatists and their allies.[9] Rather than "improving," or "making progress," the moral perfectionist—in company with a friend and helpmeet (often called a spouse and not a "scold" [*CW* 12])—will be prepared to be stopped, turned back, and humbled continually. We are far from moralism (where one speaks to another as if from on high), and well beyond the precincts of amoralism (where one speaks from nowhere, in a spirit of nihilism), but in proximity with perfectionism, which means embracing an ongoing relationship to accountability, accounting, recounting, and articulating the criteria for what counts. In this way, the moral perfectionist does "not seek to learn anything new" by our investigation, drawing a moral from Wittgenstein; instead: "We want to *understand* something that is already in plain view" (*CW* 14–15; *PI* §89, emphasis in original). As Cavell glosses the hallmark disposition: "This formulation captures the familiar fact that philosophers seem perpetually to be going back over something, something most sane people would feel had already been discussed to death. A more familiar formulation is to say that philosophy does not progress." To this end, Cavell commends us to "a mode of philosophical attention in which you are prepared to be taken by surprise, stopped, thrown back as it were" (*CW* 15). Such things happen especially when reading closely, slowly, attentively, with seriousness, with a sense of importance,[10] since "a text worth reading carefully, or perpetually, is inexhaustible" (*CW* 15). (We can see the resemblance between books and people, in this regard, as Iris Murdoch wrote in her first novel: "To find a person inexhaustible is simply the definition of love.")[11] If we want, if we insist, Cavell will allow us to think of this as a "gesture of progress," but it must involve two movements: "going back and going on" (*CW* 15).

Yet, let us not lose track: what has moral perfectionism to do with the just city, the city of words? Lukas Clark-Memler notes that "Plato regularly refers to the *Kallipolis* (city of the republic) as a 'city in words'—*Republic* 369c, 592a; *Laws* 739c—from the Greek *en logôi* translated as 'in words,' though some render it 'in theory' or 'in speech.'"[12] The shifting prepositions (viz., "of," "in") are intriguing for how we might picture such a state of affairs. Beyond that figuration we also have Cavell's pluralizing (shifting from *city* to *cities*). Let us presume, for the moment, that there is no textual or lexicographical reason (i.e., based on a reading or translation of Plato's Greek) to justify the pluralization, so we are then turned to its conceptual importance. And in this orientation (asking "why pluralize?"), we catch an instance of a modernist moment, namely, to take a phrase familiar to millennia of scholars, and, well, change it. And then, after changing, to not *explicitly* explain the change. Nowhere in the nearly five-hundred-page book does Cavell, for example, elaborate on his adaptation of *Plato's* phrase, or its meaning in the *Republic*, for the title of his book. Yet our conjectures, based on what Cavell *has* written, are nevertheless satisfying, for the presumption we may make involves the promise of (or demand for) plurality, such as we have come to know it in modernity. Indeed, the imagination of a "just city"—and of just *a* city—seems fitting for antiquity, and especially if it "makes no difference whether it exists anywhere or will exist."

Meanwhile, twenty-five hundred years later, Cavell not only has a global community to address (with its varieties of languages and mores and much else), but also the competing interests (and occasional overlapping consensus) of academic disciplines and modes of media (e.g., philosophy, literature, theology, theater, political theory, psychoanalysis, film, etc.). To paraphrase Luce Irigaray, we are coming to recognize "this city which is not one." Perhaps it can do us some good to think of our contemporary situation—in modernity—as calling for such a plurality. In this respect, we may be encouraged by Cavell to consider that it is Emerson, once again, who motivates the shift to thinking this way, namely, when he is quoted in the first selection among the book's Melvillean library of extracts: "I know that the world I converse with *in the cities* and in the farms, is not the world I *think*" (*CW* xii). The second italics are familiar, as they are found in the original, while the first italics, which I added, present to us, perhaps, with an awareness of a difference—that in America there are many cities (and farms) and no real sense of settled opinion (however much we speak of "unity" [*unum*] in these United States), much less an experience that reflects one's own mental models of the just city or "the imagination of justice" (*CW* 17). With Emerson's division of mind and world, of inner and outer, private and public, we have a new take on the ancient claim that it "makes no difference whether [the city] exists anywhere or will exist."

In this American, Emersonian, and modernist context (one defined by plurality, by tested and contested traditions), we are not only in need of words but cities in which those words can be spoken, accounted for. Perhaps too we can come to think of each of these chapters—with distinctly invoked figures and texts—as forming, unto itself, a city of words, which in turn collectively presents us with *cities* of words. In pluralizing, Cavell exploits the potential of a modernist approach for repurposing tradition (without explicit or sanctioned grounds); speaking his "latent conviction," Cavell experiments with the inherited narrative—breaks it up, loosens it, reshapes it—all in the service of prompting our further thoughts about the possible.[13] In this moment of re-writing and re-conceiving, we find Cavell's assessment of the pertinence of Plato to moral perfectionism:

> For us the text of the *Republic* represents primarily a familiar place from which to locate the full beginning of what we understand philosophy to aspire to be, the establishing of a prose, call it a set of conditions, under which we can arrive, let us say, at an understanding of our responsibilities for our words and deeds as under the assessment of reason, requiring an understanding both of the authority of reason and of the kind of creature humans are that we recognize the worth of our obedience to authority.
>
> *CW* 317

And how might all of the foregoing take place? In a word: conversation. That is, the best, say, most fitting, picture of what a city or cities of words might look like is a dialogue.[14] In an earlier book, *Conditions Handsome and Unhandsome*, which bears the subtitle "The Constitution of Emersonian Perfectionism," Cavell adduced some twenty-eight topics from Plato's *Republic* that he wished to propose as the work's "thematics of perfectionism"—beginning with a "mode of conversation" (*CW* 320; *CHU* 6–7). On this one point alone, we can marvel at the way Plato's dialogues stand in parallel to the dialogues that we find most conspicuously in what Cavell names "comedies of remarriage"—films from the Golden Age of Hollywood (in his typology, from the 1930s and 40s) in which the principal, married pair face the threat of divorce and in turn must overcome an *internal* obstacle in order to come together again, back together, "re-marry." In *Cities of Words*, Plato's continuing relevance to the exercise of contemporary conversation remains in high relief:

> A topic much on my mind as I look at that list is whether or how Plato's idea of continuous matching of a type of soul with a type of city as a city declines (or improves) applies to the aspiration of democracy I see in remarriage comedy. If I say that the aim of Emersonianism, I might say the aim of these chapters, is to suggest the richest conception of perfectionism compatible with, and indeed

essential to, a democratic disposition, then the question arises as to whether, or in what sense, the democratic city is an image of its citizens, or whether it is precisely of that city that it can be said the face of its citizens remains open to their imaginations.

CW 321

Technically, we are still trying to get a measure of the title of the book, and yet, somehow, we have entered a deep, cross-millennial analysis and integration of such disparate realms as Platonic philosophy, Ralph Waldo Emerson, and select black-and-white Hollywood movies from the 30s and 40s. How does all this hang together? I pause to ask the question (with an eye toward replying to it) as much to appreciate how a confusion or interest might have presented itself. I will elaborate a response below, but for now let us appreciate the mere act of such curation and juxtaposition—say, the sheer fact that Cavell, again with some explaining to do, has noticed a durable and meaningful connection between these disparate times and realms of human expression. Plato and Kant and . . . Henry Fonda? Cavell, like many modernists, experiments with the power of atemporality, of association, and the frisson of proximity; it is a technique familiar to filmmakers, especially since Sergei Eisenstein's experiments with cinematic montage; let us call Cavell's strategy a "Kuleshov effect" for literary-philosophical prose. Still, given the context and content of the present investigation, we find ourselves marveling at Cavell's skills for expressing his distinctively modernist sensibility—a sensibility, first, for which it seems justifiable to *make* such a connective conjecture (across time and tradition, across media and genres), and then to *back up* those associations with astute philosophical analysis. In Cavell's company, the history of philosophy is read diachronically as one of humanity's most formidable longitudinal studies, prompting us to observe, like Emerson, that "[t]he sun shines to-day also."[15]

Now to the book's subtitle. What *are* "pedagogical letters"? They too are not one thing, since the phrase encodes a double entendre. Cavell's prose forms dispatches from an older man to his (mostly) younger readers; hence the appeal to an epistolary form. The generational structure is familiar, of course, in the *Republic* and Hellenic culture generally—a social arrangement in which the teaching of boys (*pais*) by men is a vouchsafed, etymologically encoded principal of *paideia*. Meanwhile, the epistolary form, millennia later, is familiar from Benjamin Franklin's *Autobiography* ("Dear Son: I have ever had pleasure in obtaining any little anecdotes of my ancestors"[16]) to Friedrich Schiller's *On the Aesthetic Education of Man*.[17] These are, in the vernacular, "letters," which is to say part of an appeal to a kind of audience (private and sometimes public); indeed, Franklin's intimate address to his son puts the reading public (intentionally, of course) in the position of being his child, for better or worse; that is, someone to be tutored.[18] In his Preface, Cavell helps us recognize the double entendre (in "pedagogical letters") even more clearly by describing his work as a "book of letters," the latter of which calls to mind a distinctively Hebraic allusion to an alphabet, which can be invoked as easily in thinking of the Latin alphabet.

Such "pedagogical letters," on this second valence, will be the kind of alphabet that can teach us something—a function that would befit "a city of words," such as Plato imagined, where words are "lettered"—made up of letters. And so whatever we create in this city, it will be written by these means. (A geneticist might point out too that we humans are physiologically constituted by a book of [four] letters.) Meanwhile, the "collected" or "selected" *letters* of a given writer, which we customarily find in volumes of correspondence, further sustain the radiating, multiple senses of our everyday use of this word (e.g., *The Selected Letters of Ralph Waldo Emerson* [which only contains letters written by Emerson to others] and *The Correspondence of Thomas Carlyle and Ralph Waldo Emerson* [which holds a chronological repository of their two-way transatlantic communication]).

Next we turn to what a "register of the moral life" might be. "Register," in Cavell's parlance, is a decidedly musical term of art. In his California youth, he trained as a musician, studied composition at Berkeley and later at The Juilliard School in New York, and played professionally, even conceiving that he might make a life for himself in music. If his mother's perfect pitch and his own talents weighed in his favor, a childhood ear injury made his going on in music difficult, if not impossible (at least from where he stood).[19] And yet, in significant and lasting ways, Cavell has brought sound—and its musical relatives: pitch, voice, register, resonance, rhythm, pace, phrase, accent, key, tonality, measure, and so on—into the glossary of mainstream philosophical conversation.[20] In his first book, *Must We Mean What We Say?*, published in the late 1960s, Cavell declared in the title essay: "in philosophy it is the sound which makes all the difference" (*MWM* 36n31). Part of that sound involves what readers of Cavell will recognize as his preoccupation with voice—both his own (as a writer, as a philosopher) and of the filmic, philosophical, operatic, dramatic, and literary characters he explores (e.g., most conspicuously in the genre he calls "melodramas of the unknown woman," for example, where a woman's voice is suppressed or must be arrogated; in which to remain silent is to remain unknown).[21]

Part of the sound of *Cities of Words*, we are told, derives from its origins. "The book of letters you have before you," Cavell tells us—addressing his reader in the familiar second person—"follows the course of a course of lectures called Moral Perfectionism, which I gave a number of times over the last decade and a half." "The course of a course," which is to say the sequence of a given class, the order in which material will be presented, is a way of phrasing what we customarily find in a syllabus. Meanwhile, the book's table of contents invites us to consider, as the work's stated origins attest, teaching the text across an academic semester—or, more generously, across the period of an entire academic year. Yet, before we can attend to that syllabus—such as it is sketched in the book's contents—we are asked to ponder how this book is related to, is kin to or kindred with, the place in which the professor *speaks*, namely, the classroom, and if we are students, what our main activity there involves, namely, *listening*: "The idea of the book is to keep in the published chapters something of the sound of the original classroom lectures, as distinguished from the sound of a presentation to a scholarly organization or a formal talk to a general public." For Cavell's part, here imagining himself as an audience for the kinds of words or letters he promises to present, he says: "I love the sound of interesting, which means interested, academic lecturing" (*CW* ix).

In the COVID-19 era, we have renewed reason for contemplating the importance of that sound and whether it can be achieved remotely, virtually, in the distributed, asynchronous "classroom." When it seems, suddenly, that the Platonic ideal of quarantine education is MasterClass—with its ambition to "democratize access to genius"—we are forced to grapple with the meaning and possibility of "distance learning" (often without student participation). Instead of a capacious, accretive, interconnected curriculum based on the close reading of texts in community, we are presented with personality profiles built upon a hyper-distillation of life lessons learned—a mixture of advice-giving, self-mythologizing, reporting on good luck, and catalyzing the power of personal "brands." The autobiographical has been capitalized (in a double sense), yet we are left on our own to wonder what is *philosophical* about the product. In Cavell's company, in the classroom or on the page imbued with the sound of the classroom, we are instead given the terms and conditions for understanding that robust connection.[22]

In musical theory, we are told that a register is the height or range of a note; it is a term that can be used to distinguish different pitch ranges. Thus, a "register of the moral life" will invoke the notion that we are not addressing *all* moral philosophy, but some distinctive set of attributes within a discrete space or along a spectrum. The visual equivalent, which is given much use in academic settings, is "through the lens of," thus, allowing or encouraging us to see something by means of focalizing and coloring our perspective of it (e.g., classical Hollywood cinema "through the lens of" the Hays Code). To attune us to a specific "register of the moral life," then, Cavell aims to get us to hear something we may have been deaf to, but what is more, to hear its special, specific resonances—and what they might mean. (Hence, music theory, and a skill for its application, never abandoned Cavell.) Of course, by now, an audience (from the Latin *audīre*) for these letters will hear that the register in question is none other than Moral Perfectionism, often retitled Emersonian Perfectionism (while not suggesting that, somehow, "Emersonian" is a synonym for "Moral"). Rather, Cavell encourages his gathered "class" of students (another relevant and meaningful double entendre) to listen to the history of ethics with an ear for this strain of perfectionism. Importantly, though, Cavell does not *oppose* Emersonian Perfectionism with the likes of Aristotelian virtue ethics, Kantian deontology, Bentham's consequentialism, or Mill's utilitarianism, but instead notes how, for example, "Kant and John Stuart Mill both have deep perfectionist strains in their views" (*CW* 11). Thus, we are listening to familiar voices (Plato, Kant, Mill, et al.) for the way perfectionism already and always imbued their moral outlooks.

To occupy the "register of the moral life" called Emersonian Perfectionism is not to be excluded from the considerations of deontology, utilitarian theory, teleology, eudaimonia, and an ethics of care, but to hear those claims made in the context of a particular location, namely, in America ("where one can take philosophy by surprise"), with Emerson, *and* harboring a specific preoccupation: "surprise at the fact that there should be such an enterprise that measures the value of our lives" (*CW* 7). The American context or condition is, thus, a register of the moral life; we see this circumstance exemplified by the films that drew Cavell's attention. The lead characters in the comedies of remarriage, for example, are faced with the "difficulty of overcoming moral cynicism"—especially trying "after the obligations and compromises of adulthood begin to obscure the promise and dreams of youth" (*CW* 11). Still more, the kinds of problems these couples face are, in Cavell's reading, "formulated less well by questions concerning what they ought to do [say, from a Kantian deontology that generates a categorical imperative], what it would be best or right for them to do [with reference to some utilitarian calculus of relative good and goods], than by the question of how they shall live their lives, what kind of persons they aspire to be" (*CW* 11). Part of that measurement (or assessment or accounting) of one's behavior and the thoughts that motivate it, involves what Cavell, like Emerson and Thoreau before him, calls constituting. And what else is a constitution (of something) but a registration—something discoverable on a register of a moral life? Such activities call for letters, words, and conversation. Yet, we need to find a suitable place in which to conduct those proceedings. We may refer to this place as the city (or the country—often in screwball Hollywood comedies, a place called Connecticut); or the living room and the bedroom; or the book; or, in the present case, the classroom; perhaps all will be agreeable to such pursuits of happiness.

The title of Cavell's Introduction is "In the Place of the Classroom," and so yet another double entendre announces itself: "in [this] place [called] the classroom" the contents of this book were first presented, yet since we are aware that the book is *not* a classroom, it must (also) be a proxy, thus *taking the place of* the classroom it is offered to us instead of the classroom. The book in hand is a stand-in for a place called—or currently or formerly known as—the classroom. *Cities of Words* is thus a reply to the questions: "how does one make a class experience into a book?" and "how does one teach (a) film with no way of screening it?" One reply to both questions is to model the nature of attentive viewing with the care of one's prose. For example, in what might otherwise appear like plot summaries (numbered lists of descriptions placed at the head of the even chapters on film, 2–20), Cavell teaches us how to watch (or in his parlance "read") films in his company; the tuition is as educational as it is expressive of his hermeneutic virtuosity: his plot summaries are anything but summary and never plodding. The pedagogical significance of these (seemingly) humble dispatches, i.e., these plot synopses, bely the remarkable (hidden?) power of description; of *being aware* of what one is seeing "in plain view"; of *noticing* things that appear on the screen, of *hearing* things that accompany those visions (*CW* 14–15; *PI* §89). On these points, Wittgenstein's emphasis on the philosophical task of description, its vitality for philosophy—perhaps all it is capable of—comes to mind. We are familiar with the more well-known artistry of Cavell's literary-philosophical style—his long sentences, parentheticals, paraphrases, double-backing, deferrals, tacking, reference to his other works, eclectic taste in thinkers and texts, etc.—but what stands out as entirely remarkable in *Cities of Words* is the way these numbered sequences (as if mapping out a storyboard in words) arrest us with our *failure* to notice what is there—what has *been there*—before us, on the screen we are assumed to share.

It is difficult to speculate why Cavell's descriptions strike me as so accomplished, especially given the nature of his achievements elsewhere in *Cities of Words* and in his wider oeuvre. Perhaps there is something made (newly) apparent about the lost art of description (of saying what one sees or hears or otherwise perceives); that he mounts these summaries largely from memory occasions yet another aspect worth acknowledging for its virtuosity. I think it may also be the chastening effect of realizing that Cavell has stood before the same piece of art and seen things—and made connections internal to the work, to the genre, and to film and history more generally—that escaped me, us (a community that stretches back to moviegoers and critics of the 1930s and onward from there—nearly a century of *missed* observations!). I find great elation in such chastening because it reminds me what is possible for prose, and more precisely for *criticism*. A meticulous, inventive, and heartily-made description can, in fact, truly wow.

In keeping with Cavell's classroom metaphors, where intuitions are met by tuitions, we could say that *Cities of Words* is a syllabus; it is a peculiar syllabus, no doubt, in so far as it innovates from a range of disciplinary locations often unknown to one another, or that struggle to make themselves intelligible across entrenched boundaries: philosophy, literature, linguistics, religion and theology, anthropology, political theory, fine arts, theater, opera, cinema, music, psychoanalysis, poetry, and more. On another line of analogy, we could say that he issues (or pitches) a new canon, or syllabus for thought—yet even then retaining an openness to amendment, since the many works collected here are *still* "too selective to count as a proposed canon of reading in moral philosophy" (*CW* 5). If Cavell has unsettled an inherited canon, he doesn't spend much time defending his revised and expanded one. Befitting a modernist project, again in the sense that Cavell defines above, the "seriousness" and "greatness" of new works are understood to be *ipso facto* in conversation with prior works of (established) seriousness and greatness. Moreover, following Emerson, it is only in so far as we are "unsettled" that there is any hope for us.[23] Canon formation, on this reading, it turns out, is a project much in the mold of moral perfectionism—an onward process that nevertheless doubles back. If it is visionary, it is also re-visionary: it subjects the inherited world to revision and is, in turn, subject to revision. It is our privilege and responsibility, as readers and citizens (of these cities of words) to contend with this syllabus for thinking, for acting, for believing. In this respect, it may be better to speak of what Cavell has offered as not quite or not in the usual sense a syllabus or a canon but something more like a *genre* for thinking, since, as Thomas Schatz has pointed out, we are used to thinking of a genre as a phenomenon that has "static and dynamic elements."[24] Approaching *Cities of Words*, and other of Cavell's works as a kind of genre, we are more easily able to think of the ways in which its elements may be augmented, added, removed, revised, etc. A conventional syllabus can seem programmatic and linear (at times parochial or moralistic, thus compromised by omissions and distortions). Likewise, the inherited canon (of whatever kind of media) is often imposing, standing beyond the sensibilities and agency—and thus input—of any given individual reader. But to speak of a genre—to say of it that I wish this or that work to be considered for inclusion in it, to be read in a certain fashion, or to reconsider an inherited bit of patrimony from this or that source (including Cavell's own work)—suddenly fills the reader with the power and the terror of creation. The stakes of the modernist situation come into bold relief.

Placing syllabus, course, and canon in company with genre, we are profitably launched in asking what *kind* of work *Cities of Words* is or purports to be. Once we inquire after Cavell's proper discipline or field (or better, his transgression of their familiar boundaries), we are thrown back upon our training and other resources. The book occupies a genre, and we might say, it also participates in constituting one. In this respect, *Cities of Words* is not so much or so explicitly "about modernism" (e.g., Cavell does not take modernism as his key subject or point of focus) so much as the book is itself *formally* and *methodologically* a modernist work of (literary-philosophical) art—very much in keeping with Cavell's own claim that Wittgenstein's *Philosophical Investigation* was a modernist work.[25] The creation *Cities of Words*, and earlier the *Investigations*, we might say, is only possible in the context in which modernism is an issue for writers and thinkers, for artists and curators, for philosophers and essayists— that is, at such a time when the questions of what art is, can attain or aspire to, are open questions, and ones that find their way by interventions and examples. Modernism is the *condition* that makes Cavell's (modernist) experimentation possible, and it is in this way that modernism should be profitably understood as informing his work and also benefiting from his reconfiguration of what it is that philosophy counts as its business (e.g., what it thinks it has a claim upon as a special domain of investigation). As Cavell says, Emerson "describes [his work, that is, exhibits his thinking] in a way philosophers of our time will have difficulty recognizing as part of the work they are obliged to do" (*CW* 29). It turns out, under Cavell's direction, and in tension with the standard modes and definition of the profession, philosophy's purview is quite capacious indeed.

In form and spirit, *Cities of Words* is eclectic, roving, experimental, anti-foundational, anti-hierarchical, non-chronological; for Cavell is not obedient to accepted designations of high and low art, the arcane and the popular (and thus to what justifies or denies its inclusion in an academic conversation); not beholden to one tradition or another or to expertise that would settle matters or use authority as a cudgel for interpretive victory ("I am not [I know of no one who is] a scholar in all the fields touched upon in this book" [*CW* ix]); not committed to one art form (as over against another), but feels perpetually devoted to breaking or reformulating the (inherited) ranking of value (both moral and aesthetic—following Wittgenstein, who said "ethics and aesthetics are one"[26])—and thus, criteriologically questioning "what counts as." Thus, in *all* of these categories and conceptions, Cavell explores the terms and conditions of the criteria for art, literature, philosophy, etc. In this respect the labor of *Cities of Words*—where nearly half of the book is occupied with the presence of and uses of film—continues a line of questioning we find articulated in *The World Viewed* (at the conclusion of the foreword to the enlarged edition), where he points out that "the unpredictability of what we may have to count as an element of the medium of film to which significance is given in a particular film" is connected to "the unpredictability of the audience for what may be taken as the study of film" (*WV* xvi). Cavell here, as he does later in "Film in the University," an appendix to *Pursuits of Happiness*, ponders what would make film "academically or anyway intellectually respectable" (*PH* 265–74; *WV* xvi). "This is no small matter," Cavell tells us in 1979, "for as writers as different as Robert Warshow and

Walter Benjamin more or less put it, to accept film as an art will require a modification of the concept of art" (*WV* xvi–xvii). *Cities of Words*, it seems to me, undertakes yet another one of Cavell's responses to this "no small matter," and adds to it the question of accepting as philosophy figures, texts, and forms unfamiliar to philosophy. Thus, to put it as Cavell more or less put it, to accept Emerson (and Thoreau and Freud and Shaw and Shakespeare and Henry James) as philosophy will require a modification of the concept of philosophy.

Take as a sample, a vignette of the modernist confrontation with—and as Cavell understood it—the continuation of the best of tradition, his juxtaposition of lines from a film (that is, from a screenplay) with those drawn from the writer credited as founding philosophy in the Western tradition. In *The Awful Truth* (McCarey, 1937), Jerry Warriner (Cary Grant) and his wife Lucy (Irene Dunne) are alone together with just minutes to spare before their divorce is finalized (a nearby cuckoo clock provides us with means for the countdown). She says: "Things are just the same as they always were, only you're just the same, too, so I guess things will never be the same again." And he replies: "Things are different, except in a different way. You're still the same, only I've been a fool. Well, I'm not now. So, as long as I'm different, don't you think things could be the same again? Only a little different" (*CW* 377–78). As a reader, a pupil in "Moral Reasoning," where would you—or could you—go from here? If you heard a resonance with something in the history of philosophy, could you say it, make a claim to it? Cavell hears Plato, in particular lines from *Parmenides*: "Then, that which becomes older than itself, also becomes at the same time younger than itself, if it is to have something to become older than," states Parmenides. "What do you mean?" asks Aristoteles, confounded, to which Parmenides "clarifies":

> I mean this.—A thing does not need to become different from another thing which is already different; it *is* different, and if its different has become, it has become different; if its different will be, it will be different; but of that which is becoming different, there cannot have been, or be about to be, or yet be, a different—the only different possible is one which is becoming.
>
> *CW* 378

And hearing the "clear and comic resemblance" between *The Awful Truth* and Plato's dialogue, we say, like Aristoteles: "That is inevitable." But catching the edge of a resemblance is one thing, selling it another. As Cavell continues:

> The conjunction [of these texts, a Hollywood film and a Platonic dialogue] reveals, or affirms, a double revelation: first, that the thoughts of one of the most complex pieces of philosophy ever composed are recognizably recapturable in contemporary conversation, or in the representation of such conversation by a clever writer who may or may not have studied Plato in college; second, that there is something in the sublimest philosophy that can strike one as comic.
>
> *CW* 378

To repeat: Cavell's is a modernist juxtaposition *par excellence*—illumination by proximity and emergent resonances (like the medieval *florilegium*), all the while affirming the continuity of traits and tradition.[27] As such, the connection is made with Cavell's quintessential disregard for high and low, canonical and noncanonical, and without deference to what is "allowable" media or text. Since we are by now knowingly involved in a college course, "or in the representation of such" a course, let us imagine what (kind of) student could have written *The Awful Truth*. In this imagination, I would like to amplify Cavell's insight or instinct about the author of the screenplay, whom he refers to as "a clever writer who may or may not have studied Plato in college." The clever screenwriter is, in fact, Viña Delmar (née Alvina Louise Croter), the daughter of two vaudeville performers, who was educated in public schools until age thirteen. What a satisfying coda to Cavell's modernist coupling, for here Delmar—who didn't attend college, and thus who didn't read Plato there—is, nevertheless, put into conversation with Plato. Parity is not the point; this is not a contest. Rather, the point is *insight where we find it*—in a fifth-century-BCE dialogue (that often reads like a [funny] screenplay) and a twentieth-century screenplay, written by something of an autodidact with a gift for the sound of human conversation and, as it turns out, the sound of philosophy. (And if, as some sources report, Delmar was joined in writing by her [regularly] uncredited husband, Gene Delmar, it does not defeat the thesis, but compels it further, since we have further reason to cheer the insights of a screenwriting [married] couple, as we have had, more conspicuously, in the collaboration between Ruth Gordon and Garson Kanin.[28] The claim that some of the finest of Cavell's comedies of remarriage were written by a husband and wife team only seems to underscore the significance of his creation and theorization of the genre.)

Recall that for most of the life of the class, "Moral Perfectionism," the classroom was at Harvard—taught from the inside, among the elite, on grounds upon which privilege was said to be given, anointed; in the year of final composition, the classroom moved to the University of Chicago—still inside, still elite, still a sacred educational precinct. But now, "instead of" or "in place of" the Harvard (and Chicago) classroom, we have *Cities of Words*. And as the expansiveness (e.g., the plurality) of the title suggests, the book-as-classroom is out-of-school, extracurricular, liberated, democratic (as Cavell says, addressed to "an audience that extends to those past their college lives who have retained, or returned to, an interest in the college classroom" [*CW* x]). (One may think also of David Denby's *Great Books*, where memoir meets reportage, featuring his middle-aged return to the undergraduate college classroom at Columbia University, reporting, as it were from the scene of the contemporary humanities among adolescents *and also* from the sobering conditions of adulthood.[29]) We are reminded, then, how Cavell has described philosophy as "the education of grownups" (*CR* 125), and so how philosophy is necessarily (and perhaps also at its best because necessarily) poised to find an audience beyond its quarantined campus. As *Cities of Words* presents a course of study to an adult class disposed to tuition (at once paying for it and heeding it), we discover an analog incarnation of the public humanities as exercised in the nineteenth century, as Emerson practiced them on the Lyceum circuit—that is, with what Cavell calls an appeal to "an aspect of their conception of the human, at any age" (*CW* 26).

Cities of Words enacts and embodies this transformation; it promises us an extension (on) school, a continuing education. Such intellectual labors for the student—of whatever age—involve *auditing*, a cast of mind with a pertinent duplication of meaning: listening (*audīre*) and taking stock or accounting for the proceedings, letting these lessons at once become part and parcel of one's education and also act as a prompt to further study, beyond the scope of the curriculum and classroom. While we do not presume to say, much less believe, that "youth is wasted on the young," and still less squandered on the privilege of the coveted Ivy League classroom, there *is* a palpable way in which the lessons gleaned from adult life enrich and deepen one's potential for understanding *philosophy's* lessons. The so-called "real world" (that is said to exist beyond the wrought iron gates of the liberal arts quad) finds, in philosophy and its kind, much worth dwelling on anew, and perhaps for the first time. Welcome to the city of words.

One such place of welcome, here as in most books, is the Table of Contents, which in this case is an education in itself. As arranged in the first edition of the book, chapters 1 through 20 are set off in parallel columns, the odd numbers (1–19) with the names of philosophers, the even numbers (2–20) with the names of films drawn, as noted above, from the Hollywood of the 1930s and 40s. That would be enough for most books, for most college courses, but *Cities of Words* continues with a captivating comparison of Henry James's short story "The Beast in the Jungle" and Max Ophüls's film *Letter from an Unknown Woman* (1948), and is followed by an, as it were, double reading of *Pygmalion*—the George Bernard Shaw play (first performed in 1913) and the eponymous film directed by Anthony Asquith and Leslie Howard (released in 1938); Cavell doesn't mention that the Oscar-winning screenplay was adapted into the 1956 musical *My Fair Lady*, which itself was adapted (back?) to film in a 1964 film of the same name. What interests him, instead, and what should interest us, is Cavell taking seriously, "morbid[ly]" so, Shaw saying that his work "needs, not a preface, but a sequel," and that is precisely what Cavell stands to offer us (*CW* 410). And in doing so, Cavell shows us the "radicalized importance of the idea of speech or conversation as the medium of the play. There is a satisfying brilliance in using the idea of teaching phonetics as a figure for, let's say, the acquisition of speech as such, hence the idea of 'making a lady' as a figure for 'creating a woman'" (*CW* 411). Having just received tuition in the odd-numbered chapters of *Cities of Words*, a reader, and now a careful student of these films, will doubtless recognize the resonances Cavell is after. As we met an Eve (in *The Lady Eve*) and an Adam, and his rib for Amanda (in *Adam's Rib*); and as the melodramas of "unknown women" (*Gaslight* [Cukor, 1944]; *Now, Voyager* [Rapper, 1942]; et al.) introduced the project of women speaking for themselves as a way of coming to be known to themselves and the world they inhabit; so with *Pygmalion*, the teaching of the *sound* of speech makes all the difference (as it does in *Singin' in the Rain*—"round tones, round tones" [Kelly and Donen, 1952]). One more numbered chapter remains: another written text compared with a film—this time Shakespeare's *A Winter's Tale* and Éric Rohmer's *A Tale of Winter* (*Conte d'hiver*, 1992). And, as referenced above, there rests Cavell's unnumbered coda entitled "Themes of Moral Perfectionism in Plato's *Republic*," thereby ending the volume with the oldest text formally invoked in its pages (that is, aside from the likes of Hebraic scripture, Homer, and the Bible). And lastly, in a gesture of accounting for the abundant, overflowing content on offer across his two signature genres, we find nine comedies of remarriage and four melodramas of the unknown woman.

In this just-attempted one paragraph précis (or catalogue) of the book, a book set upon the task of offering a classroom experience of the history of Western philosophy coupled with the relatively new art of cinema and not a few fundamental works of literature, theater, and poetry, many unusual things can be noticed (aside from the welcome oddness of that boldest odd coupling of philosophers and movies). Even though, for Cavell, "film was as if made for philosophy," a claim that should happily divert one to his still-stunning, still-invigorating *The World Viewed*, a professionally-trained academic philosopher, educated at any time in the twentieth century, would more than likely find the conjunction of, say, Immanuel Kant and *It Happened One Night* simply baffling, utterly incomprehensible.[30] What kind of mind, what kind of philosophical temperament, can read with ready comprehension the *Critique of Pure Reason* alongside the madcap pleasures of Frank Capra's (just barely) pre-Code film, which won all five of the major Oscars the year it was released, 1934?[31] This is not a rhetorical question, though it may be a personal one for each reader of *Cities of Words*, since a reply may come in the form of saying something about the accomplishment of harmonizing these (rare) dual competencies: composing consecutive prose that does justice to the heights of modern European moral philosophy and the pinnacle of modern American cinematic entertainment—and again, not as achievements deserving high, but separate praise, as we might admire the engineering of the Golden Gate Bridge and the early Italian prose of Giovanni Boccaccio's *The Decameron*. There may be someone on earth who can make a connection between these two testaments to human imagination, and if the connection could be made, we would be duly impressed. Something along these lines—for philosophy and film, for European thinking and American thought, and for the claims of modernism—is accomplished by Cavell in *Cities of Words*.

Even (if only) as a work of canon formation (or reformation or proposition) in philosophy, *Cities of Words* would be a major intervention and contribution. Looking at the left margin of the Contents: Emerson at the beginning? Ibsen, Freud, and Henry James? Shaw and Shakespeare? This is *unlike any introduction to moral philosophy* that we have ever known. And yet, in a literal way, that's just half of the story. The other margin of *Cities of Words* is devoted to film (and as the figures selected should have us presume, dramatic, theatrical works are also party to the lessons). The Contents page offers, at a glance, then, the uncommon marriage of these "sides": philosophy and literature in conversation with cinema and theatre. Which is to say, a conversation that is, or was when Cavell started out in philosophy, almost nonexistent.[32] And if disciplinary ramparts are fortified, and we just keep to the right margin, the canon of films is a bravura presentation; it is, of course, predicated on Cavell's years of reading and research, teaching and screening, that made itself known in *The World Viewed*, *Pursuits of Happiness*, and *Contesting Tears*, among a bevy of articles, chapters, and occasional pieces. Yet, for their familiarity and impact, we can forget how inventive those earlier books are—for example, in the way they created genres where there were none (viz., comedies of remarriage, melodramas of the unknown woman).

If you were going to write a history of philosophy out of the premier Department of Philosophy in the United States, under the auspices of a world-leading university, how would you go about doing it? If we look to Frederick Copleston, Bertrand Russell, Will Durant, Alasdair MacIntyre, or any number of other historians of philosophy, chronology is typically abided by as is the cast of characters and texts—the canon. The ancient Greeks at the start . . . Augustine . . . Descartes . . . Kant, you know the moves. Meanwhile: Frank Capra, George Cukor, Cary Grant, Katharine Hepburn . . . Shakespeare, Ibsen, Freud, Rohmer . . . Emerson . . . what? These feel like category mistakes—conceptually incomprehensible on their own terms and even more so as a gathered group. A significant part of the *logic* of established (canonical) histories is their narrative flow, that ideas happen in a series or sequence, and explanations (call them arguments, call them stories) can be given for the phenomena (phenomena that abide by genre conventions and disciplinary boundaries: e.g., Plato as a philosopher rather than a dramatist; Aeschylus, Sophocles, Euripides as dramatists, not as philosophers, and so on). Imagine the undergraduate philosophy classroom in which the professor enters, distributes a syllabus entitled "Moral Reasoning," and then writes the name "Emerson" on the board. In this history of moral philosophy, not Plato, not Aristotle, but *Emerson* is the founding figure. Familiar with agitprop or avant-garde theater, with Brecht or Beckett, you might think this a stunt—in Emerson's word, something to "unsettle" his audience, a touch of *Verfremsdungeffekt* occasioning a moment of *ostranenie*. Yet, in Cavell's capable accounting for this re-founding of philosophy—and despite one's long education in established histories of philosophy—the claim to the American contribution to Western moral thought (as "preceding" or taking precedence over ancient Greek thought) seems eerily, uncannily sound. In this pedagogical (i.e., performative) act, we should take notice that we have entered modernist territory. Plato is the sequel to Emerson.

If one is predisposed to take Emerson seriously (whether from Cavell's influence, or from a conviction one held before reading Cavell), it is hard to fathom the scale of the scandal, no less the intellectual bravado, along with the attendant academic risk, in placing Emerson at the head of one's account of moral philosophy in Western civilization. And, of course, Emerson is not just the first chapter, the beginning, he is the intellectual condition *for everything* that follows, up to and including the conclusion, which is drawn directly from Plato's *Republic*. As if this Emersonian philosophy *avant la lettre* weren't enough, Cavell's inclusion of film—of many films, half-a-book's worth—on such a list signals an astonishing moment for philosophy, especially if we consider that and how he is mixing and re-conceiving media, genres, traditions, and established habits and methodologies of thought. For example, what would it mean to say (and mean) something like this: "I wish to offer a reading of classic Hollywood comedies (of the sort familiar to the 1930s and 40s) presented as 'pedagogical letters' that themselves are meant to contribute to the history of moral perfectionism, which is itself grounded in a reading of nineteenth-century essayist Ralph Waldo Emerson." How would this proposal sound to a philosopher in 1949 (the latest year in Cavell's range of films), or in 1979, the year he published his seminal study of Wittgenstein, skepticism, morality, and tragedy, *The Claim of Reason*? Indeed, even after all that has happened for philosophy and film in recent years, no doubt owing in part to Cavell's impact on these fields, how does such a strategy sound in 2018, the year of his death—or in any given time that follows? Again, I do not seek a rhetorical answer to such questions so much as I aim to invoke the peculiarity and profundity of Cavell's project in *Cities of Words*, which of course, is grounded in preceding decades of similarly made claims.

If we have grown used to Cavell's experimentalism, we should not lose sight of the fact that even if we can fathom the possibility that someone could write (and the actuality that someone did write) a work such as *Cities of Words* from a seat in Harvard University, in the same hall (Emerson Hall, we might add) that was, for many years, under the imprimatur of Willard Van Orman Quine, who said "philosophy of science is philosophy enough," we must appreciate Cavell's radical intervention into the history of (moral) philosophy—how we think about it and how we "do" it (*CW* 8). The underlying claim of the present chapter, implicit in each of its lines, and explicit in some of them, is that the institutional location, along with Cavell's bravery and imagination, are themselves conceivable *only within a modernist situation* that could both cultivate and then allow such expressions. One needs to have lived in a time when the power of institutional credentialing could be coupled with an imagination capable of rethinking the foundations of its authority. Thus, to reform a tradition from *within* that same tradition. It is as hard to do this as it is rare, and for us, difficult to find a fitting analog; present conditions in the academic humanities often betoken a much different fate for talented, heterodox experimentalists. We may speculate about receptivity to similar traits in the contemporary academy: is there more or less willingness to consider disciplinary hybridity, or because the realm is so embattled, is there increased pressure to police borders? Could Cavell's cross-fertilizing, hierarchy-dissolving approach take hold today, or was its viability a special feature, or unanticipated allowance, of his modernist condition? Then again, for some inheritors, Cavell's methodology has become, quite satisfyingly, the status quo: the operating climate made possible by his efforts and those who joined him in mounting similar tasks and treatments.[33] Typically, the revolutionary is, or is figured as, an outsider—one who is excluded, one who sees something precisely because he is not (professionally) trained and not (officially) sanctioned and not empowered by the establishment (through forms of investment and investiture). Perhaps there are "insiders," who despite accolades and accreditation somehow feel themselves, despite all appearances, to be and remain "outsiders"—and thus poised to comment trenchantly on established norms, and intentionally or not, to become reformers. Cavell earned a doctorate at Harvard, was elected to the Harvard Society of Fellows, taught at Harvard for most of his distinguished career as a scholar and teacher, was a Fellow of the American Academy of Arts and Sciences and at the Institute for Advanced Study in Princeton, received a MacArthur ("Genius") Grant, was President of the American Philosophical Association, accepted dozens of honorary degrees, awards, and invitations to speak for illustrious lectures series (the Beckman, the Carus, the Tanner, etc.), among other notable achievements. Yet, somehow, from the condition of this remarkable set of privileges, he managed, he endeavored to utterly rethink the way in which we could, or should, understand the presiding narrative of human value in Western civilization.

At this point, something explicit should be said about *why* Emerson is, in fact, so crucial, so central to Cavell's project of moral perfectionism. As part of the pre-history of *Cities of Words*, which includes Cavell's several books on or involving Emerson—*The Senses of Walden: An Expanded Edition*; *In Quest of the Ordinary: Lines of Skepticism and Romanticism*; *This New Yet Unapproachable America: Lectures after Emerson after Wittgenstein*; *Conditions Handsome and Unhandsome: The Constitution of Emersonian Perfectionism*; and *Emerson's Transcendental Etudes*—we find Cavell articulating his predicament:

> Because I have for some years seemed to myself to know, against the untiring public denials of the fact, that Emerson is a thinker with the accuracy and consequentiality one expects of a mind worth following with that attention necessary to decipher one's own, I have found myself under increasing pressure to understand what makes the fact incredible, and not just to current academic philosophical and literary sensibilities.
>
> *CHU* 1

Indeed, as Cavell writes in *Cities of Words*, "[n]othing has nourished my conviction," namely, that Emerson writes philosophy, and "calls for philosophy," "more than the number and fervor of people who have gone out of their way to deny that Emerson is capable of challenging philosophy," which arrives with a double sense: writing works of sufficient depth and sophistication that they are worthy of our attention (as philosophy), and offering works that for that same depth and sophistication can take the habits of *academic* philosophy that emerges in modernity yet has been taking on canonical force since the eighteenth century (with its legacy of professionalization, hyper-specialization, and constraints of topic and methodology) (*CW* 20). Still, being thwarted or affronted, ignored or neglected may provide a motivation for one's labors, but it does not yield a case for their legitimacy.

So, what *is* the case for Emerson? As William Rothman puts it: "Emerson is the linchpin that holds together this remarkable book, in which Cavell uses Emerson's writing, and only Emerson's, as both an object and as a 'means, or touchstone,' of interpretation—as a tool for reading, and for *teaching* reading."[34] Cavell has his own way of supplying reason and evidence for his placement (or re-placement) of Emerson at the lead of moral philosophy: "In putting Emerson first—say this making the last first, looking back over the history of philosophy from the perspective of that re-beginning—I accordingly wish here to accent that history differently from the way it presents itself to philosophers" who have understood modern philosophy (in Bacon, Descartes, and Locke) as primarily an epistemological matter motivated by the innovations of the paradigm-shifting science of Copernicus, Galileo, Newton, and others. "My claim for Emerson's achievement," Cavell continues, "is not exactly that he reverses this hierarchy [viz., where epistemology is premier and all else is 'secondary, even optional'] but rather that he refuses the breakup of philosophy into separate fields"—what we can recognize as the evolving and ongoing professionalization of academic disciplines, including the imposition and policing of boundaries between "fields" (*CW* 2–3).

As an illustration of Emerson's philosophical legacy and Cavell's modernist transformation of our reading of it, consider that Cavell not only elevates an unexpected figure (that is, unexpected for professional philosophy) for our new (and renewed) consideration, but he also traces the line of that figure's influence to a place (or places) we would not say are intuitive or deductive. Rather, we need Cavell—and *Cities of Words*, like earlier dispatches—to offer us a "course of study" (that is, a path) for making such influences plain, robust, and heritable. As we assess the "wisdom in discussing a text of Emerson's first," Cavell states that one reason to do so "is that the primary body of Hollywood films to be adduced here may be understood as inspired by Emersonian transcendentalism" (*CW* 6). Since half of *Cities of Words* is devoted to close readings of these films, and since the book is specifically understood as a series of lessons on the "register of the moral life" known as moral perfectionism, or more precisely, *Emersonian* perfectionism, then this claim for Emerson's priority is the crux of our deliberation. One question is whether one can accede to its claims for philosophy at the outset, or whether one must undertake or undergo the course in order to reach that point. Where one falls on this spectrum of response has to do with a second reason that Cavell highlights the American essayist: "that Emerson brings to philosophy dimensions of human concern that the field of philosophy [in modernity] particularly discouraged, not to say disheartened" (*CW* 6). Receptivity to Emerson as *first*, as a premier figure in the history of (moral) philosophy (as legitimate, sanctioned company for Plato, Aristotle, Kant, Mill, et al.), and then, closely following, as the progenitor of a line of thinking that finds prominent expression in Hollywood films of the 30s and 40s, may, therefore, rely a great deal on the sensibilities of one's education: what *it* valued.

Only a modernist would think it pertinent to draw from the fine arts and the popular arts to respond to the rigor and logic and purity of philosophy at mid-century. While the likes and legacies of Bertrand Russell and G. E. Moore still prevailed in England, and as W. V. O. Quine, Saul Kripke, and their company rose in America, the white heat of analytic philosophy, philosophy of mind, of science, of logic, and logical positivism burned incandescently. Cavell's gift to us, to posterity, and perhaps his greatest achievement as a *philosopher*, may be understood principally by his reaching out and back to the arts—in modern and contemporary forms (cinema, photography, painting, poetry, music), but also to Shakespearean drama, and including the *art* of Plato (e.g., helping us to remember that Plato was a dramatist and that Socrates—while based on a historical figure—was a *character* in these dramatic representations). Cavell made this reach as a *romantic*—not as an ironist or nihilist, not as a pessimist or pragmatist.[35] Though Aldous Huxley said, "[t]he right to the pursuit of happiness is nothing else than the right to disillusionment phrased in another way,"[36] as Cavell makes clear in *Cities of Words*, it is the *alternation* between desire and disappointment (which we can be sure includes disillusionment and vice versa) that sets up a dynamic of or for moral perfectionism, a kind of *fort-da* of the spirit (*CW* 2). By these means we overcome, or at least address, "a certain moral cynicism," that is, precisely at those moments when we are susceptible to "giving up on the aspiration to a life more coherent and admirable than seems affordable after the obligations and compromises of adulthood begin to obscure the dreams of youth and the rift between public demands and private desires comes to seem unbridgeable." The education we should have hoped to be prompted to—in the course we have come to call "Cities of Words"—does not concern what we "ought to do, what it would be best or right" to do, but shifts our attention, as we see in the lives of the characters on film, "to the question of how they shall live their lives, what kind of persons they aspire to be" (*CW* 11).

Cavell was, after all, known and renowned as a professor of "aesthetics and the general theory of value," and this title may be one of the few explicit moments of institutional authorization he could cite—namely, in so far as it granted him a position in which, or from which, he could legitimately *make such claims for art's essential role* in our experience and our understanding of philosophy. He was, as we are presumed to believe we all are, implicated in "an enterprise that measures the value of our lives" (*CW* 7). Cavell's measure, then, included a recalibration of forms and proportions (with roughly half of *Cities of Words* dedicated to close analysis of Hollywood films from the 30s and 40s; and even with a line-up of name-brand philosophers, we find room made, at last, at the lead for Emerson, and later for Ibsen, Freud, Henry James, Shaw, and Shakespeare—so again, half of *these* figures are drawn from beyond the bounds of traditionally acclaimed or endorsed philosophers; instead—essayist, poet, dramatist, psychoanalyst, novelist, etc.). While we can be sure that many, many academics have made significant contributions *within* their respective, highly conscribed fields (indeed, despite a heralded age of the inter- and transdisciplinary, this territoriality remains somehow the going standard for such acclaim), let us ask, with a perhaps justified and instructive degree of hyperbole: with Cavell in mind, has an academic figure of such a "resplendent academic pedigree,"[37] from an academic position of such prestige, at such an elite institution, and from the heights of professional philosophy, ever used such powers and privileges to greater effect for *contesting* the contemporary standards of what counts as the profession of philosophy—while also contributing lasting work to many of the mainstream preoccupations of the profession as he found it? (And to further enrich the question, we can look at a parallel track of his effect on the invention of disciplines and programs beyond his own and those he hybridized—for example, in helping to found at Harvard *both* the department of African American Studies and the Harvard Film Archive.) As he did in *Cities of Words*, so elsewhere in his writing and teaching, Cavell the modernist used his position as a platform upon which to create and creatively re-think what was possible for philosophy (and along the way other fields, such as English, comparative literature, cinema studies, and study of the arts more generally, and increasingly anthropology and political theory), much like Emerson and Thoreau re-conceived or re-awakened or re-began philosophy in America, for America, on new terms. Indeed, Cavell can strike us as not only a modernist philosopher, but also as an avant-garde one.

Cavell shows that being at the front guard requires a not-letting-go of the rear guard: so it is that he says "my favorite moral perfectionists are Emerson and Thoreau," who "to my mind [are] the most underrated philosophical minds (however otherwise praised) to have been produced in the United States" (*CW* 12). Full stop. From his assessment and commitment, we can appreciate that Cavell didn't hold the line, much less watch it further deteriorate under the aforementioned heat of analytic philosophy. He was not cowed, or compelled to deny his interests and affections but, in fact, instead, followed and affirmed the "gleam of light" that illuminated for him ways that Hollywood films and American philosophy and much else was pertinent to philosophy, was, indeed, itself philosophy. What did he find? That Cary Grant and Fred Astaire, Katharine Hepburn and Ralph Waldo Emerson were part of philosophy, and philosophers enough for any city of words Cavell should wish to inhabit. "Build, therefore, your own world," Emerson counseled. Cavell heeded the advice. But it is the modernist sense of *continuity* of time and tradition—"Yet line for line and point by point, your dominion is as great as theirs, though without fine names"[38]—that ratifies Stanley Cavell's experiment in heralding the undeniable reality and enduring role of Emersonian perfectionism.

Notes

1. Ralph Waldo Emerson, "A man should learn to detect and watch that gleam of light which flashes across his mind from within, more than the lustre of the firmament of bards and sages." "Self-Reliance," vol. II, 45; and "I read for the lustres," "Nominalist and Realist," vol. III, 233, in *The Complete Works of Ralph Waldo Emerson*, Centenary Edition (Boston: Houghton Mifflin, 1903–4).
2. William Rothman, "In Pursuit of *Pursuits of Happiness*," *Acknowledging Stanley Cavell, Conversations: The Journal of Cavellian Studies*, ed. David LaRocca, no. 7 (2019), 30.
3. Stanley Cavell, "Epilogue: The *Investigations*' Everyday Aesthetics of Itself," in *The Cavell Reader*, ed. Stephen Mulhall (Oxford: Blackwell, 1996), 369–70.
4. Arthur C. Danto, "In Their Own Voice: Philosophical Writing and Actual Experience," in *The Body/Body Problem: Selected Essays* (Berkeley: University of California Press, 1999), 233.
5. For remarks on Cavell and the nature of seriousness, see my "The Seriousness of Film Sustained," in *Movies with Stanley Cavell in Mind* (New York: Bloomsbury, 2021), 1–30.
6. Cavell, "Epilogue: The *Investigations*' Everyday Aesthetics of Itself," 372, emphases added.
7. Plato, *Republic*, trans. G. M. A. Grube, 1974, rev. C. D. C. Reeve (Indianapolis: Hackett, 1992), 263. In the revised edition, the phrase "city of words" is not used; instead the quoted exchange between Glaucon and Socrates reads this way:

    —I understand. You mean that he'll be willing to take part in the politics of the city we were founding and describing, the one that exists in theory, for I don't think it exists anywhere on earth.

    —But perhaps, I said, there is a model of it in heaven, for anyone who wants to look at it and to make himself its citizen on the strength of what he sees. It makes no difference whether it is or ever will be somewhere, for he would take part in the practical affairs of that city and no other.

8   Mark Greif, "The Concept of Experience," in *Against Everything: Essays* (New York: Vintage Books, 2016), 93. See also Greif's "Cavell as Educator," in *Inheriting Stanley Cavell: Memories, Dreams, Reflections*, ed. David LaRocca (New York: Bloomsbury, 2020), 69–94, and in the same volume, my "Autophilosophy," 293, 299.
9   On this point see, for example, Stanley Cavell, "What's the Use of Calling Emerson a Pragmatist?," in *Emerson's Transcendental Etudes*, ed. David Justin Hodge (Stanford: Stanford University Press, 2003), 215–23.
10 For remarks on importance, see Sandra Laugier, "The Importance of Being Alive," in *Inheriting Stanley Cavell*, 231–42, and "The Importance of Stanley Cavell for the Study of Film," in *Movies with Stanley Cavell in Mind*, xiii–xvii.
11 Iris Murdoch, *Under the Net* (New York: Penguin Books, 1954).
12 Lukas Clark-Memler, "'City in Words': Hermeneutic Analysis of Plato's *Republic*," *Ephemeris* 14, no. 1 (2014): 12n4.
13 Emerson, "Self-Reliance," in *The Complete Works*, vol. II, 45.
14 A mode that we do not have to point out, but will, is a hallmark of the way philosophy gets done in Plato; he was, after all, not just a philosopher, but a dramatist of or for philosophy—and may have, in ancient Greek antiquity, answered Cavell's modernist question "Can philosophy become literature and still know itself (as philosophy)?" (*CR* 496).
15 Emerson, *Nature*, in *The Complete Works*, vol. I, 75.
16 Benjamin Franklin, *The Autobiography of Benjamin Franklin* (Boston: Houghton Mifflin, 1906), 1.
17 Cavell cites Schiller's work as "an illustrious precursor in the line of moral perfectionism" only to add that "Schiller's views of perfectibility and of the authority of philosophy, or for that matter, the nature of morality and of aesthetics are at variance with those advanced here" (*CW* x).
18 See Kenneth Dauber, *The Idea of Authorship in America: Democratic Poetics from Franklin to Melville* (Madison: University of Wisconsin Press, 1990).
19 See Andreas Teuber, "Cavell's Ear for Things," in *Inheriting Stanley Cavell*, 199–206.
20 For more on the nature of sound in philosophy and film, see my "Contemplating the Sounds of Contemplative Cinema: Stanley Cavell and Kelly Reichardt," in *Movies with Stanley Cavell in Mind*, 274–318.
21 See *CT* and *PPh* as well as Tim Gould, *Hearing Things: Voice and Method in the Writing of Stanley Cavell* (Chicago: The University of Chicago Press, 1998). See also Catherine Wheatley, "Passionate Utterances: Cavell, Film, and the Female Voice," in *Movies with Stanley Cavell in Mind*, 175–90.
22 For more on the relationship between autobiography and philosophy, see Toril Moi, "Philosophy and Autobiography," in *Inheriting Stanley Cavell*, 269–74, and in the same volume my "Autophilosophy," 275–320.
23 Emerson, "Circles," in *The Complete Works*, vol. II, 320.
24 See, for example, Thomas Schatz, *Hollywood Genres: Formulas, Filmmaking, and the Studio System* (New York: McGraw-Hill, 1981).
25 Cavell, "Epilogue: The *Investigations*' Everyday Aesthetics of Itself," 369.
26 Ludwig Wittgenstein, *Tractatus Logico-Philosophicus*, in *Ludwig Wittgenstein Werkausgabe*, vol. 1 (Frankfurt am Main: Suhrkamp, 1984), 6.421.
27 For more on the *florilegium*, see my *Emerson's English Traits and the Natural History of Metaphor* (New York: Bloomsbury, 2013), 73, 130, 141–42, 144, 146–47, 167, 169.

28 See, for example, *The New York Times Book Review* (March 25, 1956), 30; and Cliff Aliperti, "Viña Delmar and *Uptown New York* (1932)—World Wide [Pictures]'s Bad Girl," *Immortal Ephemera* (January 4, 2016), immortalephemera.com/64040/uptown-new-york-1932-vina-delmar/. For more on Ruth Gordon and Garson Kanin, see my "On the Aesthetics of Amateur Filmmaking in Narrative Cinema: Negotiating Home Movies after *Adam's Rib*," in *The Thought of Stanley Cavell and Cinema: Turning Anew to the Ontology of Film a Half-Century after* The World Viewed (New York: Bloomsbury, 2020), 245–90.

29 David Denby, *Great Books: My Adventures with Homer, Rousseau, Woolf, and other Indestructible Writers of the Western World* (New York: Touchstone, 1996).

30 *CT*, epigraph and xii. See also "Reflections on a Life of Philosophy: Interview with Stanley Cavell," *Harvard Journal of Philosophy* 7 (1999), 25. See also Marshall Cohen, "Must We Mean What We Say? On the Life and Thought of Stanley Cavell," in *Inheriting Stanley Cavell*, 51–9, esp. 54.

31 All five "major" awards being, traditionally, Best Picture, Best Director, Best Actor, Best Actress, and Best Adapted Screenplay. Though the Hays code, or Motion Picture Production Code, was in place in 1930, it was not enforced until July 1, 1934, four months after *It Happened One Night* was released.

32 For remarks on the study of philosophy coalescing with the study of film as conducted by Cavell, see my "Introduction: Philosophy's Claim to Film, Film's Claim to Philosophy," in *The Thought of Stanley Cavell and Cinema*, 1–20. For notes on a particular instance of these relationships, see my "Thinking of Film: What Is Cavellian about Malick's Movies?" in *A Critical Companion to Terrence Malick*, ed. Joshua Sikora (Lanham: Lexington Books of Rowman & Littlefield, 2020), 3–19.

33 See, for example, Noël Carroll: "Cavell's work provided both inspiration and legitimatization to younger philosophers who grew up movie-mad and aspired to unite their love of film with their love of philosophy." "Introduction," in *The Palgrave Handbook of the Philosophy of Film and Motion Pictures*, ed. Noël Carroll, Laura T. Di Summa, and Shawn Loht (New York: Palgrave Macmillan, 2019), xxv. And see also my "The Seriousness of Film Sustained," in *Movies with Stanley Cavell in Mind*, 3–5.

34 Rothman, "In Pursuit of *Pursuits of Happiness*," 21.

35 See, for example, Áine Mahon, *The Ironist and the Romantic: Reading Richard Rorty and Stanley Cavell* (New York: Bloomsbury, 2014).

36 Aldous Huxley, "Tomorrow and Tomorrow and Tomorrow," in *Tomorrow and Tomorrow and Tomorrow, and Other Essays* (New York: Harper, 1956).

37 The phrase comes from Andrew Norris in a review of the Mahon book cited in note 34. See *Notre Dame Philosophical Reviews* (January 8, 2016).

38 Emerson, *Nature*, in *The Complete Works*, vol. I, 76.

8

Modernism: Notes Toward a Philosophical Approach

Piergiorgio Donatelli

A Premise

Modernism is not only a concept that belongs to aesthetics; it can also indicate a whole philosophical orientation. I would like to comment on this from the perspective of Stanley Cavell.[1] Cavell introduces a specific concept of modernism—on which I will dwell at the end of the chapter—but we can use the term more broadly to point to a number of authors who, at the turn of the twentieth century, both inside and outside philosophy, developed views that open up a conversation on the themes of the crisis of expression and culture, of art and morality. In this context, Austrian modernism, which has been extensively documented, especially in connection with Wittgenstein, though not always under this title, should be mentioned first.[2] Also pertinent will be the reference to other philosophical and cultural movements that, in acknowledging the crisis of traditions and artistic conventions in the passage between the two centuries, raise the problem of how the genuine expression of one's experience is possible and thereby face the problem of *forms of life*, of how human life requires a reorganization in new forms, through new connections, according to novel patterns—expressions that we find, for example, in Wittgenstein and Musil.[3]

This perspective finds a fruitful connection with the tradition of moral perfectionism established by Stanley Cavell according to a canon that begins with Plato's *Republic* and unfolds through the course of the philosophical and artistic tradition (*CHU*)—and which I would like to comment on in the light of three crucial nineteenth-century authors, Emerson, John Stuart Mill, and Nietzsche. (Furthermore, these philosophical and cultural strands can be developed in relation to twentieth-century authors such as Cavell, along with Iris Murdoch and Cora Diamond, as well as, in their proximity, John McDowell and Martha Nussbaum (among others), who can be seen as representing an alternative tradition in analytic philosophy and especially in analytic ethics. I won't discuss them here, however.) Thus, philosophical modernism can be placed in the following context of authors and perspectives: on the one hand, it is in dialogue with moral perfectionism, which in authors such as Mill and Emerson stands as an intellectual episode—historically antecedent to modernism—belonging to romanticism;

on the other hand, it is in dialogue with later developments of the philosophical tradition, especially those tied to ordinary language philosophy, where we can locate the specific contribution of Cavell's early reading of Wittgenstein in *Must We Mean* and in the first three parts of *The Claim of Reason*.

Against the background of this intersection of authors and philosophical strands, I would like to address a number of issues that form a coherent perspective. Historically they are issues, centering around Wittgenstein, that have their roots in the views which propose to contest the philosophical traditions across the two centuries and at the same time elaborate romantic themes, to be found in American Transcendentalism (Emerson and Thoreau), yet also in an author in certain respects very far from these, John Stuart Mill. They are problems, ideas, methods, and ways of dealing with them that are necessary today, in the current climate of philosophy, in which many of those who speak in the name of analytic philosophy (where we can place some of the authors mentioned here, and certainly Wittgenstein) claim that it is a specialized field of knowledge with its own problems that can be isolated from the larger domain of culture—and for whom philosophy becomes a form of knowledge that cannot conceive of its own crisis as belonging to a crisis of culture as a whole.

Philosophy as Culture

I would like to present some features of this philosophical constellation starting from the idea of modernism I have just sketched. Philosophical modernism, for our purposes here, is a perspective that seeks to offer a reconstruction of culture. It requires a conception of philosophy that does not separate itself from culture and does not turn philosophy into a specialized field, but on the contrary sees it as a form of reflection capable of responding to cultural problems and being challenged by them. In such a context, it is relevant to defend a conception of philosophy understood as a transformative activity, as opposed to theory—transformation of the self and of culture that gives voice to experience, thought as the horizon that allows experience itself to be expressed, or that shows how this may be impossible unless such a horizon is transformed, finding new words or recovering the existing vocabulary, bringing to light and broaching new modes of expression.

I will also note that a key work in this context, Wittgenstein's *Philosophical Investigations*, has been read according to (at least) two very different perspectives: some have sought in it sketches of theories (of meaning, psychology, mathematics, etc.), and some have insisted on the dissolution of philosophical problems. Elizabeth Anscombe, for example, has written that Wittgenstein's goal is to provide us with medicines that are useful for freeing us from the conceptions that hold us captive.[4] Cavell has written explicitly that "Wittgenstein has no philosophy of language at all. He can better be read as attacking philosophy's wish to provide theories of language" (*CR* 15). Cora Diamond has argued that the goal of Wittgenstein's philosophy is the transformation of philosophical desire, and has advanced the idea that philosophy does not offer doctrines, but effects changes that are revealed in our relation to language, i.e., in the phenomenology of what we are willing to read as meaning in a string of signs.[5] Moreover, John McDowell has offered his own elaboration of this anti-theoretical intent: working from a Wittgensteinian understanding of philosophy, he has argued that the goal is to deconstruct our need for theories, leading us to overcome that very need.[6]

Such various interpretations and elaborations of Wittgenstein's philosophy have contributed to the rehabilitation of a perspective that works on the clarification of problems and the transformation of the self, and that constitutes a crucial line in analytic philosophy, while the other perspective, in this contrast, is represented by the theory conception in whose light Wittgenstein has been read for many years (and which has now fundamentally rejected him). But other philosophical perspectives can also be read in the anti-theoretical light. An interpretation of the entire tradition of ancient thought and of minor but significant lines of modern philosophy in this light has been explored by Pierre Hadot and Michel Foucault, among others. Yet, in the company of Hadot, Foucault, and Cavell, it is possible to return to many classical texts that emphasize the transformative register and the critique of philosophy conceived as theory.[7]

The dispute over theory and anti-theory conceptions is important for my perspective. Only within the critique of philosophy as theory is it possible to reconstruct the space of modernist, and thus romantic and perfectionist, problematics, which see the problems of knowledge as problems of the self, concerning interest and orientation in life, and how interest can wither and orientation can be lost. However, this dispute could remain within the boundaries of philosophy, pitting those who claim that it provides real knowledge against those who claim that its task is to dissolve illusory philosophical problems, leaving us on a ground that is completely free of philosophy and about which philosophy has nothing more to say. The contrast between theory and anti-theory conceptions may not show that philosophy is nourished by problems within our culture, problems that are located in our ordinary life. One might imagine that the diagnostic and therapeutic task of philosophy concerns theoretical superfluities that, once treated, liberate the mind without touching the cultural problems that are rooted in the forms of life. Instead, I would like to propose a different view, according to which philosophy responds to cultural problems. As Cavell writes, "philosophy is the criticism a culture produces of itself" (*CR* 175), and, commenting on the *Philosophical Investigations*: "My claim is that the *Investigations* can be seen, as it stands, as a portrait, or say as a sequence of sketches (Wittgenstein calls his text an album) of our civilization, of the details of what Spengler phrases as our 'spiritual history'" (*NYUA* 59).[8]

In this light philosophy appears as a particular way of responding to cultural problems, and this view brings with it an interpretation of culture that does not confine its activities and forms of knowledge either to specialists such as scholars, critics, and various sorts of scientists, or to the specialists of the imagination (writers, film directors, etc.), but concerns us all. The members of this "all" express themselves through cultural forms and yet do not exhaust their expressive potential in them. For example, they may find that cultural forms do not give them a voice and leave them without words.[9]

If we consider philosophy as a way of responding to cultural problems, we must next address the question of its status and specificity: in this region, too, we encounter important differences and contrasts. Cavell ends *The Claim of Reason* by asking, "can philosophy become literature and still know itself?" (*CR* 496). The book ends with a question, which suggests that an answer can be offered, though never conclusively: that while the need for the transformation of philosophy into literature is important, if it were realized it would betray what motivated it in the first place. The final lines of *The Claim of Reason* return to Shakespeare's *Othello*, to Othello's failure to acquire a kind of knowledge that is too difficult for him, the knowledge of Desdemona's separateness, which is the knowledge of Othello's separateness from and dependence on Desdemona's desire, that is, the knowledge of his constitutive and vertiginous vulnerability.[10] The drama offers such knowledge, and philosophy tends to elude it, to deflect our understanding of it, whereas imaginative literature is able to grasp it with its stories, to bring it back as a fact among the many facts that inhabit the city, to find a place for it in the literary city.[11]

It seems to me, therefore, that the point of the question that brings *The Claim of Reason* to its conclusion is that philosophy lives in the dimension created by this tension. More precisely, philosophy lives in the acknowledgment of this avoidance, which is constitutive of its nature, but which, if philosophy could overcome it, if it could win it once and for all, it would lose itself: philosophy could not recognize itself, could not recognize itself as philosophy, as Cavell writes.

So a new contrast emerges here: there are those who think of philosophy as a kind of literature (Richard Rorty suggests this possibility),[12] while Cavell's point is that imaginative literature recounts what philosophy explains by avoiding it, but there is a kind of philosophy that tries to proceed in a way that is conscious of this avoidance. Philosophy has its own specificity and therefore its own internal motivation, but it would betray this very motivation (the interest that moves it) if it were to become pure, capable of flourishing on its own, separated from larger cultural problems, and also if it were to resolve itself into another pursuit, that of imaginative literature, and become indistinguishable from it.

On Cavell's view, philosophy has a motive that is personal and at the same time belongs to the discipline (to the relationship that a philosopher has with the tradition of that discipline), a motive that we want to call philosophical but which is also human: it is an interest in the world. Interest drives conceptual investigation, Wittgenstein writes: "Concepts lead us to make investigations. They are the expression of our interest and direct our interest" (*PI* §570). Philosophical interest is born in the streets, in the hallways, out of encounters and words exchanged in the circumstances of ordinary life (*PPh* 63), but what motivates philosophy is dissatisfaction with such words and circumstances; it is an interest on the side of such common interests. (Cavell discovers this sidedness—the domain of what is *next* and *besides*—in Emerson: we side against and with ourselves, we live besides ourselves. The progressive movement of the self in what Cavell calls Emersonian perfectionism is a lateral movement with respect to the self, not a vertical ascent.) It questions them anxiously because it does not consider them reliable and no longer trusts them. This is where the path of philosophy begins, nourished by the turn suffered by the common interest in life—it is Cavell's and Wittgenstein's *turn*, as when Wittgenstein writes in the *Philosophical Investigations* that we must turn our inquiry around the fixed point of our real need (*PI* §108). Such a turn is the one pressed on the common interest, and in this lies the philosophical interest, which thus appears as an inflection of common interest.

So we can say that philosophy shares the interest of imaginative literature, which is the interest aroused by stories, the wonder, the awe, the sense of the gripping and the surprising, the unspecialized interest in experience cultivated independently of explanation, as Walter Benjamin argues.[13] At the same time, it inflects such an interest: it is inflected by an interest that sides with it. But the philosophical interest loses itself when it is completely separated from common interest—in this case, the interest we have in stories. The metaphysical conception that Wittgenstein challenges imagines itself to produce such a state of purity, in a gesture of isolation that loses contact with common life: in this case, with the interests it shares with imaginative literature and with the human, nonspecialized interest in stories. But philosophy would also lose itself and its motives if it simply became literature.

Intimacy

What are the problems of a philosophy that has not separated itself from culture? Here we find the core of philosophical modernism. I will start with naturalism. Cavell describes Wittgenstein's naturalism, or rather his idea of naturalness (*CR* 86–125), as a kind of ease in speech, gesture, and thought, so that the next step is taken as a matter of course, as a foregone conclusion. More generally, we could say that it is a matter of naturalness of agreement—an attunement (*Übereinstimmung*)—of our responses, as when Wittgenstein writes: "It is not only agreement in definitions, but also (odd as it may sound) agreement in judgments that is required for communication by means of language" (*PI* §242). The activities that characterize our common life are based on agreements among us and with ourselves, like following a rule: it is natural to continue in an arithmetic series, or it is natural to use a word in a new context of application, and this finds a response, it is received by others as the natural move to make. It is a form of naturalism according to which the forms of civilization are reconstructed from the bottom up,[14] starting from agreements and intimate bonds that are natural and spontaneous: according to a *spontaneous sympathy*, as Wittgenstein writes.[15] We find this naturalism in authors such as Emerson, James, Musil, Freud, Wittgenstein, and before them, David Hume. It stands in contrast to conceptions that account for practices and institutions on the basis of intellectual constructions from above, to rationalism. Who are the rationalists? It is certainly not a predefined group, since they are internal interlocutors of this kind of problematic. The Italian philosopher Aldo Giorgio Gargani points to what he calls a classical tradition responsible for the fictitious reconstructions from above that he traces in modern philosophy, ethics, political economy, and other fields, leading up to Wittgenstein's *Tractatus*.[16] As he writes, according to the classical view, "to know something, you must know everything."[17]

However, this total knowledge is fictitious; it is only a gesture that shows the ideal transfiguration of the instinctive rejection of what is specific, different, new, and polymorphous.[18] In the modernist perspective, however, culture is reconstructed in a Humean manner as the cultivation of naturalities, of traces in the mind, as Hume would say, that we trace in common, agreements that socially conform our minds, as in his account of artificial virtues (for example, the obligation to keep our promises).[19] What is at stake is an account of practical and intellectual activities, including highly specialized pursuits such as finance, industry, and science (the examples that appear again and again in Musil), as forms of cultivated naturalness, of agreements and routes of interest that come naturally, unforcedly.

These agreements are not only natural, but also intimate, which is another aspect. What comes naturally has a certain intimate character. As Wittgenstein remarks, we become attached to our words, to faces and names, to the familiar forms of life: "It seems to us that this name is the only right one for this face"; "I feel as if the name 'Schubert' fitted Schubert's works and Schubert's face" (*PI* §171, 227). This is a crucial feature of language:

> The familiar face of a word, the feeling that it has assimilated its meaning into itself, that it is a likeness of its meaning—there could be human beings to whom all this was alien. (They would not have an attachment to their words.)
>
> *PI* 230

It is the intimacy of the touch of things in Emerson from which Cavell derives the title of his book on moral perfectionism, *Conditions Handsome and Unhandsome*. Emerson writes in his essay "Experience": "I take this evanescence and lubricity of all objects, which lets them slip through our fingers then when we clutch hardest, to be the most unhandsome part of our condition."[20] What is unpleasant and unhandsome is the inconsistency of things, people, and facts that slip from our grasp, that offer no resistance, like the grief over the death of his son Waldo, which seems to him to be nothing more than the loss of a possession: "In the death of my son, now more than two years ago, I seem to have lost a beautiful estate,—no more. I cannot get it nearer to me."[21] What is deeply unhandsome is the slipping away of things and events under the pressure of our grasp, which seeks to get hold of them, clutch them and possess them, whereas what needs to be learned is experience, conceived of as the virtue of reception and passivity, with which the essay ends: "All I know is reception."[22]

In Cavell's analysis, the unhandsome side of the human condition lies in the attempt to grasp what we must instead learn to receive and experience (*CHU* 38–42). The grasping of things is possible only as a form of reception, as an interest in things, as an incentive that comes from them and leaves them where they are in their separateness and partiality. The experience of others and of the world requires the quality of reception and passivity. Cavell comments:

> Emerson's image of clutching and Heidegger's of grasping, emblematize their interpretation of Western conceptualizing as a kind of sublimized violence. . . . The

overcoming of this conceptualizing will require the achievement of a form of knowledge both Emerson and Heidegger call reception, alluding to the Kantian idea that knowledge is active, and sensuous intuition alone passive or receptive.

CHU 39

As it gradually becomes clear in the essay "Experience" that the child Waldo is identified with the world as such, the quality of experience also takes on the meaning of acceptance of separateness and mourning. Cavell continues: "For Emerson the philosophical interpretation of experience makes it a cause for mourning, assigning to philosophy the work of accepting the separation of the world, as of a child" (*CHU* 40). We must educate experience to be worthy of trust.[23] We must educate our experience to accept the world and others—and also ourselves, as in moral perfectionism—in their separateness, to allow them to exercise the power they possess, to unfold their power of attraction, allowing us to find in them an interest and an incentive. Cavell writes:

> The reverse of the unhandsome in our condition, of Emerson's clutching and Heidegger's grasping—call the reverse the handsome part—is what Emerson calls being drawn and what Heidegger calls getting in the draw, or the draft, of thinking. Emerson speaks of this in saying that thinking is partial. . . . . Thinking *is*—at its most complete, as it were—a partial act; if it lacks something, leaves something out, it is its own partiality, what Kant calls (and Freud more or less calls) its incentive and interest (*Triebfeder*).
>
> *CHU* 41–42

The interest that drives thought and conceptual exploration is thus born out of having accepted partiality and thus the otherness of other people, of the world, and of ourselves, by having experienced such otherness. The intimacy of such an experience is delicate and difficult because it requires us to acknowledge the separateness of that which is intimate to us.

Yet touch also has the quality of pleasurable intimacy, as in Thom Gunn's poem of the same name, where the whole world seeps from touch in continuous creation. Gunn describes himself as he sinks down next to his sleeping partner:

> You are a mound
> of bedclothes, where the cat
> in sleep braces
> its paws against your
> calf through the blankets,
> and kneads each paw in turn.
>
> Meanwhile and slowly
> I feel a is it
> my own warmth surfacing or
> the ferment of your whole

> body that in darkness beneath
> the cover is stealing
> bit by bit to break
> down that chill.
>
> You turn and
> hold me tightly, do
> you know who
> I am or am I
> your mother or
> the nearest human being to
> hold on to in a
> dreamed pogrom.
>
> What I, now loosened,
> sink into is an old
> big place, it is
> there already, for
> you are already
> there, and the cat
> got there before you, yet
> it is hard to locate.
> What is more, the place is
> not found but seeps
> from our touch in
> continuous creation, dark
> enclosing cocoon round
> ourselves alone, dark
> wide realm where we
> walk with everyone.[24]

The experience of touch, which dominates and almost dissolves the personality of the two lovers, leads to a place that is nowhere, that cannot be objectified, because it is the common texture that, on the one hand, isolates and brings back to oneself, to one's dark cocoon, and, on the other hand, creates companionship. It is the basis of the agreement that is produced by walking together. This old and great place is "already there," it meets the narrator autonomously, drawing him into intimacy, making him sink and surrender in an experience of passivity and reception. Pleasure is produced by the acknowledgment of this kind of otherness.

Agreements are intimate. It is the intimacy of the senses and of human encounters. The intimate character of life is especially treated by Wittgenstein when he writes about how the world strikes us, how words and experiences are lived, in the various episodes in which our lives are filled with meaning and intensified. These are also the experiences that he calls secondary phenomena in the *Philosophical Investigations* and in the writings on the philosophy of psychology, and about which Cora Diamond has written ingeniously.[25] It seems important to remark, however, that for Wittgenstein this intimacy also touches the naturalness realized by our linguistic and normative activities, which are not characterized by these phenomena of intensification. Another name for this intimacy is the ordinary and the familiar. There is a familiar tone that permeates the agreements that come naturally to us. We might also say that Cavell and Wittgenstein encourage us to see the intimate and lived side of activities that are not in themselves intimate. They invite us to consider these activities under the aspect of what is common, familiar, and earthly—as the proximity to our body, the nearness to things in touch, the closeness to others in the complicity and the gestures, the terrestrial, that is, the familiar tone of our earthly collocation, so powerfully represented in Alfonso Cuarón's film *Gravity* (2013).[26]

Veena Das has written about the familiar tone of life. Returning to the stories of poverty and extreme hardship in India that she recounts in her work, she writes:

> I want this book to be haunted by the stories of suffering and loss but also by the courage and the stupendous efforts to affirm life made by so many of my interlocutors. And in yet another contradictory impulse I wish not to put a burden of heroic forms of self-formation on the people I encountered and lived alongside. In the end I think that if some of the poor do spend money on alcohol rather than schooling and others manage in the terrible conditions of dirt and squalor to keep their houses neat and tidy, then this diversity should be normalized as it is for those who are not poor. The phrase often used in the slums for explaining why electricity failed, or the fever returned, or the child did not feel like completing her homework is *"yeh to normal hai—this is normal."* The lives of the poor are strongly defined by living this normal—yet remaining attentive to the critical—and I have tried to think of an anthropology that would be mindful of this tonality of their lives.[27]

Das strongly criticizes the sublimation of situations of poverty, abandonment, and extreme hardship, as if they were completely separate from the ordinary conditions of life. In some cases, they do in fact mark the collapse of minimal forms of subsistence and coexistence, but often even the most extreme forms of damaged life flow according to their own rhythms, possessing their own particular normality. And the possibility of going on with one's life after a crisis (an illness, the loss of a loved one, violence, including social violence of the kind recounted in Das's work)[28] involves a return to (a kind of) normality, albeit a precarious and painful one. Normality, Das writes in this passage, has its own tonality, its own color, a sensitive and lived side that is woven into the rhythms of life.

A Difficult Naturalism

From the modernist perspective, this naturalness is under attack. The intimacy and naturalness of the stream of life in the normal steps and movements of human activity breaks down in a way that says something essential about naturalness and intimacy themselves.

Naturalness, the easy and the intimate, the proximity to oneself and to others and to the circumstances of life, seems to be too much for us. "Human kind / Cannot bear very much reality" writes T. S. Eliot in *Four Quartets*.[29] Eliot describes a crucial modernist experience. There is something we cannot accept, which takes many forms, but we can express it through the urgency of protection and at the same time the shame for what is dear and precious to us. (We are confronted here with a problematization of the Stoic question of *oikeiōsis*, that kind of intimacy and closeness to oneself that is taken for granted in the Stoic framework and later in the natural law tradition.) Shame for what seems inadequate in our eyes, not up to what it should sustain (civilization, in the end), shame for who we are, for what we know we are, considered as a private and exclusive knowledge that seems utterly incapable of standing up to who we are socially, to the tissue of relationships and activities that we support with our individual contribution. It is the obsession with privacy in Wittgenstein's *Philosophical Investigations*. One's feelings, pains, and pleasures seem so private that they are incapable of tolerating human encounter, as happens in scenes of exasperation, emphatic as they are, when someone blurts out: "But surely another person can't have THIS pain!" (*PI* §253; see *CT* 156–64). And it is also the shame that Martha Nussbaum has explored in the light of object relations theory (Melanie Klein and Donald Winnicott, among others): the shame experienced by the infant in the face of the narcissistic defeat of her need for nourishment, which is that of a special and unique being.[30] The vulnerability that comes with being dependent on someone else for sustenance is experienced with a deep sense of shame and seems unbearable.

In the modernist perspective, shame signals the way in which what is natural and intimate, easy and familiar, is transformed into something unnatural and foreign, impossible or truly difficult to endure. The familiar and the ordinary return, transformed by these experiences. Cavell uses this idea of return as transformation when he writes that "philosophy's return to the everyday is not a return but a turn; not an arrival but a coming to, a process of coming to, taking steps; a movement that presents itself sometimes as peace and sometimes as destruction" (*CT* 164).

The intimate and the natural are turned into something inadequate, incapable of withstanding the demands of life, transforming life into a difficult or unachievable task that depends on rules that must be followed forcibly and that must be motivated at every step, losing spontaneity. These are different but related phenomena: the loss of motivation, of naturalness, of happy satiety and ease, and the mechanic, the repetitive, fixation and anguish.

We find here a line of analysis that can be located in the young Nietzsche, in Wittgenstein and Freud, and then in Cavell, according to which naturalness and intimacy naturally provoke these shameful protective reactions that, by intensifying experience in this gesture of isolation, fixate it, mechanize it, and turn it into an obsession. In the perspective I am exploring here, the naturalness that has not gone along this path and has not known this suffering is not yet the naturalness that can truly host civilization. Civilization is made of agreements that are mobile and that know the experience of rupture, stumbling, and fixation; they know the naturalness that turns on itself and that leads, under happy conditions, to a mature and adult mobility. Without the experience of shame and the discovery of limitation and vulnerability, intimacy and agreement are fantastic and mythical, because they have not yet encountered reality: they inhabit the world without boundaries of infantile narcissism.

Only insofar as the human reality of agreements is finite and limited does it allow for movement—it provides the friction necessary to be able to walk, as in the famous passage from the *Philosophical Investigations*: "We have got on to slippery ice where there is no friction, and so, in a certain sense, the conditions are ideal; but also, just because of that, we are unable to walk. We want to walk: so we need friction. Back to the rough ground!" (*PI* §107). In fact, what we need is a naturalness that serves our purposes. The stream of life in which words and actions find their meaning and purpose—as Wittgenstein writes: "For words have meaning only in the stream of life"[31]—is not intact and intangible. The life to which we can contribute our part is that which we have earned as limited material (partial, in the language of Emerson and Cavell: it is always a part), composed of movements and rhythms that encounter obstacles and, for this reason, can shape our goals.

The issue here is the education of naturalness, an important concern in the philosophical tradition, beginning with Aristotle and continuing through Hume, Hegel, and Dewey. But education is permeated by the experience of crisis; it is education that calls for conversion, a turning of experience upon itself (which is the theme of moral perfectionism). Wittgenstein's and Cavell's ordinary is a condition in which the naturalness of agreements is not the immature one of the child, incapable of sustaining the encounter with reality and giving form to civilization. Rather, it is that which has returned to itself, rejected itself, and then accepted itself, that is, acknowledged itself in its limitation, finiteness, and poverty—and which is willing to travel through such refusals and acceptances, repeatedly. It is such a reality of human agreements that makes itself available as the material of the highest human constructions that Wittgenstein, Freud and Musil, Cavell and Gargani want to describe from the bottom up, from the perspective of agreements (and ruptures) that are natural and intimate.

Nor should we assume that such naturalness is *second nature*, which has experienced crisis and has treasured it profitably. The latter is the image in which everything adds up just right. Instead, the scene described by Wittgenstein and Cavell is the one in which regained naturalness takes the form of repair, of accommodation and compensation of blocks and fixations, of "domestication," to use a term of Emerson's that Cavell employs.[32] The work of domestication is daily and repetitive, and in this sense it offers a way of living in the world and with our words. The image, then, is not that of an experience that has treasured the crisis and matured in a beautiful, balanced, and excellent way, but that of a mending that works but not completely, of a compensation that makes up for a loss that leaves its mark in the new way of living. We could also say that it is a perspective that has been shaped from the point of view of the vulnerability of language and life, rather than that of achieved perfection.[33]

What we are called to do is to respond creatively, from the location in which we find ourselves. The situation of crisis requires an accommodation to the present condition—the point being that *these* are the conditions, the present, the ordinary in which we live, our self as it is now. This teaches an ability to accommodate and care for the present conditions; it teaches not to avoid the painful reality by deflecting it, getting busy about something else, because this crisis concerns our present and therefore has this concreteness.

Ordinary Language

The theme of the ordinary, in Wittgenstein and Austin, as well as in the American Transcendentalists, belongs to this scene and this context. Ordinary language is important because it shows how it is the actual words in their literality that are transformed, or rather that have the power to transform us along with them. Mobility is inscribed in ordinary language, and it is therefore important to recognize that the driving forces of change are the very words that are problematic for us, that torment us and suffocate us, or that we feel are absolutely indispensable or that we cannot say at any cost: these are the very words that change and that change us along with them.[34]

This idea of the transformative power of language has at least two opponents. On the one hand, there is the view that sees language as a set of instruments to achieve a goal. When words present difficulties, we can replace them with other words that are more functional for our purposes: words, in this view, have no weight and power of their own, they are simply at our service. Charles Taylor has criticized this view to defend another, which he calls "expressivism": language articulates human experience against a background of meanings, actions, and attitudes that shape our goals and interests. Language is not simply at our service, nor is it the background from which our goals and interests emerge.[35] Cora Diamond has offered a similar critique of this conception, which she calls "empiricist": "Empiricism makes it appear as if we could not help having whatever words we needed for our experience: words which were at least adequate to represent it to ourselves, because whenever words for a kind of experience are lacking there is no difficulty in coining new ones."[36]

On the other side, there are those who criticize the instrumentalist conception and who, along with Wittgenstein, defend the irreplaceable literality of language without recognizing its transformative power. We can read Elizabeth Anscombe and Peter Winch in this light. For them, the words of language shape a form of life. Words like "marriage" and "burial" stand for the human form of life and cannot be replaced without losing or compromising it.[37] Anscombe uses Wittgenstein (along with Aristotle and Aquinas) to draw boundaries and confidently declare who belongs to the form of life and language and who doesn't, to confidently declare that people separated by these boundaries cannot provide instruction to each other. On the contrary, the educational side of the modernist perspective consists precisely in recognizing that the education of grownups, as Cavell has glossed philosophy, passes through the experience of strangeness, of becoming strangers to ourselves, foreigners, inhabitants of the other side of the border, and hence mobile and progressive. Those who live outside, like Nora in Ibsen's *A Doll's House* (a significant example of a perfectionist text, in Cavell's reading, *CHU* 101–26), may try to explain themselves only in the words and from the point of view of the lives of those who inhabit the inside. And the one who lives inside (Torvald) may learn from those who are outside that he is living a false life, that what he calls marriage is dead, and that in order to become alive again it needs to be transfigured. The entire life-with-marriage must be reshaped around the literality of such words, the confidence in which has been shaken by the experience of those who live outside its boundaries (*SW* 92–93).

Modernism and Romanticism in Stanley Cavell

I would now like to offer some considerations on the specific use of the concept of modernism in the work of Stanley Cavell. The concept of modernism plays an important role in his writings in a certain period, in the 1960s and 1970s, in *Must We Mean* and in his book on the ontology of film, *The World Viewed*. Later, the concept is no longer significantly present, and modernist themes are developed first by examining lines of romanticism in *In Quest of the Ordinary* and then in *Conditions Handsome and Unhandsome*, where Cavell presents his viewpoint, which he now terms "Emersonian perfectionism," locating it in the region of Emerson's philosophy, that is, in this American moment of romanticism.[38]

In Cavell's treatment, modernism refers in the first place to the world of art and denotes the condition in which an artist can no longer rely on the artistic medium to express herself in poetry, music, and painting (*WV* 103). Cavell describes the problem of modernism as follows:

> [T]he modernist predicament [is one] in which an art has lost its natural relation to its history, in which an artist, exactly because he is devoted to making an object that will bear the same weight of experience that such objects have always borne which constitute the history of his art, is compelled to find unheard-of structures that define themselves and their history against one another.... When in such a state an art explores its medium, it is exploring the conditions of its existence; it is asking exactly whether, and under what conditions, it can survive.
>
> *WV* 72

For the modernist artist, what is at stake is the survival of art itself, and thus of a tradition to which she belongs, in which what she does counts as (*is*) an object of art. In order to restore this continuity and inherit the artistic tradition, she must contest the continuity of conventions and techniques and return to the power of the physical conditions of art to enable the artist to produce a work of art. The modernist situation, therefore, offers at least two crucial aspects for our consideration. First, it brings into view the theme of tradition—the necessity of belonging to expressive traditions in order to be able to express oneself. In this regard, it raises the question of the need to inherit a tradition: that is, the theme of crisis and revolution, and thus of the weight and the obligation that rests on every artist to reject a tradition when the conventions have become exhausted, in order to be faithful to it in new and unexplored ways. Secondly, the modernist situation introduces the problem of the physical conditions of artistic expression (linguistic signs, paint, sound), which is at the same time the problem of the physical conditions of humanity, the physical location of human beings. The conditions of humanity, like those of art, are not to be taken for granted, they are not a secure possession; rather, they must be earned again. In the modernist situation, the artist's task is to earn for herself the artistic power of an expressive medium, and thereby to acknowledge it as such, just as each of us earns for herself and acknowledges as such the power of the physical conditions that make us human: the fact of having a body, of being separate individuals, of expressing and communicating through gestures, words, and looks.[39] Cavell writes that a modernist painting, for example a Pollock, "may acknowledge its frontedness, or its finitude, or its specific thereness— that is, its presentness; and your accepting it will accordingly mean acknowledging *your* frontedness, or directionality, or verticality toward its world, or any world—or your presentness, in its aspect of absolute hereness and of nowness" (*WV* 110).

In this sense the modernist situation describes an epoch in the history of the arts, which in *The World Viewed* Cavell examines particularly in light of Michael Fried's treatment of modernist painting.[40] However, it also represents a kind of critical posture that elucidates and is elucidated by the condition of philosophy, as he argues explicitly in *Must We Mean*. In the introduction to this volume, Cavell writes that modern philosophy shares with modern art the fact that the relationship between the present practice of a particular intellectual or artistic enterprise and the history of that enterprise and its conventions has become problematic. The new problem posed by the modernist situation is that past and present become problematic together, that is, that the modernist faces the "difficulty of making one's present effort become a part of the present history of the enterprise" (*MWM* xxxvi). This is also the lesson of ordinary language philosophy, of Wittgenstein and Austin. In this situation, philosophy can remain faithful to itself only by acknowledging its separation from its tradition and by reclaiming new means of expression and new conventions—and thus by acknowledging its history, that is, by inheriting it again. Moreover, the theme of ordinary language philosophy brings us back to language conceived as the world, that is, to the physical conditions of human existence. Just as the "automatisms" of the medium—the conventions and genres on which a tradition is based and which allow the artist to make her own contribution[41]— have become problematic in relation to the goals of the artist, so too has the ordinary automatism of words, gestures and looks become problematic in relation to human goals. Philosophy in the modernist situation responds to this kind of problem: the loss of power suffered by linguistic and, more broadly, human automatism. The condition of humanity itself has become problematic and must be brought home from the estrangement in which it finds itself (this is the diagnosis of philosophical problems offered by Wittgenstein in the *Philosophical Investigations*).

Therefore, modernism appears in Cavell's work within a problematic that concerns the arts, but it points to crises and ways of recomposition that pertain to philosophy and that Cavell extends to religion, politics, and personal relationships, as when he writes about the truth of the artist: "In art—as now in politics, as formerly in religion, as in personal relations—finding the right to speak the truth is as difficult as finding the truth" (*WV* 98). The crisis of expressive automatism concerns the entire field of human and cultural expressions.

The next issue is that of the disappearance of the notion of modernism (or at least of its centrality) in Cavell's writings from the 1980s onward. William Rothman argues that when Cavell encounters Emerson (he had dedicated *The Senses of Walden* to the other classic Transcendentalist author in 1972),[42] he discovers a tradition in relation to which he, as a philosopher, is no longer in a "modernist situation." He once again finds a home for his thought, that of "American philosophy." We must note, however, that it is a habitation that allows him to pursue in a different way the modernist themes of crisis and rediscovery of the physical conditions of existence, which are now those of ordinary life as addressed by Emerson and Thoreau; or, as we should rather say, it is ordinary life that is conceived as the description of such conditions, thus produced as the earning and acknowledgment of them in a situation of crisis and denial. Moreover, the encounter with Emerson also marks the broaching of a kind of romanticism (which begins to find its place in the fourth part of *Claim of Reason* and is fully developed in *In Quest of the Ordinary*) from which Cavell derives an elaboration of the themes of the ordinary that he finds more effective than the one developed within ordinary language philosophy. He makes the following strong and important statement about this:

> While I find that this sense of intimacy with existence, or intimacy lost, is fundamental to the experience of what I understand ordinary language philosophy to be, I am myself convinced that the thinkers who convey this experience best, most directly, and most practically are not such as Austin and Wittgenstein but such as Emerson and Thoreau.
>
> *ETE* 23

We are thus faced with the complex problem of the relationship between what Cavell calls romanticism and modernism. Indeed, modernism is a specific cultural episode that historically comes after romanticism. But it is also clear that Cavell uses both episodes to develop his personal approach, in which modernism, if we take it as a fundamentally European artistic experience (which, however, includes the American arts), gradually becomes more and more in need of American romanticism, expressed in Transcendentalism and, further, in the experience of American popular culture, crucially represented by the Hollywood films of the 1930s and 1940s, which Cavell places in the genre of the comedy of remarriage (from which he derives the related genre of the melodrama of the unknown woman). When he comes to write *Conditions Handsome and Unhandsome*, Cavell calls Emersonian perfectionism what he considers his philosophical perspective, through which we can also read a work that precedes this elaboration, such as his book on the Hollywood comedy of remarriage, *Pursuits of Happiness*, where he splendidly works out the themes of the perfectionist conversation. However, it is also important to consider that Emersonian perfectionism and the (still unnamed) perfectionism of the Hollywood comedy of remarriage enrich and incorporate in an original way a problematic structure, that of modernism, which is not rejected but, on the contrary, regarded as necessary. As he writes in *The World Viewed*, in a passage dedicated to American modernist painting, modernism is indeed confronted with a romantic problematic:

> The works of Pollock, Louis, Noland, and Olitski achieve in unforeseen paths an old wish of romanticism—to imitate not the *look* of nature, but its conditions, the possibilities of knowing nature at all and of locating ourselves in a world. For an old romanticist, these conditions would have presented themselves as nature's power of destruction or healing, or its fertility. For the work of the modernists I have in mind, the conditions present themselves as nature's autonomy, self-sufficiency, laws unto themselves.
>
> WV 113, Cavell's emphasis

Romanticism elaborates the theme of the conditions of existence, working on the capacity of art to reproduce the creative (or destructive) power of nature, while modernism, unable to refer to artistic conventions, exhibits the artistic medium itself—the physical conditions: sound, color on canvas, the direction and location of an object, and so on—and in so doing defines *our* conditions, *our* location. In the modernist artistic experience physical conditions—nature—are experienced as autonomous and estranged. They are out there, independent of us. Nature "faces me, draws my limits, and discovers my scale; it fronts me, with whatever wall at my back, and gives me horizon and gravity" (*WV* 114). Liberated from our private possession of the world, from our self which stands between us and nature, the world returns to us in the modernist experience as a place where we find our location, as earthliness, finitude, and corporeality.

In this way of establishing the contrast with romanticism, modernism reveals its characteristic cultural experience, which is a suspicion of the spiritual (divine) creativity of art and the spiritualization of nature. Nietzsche's harsh criticism in *Human, All Too Human* of the trust in art (which he himself nurtured in the *Untimely Meditations*), which has trafficked too much with metaphysics, is a clear example of the modernist distrust of the romantic elaborations of the creative role of art. In the book that Cavell dedicates to romanticism, *In Quest of the Ordinary*, the modernist problematic (though not the designation) returns in his comments to romantic texts (by Wordsworth, Coleridge, Emerson, and Thoreau, among others). Romanticism appears as an elaboration of the loss and mourning of the world, which can be followed by an acknowledgment of its presence: a pair of attitudes that Cavell relates to what Emerson calls polarity, for example, the secret melancholy (Emerson) and the quiet desperation (Thoreau), which can be followed by hope and the reanimation of the world. In this context, Cavell uses the romantic image of the creation of the world (that the world can be recreated, reconstituted, reanimated) and the animistic mythology that runs through romanticism, but he frees them from what Nietzsche found false in them in *Human, All Too Human*.

Cavell recovers in the romantic explorations of subjectivity the way in which the world can be acknowledged in its autonomy, an acknowledgment that has the power to free us from the privacy of our grasp of reality and return us to the common world we all inhabit. It is in this light that we can read some passages from *The World Viewed*, where, traveling from Kant through Blake, he arrives at Fried and the works of art he comments on, which make possible "presentness [Fried's term—PD] to ourselves, apart from which there is no hope for a world" (*WV* 23). The romanticism Cavell explores, then, is the one that investigates subjectivity in order to recover the world; it is not the romanticism that portrays a subjectivity interposed between the self and the world. Allusively but powerfully, Cavell reformulates the path of modernity:

> At some point the unhinging of our consciousness from the world interposed our subjectivity between us and our presentness to the world. Then our subjectivity became what is present to us, individuality became isolation. The route to conviction in reality was through the acknowledgment of that endless presence of self. . . . To speak of our subjectivity as the route back to our conviction in reality is to speak of romanticism.
>
> WV 22

It is clear, however, that on this point we can leave open the question which, among other things, concerns the substance of the criticism that the later Nietzsche makes of the *Untimely Meditations* as much as it concerns the criticism that the later Wittgenstein makes of the *Tractatus*. Cavell finds in the young Nietzsche, and especially in *Schopenhauer as Educator*, the structure of perfectionism that he brings out in his work on Emerson (and that emerges very clearly also in Mill). Thus, perfectionism is elaborated by working on romantic themes, on the way in which art enables us to reanimate the world. The world is dead, it has exhausted its power over us, and we are left alone, isolated in our privacy, which as such is incapable of accomplishing anything. The private grasp of the world (also that of private property) leads us back to ourselves sterilely; it does not put us in contact with anything independent that resists us. But we can rely on the power of art, on the poetry that revives Mill after the experience he describes as dejection has exhausted the sources of his interest in life and the world (as he recounts in the *Autobiography*), on the analogous poetic investment that allows us, according to Emerson, to leave the state of secret melancholy and realize a change that takes us back to where we were all along, to everyday things and occupations, but different, awakened to them. In Nietzsche's early writings, after we have traveled through the tragic vision that makes us contemplate the horror of life, its decay and the terrible loss of form, we return to the affectionate yearning for earth, for the happiness of life in common (*Richard Wagner in Bayreuth*). In these perfectionist elaborations we can count on the expressive medium, we can count on the power that art possesses and that was once the property of religion, which has now lost it.[43]

In this light—I say this in parenthesis—we find in the perfectionist perspective and in the pertinent authors, such as Mill, Emerson, and Nietzsche of the *Untimely Meditations* (as well as Wittgenstein, Cavell, Murdoch, and Diamond), the further problem of distinguishing and at the same time overcoming the separation of the intellectual and evaluative spheres, and in particular the isolation of morality from aesthetics, which were separated—but how?—by Kant (e.g. QO 43).[44] This overcoming concerns, in particular, the importance of allowing art to make its voice heard in the other spheres (knowledge of the world and, above all, morality).[45] This is why the contrast with modernism emerges on this point in particular, since in the modernist situation and experience we cannot rely on the power of the expressive medium of art: such a power has died along with the world that art is supposed to reanimate, and so we can only count on ourselves in an effort of absolute sincerity and honesty, as Cavell writes,[46] in order to reanimate at the same time art and the world, the power of a tradition and its expressive conventions *and* the world. "Modernism signifies not that the powers of the arts are exhausted, but on the contrary that it has become the immediate task of the artist to achieve in his art the muse of the art itself—to declare, from itself, the art as a whole for which it speaks, to become a present of that art" (*WV* 103).

The theme of a world and a life that we have separated ourselves from and that are dead to us remains, while what changes is the relationship to the role of art, to the possibility of counting on an expressive sphere that we trust is still alive and effective and that retains its transformative power. In the modernist situation, it is precisely the impossibility of counting on this relationship without first having regained it personally—and thus it is the experience of the emptying of the conditions of expression, which become detached from us and strangely independent, and hence the emergence of the physical conditions of expression in such modalities—that allows us to return to ourselves, confronted with them, that is, with the world. Cinema, in particular, explores this experience in the analysis Cavell undertakes in *The World Viewed*: it explores the experience of the world that is complete without us, out there, autonomous. The experience of cinema, small and displaced in front of the big screen in the dark theater, is that of viewing unseen; the connection with the world is realized at the price of our displacement from our natural habitation in it, separated and isolated—which is precisely a description of the modernist experience (*WV* 195).

Art in Nietzsche's *The Birth of Tragedy* and the *Untimely Meditations* is immediately in service of this new settlement in the world. Wittgenstein's *Tractatus* is a modernist work, and it elaborates on the experience of the crisis of the expressive medium, of the silence of language, that is to say, of its annihilation in relation to our expressive goals, and it is in such an annihilation, in the failure of any attempt to express what we want to say, that the conditions of language and of the world are revealed. The struggle with nonsense in which our words seem to be imprisoned is such that there is nothing in our words we would be ready to accept as the expression of what we want to say. The expressions we utter are disinvested each time and turn into dead signs. It is within this experience of language, which completely loses its power to signify and disintegrates into dead signs, that we are brought back to the world and to language, which are now freed from our private grasp (this should resonate with Cora Diamond's reading of the *Tractatus*).

When we look at the *Tractatus*, we can appreciate the ambivalence of the question that Cavell poses in his writings as he moves from modernist to romantic themes. The

Tractatus experiences the exhaustion of expressive resources and the crisis of tradition (philosophical and humanistic), and thus finds itself in the "modernist situation" described in *Must We Mean* and in *The World Viewed*. At the same time, however, it is a humanistic work that appeals to the reader's ability to understand the author. It relies on the transformative power of philosophical writing, conceived as an imaginative achievement alongside that of literature and art, and in doing so uses and draws on the humanistic tradition.[47]

Notes

The present essay reproduces, with minor revisions and additions, the second chapter of Piergiorgio Donatelli, *Il lato ordinario della vita* (Bologna: Il Mulino, 2018). Translated into English by the author.

1 For modernism as an episode of literary culture in English, to be placed between 1880 and 1939, see *A Concise Companion to Modernism*, ed. David Bradshaw (Oxford: Blackwell, 2003). For European literature see *Modernism 1890–1930*, ed. Malcolm Bradbury and James McFarlane (London: Penguin, 1976). Some useful considerations on the relation between modernism and the analytic tradition are offered by John Skorupski, "The Legacy of Modernism," *Proceedings of the Aristotelian Society* 91, no. 1 (1991): 1–19.

2 Some fundamental references are: William Michael Johnston, *The Austrian Mind: An Intellectual and Social History 1848–1938* (Berkeley: University of California Press, 1972); Allan Janik and Stephen Toulmin, *Wittgenstein's Vienna* (New York: Simon and Schuster, 1973); Carl E. Schorske, *Fin-de-Siècle Vienna: Politics and Culture* (New York: Knopf, 1980); Aldo Giorgio Gargani, *Il coraggio di essere: Saggio sulla cultura mitteleuropea* (Rome: Laterza, 1992); and Gargani, *Wittgenstein: Musica, parola, gesto* (Milan: Cortina, 2008). On this specific theme, see Michael Lemahieu and Karen Zumhagen-Yekplé, eds., *Wittgenstein and Modernism* (Chicago: The University of Chicago Press, 2017).

3 For this way of putting the matter, see my *Loos, Musil, Wittgenstein, and the Recovery of Human Life*, in LeMahieu and Zumhagen-Yekpleé, eds., *Wittgenstein and Modernism*, 91–113.

4 G.E.M. Anscombe, Introduction, *Metaphysics and the Philosophy of Mind* (Minneapolis: University of Minnesota Press, 1981), viii–ix.

5 Cora Diamond, "The Tractatus and the Limits of Sense," in *The Oxford Handbook to Wittgenstein*, ed. Marie McGinn and Oskari Kuusela (Oxford: Oxford University Press, 2011).

6 John McDowell, "Meaning and Intentionality in Wittgenstein's Later Philosophy," in Peter A. French, Theodore Edward Uehling, and Howard K. Wettstein, eds., *The Wittgenstein Legacy* (Notre Dame: University of Notre Dame Press, 1992), 40–52.

7 The relation established among these authors can be criticized. See my "Moral Perfectionism and Virtue," *Critical Inquiry* 45, no. 2 (2019): 332–50.

8 On Wittgenstein and culture, see G. H. von Wright, "Wittgenstein and the Twentieth Century," in Rosaria Egidi, ed., *Wittgenstein: Mind and Language* (Dordrecht: Kluwer, 1995), 1–19.

9   On this theme see one of the inventors of the critique of popular culture, Robert Warshow, *The Immediate Experience: Movies, Comics, Theatre and Other Aspects of Popular Culture* (Cambridge, MA: Harvard University Press, 2001). The volume also contains an epilogue by Stanley Cavell, "Epilogue: After Half a Century."
10 See "Othello and the Stake of the Other," in *DK* 125–42. I have tried to follow up this reading in "Otello e la finitezza umana," *Studi di estetica* 45, no. 9 (2017): 33–47.
11 This is also the theme of an essay by Diamond on the difficulty of philosophy: "The Difficulty of Reality and the Difficulty of Philosophy," in Stanley Cavell et al., eds., *Philosophy and Animal Life* (New York: Columbia University Press, 2008), 43–90.
12 This is a crucial theme in Rorty's writings that would require a separate treatment. See e.g. *Consequences of Pragmatism: Essays, 1972-1980* (Minneapolis: University of Minnesota Press, 1982).
13 Walter Benjamin, "The Storyteller: Observations on the Works of Nikolai Leskov," in *Selected Writings*, vol. 3, ed. Howard Eiland and Michael W. Jennings (Cambridge, MA: Harvard University Press, 2001), 143–66.
14 I work on this distinction in my *La vita umana in prima persona* (Rome: Laterza, 2012), transl. as *The Politics of Human Life: Rethinking Subjectivity* (Abingdon, Oxon: Routledge, 2021).
15 Ludwig Wittgenstein, *Remarks on the Philosophy of Psychology*, vol. 2, ed. G. H. von Wright and Heikki Nyman, trans. C. G. Luckhardt and Maximilian A. E. Aue (Chicago: The University of Chicago Press, 1980), §699.
16 In interpreting the *Tractatus* I depart from Gargani; see my *Wittgenstein e l'etica* (Rome: Laterza, 1998), 92.
17 Aldo Giorgio Gargani, "Introduzione," in *Crisi della ragione: Nuovi modelli nel rapporto tra sapere e attività umane* (Turin: Einaudi, 1979), 11.
18 Gargani, "Introduzione," 14.
19 Annette C. Baier, *The Commons of the Mind* (Chicago: Open Court, 1997).
20 Ralph Waldo Emerson, "Experience," in *The Major Prose*, ed. Ronald A Bosco and Joel Myerson (Cambridge, MA: Harvard University Press, 2015), 228.
21 Ibid., 228.
22 Ibid., 244.
23 *PH* 12: "Checking one's experience is a rubric an American, or a spiritual American, might give to the empiricism practiced by Emerson and by Thoreau. I mean the rubric to capture the sense at the same time of consulting one's experience and of subjecting it to examination. . . . The moral of this practice is to educate your experience sufficiently so that it is worthy of trust."
24 Thom Gunn, *Touch* (London: Faber and Faber, 1967).
25 Cora Diamond, *The Realistic Spirit: Wittgenstein, Philosophy, and the Mind* (Cambridge, MA: MIT Press, 1991). See in particular "Secondary Sense," 225–41.
26 What is familiar does not always strike us with a familiar tone, Wittgenstein remarks (*PI* §600), but we can depict it in this way, describe it and live it in this light, under such an aspect.
27 Veena Das, *Affliction: Health, Disease, Poverty* (New York: Fordham University Press, 2015), 222.
28 Veena Das, *Life and Words: Violence and the Descent into the Ordinary* (Berkeley: University of California Press, 2007).
29 T. S. Eliot, "Burnt Norton," I, lines 44–45, in *Four Quartets* (New York: Harcourt, 1943).

30 Martha Nussbaum, *Hiding from Humanity: Disgust, Shame, and the Law* (Princeton: Princeton University Press, 2004).
31 Wittgenstein, *Remarks on the Philosophy of Psychology*, vol. 2, §687.
32 Emerson writes that the awakening of human beings to higher goals in life is a revolution: "This revolution is to be wrought by the gradual domestication of the idea of Culture" ("The American Scholar," in Emerson, *The Major Prose*, 104). Cavell comments on it as follows: "Emerson's perception of the dispossession of our humanity, the loss of ground, the loss of nature as our security, or property, is thought in modern philosophy as the problem of skepticism. The overcoming or overtaking of skepticism must constitute a revolution that is a domestication for philosophy (or redomestication)." This requires an inhabitating of the everyday: "of the *day*, today, one among others." He specifies though that for Wittgenstein in the *Philosophical Investigations* "the issue of the everyday is the issue of the siting of skepticism, not as something to be overcome, as if to be refuted, as if it is a *conclusion* about human knowledge (which is skepticism's self-interpretation), but to be placed as a mark of what Emerson calls 'human condition,' a further interpretation of finitude, a mode, as said, of inhabiting our investment in words, in the world" (*CHU* 61, Cavell's emphasis).
33 See my *Il lato ordinario della vita: Filosofia ed esperienza comune* (Bologna: Il Mulino, 2018).
34 Cavell develops this idea in *SW*.
35 This is a central concern in Charles Taylor's work. See e.g. "Language and Human Nature," in *Human Agency and Language: Philosophical Papers 1* (Cambridge: Cambridge University Press, 1985), 215–47.
36 Cora Diamond, "Losing Your Concepts," *Ethics* 98, no. 2 (Jan 1988): 255–77, here 270.
37 G. E. M. Anscombe, "The Dignity of the Human Being," in *Human Life, Action and Ethics*, ed. Mary Geach and Luke Gormally, 67–73 (Exeter: Imprint Academic, 2005); Peter Winch, "Understanding a Primitive Society," in *Ethics and Action* (London: Routledge, 1972), 8–49. I discuss these matters in *Manières d'être humain: Une autre philosophie morale* (Paris: Vrin, 2015), in particular chapters 4 and 6.
38 William Rothman, "Cavell Reading Cavell," in *The Holiday in His Eye: Stanley Cavell's Vision of Film and Philosophy* (New York: SUNY Press, 2021), 1–8.
39 William Rothman and Marian Keane, *Reading Cavell's* The World Viewed: *A Philosophical Perspective on Film* (Detroit: Wayne State University Press, 2000), 183.
40 The reference is to the paintings of Jackson Pollock, Morris Louis, Kenneth Noland, Jules Olitski, and Frank Stella; see Michael Fried, *Art and Objecthood: Essays and Reviews* (Chicago: The University of Chicago Press, 1998).
41 The notion of automatism recurs in *WV*, especially chapter 14. On this, see J. M. Bernstein, "Aesthetics, Modernism, Literature: Cavell's Transformations of Philosophy," in Richard Eldridge, ed., *Stanley Cavell* (Cambridge: Cambridge University Press, 2003), 107–42.
42 The story of this encounter emerges clearly in *ETE*. The first essay, "Thinking of Emerson," is the text of a lecture given in 1978.
43 On these issues, see Federico Vercellone, *Dopo la morte dell'arte* (Bologna: Il Mulino, 2013), especially chapter 1.
44 I have discussed this theme in relation to Mill especially: *Introduzione a Mill* (Rome: Laterza, 2007), and "John Stuart Mill perfezionista democratico," *Dianoia* 21, no. 23 (2016): 559–76.

45 One way to connect the authors who belong to the perfectionist canon with the Wittgensteinian tradition in ethics (especially Cavell, Murdoch, and Diamond), while at the same time expounding an alternative canon in analytic ethics, is precisely to show the necessity of the arts and imaginative literature in order to do philosophy (and especially moral philosophy).
46 See Cavell's "Music Discomposed" in *MWM*: "I've been insisting that we can no longer be sure that any artist is sincere—we haven't convention or technique or appeal to go on any longer: *anyone* could fake it. And this means that modern art, if and where it exists, *forces* the issue of sincerity, depriving the artist and his audience of every measure except absolute attention to one's experience and absolute honesty in expressing it" (211).
47 Piergiorgio Donatelli, "Reshaping Ethics after Wittgenstein," *Wittgenstein-Studien* 4 (2013): 207–31.

9

Modernism and Film at Criticism: Rethinking the "Aesthetic Possibilities" of the Medium

Élise Domenach

At the end of his re-reading of *Adam's Rib* (Cukor, 1950) in *Cities of Words*, some twenty-three years after the first edition of his famous book on the comedies of remarriage, *Pursuits of Happiness*, Cavell writes: "criticism, call it the reading of art, is itself an art, and one, it seems, that philosophers have not often practiced" (*CW* 81). Indeed, Cavell's unique style unites two intellectual gestures; it reconciles philosophy and criticism. By doing so, Cavell has famously kept most of the academic world as well as the film criticism world in America at a distance, if not hostile to his enterprise. His style, beautifully exemplified in his two books on the companion Hollywood genres of the remarriage comedy and the melodrama of the unknown woman (in, respectively, *Pursuits of Happiness* and *Contesting Tears*), is grounded, explained, and justified in his very first book of film philosophy: *The World Viewed*. When the first edition of the book came out in 1971, it triggered both philosophy scholars' and art critics' hostility. Nevertheless, it is clear by now that the intertwinement of film criticism and philosophy in Cavell's approach to movies is one of his method's key assets. The object of this paper is to investigate the relations between Cavell's philosophical style and his way of thinking with movies, as well as the relation between art criticism and modernism in Cavell's philosophy of film.

Indeed, Cavell claims that the philosophy of film can only be produced through the reading of particular films. And such association is even clearer in the art of film's "modernist situation," in which Cavell finds himself writing; film was "the last (traditional art) to find itself pushing itself to its modernist self-questioning," as he put it in *The World Viewed* (*WV* 215).

The famous American art critic Rosalind Krauss wrote a malicious review of Cavell's *The World Viewed* in *Artforum* in 1974, in which she criticizes Cavell's construction of an "ontology of film" for not acknowledging 1920s Soviet cinema as precursor.[1] In academia, responses to the book have not been any better. In 1973, Noël Carroll's review of *The World Viewed*[2] downplayed the originality of Cavell's conception of a "projective" relation between films and reality, by picturing it as a new version of Bazinian realism. Indeed, such a reading of Cavell's ontology of film also puts him at odds with film scholars, since various anti-realist film theories such as semiotics, deconstructionism, cultural theory, and Lacanian or Freudian theories dominated most academic work in the 1970s. All of these theories argue that films are systems of ideological signs bearing no significant relation to reality. Cavell explicitly confronts the difference of his views within the field of film studies in his 1979 supplement to *The World Viewed*, calling these anti-realist trends an "intellectual fashion":

> There is at least a double cause for finding it natural now to resist the pressure of reality upon art: there is a more or less vague and pervasive intellectual fashion, apparently sanctioned by the history of epistemology and the rise of modern science, according to which we never really, and never really can, see reality as it is; and there is an interpretation of the history of the representative arts, especially the history of painting and of the novel contemporary with the invention of photography and with the advent of motion pictures, according to which art had been withdrawing from the representation of reality as from a hopeless, but always unnecessary, task.
>
> WV 65

Such an interpretation of Cavell's philosophy of film (of his redefinition of the film-medium's relation to reality as being one of "projection") shows how out of step he was with almost all his contemporaries' film-philosophy as well as film criticism, because it associates the two in a way that was completely unheard of at the time. Indeed, Cavell associates philosophy and art criticism with what he calls a "new term of criticism with skepticism": "the modern." In the essays of *Must We Mean What We Say?*, written at the same time as *The World Viewed*, Cavell constructs the concept of modernism as a "critical category" of his "ordinary aesthetics." "Modernism" is the name of three different and interrelated topics in the book: the ordinary language philosopher's claims; modernist developments in music since 1945 and American painting and sculpture of the sixties; and more generally, all efforts aimed at meaning in the absence of given conventions or rules.[3]

I would here like to explore Cavell's modernist philosophical method for writing film criticism and philosophy of film in the same breath. This conjunction of film criticism and film-philosophy, so peculiar and idiosyncratic in Cavell, designates a set of problems found within his prose and what he calls modernism. A way to approach these issues is to question what Cavell calls the "aesthetic possibilities of the medium." He draws an unstable distinction between a "medium" and its "aesthetic possibilities" and between "automatism" and "medium," which he constantly thinks in relation to one another. In doing so, a running question arises about the articulation of film criticism— i.e. the activity of reading individual pieces of art- and film-philosophy as centrally concerned with what Cavell calls the "ontology of film" (its relation to reality, a question he famously and crucially turns into a questioning of the importance of movies, in the first paragraphs of *The World Viewed*). Conjugating film criticism with philosophy of film is crucially associated with the theme of the "importance of movies" in Cavell, since he repeatedly explains that his readings of films are based on his own experience and memories of film which are shaped by the way films "matter" to him. This theme, otherwise explored by Sandra Laugier,[4] brings us to the later developments of Cavell's philosophy of film, and particularly to the introduction to *Pursuits of Happiness*, "Words for a Conversation." But it is also in virtue of a deep reciprocal definition of an art's historical development by way of definitory masterpieces and of this art's essence that Cavell has always pursued a philosophical style that involves the reading of individual works of art. Pursuing the question of the "aesthetic possibilities of films" in *The World Viewed* uncovers complexities of Cavellian philosophical style that he himself identifies in the "Supplement" as "obscurities." They harbor the possibility of an encounter between philosophy and film criticism within the territories of modernism and skepticism.

To begin with, I will be interested in the comment Cavell later made about his own equation of philosophy of film and criticism in the "Foreword to the enlarged edition," eight years after the first edition of *The World Viewed*. Here, Cavell mentions a "theme" that he says "is explicit and is guiding in all my subsequent thinking about film": "exploring the medium of film" is a task jointly undertaken by the film director and the film critic. This task consists in conceding significance to possibilities and necessities specific to the medium. Exploring in such a way shows that the discoveries made by direction and criticism reveal what counts as an element of the medium.

> I am picking up a theme of *The World Viewed* that is explicit and guiding in all my subsequent thinking about film, namely that giving significance to and placing significance in specific possibilities and necessities (or call them elements; I sometimes still call them automatisms) of the physical medium of film are the fundamental acts of, respectively, the director of a film and the critic (or audience) of film; together with the idea that what constitutes an "element" of the medium of film is not knowable prior to these discoveries of direction and of criticism. This reciprocity between element and significance I would like to call the cinematic circle. Exploring this circle is something that can be thought of as exploring the medium of film.
>
> WV xiii–iv

Cavell then follows with the beautiful example of Malick's *Days of Heaven*, and first explains what he means by "aesthetic possibilities" by writing that Malick has been exploring "a fundamental fact of film's photographic basis: that objects participate in the photographic presence of themselves; they participate in the re-creation of themselves on film, they are essential in the making of their appearances" (*WV* xvi).

I.

In *The World Viewed*, the question of the medium's "aesthetic possibilities" first arises in chapter 5, "Types," in the context of a discussion of Panofsky's "Style and Medium in the Moving Pictures." "Possibilities" and "medium" are here defined in a mutual relation: possibilities are said to be "of" a medium. In quoting Panofsky's famous article in which he defines "the unique and specific possibilities of the new medium" as "dynamization of space and spatialization of time," Cavell is very cautious. His intuition is that this "region (is) full of traps." He wishes to ask "what it means to call them possibilities at all." Two very important paragraphs follow, in which Cavell explains what he calls a medium and what he calls its possibilities, as if to further Panofsky's intuitions. Cavell chooses to reflect on the historical discovery of "narrative film," i.e. how cinema moved from home movies to narrative movies.

> Why, for example, didn't the medium begin and remain in the condition of home movies, one shot just physically tacked on to another, cut and edited simply according to subject? ... The answer seems obvious: narrative movies emerged because someone "saw the possibilities" of the medium—cutting and editing and taking shots at different distances from the subject. But again, these are mere actualities of film mechanics: every home movie and newsreel contains them. We could say: To make them "possibilities of the medium" is to realize what will give them *significance*—for example, the narrative and physical rhythms of melodrama, farce, American comedy of the 1930s. It is not as if filmmakers saw these possibilities and then looked for something to apply them to. It is truer to say that someone with the wish to make a movie saw that certain established forms would give point to certain properties of film.
>
> This perhaps sounds like quibbling, but what it means is that the aesthetic possibilities of a medium are not a given. ... Only the art itself can discover its possibilities, and the discovery of a new possibility is the discovery of a new medium.
>
> *WV* 31–32

Giving significance to specific possibilities of a medium is therefore to create a medium; it reveals the art itself, since "Only an art can define its media" (*WV* 107). These possibilities are discovered in the process of an art's history, in its major developments. In this very early phase of the book one can already hear a sense of paradox in the way the "possibilities of the medium" are presented. They do not exist prior to their "discovery" in specific films. But in a way, we have to think of the art of film as separate from its artistic achievements. This is why Cavell will come to say that "the discovery of a new possibility is the discovery of a new medium" (*WV* 32). Even if we wish to keep the thinking of the medium as separate from its instances, we should not forget that a medium is a way of making sense, and that such expression can only be thought in the context of a specific film. It is the accomplishment of a specific artist making sense of their medium.

> A medium is something through which or by means of which something specific gets done or said in particular ways. It provides, one might say, particular ways to get through to someone, to make sense; in art, they are forms, like forms of speech. To discover ways of making sense is always a matter of the relation of an artist to his art, each discovering the other.
>
> *WV* 32

Cavell himself could sense a paradox here, and fears that this could "sound like quibbling" (*WV* 31). This is precisely one of the things Cavell retrospectively judges to be "obscurities" in his reasoning and that prompted him to write the "Supplement" in the 1979 reprint of *The World Viewed*. But Cavell wants to claim that these "obscurities" present "accurate responses to the nature of film," meaning that something in the nature of the medium itself calls for or requires this obscurity (*WV* 162). What precisely? My hypothesis is that it is the modernist dimension of art that Cavell is so interested in (a dimension in which the art itself is defined by the aesthetic possibilities of the medium that are discovered by the highest instances of art) that requires this obscurity or circularity. For in a modernist situation meaning is not assured, is no longer secured by past conventions. Meaning has to be invented, and because of this, circularity is unavoidable. The medium's aesthetic possibilities are to be defined by the highest instances (*exemplarisch*, in Kantian terms) of that art.

> I persist in the feeling asserted in the book's Preface, that its difficulty lies as much in the obscurity of its promptings as in its particular surfacings of expression. Given the feeling that a certain obscurity of prompting is not external to what I wished most fervently to say about film (and hence cannot have been cleared up before I commenced writing, nor at any time before I called the writing over), the commitments I set myself as I wrote were, first, to allow obscurities to express themselves as clearly and as fervently as I could say, and, second, to be guided by the need to organize and clarify just these obscurities and just this fervor in the progression of my book as a whole. These procedures would be pointless unless the obscurities I allowed myself were accurate responses to the nature of film and unless the expressions I found for them were accurate to those responses; and unless I did in fact manage, in the progression of the book, to bring some order and to do some justice to these expressions.
>
> *WV* 162–63

II.

The second moment in the book where the "aesthetic possibilities" are discussed is in chapter 6, where Cavell discusses Panofsky's and Bazin's analyses of the invention of film. Panofsky claims that the technical invention prompted the birth of the art of film. On the contrary, Bazin claims that the idea of film preceded the invention of cinema. To which Cavell assents, and adds: "unless film captured possibilities opened up by the arts themselves, it is hard to imagine that its possibilities as an artistic medium would have shown up as, and as suddenly as, they did" (*WV* 39).

From this discussion we understand that the possibilities of a medium can be derived from possibilities discovered by other media. Cavell's famous analysis of the way film satisfies the myth of artistic re-creation of the world in its own image follows: film satisfies the myth in an automatic, magical, way. From this, Cavell concludes that film partakes of the myth of realism as much as it connects to its magical origins.

What is cinema's way of satisfying the myth? Automatically, we said. But what does that mean—mean mythically, as it were? It means satisfying it without *my* having to do anything, satisfying it *by* wishing. In a word, *magically*, I have found myself asking: How could film be art, since all the major arts arise in some way out of religion? Now I can answer: Because movies arise out of magic; from *below* the world.

The better a film, the more it makes contact with this source of its inspiration; it never wholly loses touch with the magic lantern behind it.

WV 39

This dual origin is the basis of the development of aesthetic possibilities in the history of cinema, in the direction of realism and in the direction of the fantastic or the magical.

In chapter 7 on Baudelaire, Cavell enumerates "forms that effect cinematic possibilities" (*WV* 44) in Baudelaire's *The Painter of Modern Life*:

Read as an anticipation of film, Baudelaire's little book seems to me, in dozens of its terms, insights, and turns of phrase, to take on the power it must have had for him. Let me simply recall the titles of his chapters, pondering them against our knowledge of cinema: Fashion, The Man of the World, Crowds, The Child, War-Sketches, Pomps and Ceremonies, The Military Man, The Dandy, Cosmetics, Women and Courtesans, Carriages. Here are stores of cinematic obsession, and they are more convincingly so the more one appreciates the meaning they have for Baudelaire and the particular way they occur in movies.

WV 43

In chapter 10, "End of the Myths," the medium of film is described as mortal. And in this new context a medium is said to relate us to the world. It must "establish conviction in our presentness to the world."

I assume it is sufficiently obvious that these ways of giving significance to the possibilities of film—the media of movies exemplified by familiar Hollywood cycles and plots that justify the projection of types—are drawing to an end. And this means, in our terms so far, that they no longer naturally establish conviction in our presentness to the world.

WV 60

Cavell means that certain aesthetic possibilities of the film medium have come to an end. They are no longer efficient, believed in—and others have probably arisen.

Conviction in the movies' originating myths and geniuses—in the public world of men, the private company of woman, the secret isolation of the dandy—has been lost, or baffled.

WV 62

In the same line of thought, in chapter 11, "The Medium and Media of Film," Cavell asks what possibilities of the medium are now given significance, i.e. in the modernist situation (see page 72).

III.

The difficulties and perplexities associated with the "aesthetic possibilities" of the film medium in *The World Viewed* are finally made explicit in chapter 14, "Automatism." Cavell wants to keep distinguishing between the material basis of the film medium and the historical, artistic discoveries of what gives significance to features of its physical basis. Thus, he makes clear why he wants to keep the term "automatism" for both things, in different senses of the term.

> These mechanisms produce the physical or material basis of the medium of film, which I am articulating as successions of automatic world projections. What gives *significance* to features of this physical basis are artistic discoveries of form and genre and type and technique, which I have begun calling automatisms.
>
> WV 105, emphasis added

Later:

> It may seem perverse of me, since I am intent upon keeping these levels of artistic fact separate, to use the concept of automatism—anyway, the term automatic—also in the description of film's physical basis. I do not take the perverseness here to be of my making. In part it has to do with the identity of the art of film itself—the fact that its medium just does have this manufacturing mechanism at its basis. In part it has to do with the fate of modernist art generally—that its awareness and responsibility for the physical basis of its art compel it at once to assert and deny the control of its art by that basis. This is also why, although I am trying to free the idea of a medium from its confinement in referring to the physical bases of various arts, I go on using the same word to name those bases as well as to characterize modes of achievement within the arts. . . . It will not be dispelled by redefining or substituting some labels. It could also be said that modernist art is itself an investigation of this confusion, or of the complexities of this fact.
>
> WV 105

These complexities are crucial to what Cavell calls "aesthetic possibilities of film," because they point to the fact that these possibilities constantly reflect the basis of the medium. My reading emphasizes the role that modernism plays in uncovering this particularly deep insight into film. This is the crucial lesson from modernism that Cavell wishes to retain: the necessity to reflect on the complexities of "automatism." This is why he puts them at the heart of his reflection on movies. Cavell incorporates the modernist requirement that the medium can never be taken for granted into his philosophical thinking of film—that it is at stake in each and every authentic piece of art.

Epilogue: The "Aesthetic Possibilities" of Film and Skepticism

It is my hypothesis that this perplexity, complexity, paradox, or obscurity withheld by the notion of "aesthetic possibilities" is deeply rooted in how Cavell engages with skepticism in film-philosophy. Cavell takes the idea that a medium is, at bottom, a way of expressing something very seriously; it allows us to mean certain things in a certain way. Therefore, the investigation of the ways by which individual films *mean* will be involved with skepticism, as much as any other investigation of our ordinary ways of meaning something.

The French film director Arnaud Desplechin, famous reader of and friend to Cavell in his later years, explained his appeal for Cavell's *The World Viewed* in these terms:

> Like many French readers the first Cavell film book I read was his book on the comedies of remarriage. It has been a crucial working tool when I was shooting *Comment je me suis disputé... (ma vie sexuelle)*. I later read his other books, particularly *The World Viewed*, where a question that matters a lot to me is touched upon: how meaning comes to movies? The fact that films do mean was something that struck me when I was young. And I couldn't find any French film critic or theorist who describes as precisely as Cavell does how meaning comes to movies.[5]

Desplechin is aware of this distinctive Cavellian take on the medium of film: movies are understood as ways of meaning. And it is a fundamental point that Cavell makes extremely early in his philosophical career—as early as in his first collection of essays, *Must We Mean What We Say?*—that skepticism is at home with our claims to meaning, and that every great piece of art is simultaneously engaged in the (re)definition of its own art (in virtue of modernism) and in the uncovering of this "truth" about us: that we are tempted to withdraw from our common ways of meaning, tempted to doubt ourselves and our relation to others and to the world. Cavell's essays on *King Lear* or on Beckett's *Fin de partie*, and the first part of *The Claim of Reason* (which Cavell wrote in 1971) are in this respect very closely connected to his first philosophy of film (epitomized in *The World Viewed*). This was already the guiding hypothesis of my reading of *The World Viewed*, in *Stanley Cavell, le cinéma et le scepticisme* (Paris, PUF, 2011).[6] Today, this hypothesis is enriched with further meaning. Cavell's sense of modernity, modernism, and the modern, in *Must We Mean* and in *The World Viewed*, lead us to acknowledge this truth about the skepticism we experience: it runs through our uses of language as much as through the ordinary meaning of films.

Indeed, I would like to claim that the aesthetic possibilities of the medium are just as crucially unsettled, unstable, open to doubt, as our criteria for using language (see *The Claim of Reason*). They are open to the ordinary threat of skepticism. The aesthetic possibilities of film are not settled once and for all. Every film, as with every ordinary act of speech, renegotiates the conditions under which meaning is effective and efficient. And in the case of film, such conditions (which Cavell prefers to call criteria, rather than rules) are the "aesthetic possibilities of film." These possibilities are criteria for meaning in movies.

> Only an art can define its media. A modernist art, investigating its own physical basis, searching out its own conditions of existence, rediscovers the fact that its existence as an art is not physically assured. It gracefully accepts our condemnation to meaning—that for separate creatures of sense and soul, for earthlings, meaning is a matter of expression; and that expressionlessness is not a reprieve from meaning, but a particular mode of it; and that the arrival of an understanding is a question of acknowledgment.
>
> WV 107

Here all the crucial concepts of Cavell's redefinition of skepticism are called to bear upon the medium of film. And here medium and expression connect in a way that echoes the connection we hear between "means of expression" and "expression." This connection implies that the threat of skepticism prevails in the process of definition and invention of the "aesthetic possibilities of an art."

Cavell sums up these elements at the beginning of chapter 19, "The Acknowledgment of Silence":

> A "possibility" of a medium can be made known only by successful works that define its media; in modernism, a medium is explored by discovering possibilities that declare its necessary conditions, its limits.
>
> WV 146

In the 1979 foreword, Cavell will make it clear that the task of the film director and the film critic is to recognize the aesthetic possibilities of film. Here in chapter 19 he asks:

> What specifically movies have to acknowledge, what it is that would not exist (for it) unless admitted by it, what it is that the movie can no longer safely assume, but must declare, in order not to risk denying . . . it must acknowledge, what is always to be acknowledged, its own limits: in this case, its outsideness to its world, and my absence from it.
>
> WV 146

This final characterization of the "aesthetic possibilities of film" underlines the deep connection between film and skepticism, movies' privilege in expressing skepticism, and it explains why the aesthetic possibilities of the medium and the medium itself depend so fundamentally, by definition, upon each other. In "The Aesthetic Problems of Modern Philosophy" (in *Must We Mean*) and in *The Claim of Reason*, Cavell defines this relation of mutual definition, without basis, without rule or convention, relying upon invention and creativity alone, as one of "*claiming.*" Such *claiming* obviously operated in the absence of any given rules or border, in the context of modernist art— "lay(ing) bare the condition of art in general" (*MWM* 218) by doing so.

> In the context of his reflection on modernist music in *Must We Mean*, Cavell claimed that: Each (modernist work) is trying to find the limits or essence of its own procedures. And this means that it is not clear a priori what counts, or will count, as a painting, or sculpture or musical composition... So we haven't got clear criteria for determining whether a given object is or is not a painting, a sculpture... The task of the modernist artist, as of the contemporary critic, is to find what it is his art finally depends upon; it doesn't matter that we haven't a priori criteria for defining a painting, what matters is that we that the criteria are something we must discover, discover in the continuity of painting itself.
>
> *MWM* 219

There is no other way of thinking philosophically with films, for Cavell, than by confronting each film's way of claiming and inventing and creating new ways of expressing (and domesticating) our skepticism. This is why I believe that the Cavellian rethinking of skepticism lies at the heart of his idiosyncratic style in philosophy, at the heart of his engagement with individual film criticism. This is why I believe that film-philosophy after Cavell also requires one to critique film, in the same breath. The reading of individual films will uncover specific ways of meaning and confronting what Cavell later calls (in *Conditions Handsome and Unhandsome*) our "skeptical condition."

> I have emphasized silence, isolation in fantasy, the mysteries of human motion and separateness: such are the conditions of existence that film, in its magical reproduction of the world, tries and tries not to transgress.
>
> *MWM* 147

Notes

1 Rosalind Krauss, "Dark Glasses and Bifocals," *Artforum* 12, no. 9 (May 1974): 60.
2 Noël Carroll, "*The World Viewed: Reflections on the Ontology of Film*," reprinted in *Philosophical Problems of Classical Film Theory* (Princeton: Princeton University Press, 1988).
3 See my *Stanley Cavell, le cinéma et le scepticisme* (Paris: Presses Universitaires de France, 2011) for an exploration of the categories of Cavellian "ordinary aesthetics" as set in three contemporary Stanley Cavell books: *MWM*, *WV*, and *SW*.
4 Sandra Laugier, "L'importance de l'importance: Experiénce, pragmatisme, transcendentalisme," *Multitudes* 4, no. 23 (2005): 153–67.
5 Arnaud Desplechin and Stanley Cavell, "Pourquoi les films comptent-ils?," *Esprit* no. 347 (August/September 2018), 208–9.
6 *Stanley Cavell, le cinéma et le scepticisme*.

10

Cavell and the Modernity of Film

Eli Friedlander

Towards Film in the Time of Its Modernity

Cavell's *The World Viewed: Reflections on the Ontology of Film* has remained one of his less interpreted works. The pairing of ontology and film in its title is striking. It precludes approaching the medium of film merely in terms of the formal elements of what one might call its language (such as the form of a cinematic image, the form of the succession of images, the form of juxtaposition of images in montage). Paying attention to such formal characteristics is not so much wrong as it is too restrictive an understanding of what an artistic medium is. It would be as though what a medium is, can be separated from how it reveals to us the character of the world. I take it that the emphasis on ontology is precisely a way to undercut this primacy of the formal. Throughout the book Cavell emphasizes that the form receives its significance in so far as it allows us to recognize significant contents of our existence, of our being in the world. Writing of the ontology of film, in that sense, is meant to raise the question of the way film opens the world anew. How does film let the world, what it ultimately comes to, come into view? The identity of the medium is recognized and measured by how it reveals to us, as other arts did and still do, what a human subject is, what a body is, what are motion and action, what a place to find oneself in, what closeness and distance, human intimacy and metaphysical solitude, what is the reach and compass of our intentions and what surrounds them, what is contingent and necessary, what is living and what is automatic, what is mindful and what is mindless.

In the preface to the book, Cavell traces his use of the term "ontology" to Heidegger. This inflection is evident in Cavell's account of how the self is implicated in the recognition of the world in film. By this I mean both how film releases one from the traps of subjectivity, but also how it teaches what it is for the world to be one's own. This problematization of subjectivity is suggested by the passive voice in the title of the book: "The World Viewed" is not the same as "Viewing the World." The latter would suggest that film is an extension, by cinematic means, of the intentionality of the subject. The passive form suggests how the automatisms of cinema acquire significance precisely insofar as they allow recognition of how the world exhibits itself on its own terms. The particular inflection of passiveness is closely related to the place of the past in our experience of film. As Cavell puts it in "More of the World Viewed," "I relate that idea [of pastness of the projected world] most immediately to my passiveness before the exhibition of the world, to the fascination, the uncanniness, in this chance to view the manifestation of the world as a whole" (*WV* 212). It is not so much viewing that has taken place in the past as pastness that is internal to that which is viewed. It will take some work to understand how for Cavell this pastness is key to film's power to release us from the circle of our forced activity, from the orbit of subjectivity.

There are different levels at which it would be necessary to follow the relation Cavell establishes between film, ontology, and time. The temporal permeates *The World Viewed* first insofar as it is a book that puts together *memories* of film. It is a book constructed from recollections of viewings. In that respect it is different in character from Cavell's later books on film, *Pursuits of Happiness* and *Contesting Tears*. The latter are concerned, respectively, with the elaboration of the genres of the "remarriage comedy" and the "melodrama of the unknown woman." Each of the chapters of these books is devoted to a close reading of a single film, something one hardly finds in *The World Viewed*. It is as though in that latter book there is no unity of memory deployed in relation to a complete work. Memories are plural and localized. Sometimes it feels like the ordinary form that thoughts take in this book is of insights in memory, flashes of past experience of film. It is as though Cavell found a way to make film, in memory, constantly striking.[1] But what is indeed astounding is how a work composed of such fragments of memory comes together in a higher unity to present a constellation, the contents of the idea of film. It is the lack of mediation between these two levels, the myriad of memory—insights and the truth configuration arising out of them, that makes *The World Viewed* truly unparalleled in Cavell's corpus of writings.

Pastness is further suggested in Cavell's concern with the notion of origin. The question of origin in film should not be taken as being concerned merely with recounting the beginnings of film, as though it would be necessary to summarize the historical development of the medium in order to understand its form. The language of origin and pastness is not a reference to the past of film. One could call it the dimension of the primal, most evident in the way in which Cavell understands the pastness of film as its *mythical* conditions of existence: "There are broad hints in my book that I think the [narrative or dramatic mode of film] is more closely bound to the mythological than it is to the fictional" (*WV* 210). Myths narrate origin. It is not just that films have mythical plots as well as characters that can recall mythical heroes. Rather the primal is a dimension of our involvement with the world, say in the way our lives must address a dimension of fate, and as such it belongs to the world viewed in film.

In "More of the World Viewed," Cavell writes: "the idea of pastness threads through my books, as does the idea of presentness and of futurity" (*WV* 210). If myth is the character of pastness of film, Cavell further conceives of the pertinence of such notions as the magical, wish images, and enchantment to establish something like the form of futurity of film. The primal past, the mythical and the primal future, wish and enchantment, are always there and give film its natural power. But it is also against this original temporality that film must actualize itself and recognize, make authentically present its limits. Film's present is the problem of its modernity.

In exploring the wishes for which film finds magical fulfillment, Cavell turns to a statement of modernity in art in Baudelaire's "The Painter of Modern Life." He begins by evincing disappointment with this famous text of Baudelaire's and the way in which it so prominently makes Constantin Guys into a central figure for the modern sensibility in painting. This is for Cavell a problematic ignoring of the importance of Courbet and Manet, whose crucial place in painting's modernity was brought out in the work of Michael Fried. But Cavell adds that Baudelaire's text acquires a completely different significance when one reads it as a premonition of the world of film. It is as though Baudelaire has recognized a need, and a corresponding wish, but misplaced the form of its fulfillment. It finds realization in film.[2]

That need and that wish articulated in the most general way are for the reality of the world. Cavell evokes the deep skepticism arising from the inability to escape the mediation of subjectivity. The wish for the real is for the world showing itself without the intermediary of the subject. In this new configuration of skepticism, Cavell also includes the Romantic aftermath of Kant, and the role the arts receive in fulfilling the wish for a higher realism. It is not in painting, poetry, or theater that this wish was most powerfully fulfilled, but in film: "The idea of and wish for the world re-created in its own image was satisfied *at last* by cinema" (*WV* 39). Cinema allows the world to be recreated, reveal itself, in itself—that is not in man's image but in *its* own image.

It is against these ideas of mythical origin and wish in film that one must ask what its presentness comes to. A chapter of *The World Viewed* is devoted to the concept of presentness in painting. It is in finding significance in the automatism associated primarily with the camera that a naïve candor of film is initially distinguished from what can only be understood as an arduous and reflective task of modern painting and music.[3] This is the sense in which for Cavell, film may escape as it were naturally, automatically, what is set for the other arts as their highest achievement. This candor is nevertheless something that film must earn, as it enters the age of its modernity.

Cavell is critical of simplistic articulations of modernism in terms of self-referentiality, in which the medium is made present by consciously and symbolically being represented in the work of art. This usually gives rise to simplistic gestures of self—exhibiting, say, various ways of making reference to the presence of the camera in film. These attempts misconceive, one might say, the character of self-consciousness. They take self-consciousness to be a special moment, rather than something that is constantly reflected in the form the contents presented take. Just as there is specificity in how a self-conscious being acts, suffers, experiences, and submits to necessities of his world, so film must show by the form its contents take that it is conscious of its specific capacities.

For sure the modernist turn is closely related to the Kantian moment in philosophy, and to the possibility of critique as the acknowledgment of the constitution, i.e. the limits of a human practice. Modernism takes with the utmost seriousness the way in which conditions of possibility of an artistic practice are constituted historically, and their pertinence for that practice depends on the continuity of tradition. The modernist predicament is revealed in the threat that our relation to that tradition ceases to be given "naturally": "The essential fact (of what I refer to as) the modern lies in the relation between the present practice of an enterprise and the history of the enterprise, in the fact that this relationship has become problematic" (*MWM* xxxiii). Facing this predicament is articulated in terms of a task of acknowledgment of the medium's possibilities and limits.

Put differently, while Cavell uncovers the dimensions of the mythical and the magical in film, its "naïve" state of existence also suggests that this cannot be "naturally" sustained by film. As it develops, acquires a history, it also enters the time of its own modernism. The mythical and the magical must be themselves transformed reflectively. It is this theme Cavell calls "the end of myths," that feeds into the discussion of the task of acknowledgment in the last chapter of the book:

> I took it for granted that movies are no longer easy in the nests of wish and myth that gave its media their conviction for us, and also that their modernist fate is not yet sealed. . . . I then asked what specifically movies have to acknowledge, what it is that would not exist (for it) unless admitted by it, what is it that the movie can no longer safely assume, but must declare, in order not to risk denying.
>
> *WV* 146

The Acknowledgment of Silence

The chapter entitled "The Acknowledgment of Silence" is as dense and enigmatic a stretch of text one can find in a philosopher known for the unparalleled concentration of his writing. I will provide a commentary on this chapter, doing the best I can to carefully lay out its progress and the masterful weaving of its themes. The chapter should be read against the concern of Cavell with fundamental ontology I sketched above. Yet, precisely as a culmination of the tensions in the idea of an authentic stance that lets the world manifest or show itself, this chapter courts many dangers. This is especially evident insofar as Cavell avails himself of notions such as silence and the unsayable as well as explores how film pertains to the register of the transcendent or to the religious dimension of our existence.[4] Insofar as what is acknowledged is always our limits, the acknowledgment of silence is an acknowledgment of our finitude, of the limits of our speech, or of our words, in the world. But this occurs always against a sense of an origin beyond our words, as a wish to recover that origin. How is that dimension articulated, without making the moving picture into a mystifying picture of our relation to the transcendent?

Understanding the dimension of the acknowledgment of silence must initially take up the relation of film to its origins, to its silent era. Origin is suffused with the fantasy satisfied by the magic of film. But it is precisely for this reason that acknowledgment is not demanded in our relation to silent film. A silent film does not lack speech. On the contrary, it is rather characterized by fullness. "A world of sight is a world of immediate intelligibility" (*WV* 150). But once speech can be introduced, the character of a mismatch appears with it. It is as though now words can seem to be what draws us apart from the wholeness of world. Only now can film thematize in itself a limit to what can be expressed in words, and only now is there a necessity to acknowledge that limit as, and in, silence. The acknowledgment of silence is not demanded by silent film but only emerges as a task in relation to the talkies. It is only with the talkies that the sense of insufficiency of words to world can become part of the *ontology of film*. "With talkies we got back to the clumsiness of speech, the dumbness and duplicities and concealments of assertion, the bafflement of soul and body by their inarticulateness" (*WV* 150). Synchronization, then, is not merely a technical problem of film, but acquires metaphysical significance. It is only when the question of synchronization can be raised that we can speak of acknowledging silence, of recognizing this internal hiatus between our speech and the world bodied forth in the image. Cavell also writes of "the idea of conveying the unsayable by showing experience beyond the reach of words" (*WV* 152).

The acknowledgment of silence is the dawning in film of limits of speech. Recognizing a limit is *demanding*, first insofar as it is a demand to "remain silent" in the face of this predicament of our existence in language revealed by film. Films have ways of covering up the tense co-existence of words and world, that is of denying the anxiety that letting the world be, beyond our words, brings forth. Towards the end of the chapter, Cavell explicitly links this problem of acknowledgment to Heidegger's understanding of the disclosive character of anxiety: "According to Heidegger this means that we must be willing for anxiety, to which alone the world as world, into which we are thrown, can manifest itself" (*WV* 159). It is as though we need to leave room for the silence of the world, by respecting the limits of our words, by remaining silent. (Silence, then, is something of an imperative, in the face of the wish to cover up something with chatter.) In other words, it is precisely a certain tendency to the noisy that is I take it, then and now, part of the experience of film, through which we can indirectly sense the difficulty posed by recognizing the limits of speech.

This "covering" of anxiety comes up in a remark about the place that music (which Cavell also calls suggestively in this context "Wagnerama") sometimes has in movies: "Movie music remained in genuine continuity with its soundless era. It continued to cartoon the emotions it could accompany, and continued to use that as an excuse for the general deadening of the pain of silence" (*WV* 152). Film music, like all that belongs to the primal (or to the dimension of origin) in movies, now risks denying (i.e. covering) what demands acknowledging.[5]

With synchronization, we can make the problem of the embedding of language or of consciousness in the world a matter for acknowledgment in film. It is a limit that can come into play in the tense co-existence of the said and the viewed in film (call this the problem of saying and showing in film). The term synchronization, denoting the unity whose form is that of parallel unfolding in time, suggests the temporal inflection of the problem of attunement of words and world. We could imagine in various ways our words and the world being "out of sync." Cavell starts by dismissing some of these:

> I have in mind not the various ways dialogue can stand at an angle to the life that produces it; nor the times in which the occasion is past when you can say what you

did not think to say, nor the times when the occasion for speech was blocked by inappropriateness or fear, or the vessels of speech are pitched by grief and joy.

WV 148

These cases, one might argue, are too much a matter of one's lacking presence of mind. They are cases in which I am not representing myself as I really am, cases in which I failed to say what I should. What Cavell rather wishes to explore is a deeper sense of gap between the element (or medium) of the world and the words released to it.

The initial examples that Cavell lists are suggestive: "The curve of fingers that day, a mouth, the sudden rise of the body's frame as it is caught by the color and scent of flowers, laughing all afternoon mostly about nothing, the friend gone but somewhere now which starts from here—spools of history that have unwound for me now, and if not now, never" (WV 148). Note the following about this passage. First, the examples involve a sense of time, and mostly bring out the *contingency* of a moment, of the now. Secondly, these are examples that are wholly ordinary. They are not miraculous moments but, as it were, intimations of intimacy with the world hidden in the most ordinary. Thirdly, the contingency of the moments evoked suggests also ephemerality and the passing, an occasion ("if not now, never"), as it were locating that which is always more than our speech in the sense of the factical appearing *as an opportunity*. Finally, therefore, this passage suggests that what is at issue in acknowledging limits of speech is finding the significance of contingency in the vision of the self in time and in the world. One can call this sense of the problem of bringing together speech and world the mystery of finding my voice in my history.

Initially, Cavell identifies how a sense of contingency and of the passing, challenges the unity of consciousness of determinate and persisting objects of experience. These moments point to the *placement* of consciousness, to its being in the world, and to the world as that which is the *ground of consciousness* itself: "I am asking for the ground of consciousness, upon which I cannot but move" (WV 148). What is this coming to presence of that which does not belong to consciousness? How can the world as surroundings of the deployment of consciousness be viewed in film? Is this ground of the conscious a form of the unconscious? And, what would it be for film to make us receptive to that which escapes conscious intentionality? Wouldn't that making of the unconscious intelligible, be a wish, a fantasy of total intelligibility, and thus an attempt to transcend our finitude? And assuming this desire, how would the acknowledgement of silence emerge against this wish for total intelligibility?

Sensing the contingency of life, its felicities and accidents, reflects for us this gap between consciousness and the ground of consciousness. It is in developing this temporality that one will give the proper articulation to what we might otherwise too easily be tempted to call the ineffable: "But why the sense that words are out of reach, that there will never be the right time for them? From where the sense of the unsayable?—time's answer to the ineffable?" (WV 148). The ineffable refers us to transcendent being. As when one wants to say that some being—paradigmatically, God—*is* ineffable. It is His being in itself that is beyond the power of human comprehension. But our sense of the unsayable is inflected by the form of time: the issue is not that there are no words altogether, but rather that there might not be the *right time* for them. Tracing the sense of the contingency of meaningful existence in film will be answering the sense of unsayability in the right way, will lead a step further in what is involved in acknowledging silence.

One way in which one could attempt both to evoke the distance between speech and world, that is to evoke the way in which the world lies beyond the capacity of ordinary speech, is to make the revelation of this distance be the primary role of *another* language, the poetic. But this again risks imposing problematic pictures on the relation of language and the world. If we avail ourselves of the register of the poetic to express what goes beyond mere speech in film, it will have to be the poetry of the ordinary, what Cavell calls the "poetry of prose," or the poetry of the prosaic. For what is sought is not the mysterious and miraculous, but precisely the ordinary of one's world. It is as though the ordinary in itself precisely veils itself, so that its revelation would always be out of it, both from it and as it were appearing to us as transforming our ordinary existence. This is primarily evident in film's capacity to investigate our *embodied* existence.

The presence of the gap between the sayable and its ground can be revealed by the specific presence of the *body* in film. The body in film can take part in "conveying the unsayable by showing experience beyond the reach of words." Cavell speaks of it as "freeing the motion of the body for its own lucidity" (*WV* 152, 153). This is to be distinguished from the earlier discussion of such techniques as slow motion, that might also be modes of discovery of the intelligence of the body, and which Cavell subsumes under "the *reality* of the unsayable" (*WV* 148, my emphasis). He identifies the latter as a "release from the synchronization of speech with the speaker" (*WV* 148). Slow motion creates as it were automatically the reality of the unsayable. For it makes what we see such that speech *cannot* be synchronized with it. One can meaningfully slow human movement, but when slowing human speech accordingly it just becomes a blur. This is *not* the way into what is veiled in the ordinary. This emphasis on the *reality* of the unsayable means, I take it, that it is achieved as it were too directly. Insofar as it does not involve the actualization and struggle against fantasy, it may fascinate us, but it does *not* involve acknowledgment.[6]

Cavell emphasizes that the sense of "the body's lucidity" in film "is not dependent upon slowing and flashing and freezing it and juxtaposing it to itself over cuts and superimpositions" (*WV* 153). Such somewhat "fancy" presentations of the body are contrasted with its most prosaic presence:

> It was always part of the grain of film that, however studied the lines and set the business, the movement of the actors was essentially improvised—as in those everyday actions in which we walk through a new room or lift a cup in an unfamiliar locale or cross a street or greet a friend or look in a store window or accept an offered cigarette or add a thought to a conversation.
>
> *WV* 153

The lucidity of the body is to be understood as a particular grace it has in the contingency of its everyday moments.[7] The body moves itself in response to contingencies as it takes up improvising over and above habit. Maybe, more precisely, we become aware how much improvising there is in the habitual. This lucidity is not a matter of making split-second, reflex movements in dramatic situations (as is so prevalent in some action movies nowadays), but rather the improvisation of the body Cavell refers to belongs to the presentation of the everyday. The everyday action of walking through a room has an improvisatory lucidity when it is walking through a *new* room; the everyday action of lifting a cup has an improvisatory dimension in lifting it in an *unfamiliar* locale. These contingencies are as "small" as the greeting that comes with meeting (a friend). It is as though film offers us a vision of a myriad of crossroads at every moment, which requires not decision or choice, but the improvisation of the body: "They could all go one way or another. Our resources are given, but their application to each new crossroads is an improvisation of meaning, out of the present" (*WV* 153).

For sure, the force of using the notion of improvisation here, in part involves our sense of its pertinence in music, say in jazz, where we understand it as something like making it up as you go (rather than being led by a score). But this musical intelligence relies on capacities that are developed and trained over years of practice and playing. What is striking about film is that it is capable of revealing improvisation at the heart of what is not a special form of practice, but rather human activity as such. It is not so much that a seasoned actor would be, like an experienced musician, adept at improvising. But rather film brings out the improvisatory character of action as such.

This is in turn dependent on the way in which we think of the unity of actor and character in film. Indeed, it is precisely because so much of the presence on screen does not belong to a role one has to perform, that what becomes visible is this improvisatory dimension of "acting" itself. It is part of the peculiar unity of actor and character in film that the improvisatory presence of bodily movement shows itself over and above what is scripted by character. Calling attention to the improvisatory in the habitual is thus something that is specific to the human presence *on screen*. Cavell's discussion of actor and character in earlier parts of the book makes clear that in film, acting has a wholly different meaning than in theater. It is just as much the presence of the actor to the camera as the playing of a character that gives the figures of film their unity and consistency. This is why acting in film illuminates everyday action: "Earlier I objected to calling the subjects of film 'actors' at all. But obviously they are actors the same way any human being is" (*WV* 153). In revealing to us what human action is, film touches upon a further dimension of the unsayable. It has to do with the way it shows us how actions are "inserted" into our world.

Philosophy often conceives of action in terms of the form of practical reason. The order of reasons we give for doing such and such is distinct from the unity of events, of what happens as a matter of nature. There are obstacles in the way of realizing purposes in action. Thus actions are successful or unsuccessful, depending in part on the "co-operation" of forces that are beyond our control and might just as well set us off course. But such pictures do not capture what is truly and deeply problematic in the position of the acting self in the world. We are released to the world in language and action. Cavell writes:

The ontological fact that actions move within a dark and shifting circle of intention and consequence, that their limits are our own, that the individual significance of an act (like that of a word) arises in its being this one rather than every other that might have been said or done here and now, that their fate (like the fate of words) is to be taken out of our control—this is the natural vision of film.

WV 153

This is not just as though, when out of my hand, actions can still have effects and consequences outside my reach. It is precisely that I am responsible to their meaning that escapes my control. The meaning of my actions and words, beyond my intention, can gather back around me, and reveal what my true orbit is. It is this which makes acting in the world, as a struggle in an environment in which fate rules. Fate is a peculiar nexus of contingency and necessity. Fate would be precisely the condition that makes it possible for something contingent to have the utmost bearing on the necessity I seek, on the meaning of my existence. The meaningful unity of self and world outstrips that which is identified in the realization of intention in action. To take fate seriously is to recognize that the fulfillment of the highest meaning, my wish for total intelligibility, is precisely dependent on letting "consequences" that are in no way under our control *count* for what is most one's own. These are themes as old in art as myth and tragedy are. And therefore Cavell's question is what form these dimensions of being in the world receive in film.

What would it be to recognize the unsayable in the disparity of conscious intending and world? And what would it be to conceive of the fulfillment in meaning in intelligibility as reconciling precisely that gap? Cavell gives pregnant expression to a vision of "amor fati" where philosophy and theater play their parts and set the stage for film to intervene: "To act without performing, to allow action all and only the significance of its specific traces, the wound embracing the arrow and no self-consciousness to blunt or disperse that knowledge—that has been the explicit wish of human action since Kierkegaard and Nietzsche summed up Protestantism and Stanislavsky brought theater into line" (*WV* 153).

Whereas Nietzsche's vision for modernity harks back to the tragic theater, Cavell suggests that film might reflect more the vision of the anti-tragic theater, commonly known as "epic theater," of Brecht. This theater forgoes moments of highest significance, which can only be revealed to an ecstatically *involved* audience. It envisions the possibility of philosophical instruction in an art that produces detached contemplation. The aesthetic of detachment becomes a necessity in recognizing the alienated character of our involvements and desires. Such a theater seeks ways to dispassionately encompass precisely the ground of alienated consciousness. In Brecht's epic theater, the detachment is supposed to be in the service of recognizing the human freed from the distorting forms of existence forced on him by the social order.

Cavell, it seems, recognizes in film the power to fulfill some of these wishes of Brecht's epic theater, though not quite in the way Brecht imagines it. The mismatch revealed between the unity of consciousness (through my intentions in action and the directedness of my speech) and its material ground, is resolved by film letting us contemplate the world as it were from outside. Film offers a radical solution for the alienation of consciousness by finding a position, a place for contemplation, at a distance from the world that is viewed. One can appreciate the significance of the idea of detachment by recalling how what is called for is stepping aside, letting the world show itself on its own terms. Film's automatism provides different ways to conceive of the dissociation from the space of consciousness, letting its images be *of the world* revealing itself. (Think of this as an antidote to a constant temptation in cinema, namely the addiction to the sensational.)

In deepening his account of what detached spectatorship comes to, Cavell challenges in part the adequacy of the very language of involvement and detachment to speak of one's relations to movies: "The impact of movies is too massive, too out of proportion with the individual worth of ordinary movies, to speak politely of involvement" (*WV* 154). It would not be correct to speak merely of our involvement, as if we allow ourselves to enter into movies, because there is a sense in which movies *enter* us. Speaking no doubt in the first person, Cavell considers how movies are woven into the fabric of one's life, or become part of the pattern in the weave of one's life in memory. Such memory has an unsayable dimension to it, because its importance is not attributable to any independent significance or weight of its contents, "[l]ike childhood memories whose treasure no one else appreciates, whose content is nothing compared with their unspeakable importance for me" (*WV* 154).

I have noted that Cavell's book is a book of memories of movies. The absorbing of film into one's life makes its moments into what can receive significance much later in life, in the return of memory. In that sense the medium of memory is essential to reflect on reconciling the gap or the distance between an action or event and the recognition of its significance. That significance has to do with the place that this moment will come to have in the life of the one who experienced it. This also makes clear that the kind of detachment that we recognize in view of the world is to be understood primarily in temporal terms. We are in the same world as that of the actors of film, yet separated from them by time.

This temporal dimension is evident in the importance that the register of childhood takes. By comparing the power of film to childhood memories, Cavell suggests that there is something about film that is "infantilizing." Film, just like childhood memories, brings out the significance of childhood to meaningful existence as such. This evocation of the figure of the child in relation to the power of movies has to do in fact with "the gigantism of its figures, making me small again" (*WV* 154). But the relation to my having been a child is itself the way to sense how the world outstrips the self that is placed in it. As Cavell puts it, this sense of size "must also have to do with the world it screens being literally of my world" (*WV* 155).[8] In other words, the gigantism of the figures of a movie is not just in their being projected on a big screen. It is to be understood as the problem posed by film of "fitting" the world. There is an "analogy" between the relation I have to the unity of life that is my world in memory, and the kind of attention that is demanded in film as discontinuities of place and time are to be put into one world: "You are given bits of the world, and you must put them together into those lives, one way or another, as you have yours" (*WV* 156).

The expanse of the world is not an abstract space–time but rather is that of place and opportunity. This is another form of the unity of contingency and necessity in film. Being in a given place on earth is utterly contingent, and yet "everyone knows odd moments in which it seems uncanny that one should find oneself just here now, that one's life should have come to this verge of time and place, that one's history should have unwound to this room, this road, this promontory" (*WV* 156). This coming together of place and time may appear in film as felicitous, as the blessed unconscious skirting of the abyss in Chaplin and Keaton, or as cursed for those who find themselves in a place at the wrong time, for those Cavell calls "the men who knew too much."

This possibility of recognizing the present both as utterly contingent, yet necessary, is contrasted by Cavell to various modes of "dramatization" that require the justificatory framework of a narrative. He contrasts the Aristotelian dramatic limits of the unity of action to film's "absolute freedom of narrative" (*WV* 156). It is as though film has a particular capacity to make the contingent, the accidental, the out-of-the-way possibility, appear necessary. This means that a certain destiny that was "reserved" for gods and heroes in antiquity has become the possibility of the *ordinary* life. Or that we do not require anymore in art the great and the heroic, the traditional garbs of fate, to elicit a sense of the necessity in the contingency of life: "[W]e exist in the condition of myth: we do not require the gods to show that our lives illustrate a story which escapes us; and it requires no major recognition or reversal to bring its meaning home. Any life may illustrate any; any change may bring it home" (*WV* 157). The secularization of what the religious tradition calls fate or providence leads us to ask how film presents the redeeming unity of life. Cavell identifies this quest in the final pages of the book with the wish for total intelligibility.

The way in which we are placed in the world reflects our finitude and our partiality. The wish of film is for total intelligibility: to encompass action and its world, not from the standpoint of subjective consciousness and intentionality, but as it were from outside, as encompassing the absolute belonging together of consciousness and the ground of consciousness. Film has the capacity to present one's *placement* in meaningful surroundings. It can further study the way in which placing inflects the range of significance of the self placed, but also intimate a mysterious inflexibility of the self in whatever place it finds itself.

Cavell develops these thoughts in relation to the investigation of seeing aspects, of physiognomic understanding in Wittgenstein, to which he refers as "the knowledge of the unsayable." He is weary of mystifying attempts to load the notion of "seeing as" with the ineffability of a higher intuition. He warns "against a false idea of its importance— namely that 'seeing as' is some fancy species of seeing" (*WV* 157). At the same time, Cavell brings out the importance of this notion to the concerns of the chapter, in understanding it in terms of acknowledgment. The concept of "seeing as" has to do "with my relation to my own words and with the point at which my knowledge of others depends upon the concepts of truthfulness and interpretation" (*WV* 157). Acknowledgment would have the character of the dawning of a dimension of meaning. Seeing otherwise is not a mystical form of intuition and acknowledgment is not seeing into another. It is a form of truthfulness that has to do with accepting or refusing the meaning that dawns on me.

One could see the connection between the problematic of "seeing aspects" and the earlier concern of how film places the self in the world, by thinking how the dawning of an aspect may be precisely related to the way an image is placed in surroundings. This can be clarified by the consideration of the difference between Wittgenstein's reference to the duck-rabbit and his example of seeing a triangle as fallen on its side. In the first case the shift from one aspect to the other can occur irrespective of the surroundings of the image. But in order to see the triangle *as* fallen on one side, we need to surround it with a context, a story, a fiction (the "natural" state of this triangle is standing up like *that*, with these sides as right and left; and here we see that it has fallen on its side). This is where the supposed connection to film and montage lies. It is as though by showing an image in relation to different preceding images we can bring out different aspects of what is seen.

Cavell follows Bazin in problematizing a simplistic conception of the *determining* power of the environment of the image in montage. Bazin argues that surrounding, say, a face with a context through montage has the effect of restricting our sense of the possible. It is in effect a technique for *directing* us to see certain aspects that foregoes the capacity of film to reveal the mysterious character of the face. Indeed, surrounding the image with some reality is a necessity of film, but this need not restrict our reflection or imagination of what we see: "I must surround the face with a reality—as though the seeing of a reality is the imagining of it; and it may itself either dictate or absorb the reality with which I must surround it, or fascinate me exactly because it calls incompatible realities to itself which vie for my imagination" (*WV* 158).

One can appreciate how placement in different context can precisely establish typicality by considering the recurrence of an actor in different films. At the same time, the potentialities of a type are the background for moments of reversal that placement would allow: "The fact of recurrence of an actor in his type both limits his range of expression, the physiognomical aspects which may dawn (one film working in montage to another), and also threaten the limit. It can be internal to a character that he threatens his own limit" (*WV* 158–59). Cavell suggestively conceives of such a reversal "in character" when Harpo finds his harp. The satyr and the angel come together mysteriously.

Context may bring out typicality. It can be a way to show us the range of possibilities of a type. But it can also intimate radical individuation. Changes in surroundings might precisely be such as to bring out the inflexibility of a core of individuality. It remains singularly itself in all those shifts: "The inflection of meaning available to a type is the background against which the inflexibility of a face commands its power of mystery" (*WV* 159). The environment of a figure can be such as to bring out the isolation of the concrete existing individual, or the way it transcends any habitual surroundings. It would be as though the figure is lifted out of the unity of the world that is exhibited through the different variations of place and time. The self revealed in its isolation just is the world attaining a state of complete intelligibility. The world's complete intelligibility would mean that the partiality of the self is no more part of it, that the self is excluded from it. This would make the inflexible solitude of the self correlative with the revelation of the independent intelligibility of the world: "Film's promise of the world's exhibition is the background against which it registers absolute isolation" (*WV* 159).

The wish for the world's exhibition is correlative with the sense of the absolute isolation of the self, that one's existence has a uniqueness that transcends every part one plays. Speaking of the last scene of Carl Th. Dreyer's *La Passion de Jeanne d'Arc* (1928), Cavell relates the intense isolation and mystery of Falconetti's face to the flight of the birds above the stake. The image suggests precisely the indestructibility of the person in its freedom in its flight out of this world. It is precisely such as to suggest the freedom after "this body has been gone through" (*WV* 159). We have moved from the initial discussion of contingency, body, action, and action's environment to the utmost limit in which bare existence is literally at (the) stake.

Finitude is committed to language, to expression. This being fated to expression has two sides: it is both the essential partiality of one's position, expressed in one's words and deeds, as well as the necessity to recognize that such expression always extends beyond one's control and is to be recognized in its affinity with the world. Partiality is not a moral failing, as though a matter of one's prejudices, something one would need to get rid of, in acting in the world. Partiality is precisely a metaphysical predicament that one has to acknowledge insofar as one is alive at all. The predicament of partiality means that one's achievements are always also betrayals. The detachment in the sense of the pastness of the world contemplated in film, feeds into one's wish to overcome partiality. This is the wish for complete intelligibility.

The overcoming of partiality can be called the state in which "the self is wholly won" (*WV* 160). This is also something that can be called the disappearance of the self (as if echoing Wittgenstein's sense that solipsism and realism are one, when the self vanishes into an extensionless point). Cavell describes this as "a world complete without me, which is present to me." He calls the disappearance of the self in which experience becomes wholly world "the world of my immortality" (*WV* 160). Indeed, in viewing a world as completely intelligible, it is as though I occupy a position external to my life (which as long as I lived, was always partial).

This fantasy of complete intelligibility, of contemplating the world without me, touches upon the cursed state in which the self may be said to haunt the world: "It takes my life as my haunting of the world, either because I left it unloved (the Flying Dutchman) or because I left unfinished business (Hamlet)." One would thus wish at the same time "the camera to deny the coherence of the world, its coherence as past: to deny that the world is complete without me" (*WV* 160). It is against such wishes and fatalities that the acknowledgement of silence is film's response to Kant's question: "What may I hope for?"

Notes

1   This feature of the book might be criticized for being too personal, as though it merely deals with Cavell's personal experience of film. But this would be to be blind to the way in which Cavell harps on how the everyday response of the individual is the way

to the universal voice in art. See in this context the seminal essay "Aesthetic Problems of Philosophy," in *MWM*. I have discussed this feature of Cavell's writing at some length in my "On Examples, Representatives, Measures, Standards, and the Ideal," in Alice Crary and Sanford Shieh, eds., *Reading Cavell* (London: Routledge, 2005), 204–17.

2   Compare to Benjamin: "It has always been one of the primary tasks of art to create a demand whose hour of full satisfaction has not yet come" (Walter Benjamin, *Selected Writings*, vol. 4, ed. Howard Eiland and Michael W. Jennings (Cambridge, MA: Harvard University Press, 2003), 266). Benjamin understands in these terms Dadaism's turn to morally tinged shock-effects: "Dadaism has abounded in such barbarisms. Only now is its impulse recognizable: *Dadaism attempted to produce with the means of painting (or literature) the effects which the public today seeks in film. . . . By means of its technological structure, film has freed the physical shock effect—which Dadaism had kept wrapped, as it were, inside the moral shock effect—from this wrapping*" (266–67, emphases in original).

3   The relation of candor and fantasy is most evident in Cavell's discussion of color in film, in the chapter called "The World as a Whole: Color." The kind of original, or magical, unity of world that is candidly given to be viewed, is elaborated in regard to a film that presents one of the most destructive visions of a mind trapped in fantasy. This is Hitchcock's *Vertigo*. See in this context my "Being-in-(Techni)Color," in Katalin Makkai, ed., *Vertigo* (London: Routledge, 2013), 174–93.

4   It would be enough to suggest that danger by pointing at the disputes regarding Wittgenstein's final proposition of the *Tractatus*: "Whereof we cannot speak, thereof we must remain silent" (7). It would be enough to suggest the wishes and hopes that go into silence to point to the mystery of Hamlet's last words: "The rest is silence." (Hamlet is mentioned in the last lines of Cavell's *The World Viewed*.)

5   Cavell interestingly chooses the example of *King Kong* (Cooper and Schoedsack, 1933) to discuss this noisy character of film. That film obliquely gestures to the covering of what is original or belongs to original nature. If primal nature is the name for what is the ground of consciousness, then one could say that the fright of the movie covers the anxiety there is in relating and distinguishing our consciousness from this ground of nature. Imagining the capturing or possessing of nature would be one way of denying the interdependence of nature and spirit.

6   Which is not to say that slow motion cannot be a technical assertion that has significance. In an earlier moment in the book Cavell discusses the famous scene of the dive competition in Leni Riefenstahl's *Olympia* (1938). The question of how slow motion pertains to revealing the unconscious of the ordinary brings out affinities as well as differences between Cavell and Benjamin. See in this context Benjamin's discussion of the optical unconscious in section 13 of "The Work of Art in the Age of its Technological Reproducibility," *Selected Writings*, vol. 4, 265–66.

7   I mean this term to echo Schiller's famous essay "On Grace and Dignity," in which the idea of the expression of freedom in the movement of the human body is developed.

8   The Mount Rushmore scenes of *North by Northwest* (Hitchcock, 1959), where Cary Grant and Eva Marie Saint are exposed on the face of the earth, as she holds a small "doll" in her hand, comes to mind. See in this context Cavell's discussion of the place of childhood in *North by Northwest* in *TS*.

Part Three

Glossary

11

Claim

Sandra Laugier

Throughout his work, Cavell's goal has been to "reinsert the human voice in philosophical thinking" (*MWM* 63). For Cavell, the stakes of ordinary language philosophy (particularly Wittgenstein and Austin's work) are to make it understood that language is spoken, claimed by a human voice within a form of life. It then becomes a matter of shifting the question of the common use of language—central to Wittgenstein's *Philosophical Investigations*—toward the re-introduction of the voice into philosophy as a/the claim of subjectivity in language. From the beginning, Cavell calls into question our *criteria*—that is, our common agreement on, or rather *in*, language, and, more precisely, the *we* at stake in "what we say." What grounds the turn to ordinary language? All we have is what we say, and our agreements in language. We agree not on meanings but on usages. One determines the "meaning of a [given] word" by its uses. The search for agreement (asking "what we should say when . . .," as Austin constantly did) is grounded on something entirely other than meanings or the determination of speakers' "common sense." The agreement Austin and Wittgenstein speak of is in no way an inter-subjective agreement. It is as *objective* an agreement as possible. But what is this agreement? Where does it come from, and why accord it so much importance? This is the problem Cavell is dealing with. Throughout his work, he asks: what allows Austin and Wittgenstein to *say what they say about what we say*? For Cavell, the radical absence of any foundation to the claim to "saying what we say" (which was a first discovery of his) is not the mark of some lack of logical rigor or rational certainty (a second discovery) in the procedure (ordinary language philosophy) that starts off from this claim. This is what Wittgenstein means when he talks about our "agreement in judgments" and in language: it is founded only on itself, in the *we*. Obviously, there is material here for skepticism.

Cavell shows *both* the fragility and the depth of our agreements and focuses on the very nature of the necessities that emerge for Wittgenstein from our forms of life. This is not an "existential" interpretation of Wittgenstein but a new understanding of the fact that language is our form of life. Acceptance of this fact—which Cavell defines as the "absence of foundation or guarantee for creatures endowed with language and subject to its powers and weaknesses, subject to their mortal condition"[1]—is thus not a consolation, but an acknowledgement of finitude and of the everyday, the source of which Cavell finds in Emerson and Thoreau. It is on this condition that one can regain "lost contact with reality": the proximity to the world and words broken in skepticism.

The philosophical problem raised by ordinary language philosophy is thus double. First, as we have seen: by what right do we base ourselves on what we ordinarily say? And next: on what, or on whom, do we base ourselves to determine what we ordinarily say? But—and this is the genius of Cavell's arguments in *Must We Mean What We Say?* and in *The Claim of Reason*—these two questions are but one: the question of the relation of the I (my words) to the real (our world), that is to say, for Cavell as for Wittgenstein, the question of our *criteria*. In order to see this, let us return to his investigation of language agreements: "we share criteria by which we regulate our application of concepts, means by which, in conjunction with what Wittgenstein calls grammar, we set up the shifting conditions for conversation" (QO 5). In the *Investigations*, Wittgenstein searches out and determines our criteria, which govern what we say. But *who is he* to claim to know such things? It is this absence of any foundation to the claim to know what we say that underlies the idea of criteria and defines a claim. The central enigma of rationality and the community is thus the possibility for me to speak *in the name of others*.

It is not enough to invoke the community; it remains to be seen what authorizes me (gives me title) to refer to it.

> When I remarked that the philosophical search for our criteria is a search for community, I was in effect answering the second question I uncovered in the face of the claim to speak for "the group"—the question, namely, about how I could have been party to the establishing of criteria if I do not recognize that I have and do not know what they are. . . . [T]he claim is not that one can tell a priori who is implicated by me, because one point of the particular kind of investigation Wittgenstein calls grammatical is exactly to discover who.
>
> CR 22

That we agree *in* language is certainly not the end of the problem of skepticism, and conventionalism is not an answer to the questions asked here. Indeed, for Cavell it is crucial that Wittgenstein says that we agree *in* and not *on* language. This means that we are not agents of the agreement—that language precedes this agreement as much as it is produced by it and that this circularity constitutes an irreducible element of skepticism. I am not "by definition" representative of the human. The agreement can always be broken. I can be excluded (or exclude myself) from the community, both linguistic and political. The possibility of disagreement is inherent even to the idea of agreement, from the moment I claim (with my words) my representativeness. This ever-possible disagreement sums up the threat of skepticism: a break in the passage, a suspension of the generalization from *I* to *we*.

For Cavell, the question of the social contract underlies or defines the question of language agreements, as his wonderful analysis of Rousseau at the beginning of *The Claim of Reason* shows. If I am representative I must have my voice in the common conversation. If my society is my expression it should also allow me to find my voice.

But is this really the case? If others stifle my voice, speak for me, I will always seem to consent. One does not have a voice, *one's own voice*, by nature: it must be found so as to speak in the name of others and to let others speak in one's name. For if others do not accept my words, I lose more than language: I lose my voice.

> We do not know in advance what the content of our mutual acceptance is, how far we may be in agreement. I do not know in advance how deep my agreement with myself is, how far responsibility for the language may run. But if I am to have my own voice in it, I must be speaking for others and allow others to speak for me. The alternative to speaking for myself representatively (for *someone* else's consent) is not: speaking for myself privately. The alternative is having nothing to say, being voiceless, not even mute.
>
> CR 28, Cavell's emphasis

The error of Wittgenstein studies has been to see an alternative between private and public (this is the prejudice that underlies discussions of "the private language argument": either everything is hidden or nothing is; either I am entirely private, or I am public). Cavell explodes this alternative. To not be public is not to be *private*: it is to be *inexpressive*. "Voiceless, not even mute." If I do not speak, it is not that there is something inexpressible, but that I *have* nothing to say.

Claim: The Story of the Concept

More fundamentally than in its political use, a claim is a way of expressing oneself publicly to make a claim, a request, a right, or, quite simply, to make one's voice heard. This is the meaning of the term "claim" and the reason why Cavell has made it a central element of his philosophy of ordinary language.

From the old French word *clamer* (from Latin *clamare*, of the same semantic field as *clarus*, "clear," "strong"), to claim means in its first historically attested literary uses "to call, shout, clamor." Yet "to claim" and the noun "claim" have no parallel in French today. The current French translations of "claim," *revendication, réclamation, prétention,* all have an, if not pejorative, in any case negative tone, as if the request thus expressed needed additional justification. However, "claim," in its first legal or political uses, on the contrary raises a claim as well founded, in kind if not in law, and could be adequately rendered as "title," which refers to the notion of law which, as Alasdair MacIntyre has noted, emerges late and of which "claim" (in the sense of a claim based on a need) perhaps constitutes a first form.

In the nineteenth and twentieth centuries, "claim" moved from the political and legal fields to the theory of knowledge, and then generally to the philosophy of language. The notion is then a "claim to knowledge," a "thesis." This use raises the question, stemming from English empiricism and then taken up by Kant, of the legitimacy of knowledge, of the validity of my claims to know. There is a German lexical equivalent to this use (*Anspruch*). Finally, claim becomes an "affirmation" that must be supported and claimed.

"Claim" originally referred to a claim related to the satisfaction of a physical need or the recovery of a vital asset that has been taken from you. "Claim" is a request to obtain a title deed to an object that already legitimately belongs to me. This use of the concept is extended during the conquest of new land by pioneers: in the United States and Australia, "claim" refers to a parcel acquired by occupation (not granted nor inherited).

This "local" meaning of "claim" underlies a certain conception of the claim to property rights as fundamental rights, and perhaps also rights in general as (re)taking possession of a territory of one's own. It should be noted that a territory claimed by the native populations as the first occupants is called an "Indian claim." Thus a meaning of claim to a right is clarified: I ask what is mine and has always been mine. This refers to the request for something as it is due. A claim is then made by "requirement" or "title." This raises the question of the legitimacy of the request, which is answered with the emergence, apparently later, of the term "right." The legal (and philosophical) meaning of the notion then becomes more specific: "assertion of a right to something" (*OED*); and an entire vocabulary develops around claims, as evidenced by the multiplicity of expressions ("lay claim to," "make a claim," "enter a claim") that have penetrated ordinary language and fascinated Cavell.

The Political Claim

This claiming dimension inherent in the notion of claim extends to knowledge from the skeptical challenge. The question of empiricism, and, correlatively, that of skepticism, is that of legitimacy, of the right to know: what allows us to say that we know? Hume, examining our claim to know by reasoning from experience, wonders by what right we can say that we know anything. This question is repeated by Kant, in whom we can detect the emergence of a claim equivalent: *Anspruch*, which refers to the claim of reason to ask questions that are beyond its power but are legitimate and natural. The legal meaning of a claim, which is found in the Kantian *quid juris*, then applies to Reason, which is conceived as a claim that is both inevitable and impossible to satisfy, and therefore intended to always remain in the state of a claim.

It is this tension between the arrogance and the legitimacy of the philosophical claim to know that is at the heart of Cavell's work. Cavell defines claim from the outset as a community agreement based on singular expression and common use. From this perspective, what underlies the question of the foundation of knowledge is the political and not only epistemological question of the foundation of our common use of language. For Cavell, the claim of knowledge is the mask of a first claim: the claim to speak for others, and to accept from others that they speak on my behalf.

The philosophical invocation of "what we say" and the search for the criteria that are ours call for (are claims to) the community. However, the community claim is always a search for the basis on which it can be, or has been, established.

The legal and epistemological problems raised by the notion of claim become that of our common criteria, our agreements in language. The question becomes that of an individual's belonging to the community of a language and her representativeness as a member of that community: where does she get this *right* or claim to speak for others? In this usage, claim is inseparable from the possibility of losing my representativeness, or my belonging, of being silenced: all claims about what we say go hand in hand with the awareness that others may well disagree, that a given person or group may not share our criteria.

The political agreement is of the same nature as the language agreement: it exists only to the extent that it is claimed, invoked. "Claim" thus defines an agreement that is not psychological or intersubjective but is based on nothing more than the validity of an individual voice that claims to be a "universal voice." We find here the first meaning of "claim" (*clamer*, "to shout, call") and also the irreducibility of the cry. The voice, but also the *clamor*, thus always underlie the concept of the claim. Claim is what a voice does when it relies solely on itself to establish universal assent—a claim that, however exorbitant it may be, Cavell formulates in an even more scandalous way, that is, as not being based, as in Kant, on anything transcendental or on any condition of reason. Reason claims itself (it is the meaning of the genitive in Cavell: the claim *of* reason)—without any external warranty for the claim.

To show how the redesigned claim concept is an answer to skepticism, Cavell evokes the universality of Kant's aesthetic judgment. For him, the proximity of this approach to that of ordinary language theorists is that both of them always admit that they must rely on me to say what we say. To understand this connection, we must refer to what ordinary language philosophers mean by "what we say when . . .": the aesthetic judgment serves as a model for the kind of affirmation (claim) produced by ordinary language philosophers.

How can Kant be considered a thinker of claim? The idea of a universal agreement based on my singular voice appears in the famous §8 of the *Critique of the Power of Judgment*. In aesthetic judgment, Kant has us "discover a property of our ability to know": "the claim [*Anspruch*] to universality [*Allgemeingültigkeit*]" specific to the judgment of taste, which makes us "attribute to everyone the satisfaction brought by an object."[2] Recall that Kant distinguishes the pleasant from the beautiful (which claims universal consent) in terms of private and public judgment. How can a judgment that has all the characteristics of a private judgment claim to be public? That is the problem with the claim. The judgment of taste requires universal assent, "and, in fact, everyone assumes this assent, without the subjects who judge opposing each other on the possibility of such a claim [*Anspruch*]."[3] What supports such a claim is what Kant calls a "universal voice" (*allgemeine Stimme*).[4] This is the "voice" we hear in *übereinstimme*n, the verb used by Wittgenstein about our agreement "in language." The proximity between the universal Kantian voice and the theses of the philosophy of ordinary language appears with this ultimate meaning of *claim*, both *Anspruch* and *Stimme*: a claim, empirically unfounded, therefore threatened and raised by skepticism, to speak for all.

In his analysis of the notion of claim, Cavell identifies the different strata (legal, political, epistemic, expressive) on which the acceptable uses of the verb "to claim" are developed. The ordinary grammar he proposes suggests that our affirmations or theses (claims) are always based on an agreement in language, on a claim of my representativeness, therefore on the legitimacy of my voice as singular and universal. To recognize the intimate connection between all these uses of the notion of claim is to recognize that the expression—in the order of knowledge as well as in the order of politics and law—is always also a voice, one that wants to be heard and demands to be heard on an equal footing with other voices. And always a matter of skepticism, because this voice must constantly be reappropriated to regain a proximity to the world.

Claim and Romanticism

The search for accuracy, for absolute expression as a match between the inside and the outside, combines language, politics, and ethics. It also defines romanticism, at least insofar as it can be inherited in America according to Cavell, following Emerson and Thoreau, but also Wordsworth and Rousseau. According to Cavell, Walden is a "heroic book": it is in this sense that we can speak of a romanticism of democracy, which goes to the end of this aspiration of romanticism that is the reappropriation of the ordinary world through the accuracy of words.

The problem is not that I cannot express, externalize what I have "inside," to think or feel something without being able to say it, some pathetic infra-romantic mythology of the ineffable. The problem is the opposite: not wanting to say what I say. Not a difficulty to know but a refusal, even a fear, to want to say, and to access or expose oneself to the outside world, to be public. To accept expression, claim, is to accept the reality of the (bodily) exteriority of the meaning. "The human body is the best image of the human soul," Wittgenstein notes, not as it represents it (and what would that mean?) or possesses it, but as it gives it expression. This means that expressiveness and claim, including collective and public, are not so much the product of a will but rather a last resort; because there is no other way to make yourself heard.

Claim would be the acceptance of the expression as identically inner (it expresses me) and outer (it exposes me). This identity reveals the nature of subjectivity as reinvented by Wittgenstein: the subject is indeed the subject of language, but in the sense that it is the subject of (to) expression and claim. The subject, in Wittgenstein, exists as this claim, this voice—in and through language. That it is inseparably inner and outer means that it is obviously not a voice that assures me of my identity, my thoughts, or anything else (as soon as it is a voice, it is expression, and escapes me). The subject then defines himself in this movement of reappropriation of her voice, which is also a way of approaching, of touching reality.

Voice and Claim

Claiming is voicing. Our agreement (with others, with myself) is an agreement of voices: our *übereinstimmen*, says Wittgenstein. "That a group of human beings *stimmen* in their language *überein* says, so to speak, that they are mutually voiced with respect to it, mutually *attuned* top to bottom" (*CR* 32, Cavell's emphases). Cavell thus defines an agreement that is *not* psychological or inter-subjective and is founded on nothing but the pure validity of a voice: my individual voice claims to be, is, a "universal voice." Claiming is what a voice does when it founds itself on itself alone in order to establish universal agreement—a claim that, as exorbitant as it already is, Cavell asks us to formulate in yet more exorbitant a manner: in place and stead of any condition of reason or understanding.

In *Must We Mean What We Say?*, Cavell posed the question of the foundation of language in the Kantian terms of "universal voice," showing the proximity of Wittgenstein and Austin's methods to a paradox inherent to aesthetic judgment: basing oneself on *I* in order to say what *we* say. Kant leads us to discover "a property of our faculty of cognition that without this analysis would have remained unknown"; the "claim to universality" proper to judgments of taste, which make us "ascribe the satisfaction in an object to everyone." Kant distinguishes the agreeable from the beautiful (which claims universal agreement) in terms of *private* versus *public* judgment. How can a judgment with all the characteristics of being private claim to be public, to be valid for all? Kant himself noted the "strange," disconcerting nature of this fact, whose strangeness Wittgenstein took to the limit. The judgment of taste "demand[s] . . . assent [*Einstimmung*] universally."[5] What Kant calls the universal voice supports such a claim. We hear this "voice" in the idea of agreement, *übereinstimmen*, the verb used by Wittgenstein when he speaks of our agreement in language (*PI* §§241–42). The universal voice expresses our agreement and thus our claim to speak in the name of others—to speak, *tout court*.

The question of the universal voice is the question of the voice itself and its arrogation—an individual voice claiming to speak in the name of others. What is, then, the status of the philosophical voice? This question only receives a response in *A Pitch of Philosophy*. The philosopher speaks with ordinary words, and nothing says that others will accept these—though the philosopher claims to speak for all. By what right?

—Who is to say whether a man speaks for all men?
Why are we so bullied by such a question? Do we imagine that if it has a sound answer the answer must be obvious or immediate? But it is no easier to say who speaks for all men than it is to speak for all men. And why should that be easier than knowing whether a man speaks for me?

MWM xl

Here we may think of one of the stakes of Austin's work: the method of ordinary language philosophy. It is difficult not to notice that there is an "unhappy" dimension, a dimension of failure in ordinary language philosophy, which is obsessed—at least in the case of Austin—with instances where language fails, is inadequate, inexpressive.

Claiming the Subject

In *Must We Mean*, Cavell asks how I can mean ("to mean" here also means "to think," "to signify") what I say. He radically reverses the examination of "private language." The problem is not being able to express what I have "in me"—thinking or feeling something without being able to say it (a problem definitively dealt with by Wittgenstein in the *Tractatus*: there is the ineffable, but it most certainly cannot be thought, nor can it in some way point outside language). The problem is the inverse: not being able "to be in what I say," to *mean what I say*. Here, Austin's teaching enters in again: to say, as Austin did in *How to Do Things With Words*, that language is also action does not mean I control language, as I do (certain of my) actions. This means above all that it is possible for me to not "mean what I say." I am more possessed by language than I possess it. This point, expressed in *A Pitch of Philosophy*, makes explicit a profound intuition from *Must We Mean* about the source of skepticism: an impossibility of speaking the world that comes not from any (imaginary) distancing of the world, but from the impossibility or refusal to *mean*. "So the fantasy of a private language, underlying the wish to deny the publicness of language, turns out, so far, to be a fantasy, or fear, either of inexpressiveness, one in which I am not merely unknown, but in which I am powerless to make myself known; or one in which what I express is beyond my control" (*CR* 351). The question of the secret and the private is transformed and becomes that of the fatality of meaning, or of my "condemnation" to signification. The problem is thus not meaninglessness or the impossibility of "making sense" but rather the fatality of expression. Cavell develops the tension between the singular and the common, between the "arrogance" and the legitimacy of the philosophical claim at the political level. What underlies the question of the foundation of knowledge is the (political and not only epistemological) question of the foundation of *our* common use of language. For Cavell, the *claim to knowledge* is the mask of a prior claim: the claim to speak for others, and to accept that others speak in my name. "The philosophical appeal to what we say, and the search for our criteria on the basis of which we say what we say, are claims to community. And the claim to community is always a search for the basis upon which it can or has been established" (*CR* 20). Cavell transforms the juridical and epistemological questions raised by "claim" into the question of our shared criteria, our agreements *in* language.

> When I remarked that the philosophical search for our criteria is a search for community, I was in effect answering the second question I uncovered in the face of the claim to speak for "the group"—the question, namely, about how I could have been party to the establishing of criteria if I do not recognize that I have and do not know what they are.
>
> CR 22

It is a question of my representativeness: where does this right or this claim to speak for others come to me from? This is the question that the philosophers of ordinary language, Austin and Wittgenstein, ask, according to Cavell. The meaning of claim is inseparable from the possibility of my losing my representativeness, or my belonging—of being reduced to silence. "For all Wittgenstein's claims about what we say, he is always at the same time aware that others may not agree, that a given person or group (a 'tribe') might *not* share our criteria" (*CR* 18, Cavell's emphasis). Thus, Cavell gives an analysis of Rousseau in terms of claim: "What he *claims* to know is his relation to society, and to take as a philosophical datum the fact that men (that he) can speak for society and that society can speak for him, that they reveal one another's most private thoughts" (*CR* 25, my emphasis).

My society must be my expression. This is what theoreticians of democracy always hope, and this is the illusion Cavell denounced with regard to Rawls, for example: if others stifle my voice, claiming to speak for me, how have I consented? "To speak for yourself means risking the rebuff—on some occasion, perhaps once for all—of those for whom you claimed to be speaking; and it means risking having to rebuff—on some occasion, perhaps once for all—those who claimed to be speaking for you" (*CR* 27). Agreement between humans, linguistic or political, is as fragile as it is deep precisely because it is *always a claim*. This essential fragility of political agreement, always threatened by skepticism, constitutes the linguistic sense of claim.

Political agreement is of the same nature as linguistic agreement, which Wittgenstein calls *Übereinstimmung* (*PI* §241). This agreement only exists insofar as it is claimed, demanded, invoked: my individual voice claims to be, *is*, a "universal voice."

Here, with the appeal to voice we encounter the first meaning of claim (*clamare*: to cry, to call). The concept of voice thus always turns out to be inherent to the technical concept of a claim. Claim is what a voice does when it bases itself on itself alone in order to establish an agreement: to base oneself on *I* in order to say what *we* say. This claim is what defines agreement, and community is thus by definition something claimed, not foundational. It is I—my voice—who claim community. Finding my voice consists not in finding agreement with *everyone*, but in staking a claim.

These are themes Cavell takes from Emerson and Thoreau: Everyone is worth the same, and an individual voice claims generality. This is the principle of Emersonian *self-reliance*. (It is this possibility of a claim through the voice that makes it possible to extend the model of civil disobedience today.) Emerson and Thoreau refused the societies of their time for the same reasons America had wanted its independence and claimed the rights of liberty, equality, and the pursuit of happiness. They took the Declaration of Independence literally: "[That] to secure these rights, governments are instituted among men, deriving their just powers from the consent of the governed. That whenever any form of government becomes destructive to these ends, it is the right of the people to alter or to abolish it, and to institute new government."[6] It is here and now, every day, that my consent to my society is decided; I did not somehow give my consent once and for all. Not that my consent is calculated or conditional; it is constantly in discussion, in conversation. This is what defines the possibility of dissent, the rupture of the language agreement.

In "Civil Disobedience" Thoreau declares, "I simply wish to refuse allegiance to the State, to withdraw and stand aloof from it effectually." If the State refuses to dissolve its union with slave-owners, then let "each inhabitant of the State dissolve his union with it." Thoreau says, "I cannot for an instant recognize that political institution as my government which is the slave's government also."[7]

Those they defend—Native Americans and slaves—do not have rights (they do not have a voice in their history, Cavell says). Instead of making claims in their place, and thus, keeping them in silence, Emerson and Thoreau prefer to claim the only rights that they can defend—their own: their right to have a government that speaks and acts in their name, that they recognize and to which they give their consent and voice.

Thus the concept of democratic *conversation* (central in Rawls's liberal theory): for a government to be legitimate, everyone must have, or find, his or her voice in it, be able to stake a claim. The right to withdraw one's voice from society is based on Emersonian *self-reliance*: my private voice will be the universal feeling, for what is most intimate always ends up becoming the most public. To ensure that my private voice always be public: this is the definition of a claim and the political translation of Wittgenstein's "critique" of private language.

In both moral agreements and political claims I am brought back to myself, to the search for my position and my voice. The question of democracy is indeed the question of voice. I must have a voice in my history and recognize myself in what is said or shown by my society, and thus, in a way, give my voice to it, accepting that it speaks in my name.

The radical critique of conformism is not simply a calling into question of consent to society. To the contrary, it defines the condition of *ordinary* democratic morality. Questions of justice and injustice do not concern only those who do not speak—those who, for structural reasons, cannot speak (who have been definitively "excluded" from the conversation of justice)—but also those who *could speak* yet run up against the inadequacy of speech as it is given to them. It is in this inadequacy and misunderstanding that the political subject is defined—not in a new foundation of the subject through his or her speech, but in the suffocation and claim of his or her own voice.

A speech *claims* a voice. The subject is not a foundation; it is eternally claimed, absent, *demanded*. What must be brought out is not only the subject's fragility or plurality or obscurity, but also essential passivity: the subject must *support* the voice. The subjectivity of language is then the impossible adequacy between a speaker and his or her voice or voices. Here the terror of absolute inexpressiveness *and* of absolute expressiveness, of total exposure, come together as two extreme states of voicelessness: "I am led to stress the condition . . . [of] the terror of absolute inexpressiveness, suffocation, which at the same time reveals itself as a terror of absolute expressiveness, unconditioned exposure; they are the extreme states of voicelessness" (*CT* 43). This dissociation/dislocation of the voice is also at the heart of Cavell's autobiographical project in *Little Did I Know*, and it is a matter of claim.

> This second analyst and I eventually spent some time analyzing more or less informally my own writings. The simultaneous fear of inexpressiveness and of over-expressiveness is a recurrent topic in the material I had just decided to put aside as eluding completion by me, in its thesis form called *The Claim to Rationality*, in its revised and doubled form published as *The Claim of Reason*.
>
> LDIK 110

Notes

1 Stanley Cavell, "Préface," in *Les Voix de la raison: Wittgenstein, le scepticisme, la moralité et la tragédie*, trans. Nicole Balso and Sandra Laugier (Paris: Seuil, 2012).
2 Immanuel Kant, *Critique of the Power of Judgment*, trans. Paul Guyer and Eric Matthews (New York: Cambridge University Press, 2000), trans. mod., §8:99.
3 Ibid., trans. mod.
4 Kant, *Critique of the Power of Judgment*, §8:101.
5 Ibid., §8:99.
6 Thomas Jefferson et al., "Declaration of Independence: A Transcription," National Archives, https://www.archives.gov/founding-docs/declaration-transcript.
7 Henry David Thoreau, *Reform Papers*, ed. Wendell Glick (Princeton: Princeton University Press, 1973), 67.

12

Criteria

Martin Shuster

To get the import of the distinct context that opens Cavell's discussion of criteria, recall that the first chapter in *The Claim of Reason*, titled "Criteria and Judgment," opens with Cavell noting that he has "wished to understand philosophy not as a set of problems but as a set of texts" (*CR* 3). For Cavell, this means "that the contribution of a philosopher—anyway of a creative thinker—to the subject of philosophy is not to be understood as a contribution to, or of, a set of *given* problems, although both historians and non-historians of the subject are given to suppose otherwise" (*CR* 3). Focus especially on the way in which Cavell dismisses the idea of philosophy as a "set of *given* problems," with the obvious rejection of the idea that problems in philosophy could be given in this way (importantly, note that Cavell does not intend to dismiss the idea of philosophy as a set of problems, but rather to suggest that it is a set of texts, thereby open and variable in its constitution *and* its possible problems). I will return to these thoughts about philosophy after moving through Cavell's remarks on criteria, and especially on how he understands Wittgenstein's *Philosophical Investigations* (although my own aims here are not fundamentally to respond to Wittgenstein's text, but—in the wake of Cavell's philosophy—instead to take stock of Cavell's text). What follows is not a comprehensive account of criteria and their roles in Cavell's philosophy, a task that would far exceed the parameters of such a chapter. Instead, think of what follows as a sort of foundational blueprint that can be used to construct a proper understanding of Cavell's understanding of criteria.

Cavell's remarks on Wittgenstein and on the notion of criteria dawned to him "only after some years of acquaintance with the *Investigations*," when he realized "the trivial fact that the notion of a criterion is an everyday one and the somewhat less trivial fact that Wittgenstein's account of it, while not exactly the same notion, is dependent upon the everyday one" (*CR* 6). This relationship is one way to understand the register in which Cavell elaborates Wittgenstein's thought (and his own): for Wittgenstein, criteria are not meant to refute skepticism, as if they are some sort of antidote to epistemological problems that inherently arise for us (either in philosophy or in our everyday existence). In response to those who would read Wittgenstein in this way,[1] Cavell stresses that criteria neither can do this nor are they intended to do so. This is so much the case that Cavell claims that "the fate of criteria ... reveals, I should like to say, the truth of skepticism." He adds that "of course this may require a reinterpretation of what skepticism is, or threatens" (*CR* 6–7). I will turn to what that might mean shortly, but presently I want to register the extent to which Cavell's discussion of criteria is (1) oriented around something like our everyday experience and (2) not aimed at some epistemological solution to what might be a classical philosophical problem.[2]

Let us start then with our everyday understanding of criteria. In that sense, "criteria are specifications a given person or group sets up on the basis of which (by means of, in terms of which) to judge (assess, settle) whether something has a particular status or value" (*CR* 9). Cavell notes that it is important to distinguish between criteria on one hand and standards on the other; the former determines whether something is of the "right" kind to be labeled in a particular way, while the latter determines to what extent something satisfies particular criteria. Think here of a courtroom. The judge and/or jury in any courtroom apply certain standards, but they are unable to choose the criteria that they apply, which are given by the form of the law (of course, this isn't a perfect example: there are possible legal exceptions—like, for example, jury nullification).

Such an everyday understanding of criteria, according to Cavell, differs from Wittgenstein's understanding of criteria in two ways.[3] First, Wittgenstein's philosophical interests in and invocations of criteria never revolve around standards. The philosophically interesting cases according to him are instances where the questions are about particular criteria, not about whether criteria apply altogether, in a more general sense. As Cavell notes, "In no case in which he [Wittgenstein] appeals to the application of criteria is there a separate stage at which one might, explicitly or implicitly, appeal to the application of standards. To have criteria, in this sense, for something's being so is to know whether, in an individual case, the criteria do or do not apply" (*CR* 13). Second, Cavell notes that for Wittgenstein, the first point about criteria—that they are possibly in question with regard to a particular instance— applies across the board in our (use of) language: it is everywhere and at all times true about our existence as human agents. There is no realm of human life in which the question of criteria cannot arise. As he notes, "Wittgenstein's insight, or implied claim, seems to be something like this, that *all our knowledge, everything we assert or question* (or doubt or wonder about . . .) is governed not merely by what we understand as 'evidence' or as 'truth conditions', but by criteria" (*CR* 14, emphasis added).

These two points together lead Cavell to understand Wittgenstein's philosophy as deeply ethical and political in nature.[4] For Wittgenstein, "it is . . . always *we* who 'establish' the criteria under investigation. The criteria Wittgenstein appeals to—those which are, for him, the data of philosophy—are always 'ours', the 'group' which forms his 'authority' is always, apparently, the human group as such, the human being generally" (*CR* 18). Although I cannot develop it in proper detail here, I would suggest that this is also a way in which Cavell rejects—albeit for reasons quite different from Sellars or McDowell—any invocation of a "given."[5] A question arises, however, about how things get going here. Cavell notes two dimensions to this question:

(1) How can I, what gives me the right to speak for the group of which I am a member? How have I gained that remarkable privilege? What confidence am I to

place in a generalization from what I say to what everybody says?: the sample is irresponsibly, preposterously small. (2) If I am supposed to have been party to the criteria we have established, how can I fail to know what these are; and why do I not recognize the fact that I have been engaged in so extraordinary an enterprise?

CR 18

Let me take each question in turn.

How can I speak for others? Cavell stresses the extent to which, in matters of language, we are all each equally authoritative (*CR* 19). Of course, we may disagree, but our disagreement oftentimes—in the interesting cases—is not merely about truth or falsity. So much so that it may be the case that we *never* (come to) agree. This leads to one of Cavell's most striking conclusions in his philosophy of language:

> The philosophical appeal to what we say, and the search for our criteria on the basis of which we say what we say, are claims to community. And the claim to community is always a search for the basis upon which it can or has been established. I have nothing more to go on than my conviction, my sense that I make sense. It may prove to be the case that I am wrong, that my conviction isolates me, from all others, from myself. That will not be the same as a discovery that I am dogmatic or egomaniacal. The wish and search for community are the wish and search for reason.
>
> *CR* 20

Unpacking the various elements that make up and support the claims in the above paragraph is one way to detail Cavell's subsequent work, and especially his elaboration of moral perfectionism (most notably in *Conditions Handsome and Unhandsome*).[6] Even our reason may itself "be a set of prejudices" (*CR* 21). When we speak to each other, we have nothing to go on except ourselves: there is no universal reason that we might somehow "tap into" in order to settle matters; this does not mean, importantly, that universal reason cannot exist at all, instead it entails only that if it will exist, it must be achieved. As Cavell puts it, "community is . . . partial, always to be searched for."[7] Relatedly, this also means that if a disagreement between us persists, "there is no appeal beyond us, or if beyond us two, then not beyond some eventual us" (*CR* 19).

If I were already part of the group that established the criteria, then how might I fail to know them? Cavell takes it that the social contract tradition in (political) philosophy somehow responds to this question: I accede to such criteria in continuing to involve myself in my society, regardless of whether I am explicitly aware of every individual criterion with which I am involved. Yet Cavell also notes that such an understanding of the relationship between me and the social contract does not actually answer the question at hand. As he puts it,

> the problem is for me to discover my position with respect to these facts—how I know with whom I am in community, and to whom and to what I am in fact obedient. The existence of the prior contract is not the explanation of such facts.

> On the contrary, it is a projection from the fact that I now recognize myself to be party to some social contract [...] which explains the prior existence of the contract.
>
> CR 25

What the recourse to social contract theory does in this instance is then simply to push the problem back a step: the social contract tradition is the expression of my relationship to the criteria that I possess, not an explanation of them.

This just highlights the importance of language, and especially of speech, for speaking to others is also speaking for others, and the two just are the search for community. This fact becomes most obvious in the political realm, but it is not a fact solely about that realm (at least as it is traditionally or ordinarily conceived). The epigraph from Emerson that Cavell selects to open *The Claim of Reason* testifies to the same fact: "truly speaking, it is not instruction, but provocation" (*CR* iii).[8] Such a conception of language and speech carries with it the recognition that with any bit of speech, I may find no community. I may find myself alone; I may be alone (the application of these morally tinged remarks to the specificity of the enterprise of philosophy is now slowly coming into focus). Here's how Cavell glosses the broader point: "To speak for yourself then means risking the rebuff—on some occasion, perhaps once for all—of those for whom you claimed to be speaking; and it means risking having to rebuff—on some occasion, perhaps once for all—those who claimed to be speaking for you" (*CR* 27).

The possibility of disagreement, thereby, is central both to speech and to community. With respect to the former, the possibility of speech necessitates the possibility of disagreement. As Cavell puts it: "Dissent is not the undoing of consent but a dispute about its content, a dispute within it over whether a present arrangement is faithful to it. The alternative to speaking for yourself politically is not: speaking for yourself privately.... The alternative is having nothing (political) to say" (*CR* 27–28). With respect to the latter—the possibility of community—disagreement is also central. As Cavell puts it, both I and "my elders" (i.e., those from whom I inherited my language) have to accept each other as authoritative: I with respect to the authority of the elders (because I would not have my own words with which to form my thoughts and stake my claims) and they with respect to my authority (because to do so is to acknowledge themselves and their possession of language, which makes sense, and is of consequence and use, only to and amidst others). Cavell, in another often-cited passage, notes that:

> I would like to say: If I am to have a native tongue, I have to accept what "my elders" say and do as consequential; and they have to accept, even have to applaud, what I say and do as what they say and do. We do not know in advance what the content of our mutual acceptance is, how far we may be in agreement. I do not know in advance how deep my agreement with myself is, how far responsibility for the language may run. But if I am to have my own voice in it, I must be speaking for others and allow others to speak for me. The alternative to speaking for myself

representatively (for *someone* else's consent) is not: speaking for myself privately. The alternative is having nothing to say, being voiceless, not even mute.

CR 28, Cavell's emphasis

This is the register in which Wittgenstein's invocations of criteria must be understood.[9] What Cavell takes to be significant about Wittgenstein's work is that it shows us the extent to which there is pervasive and seemingly orderly agreement amongst ourselves; this agreement is so common that we tend to overlook it. In Cavell's words, "there is a background of pervasive and systematic agreements among us, which we had not realized, or had not known we realize" (*CR* 30). Wittgenstein alternatively calls this "agreement in judgments" or "agreement in form of life" (*PI* §241, §242). Given the discussion thus far, Wittgenstein's invocation of agreement in judgments appears to run almost exactly counter to our everyday understanding of criteria. In everyday usage, we take it that criteria are the means by which we make judgments, but Wittgenstein draws our attention to the fact that it is some sort of prior agreement in judgment or in a form of life that makes our use of criteria possible. Here's how Cavell elaborates the point: "Now the whole thing looks backwards. Criteria were to be the bases (features, marks, specifications) on the basis of which certain judgments could be made (non-arbitrarily); agreement over criteria was to make possible agreement about judgments. But in Wittgenstein it looks as if our ability to establish criteria depended upon a prior agreement in judgment" (*CR* 30).

Criteria, for Wittgenstein, then draw our eye to the fact that pervasively we do agree. The interesting philosophical questions, however, arise around the basis or means by which we come to have such agreement in judgment or forms of life. Criteria merely "call to consciousness the astonishing fact of the astonishing extent to which we *do* agree in judgment," and "eliciting criteria goes to show therefore that our judgments *are* public, that is, shared" (*CR* 31). Note though that our agreement in judgment shows that this sort of agreement cannot be mere convention, for how could we have possibly agreed upon all of the conventions necessary for every potential context?[10] Cavell puts this point forcefully when he notes the astonishment that ought to strike us about this fact about our agreement:

What makes this astonishing, what partly motivates this philosophizing on the subject, is that the extent of agreement is so intimate and pervasive; that we communicate in language as rapidly and completely as we do; and that since we cannot assume that the words we are given have their meaning by nature, we are led to assume they take it from convention; and yet no current idea of "convention" could seem to do the work that words do—there would have to be, we could say, too many conventions in play, one for each shade of each word in each context. We *cannot* have agreed beforehand to all that would be necessary.

CR 31

It is not the case, thereby, that we come to agree about these judgments and conventions piecemeal, at a certain point in time. We rather are in agreement throughout. Compare this to a harmony, as Wittgenstein's use of the German *Übereinstimmung* suggests: the idea that we are somehow "in tune" with each other, possessed of a similar "mood."[11] Note also that emergent here is a fundamentally normative dimension: this sort of pervasive agreement in judgment allows for the possibility of disagreement, and it just is the case that it is always up to me to take a particular relation to this agreement. Another way to put the significance of this point is to note that even if there emerged some sort of linguistic or biological explanation for this agreement, it would not—unless we allow it to—change how we relate to those explanations, a point Cavell raises when he notes that we'd still have to go "on the old things we say and do, bring to light the consequences of our old agreements" (*CR* 32). All of this raises questions about what sort of necessity is involved here, in our agreements in judgments, or in the criteria that they allow us to share.

One way to approach this question—we might call it the "Malcolm-Albritton view," as Cavell does—is to see criteria as providing us something like "almost certainty" and/or justification for our claims. The fact that someone is, say, behaving as if they have a toothache—exhibiting "pain criteria"—in Albritton's words

> can entail that anyone who is aware that the man is behaving in this manner, under these circumstances, is justified in saying that the man has a toothache, in the absence of any special reason to say something more guarded (as, for example, that there is an overwhelming probability that the man has a toothache). Even more roughly: That a man behaves in a certain manner, under certain circumstances, can entail that he almost certainly has a toothache.[12]

Note the way in which Albritton hedges here; terms like "almost certainly" and "under these circumstances" and "overwhelming probability" all are vague, we might even say empty in this context. We seem only able "to preserve the certainty of the connection between a criterion and what it is a criterion of only at the price of never knowing with certainty that the criterion is satisfied" (*CR* 41). What's emerging here is the importance of context to our linguistic capabilities and actualizations. The question of context, however, cannot be settled solely by philosophy, as if we might sketch the context—once and for all—in the way in which philosophers sketch thought experiments in their latest articles. We simply cannot learn what the relevant circumstances are—for us, for the present moment—until we talk to each other, and that's potentially the case every single time we talk. And *that* is no different from "coming to know what things are, what people do" (*CR* 43). Part of grasping a concept is also grasping the sorts of circumstances that allow you to use it (of course the use of a particular concept may be hesitant or slow-going—*is* this artwork beautiful? *Is* he an evil man? *Was* that an insult?).

Putting things in this way just seems to raise a variety of new questions, especially about how we do come to learn such things. Note also, though, that it fundamentally alters the epistemological tenor of the sort of questions that Malcolm and Albritton raised about their foundational example of the criteria of pain. Cavell broaches this point by asking whether the view that's emerged implies that there are "no criteria for the existence, the occurrence, of the pain itself?" He continues by pointing out that in such a case:

> I might ask what "the pain itself" is. Or I could say: There are none that go essentially beyond the criteria for the behavior's being pain-behavior. Then how can we ever know whether another person is actually *suffering* pain? If I had truly motivated the appearance of that question, we would now wish to give full, not what is called "rhetorical," force to the question, What makes us think we might never know? That is to say, we would at such a point be moved to investigate, to try to uncover the source of our disappointment with human knowledge as such. *That is a way of putting what it is I take criteria, conceived as Wittgenstein conceived them, to enable us to do.*"
>
> CR 44, second emphasis added

What I take Cavell to highlight is that these sorts of skeptical questions are the beginning of any investigation. It is up to us to investigate why we are talking, to what ends, and how—indeed, even for how long. In what sort of situations would questions around the application of criteria—especially the criteria of pain—emerge as (strictly) epistemological questions? Another way to put this point is to stress that criteria "do not determine the certainty of statements, but the application of the concepts employed in statements" (*CR* 45). If that's so, then in such cases, the criteria for the application of a concept are satisfied: the alternative context is dependent on or derivative from— parasitic, we might say— the original context. What emerges in these types of imagined scenarios is in fact a revelation that these are not questions exclusively of knowledge, and this is why Cavell suggests that Wittgenstein affirms the thesis of skepticism, "takes it as *undeniable*, and so shifts its weight" (*CR* 45).

Another way to register the question that's appeared here is to ask whether Cavell is simply pursuing the route that many others before him—from pragmatists to certain ordinary language philosophers—have: is Cavell here merely denying the forcefulness of the skeptical position? On such a view, skepticism is a standing possibility, but it is one that—to speak with Hume—is essentially irrelevant to our everyday existence, where skeptical concerns "vanish like smoke and leave the most determined skeptic in the same condition as other mortals."[13] Quite the opposite. While Cavell views skepticism as a "*natural* possibility" of the human condition, he concludes from this that thereby no *particular* case of skepticism could serve as a paradigm case for refuting or confirming skepticism. Skepticism is a global phenomenon, and *any* instance of language is possibly subject to skepticism. That is our (human) condition—our fate. None of this, however, means that *every* case is *always* so subject, only that the skeptical problematic can emerge with any linguistic operation.

Putting things in this way, at a certain high-altitude view, raises questions about the general relationship between skepticism and the everyday. To pursue the thought that we might refute or dismiss the skeptic—pursued in various ways by figures as diverse as Hume, Kant, Moore, and Austin—would be to misunderstand or to warp what the everyday is like, especially to fail to understand what our linguistic lives and capacities amount to, what they ultimately *are* for and to us. Cavell thereby blocks any dismissal of the skeptic; the skeptic's concerns are not unwarranted. At the same time, Cavell refuses the skeptic's conclusion; it just is not the case that such a global condemnation of our powers of knowledge is warranted. Such a strategy is also one that Cavell finds in Austin's work. When Austin, in his examples involving goldfinches, raises various questions about their modes of existing (is it a live goldfinch? a painting of one? a stuffed goldfinch? We might now add: a hologram or robot goldfinch?), he uses those examples to note the extent to which context deeply matters to the possibility of skepticism altogether (*PP* 77–89). When we are discussing particular objects, Cavell—following Austin—notes that "the difference between real and imaginary, between existence and absence, is not a criterial difference, not one of recognition." In such a case, answering the question of whether we are wrong about any particular object "depends on whether the question I am asked is one of identification or of something else (something I waver between calling existence and reality). The problem, or something I am trying to make a problem, is: How do I know whether I am asked the one or whether the other?" (*CR* 51). Austin puts a related point in a characteristically concise way when he highlights that language is not predictive, the "future can always prove it wrong." With respect to goldfinches, but also to any object or concept we might employ, the future "can always . . . make us *revise our ideas*" (*PP* 88–89, Austin's emphasis).

In reviewing how doubts can arise, however, Cavell notices an interesting fact about the sort of examples that Austin marshals and the sorts of examples that arise in traditional epistemology. When it comes to the latter's concerns, the objects in question "are ones specifically about which there just is no problem of recognition or identification or description . . . the only 'problem,' should it arise, would be not to say what they are but to say whether we can know that they exist, are real, are actually there" (*CR* 52). The same is not true of Austin's examples, where the whole point of the examples is always about recognition, identification, and/or description. In order to countenance the contrast that his discovery reveals, Cavell introduces a distinction between what he terms "generic objects" and "specific objects." A specific object maps onto our everyday conception of a particular object. A generic object, however, raises

> the problem, one might say, of the phenomenology of materiality. When those objects present themselves to the epistemologist, he is not taking one as opposed to another, interested in its features as peculiar to it and nothing else. He would rather, so to speak, have an unrecognizable *something* there if he could, an anything, a that-ness. What comes to him is an island, a body surrounded by air, a tiny earth. What is at stake for him in the object is materiality as such, externality altogether.
>
> *CR* 53

The generic nature of such an object is exactly the point, since it guarantees that no person's particular context is necessary for recognizing them. Indeed, "*no one's position, with respect to identifying them, is better than anyone else's* (*CR* 56, Cavell's emphases).

Leaning on this discovery, Cavell proposes another insight: neither the traditional epistemologist (here a stand-in for anyone who raises such "general" sorts of questions about "general objects") nor the ordinary language critic of such procedures (Austin, with his targeted invocation of "specific" objects) provides a plausible, compelling—we might say: accurate—explanation of how skeptical doubts arise. Both of them, in a deep sense, have strayed far from a proper understanding of how language works, where there is always a *point* to someone saying something. As Cavell puts it, "'because it is true' is not a *reason* or basis for saying anything, it does not constitute the point of your saying something" (*CR* 206). Cavell thus asks of Austin:

> What did I want to know? What, or how much, did I claim to know when I claimed there was a goldfinch in the garden? Did I take my claim to penetrate the bird and to stake a claim against anything untoward inside it? What extent of power have I given over to reality in opening my judgment toward it? What stake have I made in earning the claim's attention upon reality at all?—What is an empirical judgment?
> *CR* 58

An empirical judgment is always context-dependent: sometimes we claim things because they're true, other times because they're absurd. Sometimes we speak because we want to know, sometimes we want to laugh or cry or be outraged. Sometimes we speak and make claims in order to figure out where we stand, other times to determine where our interlocutors stand. Sometimes we merely play with our words, bored as we are, while at other times, a wrong word could end the relationship between us, indeed might end either one of us (the world just is oftentimes cruel, and people sometimes destroy for very little). The contexts that determine what we say, and how, are so variable that we can never decide how or what we are claiming once and for all—as Cavell puts it, "making sure . . . is not done once and for all, not by human kind" (*CR* 59). This is why Cavell concludes his thoughts with the idea that we might understand what I have been describing here as a "field of sense," where that is meant to suggest that what matters—what such a field opens up—are the plethora of ways in which we can make sense to each other and to ourselves. Such a field, importantly, "is broader than any a priori bargain knows. Science, history, magic, myth, superstition, religion, are all in that field" (*CR* 63).[14]

Taking such a point seriously is to be drawn to Wittgenstein's (and Cavell's) focus on grammar. No object in our world has a solitary existence (even objects that are one of a kind); rather there is a holism that animates our entire world and the things that we might say about it.[15] Cavell marshals the example of a chair:

> It is part of the grammar of the word "chair" that *this* is what we call "to sit on a chair" [. . .]. That you use this object *that* way, sit on it *that* way, is our criterion for calling it a chair. You *can* sit on a cigarette, or on a thumb tack, or on a flag pole, but not in *that* way. Can you sit on a table or a tree stump in that (the "grammatical") way? Almost; especially if they are placed against a wall. That is, you can *use* the table or a stump *as* a chair (a place to sit; a seat) in a way you cannot use a tack as

a chair. But so can you use a screw-driver as a dagger; that won't make a screwdriver a dagger. What can *serve as a chair* is not a chair, and nothing would (be said to) serve as a chair if there were no (were nothing we called) (orthodox) chairs. We could say: It is part of the grammar of the word "chair" that *this* is what we call "to serve as a chair."

CR 71, Cavell's emphases

With regard to the chair, "if you don't know all this, and more, you don't know what a chair is; what 'chair' 'means'; what we call a chair; *what* it is you would be certain of ... if you were certain ... that something is a chair" (*CR* 71). Any uncertainty about grammar produces not only an uncertainty in the agent, but in fact, an uncertainty in her world. Holism animates grammar. In a related example, Cavell notes that when the child asks if *this* is Manhattan, we are tempted to point to *something*, but that any such pointing is arbitrary, incomplete, not liable to capture what the child is asking after (or what we take the child to be asking). That is because one needs a wide range of other concepts, grammatical nuances, and moves in order to understand the concept of Manhattan (cities, people, location, time, space, and so forth) (*CR* 74). In this sense, criteria "establish the position of the concept of an 'object' in our system of concepts" (*CR* 76).

In such a case, there is an important distinction that emerges between the way in which Austin and Wittgenstein deploy criteria. For the former, if you lack a certain criterion, you are merely missing a piece of information. For the latter, on the other hand, you lack a piece of a (the) world. As Cavell puts it,

> but if you do not know the grammatical criteria of Wittgensteinian objects, then you lack, as it were, not only a piece of information or knowledge, but the possibility of acquiring any information about such objects *überhaupt*; you cannot be told the name of that object, because there is as yet no *object* of that kind for you to attach a forthcoming name to: the possibility of finding out what it is officially called is not yet open to you.

CR 77

The child simply cannot be told what Manhattan is because the child's world as yet has no cities.

To begin to conclude, it is important to understand that in a deep sense, for Cavell (and allegedly for Wittgenstein) such an understanding of criteria is the beginning of our inquiry into language, but this is exactly because the inquiry is now no longer (artificially) constrained merely to epistemological concerns. Nonetheless, it also just is the case that criteria are ultimately disappointing, and this is so for at least two reasons. On one hand, criteria are never exhaustive because they change as our grammar changes, as our world changes, as we change. On the other hand, they are never exhaustive because they are normative: each one of us, in deploying them, has a say in what they *ought* to be. With any interlocutor, and with regard to any criteria deployed between the two of us, "adding what he *says* just makes matters even worse; for now I have to *believe* him, and determine whether he means by his descriptions what I would mean if I gave them" (*CR* 79, Cavell's emphases). But believing him is just the beginning of a possible range of responses. Imagine someone in front of you is in pain: groaning, wincing, howling, and so forth. Make the description as fine-tuned as you would like: import, to speak with Theodor W. Adorno, as much "carrion, stench, and putrefaction" as you would like.[16] One thing that the grammar of pain always implies, that simply cannot be left out in any serious investigation—although it can always be elided or overlooked or ignored—is the call for a response. Pain demands a response (of course, the nature of that response can be varied: from pity to fury to laughter to satisfaction to shock to compassion to whatever else besides). Part of knowing what pain is, is knowing that it demands a response (*CR* 82).

Talk of a response, though, just highlights the extent to which what is emerging here is a problem of acknowledgment. As Cavell puts it, "my condition is not exactly that I have to *put* the other's life there; and not exactly that I have to *leave* it there either. I (have to) *respond* to it, or refuse to respond. It calls upon me; it calls me out. I have to acknowledge it" (*CR* 84, Cavell's emphases). Note the extent to which I am at the center of this drama. In one of his last published works, Cavell will simply claim that "I am the scandal" of skepticism (*PDAT* 151). In *The Claim of Reason,* Cavell notes that his discussion "makes it seem that the philosophical problem of knowledge is something I impose on these matters; that I am the philosophical problem." He responds: "I am. It is in me that the circuit of communication is cut; I am the stone on which the wheel breaks. What is disappointing about criteria?" (*CR* 83). We might as well rephrase Cavell's question as: *who* is disappointing? In this context, note how Cavell frames Wittgenstein's project, noting that "what interests Wittgenstein about philosophizing is that it does tend to put the one philosophizing out of agreement with ordinary words (i.e., with his own words when he is not philosophizing)." Because others are involved in our words, though, because a relationship—the acknowledgment between us—is at stake, what someone philosophizing has said is not thereby "meaningless," indeed the words spoken are "compulsively true" (*CR* 34). There is a distinct and important *ethical* project coming into focus.[17]

We are thereby back to where we started, but our question—how is it that we as much as come to understand each other?—is now inflected in ethical terms. Criteria simply cannot guarantee that we come to agreement, and yet this can seem to us "essential" about what they ought to do. When it comes to criteria, "I have to know what they are for; I have to accept them, use them. This itself makes my use of them seem arbitrary, or private—as though they were never shared, or as if our sharing of them is either a fantastic accident or a kind of mass folly" (*CR* 83). Yet, it is only in sharing them that I could come to have them in the first place; but my fate—our fate—is not to share them forever.

In a deep sense, our linguistic condition is thereby also our philosophical condition, what it means to *do* philosophy, what the "education of grownups" is (*CR* 125). There is in such a conception—like in Cavell's invocation of criteria—a deeply ethical commitment, one that requires us to take responsibility for who we are, for what we say and why (and what we read and why), and also to take responsibility for those that we talk to and why (and those we read and why). To conceive of philosophy as a set of given problems is analogous to conceiving of criteria as already set, thereby warping what our present experience might be (both of the world and of philosophy, and of the relationship between the two, ultimately of each other). On such a view, we locate criteria, as much as philosophical problems, solely in the past, and thereby render our experience of the present impossible, since the past may or may not be applicable or proper to and in the present. Analogously, we might push the discovery of criteria or philosophical problems to the future ("outsourcing" them to others), thereby equally voiding possible experience in the present. In either case, our choices have an effect equally on who we are, and on who you are and can be. Our words—as much as our philosophical canons—exclude and include, sever and connect. Our learning is thereby never over, not even when the conversation ends (not even when we end it)—and that for better or for worse.[18]

Notes

1   The two pieces that Cavell cites explicitly (*CR* 7) are Norman Malcolm, "Wittgenstein's Philosophical Investigations," *The Philosophical Review* 63, no. 4 (1954): 530–59, and Rogers Albritton, "On Wittgenstein's Use of the Term 'Criterion,'" *The Journal of Philosophy* 56, no. 22 (1959): 845–57.
2   As they are on Albritton's reading, where because of this epistemological register—because of the idea that criteria are "a phenomenon by which one may know"— Albritton is led to conclude that, in the case of the phenomena he was considering (most notably, a toothache), he "cannot discuss here the question whether there *are* criteria." See Albritton, "On Wittgenstein's Use of the Term 'Criterion,'" 855 (emphasis removed), 856 (emphasis in original). For Albritton, then, Wittgenstein's criteria are aimed at granting us knowledge and are also seemingly suggested to be inadequate for that task.
3   In the rest of the essay, I will generally refer to "Wittgenstein," not bothering with the specification "Cavell's Wittgenstein," although that should be taken as given. It is simply not possible for me to engage the massive corpus of scholarship on Wittgenstein here, except as necessary in order to clarify Cavell's views.
4   I register this point several ways in my "Nothing to Know: The Epistemology of Moral Perfectionism in Adorno and Cavell," *Idealistic Studies* 44, no. 1 (2015), and "Education for the World: Adorno and Cavell," in *Dissonant Methods: Undoing Discipline in the Humanities Classroom*, ed. Ada Jaarsma and Kit Dobson (Alberta: University of Alberta Press, 2020). For explorations and a book-length elaboration, see Andrew Norris, ed., *The Claim to Community: Essays on Stanley Cavell and Political Philosophy* (Palo Alto: Stanford University Press, 2006), and *Becoming Who We Are: Politics and Practical Philosophy in the Work of Stanley Cavell* (Oxford: Oxford University Press, 2017).
5   The difference is captured quite well by Avner Baz, who writes:

> One recurrent metaphor in McDowell is that of "our space of reasons." And what I've said so far seems to me to suggest that if that metaphor is to be truly helpful to us for understanding our wording of our world, then we would need

to think of our space of reasons as including reasons, not just for "holding a belief" or for "taking something to be true," but also for noting, or remarking, or claiming, or otherwise saying something about something, here and now.

See Avner Baz, "On When Words Are Called For: Cavell, McDowell, and the Wording of the World," *Inquiry* 46 (2003): 494. I return to this point below.

6   On this point, see also Norris, *Becoming Who We Are*, 95ff.
7   Stanley Cavell, "Philosophy as the Education of Grownups," in Naoko Saito and Paul Standish, eds., *Stanley Cavell and the Education of Grownups* (New York: Fordham University Press, 2012), 29.
8   See Norris, *Becoming Who We Are*, 100.
9   This is still a controversial point in the scholarship on Wittgenstein. For example, see Daniele Moyal-Sharrock, "Too Cavellian a Wittgenstein: Wittgenstein's Certainty, Cavell's Scepticism," in Anat Matar, ed., *Understanding Wittgenstein, Understanding Modernism* (London: Bloomsbury, 2017), 92–110. Moyal-Sharrock notes that "to think that for Wittgenstein, the end of justification means the beginning of skepticism, is to understand the opposite of what Wittgenstein means" (107). This is hardly Cavell's suggestion: skepticism doesn't (always) "begin" here (it may or it may not—thus its constant truth), but rather skepticism just is the fact that justifications can always come to an end.
10 The same sort of insight about how forms of life function writ large is what allows us to make sense of how the social contract tradition can be leveraged for understanding ways in which a form of life may be said to be pathological, as in the work of Carole Pateman (the sexual contract) and Charles W. Mills (the racial contract). See Carole Pateman, *The Sexual Contract* (Cambridge: Polity, 1988), and Charles W. Mills, *The Racial Contract* (Ithaca: Cornell University Press, 2014).
11 For an excellent overview of the difficulty of translating this German word, see David Wellbery, "Stimmung," trans. Rebecca Pohl, *New Formations* 93, no. 93 (2018): 6–45. There are, of course, also deep resonances here between Wittgenstein and Heidegger. On this point, see Lucilla Guidi, "Moods as Groundlessness of the Human Experience. Heidegger and Wittgenstein on *Stimmung*," *Philosophia* 45, no. 4 (Dec 2017): 1599–1611. More broadly, see Lee Braver, *Groundless Grounds: A Study of Wittgenstein and Heidegger* (Cambridge, MA: MIT Press, 2012); Richard Rorty, "Wittgenstein, Heidegger, and the Reification of Language," in *Philosophical Papers, Volume 2: Essays on Heidegger and Others* (Cambridge: Cambridge University Press, 1991), 50–65.
12 Albritton, "On Wittgenstein's Use of the Term 'Criterion,'" 856.
13 David Hume, *An Enquiry Concerning Human Understanding*, ed. Eric Steinberg (Indianapolis: Hackett, 1993), 110.
14 For an excellent elaboration of the full scope of what such a position implies, see Avner Baz, *When Words Are Called For: A Defense of Ordinary Language Philosophy* (Cambridge, MA: Harvard University Press, 2012).
15 It is this aspect of Wittgenstein that has made him amenable to contemporary Hegelians like Robert Brandom and John McDowell. For more on the analogies between Wittgenstein and Hegel, especially on this point, see Terry Pinkard, "Innen, Aussen und Lebensformen: Hegel und Wittgenstein," in Christoph Halbig, Michael Quante, Ludwig Siep, eds., *Hegels Erbe* (Frankfurt am Main: Suhrkamp, 2004), 254–92.
16 Theodor W. Adorno, *Metaphysics: Concepts and Problems*, ed. Rolf Tiedemann, trans. Edmund Jephcott (Stanford: Stanford University Press, 2000), 117.

17 See my "On the Ethical Basis of Language: Some Themes in Davidson, Cavell, and Levinas," *Journal for Cultural and Religious Theory* 14, no. 2 (Spring 2015): 241–66.
18 In this way, there are deep analogies here with Rorty's stress on conversation despite the important difference (of course, one among many) that for Cavell there is no point at which we—or at least not we as linguistic agents—might conceive of a world where "love is the only law." See Richard Rorty, Gianni Vattimo, and Santiago Zabala, "Dialogue: What Is Religion's Future after Metaphysics?," in *The Future of Religion*, ed. Santiago Zabala (New York: Columbia University Press, 2005), 55–82. For more on this point (without reference to Cavell), see my "Rorty and (the Politics of) Love," *Graduate Faculty Philosophy Journal* 40, no. 1 (2019): 65–78.

13

Skepticism

Jeroen Gerrits

Introduction: Cavellian Skepticism in Three Steps

The issue of skepticism, broadly understood as the philosophical challenge to the possibility of establishing human knowledge and beliefs beyond doubt, motivates Stanley Cavell's entire oeuvre and deeply informs his take on the modern arts (among which film, literature, theater, music, and painting receive most attention). While Cavell's writing is grounded historically and in constant conversation with contemporary scholars and philosophers, his approach to skepticism is quite idiosyncratic. Here I will elaborate how Cavell's singular view on the matter emerges from three moves or steps. The first step concerns a critical differentiation between three positions regarding skepticism: its impetus, its conclusion, and its defeat or repudiation. While skeptical arguments usually play out amongst proponents defending either of the latter two positions, Cavell warns against both the skeptical conclusion and its defeat, even while embracing the impetus. Cavell's second step, which follows from this first, turns skepticism from an epistemological problem to a moral concern. Cavell evaluates the three positions accordingly. Finally, Cavell differentiates between epistemological skepticism, which centers on knowledge of objects or of the world as a whole, and skepticism about other minds, whereby the latter engages the question whether we can know others to be human beings (rather than, say, animated dolls, perfected robots, or demons in disguise). Regarding skepticism with respect to other minds Cavell again draws out the moral consequences.

The following looks at these three steps in more detail. Since the concept and application of the criterion underlies each of them, I will begin by outlining its significance in light of Cavell's approach to skepticism.

On Recognition and Existence: The Use of Criteria

Cavell initially approaches the question of skepticism obliquely. During his early career his primary philosophical interests center on ordinary language philosophy, most notably Ludwig Wittgenstein's *Philosophical Investigations* and the teachings of J. L. Austin (whose classes at Harvard University Cavell attended while completing his graduate studies there). The question of skepticism impresses itself on him when he encounters scholars (Cavell specifically has the "Malcolm-Albritton view" in mind [*CR* 37]) who take ordinary language philosophy to refute skepticism. In his earliest writings, collected in *Must We Mean What We Say?*, but also including sections of his magnum opus, *The Claim of Reason*, Cavell argues against the idea that Wittgenstein and Austin take the actual use of language to counter the skeptical idea that we reach a point at which we can no longer justify what we say and do. Cavell thus enters the debate not by making a case for or against skepticism per se, but by countering what others might construe as the overcoming of skepticism.

An important argument among the various objections Cavell brings to bear against the idea of ordinary language philosophy as a bulwark against skepticism revolves around the use of criteria (the sufficient condition, ground, or basis of a knowledge claim), a topic discussed by both Wittgenstein (as part of his private language argument in *Philosophical Investigations*) and Austin (especially in the essay "Other Minds").[1]

From Wittgenstein, Cavell picks up the question how I can know someone to be in pain. While an expression of pain (say, groaning) may well mean something else in other contexts (clearing one's throat, responding to a joke), Cavell understands Wittgenstein as positing that I should not have problems, considering the circumstances in which I engage with a groaning person, to determine whether its current expression is one of pain indeed. However, knowing that the expression is one of pain does not mean that I know the groaning person to *be* in pain: she may be well be feigning. The point about criteria is that they can help us recognize *what* something is, not *that* it is. They tell us, in other words, of something's *identity* rather than its *existence*; they speak, as Cavell writes, "not of its *being* so, but of its being *so.*" Even if someone were feigning or rehearsing pain-behavior, we can know that it is *pain* the groan expresses. Hence Cavell writes, "We *retain the concept* (here, of pain) whose application these criteria determine... Criteria do not determine the certainty of statements, but the application of the concepts in the statements" (*CR* 45, Cavell's emphases).

Cavell further explains that criteria crucially apply to the recognition or identification of things rather than to their existence by distinguishing between what he calls specific and generic objects, arguing that skeptics have a preference for using the latter in their arguments. The differentiation between specific and generic objects does not imply that world falls apart into two classes or categories of objects: in principle, any object can be regarded as either. The distinction rather marks "the spirit in which an object is under discussion, the kind of problem that has arisen about it" (*CR* 53). The kinds of problems that arise with specific objects are ones of identification, as in the example of recognizing a goldfinch, which Cavell takes from Austin.[2]

> Claim: There is a goldfinch in the garden.
> Request for Basis: How do you know?
> Basis: From the red head.
> Ground for Doubt: But that's not enough; woodpeckers also have red heads.
>
> *CR* 132

To Cavell it is no surprise that skeptics don't bring up examples such as this. For, as Austin argues, in a specific case like the goldfinch there is a point at which grounds for doubts lose their pertinence, when "enough is enough," namely when our bases are covered by sufficient marks and features (new basis: from its eye markings, the shape of its head) to rule out other possible identifications. Moreover, if I fail to justify my initial claim of seeing a goldfinch, all we have discovered is that I have more to learn in the realm of ornithology; nothing, so far, leads me to doubt the existence of the bird or anything beyond this bird.

This is different in the case of generic objects, which are objects whose features are not peculiar to it (or anyway they are not at stake) and which are not opposed to other objects that may share some of those features. The traditional epistemologist, Cavell writes, "would rather, so to speak, have an unrecognizable *something* there if he could, an anything, a thatness" (*CR* 53, Cavell's emphasis). In want of such generic anythings, skeptics (and epistemologists trying to defeat them) rather stick to second best examples, such as pieces of wax, tomatoes, tables, or envelopes (all of which have indeed been brought up by various philosophers). These are most ordinary objects anyone would recognize precisely because they have nothing special about them. Now if someone doubts my claim that "I see a tomato on the countertop" when the tomato is in plain sight for both of us, the point of the question "How do you know?" would be missed if I would now aim to rule out other red vegetables or round objects. By contrast, the more relevant, if all but redundant, basis "because I see it" may now give rise to different grounds for doubt, such as "Do you see *all* of it?" (meaning the inside, the backside) or "Aren't you hallucinating?" For the real question when it comes to "an anything" is whether we can know anything at all. That is: can we know for sure that it exists, whatever it is?

This discussion of Austin points out, then, that criteria apply to specific objects, which give rise to problems of identification, whereas generic objects give rise to problems of existence, for which there are no criteria. Put more generally, *there are no criteria* for distinguishing between reality and dreams (or hallucinations, simulations, etc.). Hence Cavell concludes that ordinary language philosophy's "appeal to criteria, though it takes its importance from the problem of skepticism, is not, and is not meant to be, a refutation of skepticism ... That is, it does not negate the concluding thesis of skepticism, that we do not know with certainty of the existence of the external world (or of other minds)" (*CR* 37).

Three Positions Regarding Skepticism

That concluding remark features two of the three positions Cavell distinguishes vis-à-vis skepticism: its conclusion and its refutation. The conclusion the skeptic arrives at by methodically applying doubt to generic objects is that we cannot know anything at all (with certainty), so that, for all we know, the world may just as well not exist. When Austin and Wittgenstein come to the defense of our use of criteria, they do not refute the skeptic's concluding thesis, because criteria do not apply to the existence of (things in) the world itself.

Crucially, however, Cavell further argues that it does not follow from this double negation (the repudiation of the claim that the skeptic's repudiation of knowledge has been overcome by ordinary language philosophy) that we are to affirm, or are forced to accept, the skeptical conclusion instead. Rather than getting stuck on the question how we can *ever* know (that another is in pain, that the world exists, anything at all), Cavell suggests that we need to investigate the reasons for our disappointment in our response. It is as though we think we ought to have a definitive answer but fail to come up with one. Hence the disappointed concerns human knowledge as such, if not ourselves, as creatures with the capacity for knowledge, for failing to live up to its (or our) full capacity. To Cavell, however, the *limitations* of knowledge are not *failures* of it.

This leads to the third position Cavell distinguishes from both the skeptical conclusion and its refutation, namely its impetus, which contains what Cavell, not without irony, dubs the "truth of skepticism." Starting from an attempt to justify our very conviction in the existence of a generic object, the skeptic, failing to do so, concludes with the thesis that we do not and cannot know (with certainty) that the external world exists, or that anything is real. The skeptic, in other words, argues not just for the want of a *justification* of the initial conviction; she concludes against this very *conviction* itself (*WV* 188–89).

While Cavell responds critically to this conclusion, as we shall see shortly, it is hard to overestimate the importance of this impetus for Cavell's overall assessment of skepticism. The attempt to justify our conviction in the reality or existence of anything runs up against the limitations of knowledge. By "limitations of knowledge" Cavell not only means that there are things beyond its reach, as opposed to things human beings are capable of knowing (with certainty). The Kantian defense against skepticism, which claims that we may not know the nature of things in themselves but can acquire knowledge of the way things appear to us, would be one variation of limitations in this sense. For Cavell, the idea of "limitations of knowledge" further means that there are human ways of relating to the world "which are not exhausted in the capacity of knowing things" (*CR* 54). This, Cavell writes, is "what I have called the truth of skepticism, or what I might call the moral of skepticism, namely, that the human creature's basis in the world as a whole, its relation to the world as such, is not that of knowing, anyway not what we think of as knowing" (*CR* 241). Or, as he specifies in an early essay on *King Lear*:

> [W]e think skepticism must mean we cannot know the world exists, and hence that perhaps there isn't one... Whereas what skepticism suggests is that since we cannot know the world exists, its presentness cannot be a function of knowing. The world is to be *accepted*; as the presentness of other minds is not to be known, but acknowledged.
>
> *MWM* 324, Cavell's emphasis

Accepting the World: From Epistemology to Morality

The question of acknowledgment of other minds will be discussed in the next section. Let us first look more closely at the reason for Cavell to state that the world is to be accepted. For this is the pivot around which skepticism turns from an epistemological into a moral concern.

That the world *is* to be accepted does not means that it *has* to be accepted, if by the latter we mean that we have no choice about it. What we have no choice about is that the world's existence is a matter of accepting it (or not), rather than a matter of knowing it (or failing to). Put in Wittgensteinian terms, we could say that the world's existence falls under the *grammatical* scope of the word "acceptance." Indeed, that the world *is* to be accepted precisely means that we *do* have a choice about it—this is what makes it a moral issue. It is not moral in the sense that we are to accept the world *as* it is—as though Cavell were a conservative defender of the status quo—only *that* it is; we are to accept its *being*, not its being *so*. (The only aphorism from Wittgenstein's *Tractatus Logico-Philosophicus* Cavell occasionally cites, for example at *WV* 113, is aphorism 6.44: "Not *how* the world is, but *that* it is, is the Mystical.")

If we were to accept the world beyond our knowing it, we would primarily accept its "standoffishness" (*NYUA* 86), its autonomous existence at a (metaphysical) distance from us. Cavell indeed practically defines skepticism in terms of this distance: "The name skepticism speaks, as I use it, of some new, or new realization of, human distance from the world, or some withdrawal of the world" (*CF* 116). Given this context we can now see that drawing the skeptical conclusion implies a choice, in the absence of knowing, *not to accept* the world's existence. Not to do so, however, amounts to a withdrawal in isolation, Cavell argues, as it renders the metaphysical distance to the world absolute. It is on that ground that Cavell rejects the skeptical conclusion: to proclaim that the world may just as well not exist amounts, before all else, to a declaration of *our* absence from it. "The world's absence," Cavell writes, "is only the history of our turnings from it" (*WV* 114).

Cavell further argues that the attempt to defeat the skeptic, by contrast, amounts to a denial of our distance to the world, or postulates that it is to be overcome once and for all. This would require that we grasp the world in thought, hence a mode of "thinking as clutching" which Cavell, in his reading of Emerson's essay "Experience," compares to the effort of trying to catch smoke with our fists, calling it "the most unhandsome part of our condition" (*NYUA* 86). To Cavell, this mode of thinking not only amounts to a denial of *the world's* standoffishness, it denies *our own* humanity, or our subjectivity, as it would require an overcoming of human finitude to cover the distance. Adding that the desire to overcome skepticism "is human, it is the human drive to transcend itself, make itself inhuman, which would not end until, as in Nietzsche, the human is over," Cavell concludes that "this struggle with skepticism, with its threat or temptation, is endless" (*NYUA* 57).

Warning against the moral implications of both the skeptical conclusion and the desire to overcome skepticism as such, Cavell does embrace the skeptical impetus insofar as it accepts the world's autonomy, its independence from our thought, its distance from each one of us. Rather than withdrawing in isolation or demanding that the human transcend its limitation, Cavell posits that each of us remains responsible for finding connections to the world. The endlessness of the struggle notwithstanding, he suggests that we reverse the mode of thinking into clutching's opposite by allowing ourselves to be attracted to the world, to be drawn to it. Doing so, we may not live without doubt. Rather, to live "in the face of doubt, eyes happily shut, would be to fall in love with the world" (*CR* 431). The world, at any rate, will be dead to us should we fail to keep turning towards it.

Skepticism about Other Minds

That the three positions regarding skepticism are evaluated based on their moral implications, and that they place a call upon each one of us, becomes even more pertinent in the case of skepticism about other minds, which Cavell distinguishes from epistemological skepticism. The Wittgensteinian case discussed above—whether I can know someone to be in pain—is already an example of skepticism of this kind. We should indeed note from the outset that Cavell concludes towards the end of *The Claim of Reason*: "Over and over, an apparent symmetry or asymmetry between skepticism with respect to the external world and skepticism with respect to other minds has collapsed, on further reflection, into its opposite" (*CR* 451). While important differences nevertheless remain worthy of consideration, the basic approach to the two forms of skepticism is indeed similar, as can be gleaned from the following passage from the early essay "Knowing and Acknowledging," which brings up the example of pain:

> The skeptic comes up with this scary conclusion—that we can't know what another person is feeling because we can't have the same feeling, feel his pain, feel it the way he feels it—and we are shocked; we must refute him, he would make it impossible ever to be attended to in the right way. But he doesn't *begin* with a shock. He begins with a full appreciation of the decisively significant fact that I may be suffering when no one else is, and that no one (else) may know (or care?); and that others may be suffering and I not know, which is equally appalling.
>
> *MWM*, 246–47

As in the case of epistemological skepticism, then, we can distinguish in skepticism about other minds the three positions discussed previously: the conclusion, its defeat, and the impetus. The concluding thesis of the skeptic of other minds is that I may never know that another is in pain, that the other ever has any genuine human feelings, or that she is a human being at all (rather than a perfected automaton, a non-human in human guise, a humanoid something simulating human expressions, say of pain). To (satisfy the human desire to) refute this conclusion, I would need to feel what you feel, suffer your pain, *be* you. In short, I would have to deny the truth that initially inspired the skeptic's inquiry: the fact of human separateness, the (metaphysical) distance between us.

When you express suffering, however, my task at hand is not to verify or ascertain my knowledge of your being in pain: I am called upon to *do* something. Indeed, Cavell argues that my knowledge is not enough here: I need to go beyond it by *acknowledging* your being in pain. Crucially, acknowledgment takes a different form than knowledge.

To acknowledge your pain does not imply that I feel what you feel or that I express it the way you do. Far from being an expression of pain, my acknowledgment of yours is an expression of sympathy. Moreover, it is not expressed by proving something about you, but by revealing something about me, and, as such, Cavell writes, it is "evidenced equally by its failure as by its success" (*MWM* 263). Whereas a failure of knowledge may be a piece of ignorance, a mere absence or blank, a failure of acknowledgment marks the presence of something on my part: perhaps I am confused, indifferent, exhausted, or cold. A refusal or inability to acknowledge someone else's pain, at any rate, is a matter of avoidance rather than ignorance. Consequently "the slack of acknowledgment can never be taken up by knowledge" (*CR* 338).

Empathic Projection

An important difference between epistemological skepticism and skepticism about other minds comes to the fore when considering failed cases. In epistemological skepticism, as we have seen, Cavell distinguishes between specific and generic objects. If on occasion I fail to recognize a specific object, nothing of major consequence follows beyond that occasion (what I thought was a goldfinch turns out to be a woodpecker). But when I fail to respond satisfactorily to your question of how I know that a generic object exists when I am in a best case of knowing it (e.g. when nothing specifically prevents me from seeing it)—if I fail, for example, because it turns out you had hypnotized me when I was sure to see a tomato on the countertop—the skeptic will be quick to infer that I can never rule out the possibility that I am hypnotized, and hence that I cannot know anything with certainty.

As discussed, when it comes to your pain, I cannot, from your expression of it, know that it exists—meaning that you are actually in pain, suffering from it. It is a matter of acknowledgment. Of course I can choose not to acknowledge your pain, but then I am still doing something by withholding it—being cold towards you, for example—which reveals something about me. Now if I do acknowledge your pain by expressing sympathy, and you slap me on the back laughingly because you just fooled me into believing you were in pain, will I, in my surprise (or hurt), further doubt that you are having fun at my expense? Do I continue to doubt that you have any genuine human feelings at all? If not, I apparently do not infer from a failed case that I may *never* be right to acknowledge someone else's humanness.

Recognizing someone as a human being is not analogous to recognizing a specific object, then, since the identification is not merely *of* someone but *with* someone. We recognize objects by seeing them, but the identification of human beings requires something more than mere seeing. While we may not, strictly speaking, *acknowledge* the existence of human minds in a general manner, Cavell does suggest that we do, and have to, *project* humanness onto others around us. This something more than merely seeing others is what he calls *empathic projection*.

The concept of empathic projection of otherness can help us see that the existence of other minds is not subject to the same inductions as generic objects are in the hands of the skeptic. If I cannot rule out the possibility that I am hallucinating when I claim to see a tomato here on this countertop, the impact of my "failure" does not stop at the tomato. In the absence of marks or features that allow me to distinguish the real from the unreal, the possible hallucination includes the countertop, the whole kitchen, indeed the whole world. Cavell writes: "Hallucination and dreaming happen all at once, seamlessly; they are world-creating, hence they are world-depriving," only to add: "I find that I do not accept this idea of seamlessness of [empathic] projection" (*CR* 424).

The projection of humanness on beings around us always already implies a seam: I, for one, do not project it on tomatoes or goldfinches. It is not unimaginable, however, that on occasion I project humanness on the wrong side of the seam. We should note here that, just as there is no criterion to distinguish the unreal from the real, Cavell argues that there is no criterion, or set of criteria, for what exhibits a human form of life, or states of consciousness (*NYUA* 43). Without claiming that humanoid non-humans exist, he writes:

> [T]he presence of mutants, automata, zombies, androids, etc. would mean that I am almost certainly projecting humanness where it is inappropriate; certainly it would mean that I cannot be certain that I never am. But would this cause me to wonder whether I am ever right to project? The *fact*, so far at least, is that I do not doubt, anyway that I am not prey to skeptical doubt. The others do not vanish when a given case fails me. My experience continues to affix the seam.
>
> *CR* 425, Cavell's emphasis

Cavell thus argues that if what I accepted as a human being "turns out" to be an android or alien, I would not infer that perhaps there are no human beings at all; perhaps everyone is an android. If that were the case, how did I end up with so much as an idea of humanness in the first place? Moreover, were I to stop projecting altogether, I would no longer take any being as a human. But to treat (possible) humans like objects just makes *me* inhuman, immoral. The moral Cavell draws from this imaginary situation is that a given failed case of empathic projection does not lead to the same entailments as a failed case of knowing a generic object. I am not prey to skeptical doubt; not, at least, to the extent that I do not conclude from the presence of a demon that, for all I know, human beings may not exist at all. This in turn is not to deny that there is a skepticism about other minds, for it remains the case that I cannot know (with certainty) that anyone is a human being or not. It is, Cavell concludes, a "limited skepticism" (*CR* 426).

Conclusion: A Death-Dealing Passion

Cavell initially engages skepticism by countering arguments that claim (ordinary language philosophy helps) to overcome the threat of skeptical doubt. Embracing the truth of skepticism by accepting the limitations of human knowledge instead, he nevertheless challenges the skeptical conclusion as well as attempts at repudiating skepticism, and he does so primarily on moral grounds.

Having thus differentiated various positions regarding skepticism generally, Cavell further distinguishes skepticism about other minds from skepticism about the external world. In both cases, Cavell insists that knowledge has its limitations. When we run up against these limitations, we are confronted with a choice that turns skepticism from an epistemological into a moral issue. Having shown that criteria apply neither to the existence of the world nor to the existence of other minds, Cavell's claims that "[t]he world is to be accepted; as the presentness of other minds is not to be known, but acknowledged" (*DK* 95).

Acknowledgement can, in fact, be seen as a special case of acceptance, and its difference from the acceptance of the world is perhaps one of degree rather than of kind. Cavell suggests as much when he writes: "whether I accept the (independent; non-projected) existence of other minds seems *more deeply* up to me, to my attitudes and sensibility, than whether I accept the (independent; non-hallucinated) existence of material objects" (*CR* 42, my emphasis). Even if this difference underlies the further claim that skepticism with respect to other minds is of a more limited kind than external world skepticism, the consequence of failing to accept the existence of either mind or world would render my isolation complete and challenge my sanity. Likewise, an overcoming of either form of skepticism implies an overcoming of separateness, a denial of human distance to the world and to one another, which comes with full potential for tragedy. Despite the fact that the two forms of skepticism are not symmetrical and do not follow identical lines of inquiry, the one does share features that are inflected in the other. Provocatively and imaginatively, Cavell suggests "a death-dealing passion" to exist between the two directions of skepticism, as he finds implied in his suggestion "of the possibility of falling in love with the world" (*CR* 452).

Notes

1 For Austin's essay, see *PP* 76–116.
2 See *MWM* 92.

Notes on Contributors

Andrew Brandel is Associate Instructional Professor of the Social Sciences University of Chicago. His research focuses particularly on the politics of literature and philosophy and on the continued relevance of Romanticism to contemporary social theory. He is the series co-editor of *Thinking from Elsewhere*, Fordham University Press and Associate Editor, *American Anthropologist*. His publications include: *Moving Words: Literature, Memory, and Migration in Berlin* (University of Toronto Press, 2023), which received the DAAD/GSA Prize for the Best Book in Literature and Cultural Studies, Honorable Mention; "A Poet in the Field. The Companionship of Anthropology and Literature" in *Anthropology of this Century* 21 (2018); "The Art of Conviviality" in *Journal of Ethnographic Theory* 6, no. 2 (2016); "Triste Romantik: Ruminations on an Ethnographic Encounter with Philosophy" in *Wording the World: Veena Das and Scenes of Inheritance* (Fordham, 2015); and "Anthropology, Governance and the State" in *The Oxford Handbook of Governance and Limited Statehood* (Oxford, 2018).

Hugo Clémot is Lecturer in Philosophy at Tours University and Researcher at the Center for the Study of Contemporary Philosophy of Paris 1 Sorbonne University. He is interested in aesthetics and moral philosophy, in particular in relation to cinema and TV series. His publications include: *Cinéthique* (Vrin, 2018); *La philosophie d'après le cinéma: une lecture de la Projection du Monde de Stanley Cavell* (Presses Universitaires de Rennes, 2014); *Les jeux philosophiques de la trilogie Matrix* (Vrin, 2011); and *La perception de l'image selon Wittgenstein* (M-Editer, 2010), as well as numerous articles on cinema, TV series, and philosophy.

Élise Domenach is Associate Professor of Film Studies at the Ecole Normale Supérieure in Lyon and member of the editorial board of *Positif* and *Esprit*. She is a philosopher and film critic. Her publications include: *Stanley Cavell. Le cinéma et le scepticisme* (Presses Universitaires de France, 2011); editor and translator of Stanley Cavell, *Le cinéma nous rend-t-il meilleurs?* (Bayard, 2003); and *Le paradigme Fukushima au cinema. Ce que voir veut dire* (Mimesis, 2022).

Piergiorgio Donatelli is Professor of Moral Philosophy at La Sapienza University of Rome. He chairs the PhD program in Philosophy and the History of Philosophy and is the director of the Master in Applied Ethics and Bioethics. He has written on the history of ethics and contemporary moral theory, as well as on J. S. Mill, Cavell, Wittgenstein, Diamond, and Foucault. He is the editor of the journal *Iride. Filosofia e discussione pubblica/Philosophy and Public Discussion*. His publications include: *Manières d'être humain. Une autre philosophie morale* (Vrin, 2015); *Wittgenstein e l'etica*

(Laterza, 1998); *La filosofia morale* (Laterza, 2001, 2nd ed. 2012); *Introduzione a J. S. Mill* (Laterza, 2007); *The Politics of Human Life* (Routledge, 2021)

Eli Friedlander is Laura Schwarz-Kipp Professor of Modern Philosophy at Tel Aviv University. He received his PhD from Harvard, writing his dissertation under the supervision of Stanley Cavell and Burton Dreben on the different manifestations of the distinction between showing and saying in logic, ethics, and aesthetics. His publications include: *Signs of Sense: Reading Wittgenstein's Tractatus* (Harvard, 2000); *J. J. Rousseau: An Afterlife of Words* (Harvard, 2005); *Walter Benjamin: A Philosophical Portrait* (Harvard, 2011); *Expressions of Judgments: An Essay on Kant's Aesthetics* (Harvard , 2015).

Jeroen Gerrits is Associate Professor of Comparative Literature at Binghamton University. His research centers on intersections between film, new media, literature, and philosophy. He is the author of *Cinematic Skepticism: Across Digital and Global Turns* (SUNY Press, 2019) and of a variety of essays on cinema, TV series, and the relation between cinema and philosophy.

Sandra Laugier is Professor of Philosophy at the University of Paris 1 La Sorbonne, Senior Member of Institut Universitaire de France, and Scientific Deputy Director at the Institute for Humanities & Social Sciences (INSHS, *Institut des sciences humaines et sociales*) of the CNRS (the French National Center for Scientific Research). Her interests include moral philosophy, ordinary language philosophy, feminism, and television studies. She has been instrumental in introducing and translating the works of Stanley Cavell in France. Her most recent publications include: *Why We Need Ordinary Language Philosophy* (University of Chicago Press, 2013); *Wittgenstein. Le mythe de l'inexpressivité* (Vrin, 2010); *Pourquoi désobéir en démocratie?* with Albert Ogien (La Découverte, 2010); the collective volume, with contributions by Anne M. Lovell, Stefania Pandolfo, Veena Das and S. Laugier, *Face aux désastres. Une conversation à quatre voix sur la folie, le care et les grandes détresses collectives* (Ithaque, 2013); and editor with Nancy Bauer and Alice Crary of Stanley Cavell, *Here and There: Sites of Philosophy* (Harvard University Press, 2022).

David LaRocca is author, editor, or coeditor of more than a dozen books and a member of the advisory board at *Conversations: The Journal of Cavellian Studies*. He edited *The Thought of Stanley Cavell and Cinema: Turning Anew to the Ontology of Film a Half-Century after* The World Viewed (Bloomsbury, 2022); *Inheriting Stanley Cavell: Memories, Dreams, Reflections* (Bloomsbury, 2020); and *Movies with Stanley Cavell in Mind* (Bloomsbury, 2021). He served as guest editor of a commemorative issue of *Conversations, Acknowledging Stanley Cavell* (no. 7). He edited, annotated, and indexed Stanley Cavell's *Emerson's Transcendental Etudes*; subsequently edited additional books featuring Cavell's work, including *Estimating Emerson: An Anthology of Criticism from Carlyle to Cavell* and *The Bloomsbury Anthology of Transcendental Thought: From Antiquity to the Anthropocene*; and contributed chapters to *Stanley Cavell, Literature,* *and Film: The Idea of America* and *Stanley Cavell and Aesthetic Understanding*. www.DavidLaRocca.org, DavidLaRocca@Post.Harvard.Edu

Paola Marrati is Professor of Humanities and Philosophy at Johns Hopkins University. Her main interests are in Modern and Contemporary French philosophy, Anglo-American philosophy, phenomenology, film and philosophy, and feminist and queer theory. She is member of the Scientific Board of the Center for the Study of French Contemporary Philosophy at the Ecole Normale Supérieure of Paris and other international research networks. Her publications include: *Genesis and Trace. Derrida Reader of Husserl and Heidegger* (Stanford University Press, 2005), *Gilles Deleuze. Cinema and Philosophy* (Johns Hopkins University Press, 2008), and numerous articles and contributions to collective volumes.

Naoko Saito is Associate Professor at the Graduate School of Education, University of Kyoto. Her area of research is American philosophy and pragmatism and its implications for education. She writes in Japanese and English, with a commitment to crossing cultural borders. Her publications include: *The Gleam of Light: Moral Perfectionism and Education in Dewey and Emerson* (Fordham, 2005); Naoko Saito and Paul Standish, eds., *Stanley Cavell and the Education of Grownups* (Fordham, 2012); Paul Standish and Naoko Saito, eds., *Stanley Cavell and Philosophy as Translation: The Truth is Translated* (Rowman & Littlefield, 2017).

Martin Shuster is Professor of Philosophy and Isaac Swift Distinguished Professor of Jewish Studies at the University of North Carolina. His main interests are in ethics, political philosophy, aesthetics, critical theory, and philosophy of religion. His publications include: *New Television: The Aesthetics and Politics of a Genre* (University of Chicago Press, 2017) ; *Autonomy after Auschwitz: Adorno, German Idealism, and Modernity* (University of Chicago Press, 2014); and with Anne O'Byrne *Logics of Genocide: The Structures of Violence and the Contemporary World* (Routledge, 2020).

Paul Standish is Professor of Philosophy of Education and Chair of the Institute for Education at University College London. His publications include: *Beyond the Self: Wittgenstein, Heidegger and the Limits of Language* (Avebury, 1992); Naoko Saito and Paul Standish, eds. *Stanley Cavell and the Education of Grownups* (Fordham University Press, 2012); Paul Standish and Naoko Saito, eds., *Stanley Cavell and Philosophy as Translation: The Truth is Translated* (Rowman & Littlefield, 2017).

Index

acknowledgment 40–1, 92, 97, 104, 129
  film 202, 203
  politics of 104–6
  of silence 202–11
acting 61, 206–7, 210
action 60, 206–7
active/passive voice 24
Adam's Rib (Cukor, George) 157, 189
aesthetics 2, 8
  aesthetic possibilities of a medium 190, 191–8
  judgment 21–2, 56
  Kant, Immanuel 21–2
agreement 15, 21, 90–1, 176–7
  intimacy 171, 172, 174, 175
  language 13, 17, 18, 20, 21
  naturalism 171, 172
alphabet s149
America 50, 147–8
  identity 47–8, 49, 53
  literature 52
  philosophy 48, 130, 138, 181
  politics 95, 96
  Romanticism 113, 181
American Humor: A Study of the National Character (Rourke, Constance) 53
American Romanticism 113, 181
an-archic perfectionism 97, 106
  analytic judgment 76
  analytic philosophy 9, 11
  animism 119–20, 124
Anscombe, Elizabeth 168, 178
anti-foundationalist perfectionism 98
anti-realism 189–90
anti-theory conceptions 169
anxiety 203
appearance 115
art 2 *see also* film
  automatisms 37–8
  common purpose 38
  criticism 56
  definition 40
  expression 183–4
  history of 180
  importance 16, 29, 30
  judgment 56
  media 38, 49
  modernism 33–4, 38–41, 43, 57, 58, 144, 179–80, 184, 193
  modernist painting 40–1, 180, 182
  modifying the concept of 155
  physical conditions of expression 180
  power of 183
  presentness in painting 201
  Rothman, William and Keane, Marian 41
  Tolstoy, Leo 16, 29, 30
  truth in 181
Art and Objecthood (Fried, Michael) 35
artistes 65 n. 36
  Asquith, Anthony and Howard, Leslie *Pygmalion* 157
Augustine, Saint 81
  Confessions 80
Austin, J. L. 1, 8, 10, 12
  artistes 65 n. 36
  backstage 65 n. 36
  criteria 86
  distinctions 13–14
  failures of performatives 22
  How to Do Things with Words 14, 22, 23, 67
  knowledge 85–7
  language functions 46–7
  linguistic phenomenology 13
  moral philosophy 67
  "Other Minds" 85
  realism 13
  skepticism 85–6, 87, 119
  authority 90
autobiography 21, 30
Autobiography (Franklin, Benjamin) 149

Autobiography (Mill, John Stuart) 183
automatism/s 36–40, 195
"Availability of Wittgenstein's Later Philosophy, The" (Cavell, Stanley) 1, 11, 17–18, 19–20, 25
language learning 18, 19, 82–3
"Avoidance of Love, The" (Cavell, Stanley) 24
Awful Truth, The (McCarey, Leo) 155, 156

backstage 65 n. 36
baptism 51
Baudelaire, Charles
Painter of Modern Life, The 33, 194, 201
Bauen Wohnen Denken (Heidegger, Martin) 48
Bazin, André 31, 193, 210
Bearn, Gordon 57–61
"Staging Authenticity: A Critique of Cavell's Modernism" 57
"Beast in the Jungle, The" (James, Henry) 157
Beckett, Samuel
Fin de partie 196
Beckman Lectures (Cavell, Stanley) 119, 121, 128
Becoming Who We Are (Norris, Andrew) 43
Behmen, Jacob 118
Bernstein, J. M. 55–6, 57, 104
Bhagavad Gita 48
Bible, the 50–1
Biographia Literaria (Coleridge, Samuel Taylor) 118
Birth of Tragedy (Nietzsche, Friedrich) 184
Blake, William 52–3
Blue Book (Wittgenstein, Ludwig) 11, 30, 77
Boccaccio, Giovanni
Decameron, The 158
boredom 131
Brecht, Bertholt 207
British Romanticism 44, 52–3 *see also* Romanticism

Carroll, Noël 189
Cassin, Barbara 140 n. 37

castration complex 133
Cavell, David 61
Cavell, Stanley 1 *see also* Cavell, Stanley, works
career, 7, 8–9, 160, 163
criticism 10, 57–9
early period 9–11
family 125–6
as musician 63, 150
politics 26
writing style 49, 152
Cavell, Stanley, works 2, 3
"Availability of Wittgenstein's Later Philosophy, The" 1, 11, 17–18, 19–20, 25
"Avoidance of Love, The" 24
Beckman Lectures 119, 121, 128
Cities of Words: Pedagogical Letters on a Register of the Moral Life. See *Cities of Words: Pedagogical Letters on a Register of the Moral Life*
Claim of Reason, The. See *Claim of Reason, The*
Claim to Rationality, The 68
Conditions Handsome and Unhandsome: The Constitution of Emersonian Perfectionism. See *Conditions Handsome and Unhandsome: The Constitution of Emersonian Perfectionism*
Contesting Tears 158–9, 189, 200
Disowning Knowledge 9
Emerson's Transcendental Etudes 161
In Quest of the Ordinary. See *In Quest of the Ordinary*
Lectures after Emerson after Wittgenstein 161
Lines of Skepticism and Romanticism 161
Little Did I Know 7, 8, 22, 24, 26, 125
"Moral Reasoning: Moral Perfectionism" class/lectures 143–4, 145, 150, 156
"Must We Mean What We Say?" 7–8, 11, 30–1
Must We Mean What We Say?. See *Must We Mean What We Say?*

"Passionate and Performative
    Utterance" 22
Pitch of Philosophy, A 9, 12, 22, 24
Pursuits of Happiness 9, 12, 154, 158–9,
    181, 189, 191, 200
Senses of Walden, The. See *Senses of
    Walden, The*
This New Yet Unapproachable America
    9, 18, 115, 161
"What Becomes of Things on Film" 16
*World Viewed: Reflections on the Ontology
    of Film, The.* See *World Viewed:
    Reflections on the Ontology of Film,
    The*
ceremony 140 n. 30
certainty 69–70, 74
child, the/childhood 80–3, 121–2, 125–6,
    173
    film 208
    memories 208
"Circles" (Emerson, Ralph Waldo) 60
cities 145, 147, 148–9
*Cities of Words: Pedagogical Letters on a
    Register of the Moral Life* (Cavell,
    Stanley) 67, 143, 145–55, 156–60,
    162–4, 189
    criticism 189
    education 157
    Emerson, Ralph Waldo 159, 161–2,
        164
    film 148, 149, 152, 154–5, 157–8,
        159–60, 162, 163
    genre 154
    moral perfectionism 146
    "Moral Reasoning: Moral
        Perfectionism" class/lectures 143–4,
        145, 150, 156
    pedagogical letters 149–50
    plurality 147, 148
    register of the moral life 150, 151–2,
        162
    Republic, The 145–6, 147, 148–9,
        157–8, 159
    speech 157
    structure 152
    as a syllabus 153
    Table of Contents 150, 157, 158
    title meaning 147
    women 157–8
    claim/claiming 197–8, 215–24
Bernstein, J. M. 56
voice 21
Claim of Reason, The (Cavell, Stanley)
    9, 11, 43, 47, 67–92, 160, 170
    acknowledgment 129
    agreement 90–1
    child, the 80–3
    claiming 197–8
    community 91–2
    criteria 72–4, 83–4, 86, 90
    education 49
    expression 132
    film 196
    fragmentary structure of 57
    judgments 73–5
    knowledge 74–7, 85–8
    metaphysical solitude 88–90
    modernism 68
    morality 67
    objectivity/subjectivity 57
    objects 77–80
    Romanticism 181
    self-knowledge 25
    skepticism 69–73, 83–5, 87–8, 89,
        128
    universal voice 21
    Wittgenstein, Ludwig 68–9, 71–5,
        77–81, 82–5, 87–8, 89–92, 168
    words, 60
Claim to Rationality, The (Cavell, Stanley)
    68
Clarke, Thompson 67
classrooms 150–1, 152, 156
cinema. *See* film
civilization 176–7
Coleridge, Samuel Taylor 52–3
    Biographia Literaria 118
    Kant, Immanuel 118–21
    Lyrical Ballads 130
    Ode to Dejection 53
    Rime of the Ancient Mariner, The
        119–21
community 91–2, 114 *see also* society
Concord, Massachusetts 50

condition/s 50, 116–17 *see also* human condition
Conditions Handsome and Unhandsome: The Constitution of Emersonian Perfectionism (Cavell, Stanley) 96, 97–104, 106, 148, 161
   Emersonian perfectionism 179, 181
   intimacy 172
   skepticism 198
Confessions (Augustine, Saint) 80
consciousness 204
Contesting Tears (Cavell, Stanley) 158–9, 189, 200
conversation 94 n. 21, 106–7, 148, 157
conversation of justice 107
conviction 49, 91
correct blindness 103, 105
correspondence 150
Correspondence of Thomas Carlyle and Ralph Waldo Emerson, The (Carlyle, Thomas and Emerson, Ralph Waldo) 150
counting 125, 146
COVID-19 pandemic 151
"Creative Democracy—The Task Before Us, The" (Dewey, John) 96
crisis 177–8, 180–1
criteria 17, 31, 69, 116, 144, 227–38
   Austin, J. L. 86
   Claim of Reason, The 72–4, 83–4, 86, 90
   Mulhall, Stephen 93 n. 13
   ordinary 78–9
   Wittgenstein, Ludwig 69, 72–4, 75, 77–9, 83, 84, 87–8, 90, 91
criticism 16–17, 56, 189
Critique of Judgment (Kant, Immanuel) 2, 21
Critique of Pure Reason (Kant, Immanuel) 75, 158
Cuarón, Alfonso
   Gravity 175
cultural renewal 55
culture 55, 130, 168
   philosophy as 168–71
   popular 61

Danto, Arthur 144
Das, Veena 19, 132, 175
Days of Heaven (Malick, Terrence) 191
death 119, 122
Decameron, The (Boccaccio, Giovanni) 158
Delmar, Gene 156
Delmar, Viña (Alvina Louise Croter) 156
democracy 95–7, 99, 100, 102–3, 104, 106
Denby, David
   Great Books 156
Derrida, Jacques
   Specters of Marx 48
Descartes, René 69, 70, 88–9, 136
   Meditations 89
description 152–3
despair 104, 126
Desplechin, Arnaud 196
detachment 207–8
devastation 125–6
Dewey, John 95–6, 97, 99, 100–1
   "Creative Democracy—The Task Before Us, The" 96
   Emerson, Ralph Waldo, compared with 101–3
   Experience and Nature 100
   science 101–2
Diamond, Cora 168–9, 178
disequilibrium 106
Disowning Knowledge (Cavell, Stanley) 9
Doll's House, A (Ibsen, Henrik) 179
Domenach, Élise 34
domestication 177
doubt 86–7, 103, 104–5, 119, 124
Dreyer, Carl Theodor
   Passion de Jeanne d'Arc, La 211

Eddie Diptych (Lichtenstein, Roy) 60–1
edification 132
education 49, 106, 157
   classrooms 150–1, 152, 156
   COVID-19 pandemic 151
   language learning 18, 19, 81–3, 106
   modernism 178–9
   mutual learning 96
   naturalness 177
   pedagogical letters 149

Index

political 106–7
Eldridge, Richard 114
Eliot, T. S.
  Four Quartets 176
Emerson, Ralph Waldo 44, 47–50, 57, 136, 159, 181 *see also* Emersonian moral perfectionism
  "Circles" 60
  conversation 107
  Correspondence of Thomas Carlyle and Ralph Waldo Emerson, The 150
  Dewey, John, compared with 101–3
  "Experience" 172, 173
  "Fate" 136
  genius 99
  human condition 116
  importance of 161–2
  intimacy 172, 181
  modernism 181
  negativity/affirmation 105
  polarity 182
  "Over-Soul, The" 99
  reading 131
  revolution 187 . 32
  science 101–2
  Selected Letters of Ralph Waldo Emerson, The 150
  self, the 99
  "Self-Reliance" 100, 117, 135
  skepticism 187 n. 32
  tragedy 104
Emersonian moral perfectionism 48–9, 96–107, 146, 151, 167, 181–2
  action 60
  education 106–7
  Romanticism 167, 179, 181
  self, the 170
  skepticism 103
Emerson's Transcendental Etudes (Cavell, Stanley) 161
Emile (Rousseau, Jean-Jacques) 49
emotions 100
  negative 104, 105, 106
  political 100, 106–7
empiricism 178
epic theater 207
epistolary literature 149–50

existence 70, 86, 88–9
laughter 135–6
experience 102, 115–16, 173, 184
"Experience" (Emerson, Ralph Waldo) 172, 173
Experience and Nature (Dewey, John) 100
expression 24–5, 61–2, 183–4, 197, 211
expressivism 178
Ezekiel 50–1

Fahrenheit (Moore, Michael) 95
familiar, the 137, 175
fate 207, 209
"Fate" (Emerson, Ralph Waldo) 136
film 24, 148, 149, 154, 157–8, 162, 189–98
  see also *World Viewed: Reflections on the Ontology of Film, The*
  acknowledgement 202, 203
  acting 206–7, 210
  aesthetic possibilities of 191–8
  as art 155
  automatism/s 36–40, 195
  body in 205–6
  candor of 201
  child, the 208
  cinematic circle 191
  criticism 190
  definition 36
  detached contemplation 207–8
  experience 184
  fate 207, 209
  grammar 31
  importance of 190–1
  improvisation 205–6
  invention of 193–4
  investigating 30–1
  memory 200, 208
  as modern art 35
  modernism 34, 36–41, 185, 189–98, 196
  modernity of 199–211
  montage 210
  music 203
  mythical origin 200–2
  myths, end of 36
  narrative 192, 209
  ontology of 16, 189, 190, 199, 203

ordinary of 30
pastness of 199–200
philosophy and 158, 159–60
philosophy of 190–1
place 208–9
reading 31
realism 189–90, 201
remarriage 181, 182
seeing 210
self-consciousness 201
silence, acknowledgement of 202–11
silent 202–3
skepticism 32, 196–8
slow motion 205
speech in 202–5
synchronization 203–4
theories 189–90
time 200, 204–5, 208–9
as way of meaning 196
Fin de partie (Beckett, Samuel) 196
forgiveness 127
forms of life 18–20, 167
  language 81, 82, 83, 178
Foucault, Michel 169
foundationalist epistemology 124
Four Quartets (Eliot, T. S.) 176
Fox, George 118
fragmentary structure 57
Franklin, Benjamin
  Autobiography 149
Freud, Sigmund 133–4
Fried, Michael 40, 183
  Art and Objecthood 35

Gargani, Aldo Giorgio 171–2
Gaslight (Cukor, George) 157
Gellner, Ernest
  Words and Things: An Examination of, and an Attack on Linguistic Philosophy 10
generic objects 79, 87, 90
genius 99
German Romanticism 57
givens 13–14
God 50–1, 89
Gombrich, Ernst
  Story of Art, The 39

grammar 19, 30, 117
  film 31
  Wittgenstein, Ludwig 19, 30, 72, 73, 75, 77–8, 82, 83
grasping 172–3
Gravity (Cuarón, Alfonso) 175
Great Books (Denby, David) 156
Gunn, Thom
  "Intimacy" 173–4

Hadot, Pierre 169
Hamlet (Shakespeare, William) 129
happiness 100, 105
Heidegger, Martin 48, 83, 132, 134, 137, 172–3, 199, 203
  anxiety 203
  Bauen Wohnen Denken 48
  language 83
  "Purloined Letter, The" 135
  skepticism 70
  "Ursprung des Kunstwerkes, Der" 133
Hoffman, E. T. A.
  "Sandmann, Der" 133, 134
Hollywood myths 36
Homer
  Iliad 52
hopelessness 105
How to Do Things with Words (Austin, J. L.) 14, 22, 23
Human, All Too Human (Nietzsche, Friedrich) 182
human condition 83, 89–90, 116, 180
humanity 39, 90
  two worlds split 116
Hume, David 70, 172

Ibsen, Henrik
  Doll's House, A 179
Iliad (Homer) 52
improvisation 205–6
In Quest of the Ordinary (Cavell, Stanley) 115, 133, 138
  child, the 121
  modernism 182
  Romanticism 113, 128, 179, 181, 182
  voice 9
indebtedness 127

individuality 210
infelicities 22–3
Information Please quiz show 126
intelligence 102
intimacy 172–6, 181
"Intimacy" (Gunn, Thom) 173–4
"Intimation of Immortality from Recollections of Early Childhood" (Wordsworth, William) 121
intuition 115
isolation 210–11
It Happened One Night (Capra, Frank) 158

James, Henry
    "Beast in the Jungle, The" 157
judgment
    aesthetics 21–2, 56
    analytic 76
    art 56
    Claim of Reason, The 73–5
    Kant, Immanuel 76–7
    synthetic 76
    synthetic *a priori* 76–7
just city, the 145, 147, 148

Kant, Immanuel 21–2, 70, 115–17
    Coleridge, Samuel Taylor 118–21
    Critique of Judgment 2, 21
    Critique of Pure Reason 75, 158
    judgment 76–7
    Kantian bargain 115, 119
    knowledge 75–7, 79
    noumena 113, 115, 118
    Romanticism 113, 114
    schematism 117
    self, the 99
    skepticism 113–14, 120, 123, 124
    subjectivity 76
King Lear (Shakespeare, William) 24, 196
knowledge 69–70, 74–6, 79, 85–9, 124
    Austin, J. L. 85–7
    Descartes, René, 88–9
    Dewey, John 101
    failure of 87
    Gargani, Aldo Giorgio 171–2
    hierarchy 135
    Kant, Immanuel 75–7, 79
    Wittgenstein, Ludwig 79–80, 84, 87, 88, 89–90
Krauss, Rosalind 189
Kripke, Saul 162

Lacan, Jacques 134–5
Lady Eve, The (Sturges, Preston) 157
language 1, 11–14, 114 *see also* grammar; ordinary language philosophy
    aesthetics 8
    agreement 13, 17, 18, 20, 21, 117
    child, the 80–3
    control 23
    criteria and 83–4
    deduction 116
    distinctions 13–14
    double relation to 137
    forms of life 18, 81, 82, 83, 178
    givens 13–14
    infelicitous 22–3
    intimacy 172
    learning 18, 19, 81–3, 106
    lifeforms 15
    ordinary 128–30
    passionate utterances 106, 107
    performative utterances 106–7
    poetic 205
    projection 18
    transformative power of 178
    unctions 46–7
    Wittgenstein, Ludwig 72, 75, 80–1, 82, 83, 168–9
Laocoön (Lessing, Gotthold Ephraim) 38
laughter 135–7
Laugier, Sandra 114, 116
Lectures after Emerson after Wittgenstein (Cavell, Stanley) 161
Lessing, Gotthold Ephraim
    Laocoön 38
Letter from an Unknown Woman (Ophüls, Max) 157
letters 149–50
Lichtenstein, Roy
    Eddie Diptych 60–1
lifeforms 18, 19, 20 *see also* forms of life

Lines of Skepticism and Romanticism (Cavell, Stanley) 161
  linguistic phenomenology 13
literalism 35
literature 52, 128, 130–1, 133–4, 138
  epistolary 149–50
  philosophy and 128, 130–1, 133, 138, 170, 171
Little Did I Know (Cavell, Stanley) 7, 8, 22, 24, 26, 125
Lyrical Ballads (Wordsworth, William and Coleridge, Samuel Taylor) 130

McDowell, John 169
Malcom, Norman and Albritton, Roger 72
Malick, Terrence
  Days of Heaven 191
Marrati, Paula 43
marriage 121, 148, 152, 156 *see also* remarriage
Mates, Benson 7, 30
media 38, 49
Meditations (Descartes, René) 89
medium 191–2
  aesthetic possibilities of a 190, 191–8
  obscurities in a 193
  significance of a 192
metaphysical solitude 88–9, 90, 91
Mill, John Stuart 167, 168, 183
  Autobiography 183
Milton, John 52
  Paradise Lost 44, 52
modernist/modernism 2, 17, 29, 167–8, 179–85, 190, 201–2
  art 33–4, 38–41, 43, 57, 58, 144, 179–80, 184, 193
  Cities of Words: Pedagogical Letters on a Register of the Moral Life 144–5, 154, 160
  conventions 68
  definition 144–5
  disappearance of 181
  education 178–9
  film 34, 36–41, 185, 189–98, 196
  film as modern art 35–6
  Fried, Michael 35
  importance 33–4

intimacy 172–6, 181
Marrati, Paula 43
naturalism 171–2, 175–8
nature 182
ordinary language 178–9
painting 40–1, 180
philosophical 168
Romanticism, relationship with 55, 181–2
seriousness 55
shame 176
World Viewed: Reflections on the Ontology of Film, The 34, 36–41, 179, 185, 189, 196
modernity 33–4, 144
  film 199–211
modernizing 145
Moore, G. E. 70, 162
Moore, Michael 96
  Fahrenheit 95
moral perfectionism 67, 146–7, 162, 167
  see also Emersonian moral perfectionism
"Moral Reasoning: Moral Perfectionism" class/lectures (Cavell, Stanley) 143–4, 145, 150, 156
morality 67, 98, 100
Mulhall, Stephen 31, 33, 93 n. 13
music 38, 63, 150, 151, 203
  improvisation 206
"Must We Mean What We Say?" (Cavell, Stanley) 7–8, 11, 30–1
Must We Mean What We Say? (Cavell, Stanley) 7–16, 18, 23–6, 43, 168, 179
  sound 150
  skepticism 196
  modernism 179, 180, 185, 190, 196
  claiming 197–8
  universal voice 20–2
My Fair Lady (Cukor, George) 157
My Fair Lady (Lerner, Alan Jay and Loewe, Frederick) 157

nature 182
naturalism/naturalness 171–2, 175–8
negativity/affirmation 105

New England 50
Nietzsche, Friedrich 99, 125
   Birth of Tragedy 184
   Human, All Too Human 182
   Richard Wagner in Bayreuth 183
   Schopenhauer as Educator 183
   Übermensch 99
   Untimely Meditations 182, 183, 184
normality 175
Norris, Andrew 104
   Becoming Who We Are 43
noumena 113, 115, 118
Now, Voyager (Rapper, Irving) 157

objectivity 41, 55, 56–7
   objects
   criteria 90
   generic 79, 87, 90
   specific 79, 87
   Wittgenstein, Ludwig 74, 75, 77–80, 90
obscurities 193
Ode to Dejection (Coleridge, Samuel Taylor) 53
On the Aesthetic Education of Man (Schiller, Friedrich) 149
ontology 199
   of film 16, 189, 190, 199, 203
opera 24
Ophüls, Max
   Letter from an Unknown Woman 157
ordinary, the 12, 24–5, 46, 60
   Laugier, Sandra 116
   normativity of 13
   uncanniness of 133
ordinary language 128–30, 178–9
ordinary language philosophy 7–9, 10–11, 12–13, 56, 180
   failure 22
   intimacy 181
   others, relation to 47
   "Purloined Letter, The" 135
   revival 26
   voice 15
   World Viewed: Reflections on the Ontology of Film, The 30–1
ordinary realism 16–17
ordinary world 9

Othello (Shakespeare, William) 170
"Other Minds" (Austin, J. L.) 85
"Over-Soul, The" (Emerson, Ralph Waldo) 99

Painter of Modern Life, The (Baudelaire, Charles) 33, 194, 201
Panofsky, Erwin 193
   "Style and Medium in the Motion Pictures" 35, 191–2
Paradise Lost (Milton, John) 44, 52
Parmenides (Plato) 155
partiality 211
Passion de Jeanne d'Arc, La (Dreyer, Carl Theodor) 211
"Passionate and Performative Utterance" (Cavell, Stanley) 22
pedagogical letters 149–50
perfect pitch 63
perfectionism 57–8, 59–60, 151 *see also* Emersonian moral perfectionism
   an-archic 97, 106
   anti-foundationalist 98
   moral 67, 146–7, 162, 167
   Romanticism 183
Philosophical Investigations (Wittgenstein, Ludwig) 16, 34, 45–6, 57, 169, 171
   Anscombe, Elizabeth 168
   autobiographical tone 21
   criteria 69, 72–3, 77, 79, 84, 90, 91
   Dewey, John, compared with 101
   Diamond, Cora 168–9
   disagreement 91
   friction 177
   grammar 73
   influence 1
   intimacy 174–5
   language 80, 168–9
   laughter 136–7
   as literary art 144
   Malcom, Norman and Albritton, Roger 72
   McDowell, John 169
   as modernist 154
   privacy 176
   readings 168–9
   self-knowledge 25

264 Index

skepticism 67, 68, 72, 89, 103–4, 187 n. 32
waiting 132
philosophy 1, 2, 43, 135 *see also* ordinary language philosophy
  actions 206–7
  America 48, 130, 138, 181
  analytic 9, 11
  anti-theory and theory conceptions 169
  audience 2–3
  canon 153, 158–9
  Coleridge, Samuel Taylor 118
  as culture 168–71
  distinctions 13–14
  film and 158, 159–60
  history 143, 159, 161, 180
  literature and 128, 130–1, 133, 138, 170, 171
  modernism 34, 168
  modifying the concept of 155
  philosophical interest 170
  reading 131–2
  skepticism 70–1
  writing 68, 131
Pilgrim Fathers 50
Pitch of Philosophy, A (Cavell, Stanley) 9, 12, 22, 24
Plato 131, 155, 156
  just city, the 147
  Parmenides 155
  Republic, The 49, 145–6, 147, 148–9, 157–8, 159
plurality 147, 148
Poe, Edgar Allan
  "Purloined Letter, The" 134–5, 136–7
poetry 129–30
polarity 182
politics 15, 26, 47, 56, 100
  democracy 95–7, 99, 100, 102–3, 104, 106
  education 106–7
  emotions 100, 106–7
  Moore, Michael 95
politics of acknowledgment 104–6
Pollock, Jackson 40
popular culture 61

possibilities 191–8
poverty 175
pretense 61–2
psychoanalysis 102
psychology
  psychologizing of 56, 62–3
Puritanism 50, 51–2
"Purloined Letter, The" (Poe, Edgar Allan) 134–5, 136–7
Pursuits of Happiness (Cavell, Stanley) 9, 12, 154, 158–9, 181, 189, 191, 200
Pygmalion (Asquith, Anthony and Howard, Leslie) 157
Pygmalion (Shaw, George Bernard) 157

Quine, W. V. O. 162

rationalism 171
Rawls, John 99, 100
  Theory of Justice 98
  "Two Concepts of Rules" 15
reading 47, 131–2, 138, 147
real, the 85–6
realism 23, 189–90, 201
  ordinary 16–17
reason 92, 115
"Rebuking Hopelessness" (Standish, Paul) 105
reception 172–3
redemption 51
register of the moral life 150, 151–2, 162
relevance 11–14, 16
religion 50–2, 53
remarriage 148, 152, 181, 182, 189 *see also* marriage
repetition 134
Republic, The (Plato) 49, 145–6, 147, 148–9, 157–8, 159
responsiveness 132
  Romanticism 113–14, 115, 116, 118–19, 127, 128–30, 132
  skepticism 113, 114, 120, 123–4, 128–9
revenge 122, 127
revolution 187 . 32
Richard Wagner in Bayreuth (Nietzsche, Friedrich) 183

Rime of the Ancient Mariner, The
(Coleridge, Samuel Taylor) 119–21
Rohmer, Eric
  Tale of Winter, A 157
Romanticism 44, 52–3, 55–9, 113–16, 179, 181–3
  America 113, 181
  animism 119–20, 124
  modernism, relationship with 181–2
  response 113–14, 115, 116, 118–19, 127, 128–30, 132
Rothman, William 144, 161, 181
Rothman, William and Keane, Marian 41
Rourke, Constance
  American Humor: A Study of the National Character 53
Rousseau, Jean-Jacques
  Emile 49
rules 15
Russell, Bertrand 162

"Sandmann, Der" (Hoffman, E. T. A.) 133, 134
Sartre, Jean-Paul 39
saying 14–15 *see also* voice
schematism 117
Schiller, Friedrich
  On the Aesthetic Education of Man 149
Schopenhauer as Educator (Nietzsche, Friedrich) 183
science 101–2, 118
seeing 209–10
Selected Letters of Ralph Waldo Emerson, The (Emerson, Ralph Waldo; ed. Myerson, Joel) 150
self, the 67, 98, 210–11
  aristocracy of 99
  disappearance of 211
  dual nature of 99
self-consciousness 201
self-knowledge 25–6, 103, 146
"Self-Reliance" (Emerson, Ralph Waldo) 100, 117, 135
Senses of Walden, The (Cavell, Stanley) 10, 16, 21, 43–5, 54–5, 63, 161
  America 47–8
  dedication 181

separation theme 121
seriousness 57–8, 60, 61, 62
sermons 51–2
Shakespeare, William
  Hamlet 129
  King Lear 24, 196
  Othello 170
  Winter's Tale, The 115, 122–5, 127, 134, 157
shame 100, 136, 176
Shaw, George Bernard
  Pygmalion 157
significance 192
silence 203
  acknowledgement of 202–11
Singin' in the Rain (Kelly, Gene and Donen, Stanley) 157
skepticism 12, 15, 23, 45–7, 69–72, 133, 241–9
  Austin, J. L. 85–6, 87, 119
  Claim of Reason, The 67, 68
  Emerson, Ralph Waldo 187 n. 32
  film 32, 196–8
  film, aesthetic possibilities of 196–8
  Kant, Immanuel 113–14, 120, 123, 124
  response to 113, 114, 120, 123–4, 128–9
  Romanticism 119
  skeptical doubts 86–7 i
  truth of 92, 103–4, 114, 244
  Winter's Tale, The 123, 125
  Wittgenstein, Ludwig 67, 68, 72, 83–4, 87–8, 89, 90, 91, 92, 103–4, 128, 187 n. 32
  world, existence of 119
social contracts 94 n. 20
society 103, 104 *see also* community
Socrates 3
solitude 88–9, 90, 91
soul, the 99
sound 150–1, 157
specific objects 79, 87
Specters of Marx (Derrida, Jacques) 48
speech 157, 202–5 *see also* voice
staging, 61, 62–3
"Staging Authenticity: A Critique of Cavell's Modernism" (Bearn, Gordon) 57

standards 73–4
Standish, Paul 98
    "Rebuking Hopelessness" 105
Stanley Cavell, le cinéma et le scepticisme (Domenach, Élise) 196
Story of Art, The (Gombrich, Ernst) 39
"Style and Medium in the Motion Pictures" (Panofsky, Erwin) 35, 191–2
subjectivity 16, 20, 37, 55, 56–7, 183
    film 199
    Kant, Immanuel 76
    Romanticism 114
    voice 15, 24
synchronization 203–4
synthetic *a priori* judgment 76–7
synthetic judgment 76

Tale of Winter, A (Rohmer, Eric) 157
Taylor, Charles 178
telling 125
theater 24
    acting 61
    artistes 65 n. 36
    backstage 65 n. 36
    epic 207
theatricality 58, 60, 61, 62–3
theory conceptions 169
Theory of Justice (Rawls, John) 98
This New Yet Unapproachable America (Cavell, Stanley) 9, 18, 115, 161
Thoreau, Henry David 16, 25, 48–50, 137
    intimacy 181
    reading 131
    Walden. See *Walden*
    "Walking" 60
Thoyras, Paul Rapin de 118
time 200, 204–5, 208–9
Tolstoy, Leo 16, 29, 30
    What is Art? 30
tone 12, 14
Tractatus Logico-Philosophicus (Wittgenstein, Ludwig) 13, 69, 171, 183, 184–5, 222, 245
tradition 179–80
tragedy 91, 104–5
transcendental logic 77

transcendentalism 77
Trump, Donald 95, 96
truth 13, 14, 16, 25
    in art 181
"Two Concepts of Rules" (Rawls, John) 15
two worlds split 116
typicality 210

Übermensch (Nietzsche, Friedrich) 99
uncanniness 133, 137
uncreatedness 136
universal voice 20–1
Untimely Meditations (Nietzsche, Friedrich) 182, 183, 184
"Ursprung des Kunstwerkes, Der" (Heidegger, Martin) 133

voice 12, 14, 15, 150
    active/passive 24
    conversation 94 n. 21, 106–7, 148, 157
    Emersonian moral perfectionism 98
    expression 24–5
    passionate utterances 106, 107
    performative utterances 106–7
    saying 14–15
    speech 157, 202–5
    universal 20–2

waiting 132
Walden Pond, Massachusetts 50, 55
Walden (Thoreau, Henry David) 16, 25, 43–5, 47, 49
    America 48
    animal symbolism 53–4
    dwelling 132
    economic terms 54
    imagery 53–4
    journal form of 57
    literary context 52–3
    pastoral reading 48, 53
    philosophy 130
    religious context 44, 50–2, 53
    staged expression 61
    tourism, 55
    words 60
"Walking" (Thoreau, Henry David) 60
wandering 60

Weber, Max 140 n. 38
West, Cornel 26
"What Becomes of Things on Film" (Cavell, Stanley) 16
What is Art? (Tolstoy, Leo) 30
Winch, Peter 178
Winter's Tale, The (Shakespeare, William) 115, 122–5, 127, 134, 157
Wittgenstein, Ludwig 1, 10, 20–1, 23 *see also* "Availability of Wittgenstein's Later Philosophy, The"
  Blue Book 11, 30, 77
  child, the 80–1
  criteria 69, 72–4, 75, 77–9, 83, 84, 87–8, 90, 91
  grammar 19, 30, 72, 73, 75, 77–8, 82, 83
  human condition 83
  intimacy 172, 174–5
  knowledge 79–80, 84, 87, 88, 89–90
  language 72, 75, 80–1, 82, 83, 168–9
  metaphysical solitude 88, 91
  naturalism 171
  objects 74, 75, 77–80, 90
  Philosophical Investigations. See *Philosophical Investigations*
  pretense 61–2
  psychology 62–3
  "Purloined Letter, The" 135
  seeing 210
  skepticism 67, 68, 72, 83–4, 87–8, 89, 90, 91, 92, 103–4, 128, 187 n. 32
  therapy of philosophy 46
  Tractatus Logico-Philosophicus 13, 69, 171, 183, 184–5, 222, 245
  transcendentalism 77
Wizard of Oz, The (Baum, L. Frank) 12
women 157–8
words, 60
Words and Things: An Examination of, and an Attack on Linguistic Philosophy (Gellner, Ernest) 10

Wordsworth, William 52–3, 121–2, 129
  "Intimation of Immortality from Recollections of Early Childhood" 121
  Lyrical Ballads 130
world, the 32, 92, 116
  automatism 36–7
  conceptualizing 79–80
  death 119
  film 36, 37
  intelligibility of 210–11
  judgments 76–7
  knowledge 85–8
  language and 12–14
  life, bringing to 127, 133
  objects 74–5
  ordinary world 9
  perspectives on 116
  recovery 119
  skepticism 70–1, 119
  two worlds split 116
World Viewed: Reflections on the Ontology of Film, The (Cavell, Stanley) 10, 12, 16, 29–41, 158–9
  acknowledgement of silence 202–11
  aesthetic possibilities 192–5
  automatism/s 36–40
  criticism of 189–90
  Desplechin, Arnaud 196
  experience 184
  film 154, 191
  film as modern art 35
  Krauss, Rosalind 189
  memories 200
  modernism 34, 36–41, 179, 185, 189, 196
  modernist art/painting 40–1, 144, 180, 182
  ordinary language philosophy 30–1
  ordinary of film 30
  presentness in painting 201
  Romanticism 183
  structure of, 32–3
  "Supplement" 190, 193
  time 200
  writing 68, 131

Made in the USA
Monee, IL
09 September 2025

cb457c1a-1601-403f-8cf5-0b7ff1eb6cc5R02